BIBLICAL RESEARCH INSTITUTE STUDIES , vol. 2

Interpreting Scripture
Bible Questions and Answers

Gerhard Pfandl, Editor

Biblical Research Institute
Silver Spring, MD 20904

2010

Layout   Marlene Bacchus
Cover design   Tina M. Ivany
Copy editor   Soraya L. Homayouni

Printed in the U.S.A. by the
Review and Herald Publishing Association
Hagerstown, MD 21740

ISBN 978-0-925675-19-4

Contributors

Roberto Badenas	Director of Education, Euro-Africa Division, Switzerland
John T. Baldwin	Professor of Systematic Theology, Andrews University
Ivan T. Blazen	Professor of New Testament, Loma Linda University
S. Quezada Case	Professor of New Testament, Union College
P. Richard Choi	Professor of New Testament, Andrews University
Richard M. Davidson	Professor of Old Testament, Andrews University
A. Ganoune Diop	Director, Global Mission Study Centers, General Conference
Kwabena Donkor	Associate Director, Biblical Research Institute
Ron du Preez	Pastor, Michigan Conference
Roy E. Gane	Professor of Old Testament, Andrews University
Erno Gyeresi	Ph.D. Student, Andrews University
Frank M. Hasel	Professor of Systematic Theology, Seminar Bogenhofen, Austria
Michael G. Hasel	Professor of Old Testament, Southern Adventist University
Robert M. Johnston	Professor of New Testament, Emeritus, Andrews University
Grenville J. R. Kent	Professor of Old Testament, Wesley Theological College, Sydney, Australia.
Gregory A. King	Professor of Old Testament, Southern Adventist University
Miroslav M. Kiš	Professor of Systematic Theology, Andrews University
Gerald A. Klingbeil	Associate Editor, Adventist Review, Research Professor of Old Testament, Andrews University

Martin G. Klingbeil	Professor of Old Testament, Helderberg College, South Africa
Samuel Koranteng-Pipim	Pastor, Michigan Conference
Donn W. Leatherman	Professor of Old Testament, Southern Adventist University
Tarsee Li	Professor of Old Testament, Oakwood University
Larry L. Lichtenwalter	Professor of Systematic Theology, Andrews University
Pedrito Maynard-Reid	Professor of New Testament, Walla Walla University
Robert K. McIver	Professor of New Testament, Avondale College, Australia
John K. McVay	Professor of New Testament, Walla Walla University
P. David Merling	Pastor, New Mexico
Jiří Moskala	Professor of Old Testament, Andrews University
Ekkehardt Mueller	Associate Director, Biblical Research Institute
The late Kenneth Mulzac	Professor of Old Testament, Andrews University
Afolarin O. Ojewole	Professor of Old Testament, Babcock University, Nigeria
Kim Papaioannou	Professor of New Testament, Adventist International Institute of Advanced Studies, Philippines
Wilson Paroschi	Professor of New Testament, Brazil Adventist University, Brazil
Jon K. Paulien	Professor of New Testament, Loma Linda University
Gerhard Pfandl	Associate Director, Biblical Research Institute
Martin Pröbstle	Professor of Old Testament, Seminar Bogenhofen, Austria
Leo Ranzolin, Jr.	Professor of New Testament, Pacific Union College
Teresa Reeve	Professor of New Testament, Andrews University
Edwin Reynolds	Professor of New Testament, Southern Adventist University

W. Larry Richards	Professor of New Testament, Emeritus, Andrews University
Ángel M. Rodríguez	Director, Biblical Research Institute
William H. Shea	Former Associate Director, Biblical Research Institute
Tom Shepherd	Professor of New Testament, Andrews University
Ranko Stefanovic	Professor of New Testament, Andrews University
Peter M. van Bemmelen	Professor of Theology, Emeritus, Andrews University
Winfried Vogel	Professor of Old Testament, Seminar Bogenhofen, Austria
Clinton Wahlen	Associate Director, Biblical Research Institute
Lloyd Willis	Professor of Old Testament, Southern Adventist University
Randall W. Younker	Professor of Old Testament, Andrews University

Gratefully dedicated to

GEORGE W. REID

A scholar and a gentleman.
In recognition of his leadership of the Biblical Research Institute
from 1984 to 2001, his commitment to the message, mission, and
unity of God's remnant people and his positive spiritual influence in the
world church.

George W. Reid served the Seventh-day Adventist Church for 48 years as
pastor, teacher, editor, and director of the Biblical Research Institute
of the General Conference of Seventh-day Adventists.

The members of the Biblical
Research Institute Committee

Contents

Contents

Contents

Contents

Pictures, Tables, and Notes

Picture credits

Ekkehardt Mueller, 296.

Gerhard Pfandl, 49, 58, 168, 184, 187, 219, 241, 262, 276, 292, 339, 365, 390, 437, 443.

Review and Herald, 161, 253, 359.

Efrain Velazquez, 368.

Page 31 – Codex Leningradensis. Photograph by Bruce and Kenneth Zuckerman, West Semitic Research, with the collaboration of the Ancient Biblical Manuscript Center. Courtesy Russian National Library (Saltykov-Shchedrin).

Page 236 – Map of ancient Tyre. Copyright Hammond World Atlas Corporation – Reprinted with Permission.

Page 320 – Papyrus P52. Reproduced by courtesy of the University Librarian and Director, The John Rylands University Library, The University of Manchester.

Preface

As a young minister in the early 1970s, I was grateful for the book *Answers to Objections* by F. D. Nichol that provided short answers to difficult Bible texts. Nichol's book is no longer in print, and no other Adventist book has taken its place; the need for such a book, however, has not disappeared. On the contrary, the larger the church becomes, the greater the need for such a volume. Difficulties in understanding some biblical texts may be due to differences in culture and time, or because they challenge the way we think and act.

In 2006, the Biblical Research Institute published the book *Understanding Scripture: An Adventist Approach,* which outlined the principles of biblical interpretation. The present volume applies these principles to difficult texts in the Old and New Testaments. In addition, the first section of this volume addresses a number of general questions concerning the Bible, such as "Who is the author of the Bible?" "Are there mistakes in the Bible?" and "Why do Christian scholars interpret Scripture in so many different ways?"

The forty-nine authors who contributed to this volume are all highly qualified Seventh-day Adventist scholars who share the conviction that the Bible is God's inspired and authoritative Word. Coming from many countries and cultures, they share a common commitment to Christ and His church. Although each article is signed, each one has been reviewed and revised by the members of the Biblical Research Institute Committee (BRICOM), a group of about forty scholars and administrators from around the world. Hence, no part of this volume is the work of a single author. The individual chapters and the book as a whole profited from this cooperative approach. While the authors and members of BRICOM worked hard to explain the difficult Bible texts collected in this volume, they do not claim to have spoken the last word on any them, i.e., the answers do not represent an official position of the church but reflect the authors' understanding of the passages. Nevertheless, it is hoped that this book will be a help to many who are struggling with some of the difficulties found in Scripture.

I would like to express my appreciation to the authors who contributed to this volume, to the associate editors Kwabena Donkor, Michael G. Hasel, and Tom Shepherd, as well as to my colleagues at the Biblical Research Institute and to the members of BRICOM whose input and critique, over the years this book have been in the making, has been invaluable.

A special tribute is due to Marlene Bacchus, our desktop publishing specialist, without whose expertise and dedication to the task this volume would not have seen the light of day. I also would like to thank Soraya Homayouni, our copy editor, Tina M. Ivany, who designed the cover, and the staff of the Review and Herald Publishing Association for their help in the production of *Interpreting Scripture*.

Gerhard Pfandl
Associate Director
Biblical Research Institute

Abbreviations

Bibles

ASV	American Standard Version
CEV	Contemporary English Version
CJV	Complete Jewish Bible
ESV	English Standard Version
GNB	Good News Bible
HSCB	Holman Christian Standard Bible
JPS	Jewish Publication Society Version
KJV	King James Version
LXX	Septuagint – the translation of the Old Testament into Greek (2nd century B.C.)
NCV	New Century Version
NKJV	New King James Version
NAB	New American Bible
NASB	New American Standard Bible
NEB	New English Bible
NET	New English Translation
NIV	New International Version
NJB	New Jerusalem Bible
NLV	New Life Version
NRSV	New Revised Standard Version
REB	Revised English Bible
RSV	Revised Standard Version
RV	Revised Version
TEV	Today's English Version
TNIV	Today's New International Version
YLT	Young's Literal Translation

*Unless otherwise noted the NASB text (1975,1995) has been used in this volume.

Biblical Books

Gen	Genesis	Deut	Deuteronomy
Exod	Exodus	Josh	Joshua
Lev	Leviticus	Judg	Judges
Num	Numbers	Ruth	Ruth
		1-2 Sam	1-2 Samuel

1-2 Kgs	1-2 Kings	Zech	Zechariah
1-2 Chron	1-2 Chronicles	Mal	Malachi
Ezra	Ezra	Matt	Matthew
Neh	Nehemiah	Mark	Mark
Esth	Esther	Luke	Luke
Job	Job	John	John
Ps(s)	Psalms	Acts	Acts
Prov	Poverbs	Rom	Romans
Eccl	Ecclesiastes	1-2 Cor	1-2 Corinthians
Song	Song of Solomon	Gal	Galatians
Isa	Isaiah	Eph	Ephesians
Jer	Jeremiah	Phil	Philippians
Lam	Lamentations	Col	Colossians
Ezek	Ezekiel	1-2 Thess	1-2 Thessalonians
Dan	Daniel	1-2 Tim	1-2 Timothy
Hos	Hosea	Titus	Titus
Joel	Joel	Phlm	Philemon
Amos	Amos	Heb	Hebrews
Obad	Obadiah	Jas	James
Jonah	Jonah	1-2 Pet	1-2 Peter
Mic	Micah	1-2-3 John	1-2-3 John
Nah	Nahum	Jude	Jude
Zeph	Zephaniah	Rev	Revelation
Hag	Haggai		

Ellen G. White References

1-3 SM	Selected Messages, vols. 1-3
1-4 SG	Spiritual Gifts, vol. 1-4
1-9 T	Testimonies for the Church, vols. 1-9
AA	Acts of the Apostles
AG	God's Amazing Grace
AH	Adventist Home
CC	Courage and Conflict
CE	Christian Education
CG	Child Guidance
CH	Counsels on Health
COL	Christ's Object Lessons
CSA	A Call to Stand Apart

CSW	Counsels on Sabbath School Work
DA	Desire of Ages
Ed	Education
Ev	Evangelism
FE	Fundamentals of Christian Education
FLB	The Faith I Live By
GC	The Great Controversy
LHU	Lift Him Up
MB	Thoughts from the Mount of Blessing
MH	Ministry of Healing
ML	My Life Today
MM	Medical Ministry
MYP	Messages to Young People
PK	Prophets and Kings
PP	Patriarchs and Prophets
RH	Review and Herald
SR	Story of Redemption
ST	Signs of the Times
TM	Testimonies to Ministers and Gospel Workers
Visitor	The Columbia Visitor
YI	Youth Instructor

Other Abbreviations

1-11Q	Qumran Caves 1-11
1-QS	Qumran Rule of the Community
A.D.	Anno Domini (Latin for "in the year of the Lord")
B.C.	Before Christ
cf.	*confer* (Latin for compare)
Gr.	Greek
Heb.	Hebrew
MSS	Manuscripts
NT	New Testament
OT	Old Testament
s.v.	sub verbum (Latin for "look under the word")

Frequently Cited Sources

Josephus, *The Works of Josephus,* trans. W. Whiston (Peabody, MA, Hendrickson, 1987)

F. D. Nichol, *Answers to Objections* (Washington D.C.: Review and Herald, 1952)

F. D. Nichol, ed., *Seventh Day Adventist Bible Commentary,* 7 vols. (Washington, D.C.: Review and Herald, 1956, 1980)

Questions on Doctrine (Washington D.C.: Review and Herald, 1957)

Quotations from *Signs of the Times* or *Review and Herald* are always Ellen White quotations.

WHO IS THE AUTHOR OF THE BIBLE?

According to the traditional understanding, held by most biblical scholars until the rise of historical criticism during the Enlightenment (seventeenth century), the Bible was written by some thirty-five named individuals over a period of 2500 years. Old Testament Bible writers include: Moses (the Pentateuch, the book of Job, and Ps 90), Joshua (the book of Joshua), Samuel (the books of Judges, Ruth, perhaps 1 Samuel), David (the majority of the book of Psalms), Asaph (Pss 50, 73-83), the sons of Korah (Pss 42-49, 84, 85, 87), Heman (Ps 88), Ethan (Ps 89), Solomon (Pss 72 and 127, the majority of the book of Proverbs, the books of Ecclesiastes, Song of Solomon), Agur (Prov 30), Lemuel (Prov 31), the four "Major Prophets" (Isaiah, Jeremiah, Ezekiel, Daniel) and twelve "Minor Prophets" (whose books are named after them, plus Jeremiah writing also Lamentations and possibly editing 1–2 Kings), and Ezra (the books of Ezra and Nehemiah and 1–2 Chronicles). New Testament writers include Matthew and Mark (the Gospels named after them), Luke (Luke and Acts), John (the Gospel of John, 1–3 John, and Revelation), Paul (the fourteen epistles attributed to him), Peter (1 and 2 Peter), James and Jude (the epistles named after them). Although modern critical scholarship has questioned the authenticity of many of these claims, there is solid support for the traditional understanding.

The ultimate author of the Bible is God – While the Bible was *written* by numerous individuals, the question remains: who really *authored* the Bible? By many and various means the Bible makes clear that the ultimate *Author* of Scripture is God Himself.

The self-testimony of Scripture regarding its ultimate divine authorship is summarized in 2 Timothy 3:16, 17, "All Scripture is inspired by God and profitable for teaching, for reproof, for correction, and training in righteousness, that the man of God may be adequate, equipped for every good work." It is "inspired by God," Gr. *theopneustos*, literally "God-breathed." The picture here is that of the divine "wind" or Spirit coming upon the prophet so that Scripture is a product of the divine creative breath.

All Scripture—not just a part—is God-breathed. This certainly includes the whole Old Testament, the canonical Scriptures of the apostolic church (see Luke 24:32, 44, 45; Rom 1:2; 3:2; 2 Pet 1:21; etc.). But for Paul it also includes the New Testament sacred writings as well. His use of the word "Scripture" (Gr. *graphe*, "writing") in his first epistle to Timothy (5:18) points in this direction. There he introduces two quotations with the words "Scripture says," one from Deuteronomy 25:4, in the Old Testament, and the other from the words of Jesus, recorded in Luke 10:7. Thus "Scripture" is used to refer to both the Old Testament and the Gospel accounts as "inspired, sacred, authoritative writings."

Numerous passages in the Gospels assert their truthfulness and authority on the same level as the Old Testament Scriptures (e.g., John 1:1-3 paralleling Gen 1:1; John 14:26; 16:13; 19:35; 21:24; Luke 1:2-4; Matthew 1 paralleling Genesis 5; Matt 23:34). Peter's use of the term "Scriptures" for Paul's writings also supports this conclusion (2 Pet 3:15, 16). By comparing Paul's letters to the "rest of the Scriptures," Peter implies that Paul's correspondence is also a part of Scripture. Thus "all Scripture," both the Old and the New Testament, is "God-breathed."

> The Bible was written in three languages (Hebrew, Aramaic, and Greek) over about a period of fifteen-hundred years. Nevertheless, it displays a remarkable unity. Its writers came from every walk of life. They included kings, military leaders, priests, prophets, fishermen, poets, musicians, statesmen, shepherds, a tax collector, a physician, and a tentmaker-theologian.

The Holy Spirit inspired the biblical writers – A key biblical passage which clarifies the ultimate divine origin of Scripture in relation to the human dimensions of the biblical writers is 2 Pet 1:19-21,

> And we have the word of the prophets made more certain, and you will do well to pay attention to it as to a light shining in a dark place, until the day dawns and the morning star rises in your hearts. Above all you must understand that no prophecy of Scripture came about by the prophet's own interpretation. For prophecy never had its origin in the will [*thelema*] of man, but men spoke from God as they were carried along [*phero*] by the Holy Spirit (NIV).

Several related points are developed in these verses. Verse 19 underscores the trustworthiness of Scripture; it is "the prophetic word made more certain." In verse 20 we learn why this is so; because the prophecy is not a matter of the prophet's own interpretation, i.e., the prophet does not intrude his own ideas. Verse 21 elaborates on this point: prophecy does not come by the *thelema*—the initiative, the impulse, the will—of the human agent; the prophets are not communicating on their own. Rather, the Bible writers were prophets who spoke as they were moved, carried along, even driven [*phero*] by the Holy Spirit. Peter's statement makes clear that the Scriptures did not come directly from heaven, but rather God used human authors to write His Word.

A close study of the biblical writings confirms that the Holy Spirit did not abridge the freedom of the biblical writers, did not suppress their unique personalities, and did not destroy their individuality. Their writings sometimes involved human research (Luke 1:1-3); they sometimes gave their own experiences (Moses in Deuteronomy, Luke in Acts, the Psalmists); they present differences in style (contrast Isaiah and Ezekiel, John and Paul); they offer different perspectives on the same truth or event (e.g., the four Gospels). And yet, through inspiration, the Holy Spirit was carrying along the biblical writers, guiding their minds in what to speak and write so that what they presented is not merely their own

> **The Holy Spirit guided the biblical writers in what to speak and write.**

interpretation but the utterly reliable word of God, the prophetic word made more certain. The Holy Spirit imbued human instruments with divine truth and assisted them in writing so that they faithfully committed to apt words the things divinely revealed to them (1 Cor 2:10-13).

The human and divine elements in Scripture, the written word of God (Heb 4:12), are inextricably bound together just as they are in Jesus, the incarnate "Word of God" (Rev 19:13). Just as Jesus, the incarnate Word of God, was fully God and fully man (John 1:1-3, 14) so the written word is an inseparable union of the human and the divine.

The words of the prophet are called the Word of God – Though the Bible was not verbally dictated by God so as to bypass the individuality of the human author, except in rare cases, and thus the specific words are the words chosen by the human writer, yet the human and divine elements are so inseparable, the human messenger so divinely guided in his selection of apt words to express the divine thoughts that the words of the prophet are called the Word of God. The individual words of Scripture are regarded as trustworthy, accurately representing the divine message.

This is illustrated by a number of New Testament references. Jesus says, quoting Deuteronomy 8:3, "Man shall not live by bread alone, but by every word [Gr. *rhema*, "word," translating Heb. *qol* "everything"] that proceeds from the mouth of God" (Matt 4:4 RSV). Paul says of his own inspired message: "And we impart this in words not taught by human wisdom but taught by the Spirit, interpreting spiritual truths to those who possess the Spirit" (1 Cor 2:13). Again Paul writes: "And we also thank God constantly for this, that when you received the word of God which you heard from us, you accepted it not as the word of men but as what it really is, the word of God, which is at work in you believers" (1 Thess 2:13).

What is stated explicitly in the New Testament is also indicated by the instances in which Jesus and the apostles base an entire theological argument upon a crucial word or even a grammatical form in the Old Testament. For example, in John 10:34 Jesus appeals to Psalm 82:6 and the specific word "gods" to substantiate His divinity. Accompanying His usage is the telling remark: "The Scripture cannot be broken . . ." (v. 35); it cannot be loosed, broken, repealed, annulled, or abolished. In Matthew 22:41-46, He grounds His final, unanswerable argument to the Pharisees upon the reliability of the single word "Lord" in Psalm 110:1.

The self-testimony of Scripture is overwhelming and unequivocal: it is the Word of God. In the Old Testament there are about sixteen hundred occurrences of four Hebrew words (in four different phrases with slight variations) that explicitly indicate that God has spoken: (1) "the utterance/ declaration [*n^{ec}um*] of Yahweh," some 361 times; (2) "thus says [*'amar*] the Lord," some 423 times; (3) "and God spoke [*dibber*]," some 422 times; and (4) the "word [*dabar*] of the Lord," some 394 times. Numerous times the equivalency between the prophet's message and the divine message is indicated: the prophet speaks for God (Exod 7:1, 2; cf. Exod 4:15, 16), God puts His words in the prophet's mouth (Deut 18:18; Jer 1:9), the hand of the Lord is strong upon the prophet (Isa 8:11; Jer 15:17; Ezek 1:3; 3:22; 37:1), or the word of the Lord comes to him (Hos 1:1; Joel 1:1; Mic 1:1; etc.). Jeremiah (chap. 25) rebukes his audience for not listening to the prophets (v. 4), which is equated with not listening to the Lord (v. 7) and further equated with "His words" (v. 8).

Summarizing the prophetic messages sent to Israel, 2 Kings 21:10 records, "And the Lord said by his servants the prophets," and 2 Chronicles 36:15, 16 adds: "The Lord, the God of their fathers, sent persistently to them by his messengers . . . ; but they kept mocking the messengers of God, despising his words, and scoffing at his prophets. . . ." The prophets' message is God's message. For this reason the prophets often naturally switch from a third person reference to God ("He") to the first person direct divine address ("I"), without any indication of such a switch (see Isa 3:1-4; 5:1-3; 27:1-3; Jer 16:19-21; Hos 6:1-5; Joel 2:23-25; Zech 9:4-7). The Old Testament prophets were sure that their message was the message of God!

Numerous times in the New Testament "it is written" is equivalent to "God says." For example, in Hebrews 1:5-13, seven Old Testament citations are said to be spoken by God, but the Old Testament passages cited do not always specifically ascribe the statement directly to God (see Ps 104:4; Ps 45:6-7; Ps 102:25-27). Again Romans 9:17 and Galatians 3:8 (citing Exod 9:16 and Gen 22:18 respectively) reveal a strict

> In the New Testament "it is written" is equivalent to "God says."

identification between Scripture and the Word of God: the New Testament passages introduce the citations with "Scripture says," while the Old Testament passages have God as the speaker. The Old Testament Scriptures as a whole are viewed as the "oracles of God" (Rom 3:2). Likewise, the New Testament as a whole is "God-breathed" Scripture. While the Bible had many human *writers*, it has only one ultimate *Author* – God Himself!

Richard M. Davidson

The Bible is God's voice speaking to us, just as surely as if we could hear it with our ears.

ML 283

WHO DECIDED WHICH BOOKS SHOULD BE INCLUDED IN THE BIBLE?

The process by which books were included or excluded from the Bible has come to be known by the term "canonization." The word canonization is derived from the Greek word *kanon* whose basic meaning is that of a "rule." Sometimes the books included in our Bible are, therefore, called "canonical books." While canonization has to do with a specific list of books, it deals with more than a mere list of books.

Canonization is really a question about the reasons for which certain books came to be regarded as sacred and authoritative in the early Christian communities. The question is important because the answer to it indicates whether the Bible, as we have it, came into being as a result of the guidance of the Holy Spirit in the early church or whether political forces in the time of Constantine were responsible, as some people claim. Since the Bible consists of the Old and New Testaments, the question will be answered in two parts.

The Old Testament Canon

The thirty-nine books of the Hebrew Old Testament are arranged in three major divisions: the Law, the Prophets, and the Writings. In response to the question as to who decided which books should be included in the Old Testament, we have to acknowledge that due to the lack of historical sources we cannot give a definitive answer. The same applies to the question regarding what time the decision was made. Historical-critical scholars believe the Bible gained its authority progressively. They suggest that the three parts of the Hebrew Bible indicate a three-step development in the canonization of the Hebrew Old Testament. According to this view, the Law—meaning the books of Moses, also called the Pentateuch—was canonized by about 400 B.C., then the Prophets during the first century B.C., and the Writings during the first century A.D.[1]

A conservative perspective – From a conservative perspective, the story is quite different. There is little doubt that the book of the Law (the Pentateuch) was regarded as the word of God from its earliest existence.

Several biblical passages point to the self-authenticating authority of the law from the very beginning. Moses at the foot of Mount Sinai "took the book of the covenant and read it in the hearing of the people; and they said, 'All that the LORD has spoken we will do, and we will be obedient!'" (Exod 24:7). Centuries later, after the Babylonian Exile, Ezra read from the "book of the law of Moses" and the people adopted it as the constitution of their restored commonwealth (Neh 8:1-8). The reverence shown by the Jews to the books of Moses, variously called "the Law of Moses" (Neh 8:1), "the Book of the Law" (v. 3), and "the Law of God" (v. 8), points to the honored status of the books of Moses.

Ezra and Nehemiah may have been involved with the collection of the books comprising the Old Testament canon, but it was not one person, or

The Hebrew Canon		
Law	**Prophets**	**Writings**
Genesis	Joshua	Psalms
Exodus	Judges	Proverbs
Leviticus	1–2 Samuel	Job
Numbers	1–2 Kings	Song of Songs
Deuteronomy	Isaiah	Ruth
	Jeremiah	Lamentations
	Ezekiel	Ecclesiastes
	The twelve Prophets	Esther
	(Hosea – Malachi)	Daniel
		Ezra
		Nehemiah
		1–2 Chronicles

even several, that decided which books should be included in the Old Testament. The story of Israel shows that throughout its history there were individuals who were recognized as prophets of God, and what these people said and wrote was considered the Word of God. The writers did not have to wait for their work to pass the test of time for their authority to be acknowledged. Their work was received as Scripture because what they said and wrote was believed to be from God.

When did the Hebrew canon come into being? – According to Jewish tradition the greater part of the Hebrew canon came into being with Ezra and Nehemiah. The non-canonical book 2 Maccabees refers to records and memoirs of Nehemiah, as well as to his library with books about the kings, prophets, and the writings of David (2 Macc 2:13). The Jewish historian Flavius Josephus argues that unlike the Greeks, who had an innumerable multitude of books, the Hebrews had only twenty-two books;[2] he noted that these books

> contain the records of all the past times; which are justly believed to be divine; and of them five belong to Moses, which contain his laws and the traditions of the origin of mankind till his death . . . but as to the time from the death of Moses till the reign of Artaxerxes, king of Persia, who reigned after Xerxes, the prophets, who were after Moses, wrote down what was done in their times in thirteen books. The remaining four books contain hymns to God, and pre-cepts for the conduct of human life.[3]

Josephus clearly implies that the "prophets" were in place as a body of writings by the time of Ezra and Nehemiah. His subsequent remarks also point to the status of this literature as Scripture. He notes, "It is true, our history hath been written since Artaxerxes very particularly, but hath not been esteemed of the like authority with the former by our forefathers, be-cause there hath not been an exact succession of the prophets since that time."[4] No doubt, the prophetic books like the Pentateuch were considered authoritative from the moment they were written.

Internal evidence indicates that by the time of Daniel and Zechariah the Law and the earlier prophets (Joshua–Kings) were regarded as Scrip-ture. For example, Zechariah 7:12 (c. 518 B.C.) mentions the hardness of the hearts of the people "so that they could not hear the law and the words which the LORD of hosts had sent by His Spirit through the former prophets." And Daniel considered the book of Jeremiah as well as the law of Moses as authoritative (Dan 9:2, 11).

The third division of the Hebrew Bible, the "Writings," as a complete collection dates somewhat later than the "Prophets." The prologue to the Greek translation of *Ecclesiasticus* (an apocryphal book from the second century B.C.) refers repeatedly to the three sections of the Old Testament, indicating that the third section of the Old Testament was already recog-nized as canonical at that time.

The New Testament Canon

The Christian church began with the Old Testament as its Bible. This was in accordance with the practice of Jesus who regarded the Old Testament as authoritative (Matt 5:17-19; 21:42; 22:29; Mark 10:6-9; 12:29-31). Along with the Old Testament, the early church revered the words of Jesus with equal authority (1 Cor 9:14; 1 Thess 4:15). It could not have been otherwise since Jesus was perceived not only as a prophet but also as the Messiah, the Son of God. With the death and resurrection of Jesus, the apostles came to occupy a unique position in spreading and bearing witness to the words of Jesus. Indeed Christ had said of them that because they had been with Him from the beginning they would be His witnesses (John 15:27). As the church grew, and as the apostles became conscious of the prospect of their own death, obviously the need was felt for the words of Jesus to be recorded (2 Pet 1:12-15). The apostles as witnesses of the salvation of God in Jesus Christ were keen to preserve and communicate authoritatively what had happened. Thus, the stage was set for the development of books that, under the guidance of the Holy Spirit, would in time become the New Testament canon.

> **The Christian church began with the Old Testament as its Bible.**

For about two decades after the cross, the message of Jesus was proclaimed orally. Then, from the mid-first century on, Paul's letters began to appear. Somewhat later the three synoptic Gospels and the book of Acts were written and by the end of the first century, when John wrote the book of Revelation, all the books of the New Testament were completed. Throughout the New Testament the focus is on what God had done in Christ (1 Cor 15:1-3; Luke 1:1-3).

The New Testament books acknowledged as Scripture – As was the case with the books of the Old Testament prophets, the writings of Paul and the other apostles were immediately accepted as authoritative because the authors were known to be authentic spokesmen for God. And they themselves were conscious of the fact that they were proclaiming God's message, not merely their own opinions. Paul in 1 Timothy 5:18 follows up the formula "Scripture says" with a quote from Deuteronomy 25:4 and Luke 10:7, thereby placing the Old Testament Scriptures and the New Testament Gospels on the same level of authority; and in 1 Thessalonians 2:13 Paul commends the Christians in Thessalonica for accepting his words as "the word of God." Peter in 2 Peter 3:15, 16 also considered Paul's writings as Scripture.

During the second century most churches came to possess and acknowledge a collection of inspired books that included the four Gospels, the book of Acts, thirteen of Paul's letters, 1 Peter, and 1 John. The other seven books (Hebrews, James, 2 Peter, 2 and 3 John, Jude, and Revelation) took longer to win general acceptance. The early Church Fathers—e.g., Clement of Rome (flourished c. 100), Polycarp (c. 70-155), and Ignatius (died c. 115)—quoted from most of the New Testament books (only Mark, 2 and 3 John, and 2 Peter are not attested) in a manner indicating that they accepted these books as authoritative. Quite clearly, the authority that the books of the New Testament had was not subsequently attributed to them but inherently present in them from the beginning.

Reasons for the New Testament canon – The period during which the New Testament canon took shape (specifically defining the list of books) occupied four centuries and involved a number of factors. While, the primary reason for the inclusion of the New Testament books in the canon was the self-authenticating nature of the books, i.e., their inspiration, other issues contributed to it.

The second century witnessed the development of several heretical movements in Christianity. When the prominent heretic Marcion broke with the church around A.D. 140, he drew up his own list of Christian books that would provide a canon for faith and worship. Marcion, however, accepted only a modified version of Luke's Gospel and ten of the Pauline Epistles as inspired. At the same time, a growing number of Christian writings appeared that claimed to relate unknown details about Christ and the apostles. Many of these books were written by individuals who belonged to a heretical movement called Gnosticism. The Gnostics

> The driving force behind the history of the canon was the faith of the church.

stressed salvation through secret knowledge (Gr. *gnosis*). A number of "infancy" gospels supplied details from the hidden years of Christ's life. Numerous apocryphal books of Acts related the deeds of Peter, Paul, John, and most of the other apostles, and several apocalypses described accounts of personally conducted tours of heaven and hell by the apostles. Today, these writings are known collectively as the New Testament Apocrypha.

11

This period also saw the publication of lists of books known to have been written by the apostles or their associates. Among these lists were the Muratorian Canon, dated towards the end of the second century, the list of Eusebius of Caesarea from the early part of the fourth century, and the list of Athanasius of Alexandria from the middle of the fourth century. The first two lists were still incomplete, listing only about twenty of the twenty-seven New Testament books. The complete New Testament canon is set out in detail in Athanasius' Easter Letter of 367 which contains the twenty-seven New Testament books to the exclusion of all others. During the fourth century several church synods, such as the councils of Rome (382), Hippo (393), and Carthage (397), accepted all 27 books of the New Testament as canonical.

While heretical movements and church councils played a certain role in the formation of the canon, the desire to preserve faithfully the events of what God had done through Christ, already evident in the New Testament, means that the driving force behind the history of the New Testament canon was the faith of the church. In fact "much of what became the core of the New Testament canon . . . had already been unofficially and generally recognized as Scripture as the church began to consider making and approving a list that would set the limits of Christian Scripture."[5] In reference to the New Testament canon Bruce Metzger correctly says of the Synod of Laodicea, "The decree adopted at this gathering merely recognized the fact that there are already in existence certain books, generally recognized as suitable to be read in public worship of the churches, which are known as the 'canonical' books."[6]

> For both Testaments the books which came to be part of the biblical canon had their own self-authenticating authority.

Summary – Who decided which books should be included in the Bible? Our brief discussion has shown that for both Testaments the books that came to be part of the biblical canon had their own self-authenticating authority. The Old Testament books carried their own authoritative credentials by virtue of the writers who unequivocally declared that what they said and wrote was from God. The New Testament books by and large had immediate authority as faithfully witnessing to the events and meaning of God's action through Christ.

The Old Testament canon was, for the most part settled within Judaism by the second century B.C., though discussions concerning it continued for several centuries. From history we know that the final shape of the New Testament canon existed by the fourth century A.D. Although heretical movements and church councils played a role in the actual formation of the New Testament canon, it was not the church who decided which books should be included in the canon. The church recognized and acknowledged the inspiration and self-authenticating authority of the 27 New Testament books and limited the canon to these books.

Kwabena Donkor

References

[1]James A. Sanders, "Canon," *The Anchor Bible Dictionary*, 6 vols. (New York: Doubleday, 1992), 1:843.

[2]Among the Jews the twelve Minor Prophets were counted as one book, as were 1 and 2 Samuel, 1 and 2 Kings, Ezra-Nehemiah, and 1 and 2 Chronicles. Josephus may have counted Ruth as part of Judges and Lamentations as part of Jeremiah, but we do not really know how Josephus divided or grouped the books of the Old Testament to arrive at twenty-two.

[3]Josephus *Against Apion* 1.38-40.

[4]Ibid, 1.41.

[5]Steven M. Sheeley, "From 'Scripture' to 'Canon': The Development of the New Testament Canon," *Review and Expositor* 95 (1998): 518.

[6]Bruce M. Metzger, *The Canon of the New Testament* (Oxford: Clarendon Press, 1997), 210.

The Bible needs fewer defenses and more practice.

Anonymous

WHY DO SOME CHRISTIANS HAVE A LARGER BIBLE?

The three major sections of Christianity—Eastern Orthodox, Roman Catholic, and Protestant—agree about the content of the New Testament canon, but they differ on the number of books included in the canon of the Old Testament. Whereas Protestants recognize thirty-nine books as forming the canon of the Old Testament, Roman Catholics accept forty-six books plus additions to the books of Esther and Daniel. Protestants refer to the seven additional books as Apocrypha while Catholics refer to them as Deuterocanonical. The Eastern Orthodox Churches have traditionally included an even larger number of apocryphal books in the Old Testament canon.

The apocryphal books – Because the books of the Apocrypha are not included in many Protestant Bibles it may be helpful to enumerate their names. First of all there are two narratives entitled Tobit (sometimes also called Tobias) and Judith. Of a somewhat similar nature are three additions to the Book of Daniel known as "Susanna,". . . . "The Prayer of Azariah and the Song of the Three Young Men," and "Bel and the Dragon." There are six additions to the Book of Esther; however, they are not usually given separate names. Then there are two wisdom books among the Apocrypha entitled Wisdom (of Solomon) and Ecclesiasticus [not to be confused with the canonical book Ecclesiastes], also known as The Wisdom of Jesus the Son of Sirach (or, for short, Sirach). Then there is the Book of Baruch and two books of Maccabees; the latter describe, from two different perspectives, the revolt of the Jews against Antiochus IV in the second century B.C. Sometimes other books are mentioned among the Apocrypha, such

> *Apocrypha* – a Greek term meaning "hidden" or "secret." It refers to a collection of books dating from about the third century before Christ to until roughly A.D. 100.
>
> *Deuterocanonical* – is a Greek term meaning literally "second canon." Since the Council of Trent (1545–1563), it is used by Roman Catholics to describe the seven books and additions to Daniel and Esther called Apocrypha by Protestants.

15

as First and Second Esdras and the Prayer of Manasseh, but these are not included in the Roman Catholic canon of the Old Testament.

Historical Review

Although there are various views concerning what time the content of the Old Testament canon was finalized among the Jews, there is weighty evidence that the Hebrew Scriptures, held as sacred by them in the time of Christ and the apostles, contained the same books that are accepted as canonical in the Old Testament of Protestant Bibles today. Neither the Jewish nor the Protestant canon includes the Apocrypha. How then did they come to be included as canonical in Roman Catholic Bibles? The process by which this happened is difficult to trace with exactness. There is enough evidence, however, to provide us with clues as to how the difference came about.

> There are no quotations from the Apocrypha in the Gospels or in any other books of the New Testament.

References to apocryphal books – The first major fact to be stated is that there are no quotations from the Apocrypha in the Gospels or in any other books of the New Testament while there are quotations from or references to most of the thirty-nine books of the Old Testament, quite often quoting them as Scripture. In Christian writings of the second century there are some quotations from or allusions to the Apocrypha, but with few exceptions they are not quoted as Scripture. Most of these quotations or allusions are taken from three books of the Apocrypha: Wisdom, Tobit, and Ecclesiasticus.

The list of Melito – Very significant is the fact that the earliest list of Old Testament books by a Christian writer, Melito, who was bishop of Sardis in the second half of the second century, does not contain the Apocrypha. He went to the East to make himself "accurately acquainted with the books of the Old Testament," which he lists as follows:

The five *books* of Moses—Genesis, Exodus, Leviticus, Numbers, Deuteronomy; Joshua, Judges, Ruth, the four *books* of Kings [now called the books of Samuel and Kings], the two of Chronicles, the *book of the* Psalms of David, the Proverbs of Solomon, also called

16

the Book of Wisdom [not to be confused with the apocryphal book called Wisdom], Ecclesiastes, the Song of Songs, Job, *the books of* the prophets Isaiah, Jeremiah, of the twelve contained in a single book, Daniel, Ezekiel, Esdras [Ezra and Nehemiah].[1]

This list, though slightly different as to the order of the books, is identical with the list of Old Testament books in Protestant Bibles, except that the book of Esther is missing from Melito's list.

Quotations from the Apocrypha in the Church Fathers – From the end of the second century A.D. onward, we find that some apocryphal books begin to be quoted more frequently and are sometimes quoted as Scripture. Clement of Alexandria (c. 150– c. 215), for instance, treats the apocryphal books Tobit, Ecclesiasticus, and Wisdom as Scripture. During the third and fourth centuries a number of Christian writers, both Eastern (Greek) and Western (Latin), follow the same practice. What caused this change in attitude towards the Apocrypha? There is no easy, clear-cut answer to this question. One theory holds that the Jews in Alexandria accepted the Apocrypha as part of the Greek Old Testament (called Septuagint or LXX) in contrast to the Hebrew Old Testament of the Jews in Palestine. Supposedly Christian scholars like Clement of Alexandria then received this expanded Old Testament canon from the Alexandrian Jews.

However, the available evidence suggests that the Jews in Alexandria had the same canon as the Jews in Palestine. The Jewish philosopher Philo (c. 20 B.C.– c. A.D. 50), foremost among Alexandrian Jewish scholars, never once quoted from the Apocrypha. Why, then, did a number of Christian writers in the third and fourth centuries begin to quote the Apocrypha as part of the Old Testament canon? And what led to a fairly general acceptance of the Apocrypha into the canon towards the end of the fourth century?

Inclusion of the Apocrypha in the Greek Old Testament – A number of factors may have contributed to the inclusion of the Apocrypha in the Greek Old Testament. It is important to understand that in the early centuries of the Christian era there existed no Bibles in one unit as we have them today. Individual books were written on scrolls, and it took many scrolls to form a collection of all the books of the Bible. It was therefore easier to mix apocryphal books with canonical books. That a pagan mindset infiltrated Christianity when it replaced pagan religion as the state religion in the Roman Empire during the fourth and fifth centuries is another possible contributing factor, because the apocryphal books contain stories and teachings suited to that pagan mindset. The Septuagint became the Scriptures universally used by Christians, and often they considered them as more inspired than the Hebrew Scriptures, which were used by the Jews. This is illustrated in the case of the disagreement between the Church Fathers Jerome (c. 342–420) and Augustine (354–430).

Jerome, who was born in Italy, spent much of his life in Palestine where he became proficient in the knowledge of the Hebrew language. In A.D. 382 a synod in Rome under the leadership of pope Damasus I (A.D. 304–384) issued a statement on "The Canon of Sacred Scripture," which included the apocryphal books Wisdom, Ecclesiasticus, Tobias, Judith, and two books of Maccabees. The statement is part of the so-called "Decree of Damasus."[2] This is the first Catholic synod that voted to include apocryphal books in the Old Testament canon.

Damasus requested Jerome, who was his secretary from A.D. 382 until 384, to make a new translation of the Old Testament into Latin. Jerome, who after the death of Damasus returned to Palestine, spent many years on this task. He decided to make his translation from the original Hebrew text rather than from the Greek text. When Augustine came to know this he exhorted Jerome to give preference to the Greek text of the Septuagint, "which has the very weightiest authority."[3] Jerome, who knew both the Hebrew and Greek texts well, disagreed with Augustine. He was convinced that books not found in the Hebrew Scriptures "must be placed amongst the Apocryphal writings."[4] However, Augustine, who was bishop of Hippo in North Africa, took a leading part in the Third Council of Carthage in A.D. 397, which voted a statement, "The Canon of the Sacred Scripture" that included the same apocryphal books as did the statement issued by the synod in Rome in 382. These and similar statements came to define the canon of the Latin Bible, the Vulgate, as used in the Roman Catholic Church for more than a thousand years until the time of the Protestant Reformation.

The Protestant Reformation and the Apocrypha – From time to time the inclusion of the Apocrypha in the canon of the Old Testament was questioned in medieval times, but the decisions concerning the canon made in earlier centuries seemed to guarantee their permanent status as part of the canonical Scriptures. This acceptance changed with the rise of the Protestant Reformation. The appeal of Martin Luther (1483–1546) to Holy Scripture as the final authority by which all doctrines and teachings should be judged pressed the issue as to which books constituted Holy Scripture. In his German translation of the Bible, published in 1534, Luther placed the apocryphal books in a separate section entitled, "Apocrypha: these books are not held equal to the Scriptures but are useful and good to read."[5]

Other Protestant translations of the Bible, published even before Luther's German Bible, separated the apocryphal books from the canonical books, not because they despised them, but as the Reformer John Oecolampadius (1482–1531) stated, because "we do not allow them divine authority with the others."[6] The Reformers appealed to the facts that the Hebrew Scriptures did not contain the Apocrypha, that the Church Fathers were not in agreement about their inclusion in the canon, and especially that Jerome had objected to their inclusion when he translated the Old Testament into Latin.

The Council of Trent defended the Apocrypha – The Roman Catholic Church reacted to all of this in the Council of Trent, which convened intermittently from 1545 until 1563. During its fourth session it issued, on April 8, 1546, a "Decree Concerning the Canonical Scriptures." Besides declaring that the Council "receives and holds in veneration with an equal affection of piety and reverence" all the books of the Old and New Testaments as well as the unwritten traditions, it added a list of the sacred books to be included in the canon. The list included the traditional list of Apocrypha and the decree declared that if anyone "should not accept the said books as sacred and canonical, entire with all their parts, . . . as they are contained in the old Latin Vulgate edition, . . . let him be anathema."[7] From Trent onwards all Catholic Bibles include the Apocrypha as part of the Old Testament. More than three centuries later Vatican Council I in its "Dogmatic Constitution Concerning the Catholic Faith," issued on April 24, 1870, strongly affirmed the decree issued by the Council of Trent.

> Martin Luther placed the apocryphal books between the Old and New Testaments and stated that "these books are not held equal to the Scriptures but are useful and good to read."

Many Protestant Bibles, published during the seventeenth and eighteenth centuries, would insert the Apocrypha as a separate section between the Old and New Testaments. Admittedly, there also were editions that did not include the Apocrypha at all. A definite change came in the nineteenth century when, in 1827, the British and Foreign Bible Society, after considerable debate, decided no longer to include the Apocrypha in any of their

Bibles. This decision was followed by other Bible societies in Europe and North America. As a result most Protestant Bibles in the last two centuries have been printed without the Apocrypha. However, the second half of the twentieth century has seen a renewed interest in the Apocrypha among Protestants due to an increasing emphasis on the critical scholarly study of biblical and apocryphal literature and a greater ecumenical interaction between the three major branches of Christianity: Protestantism, Catholicism, and the Orthodox churches. Consequently, while most Protestant Bibles are still printed without the Apocrypha, there is a tendency, especially in scholarly circles, to blur the difference between the canonical books and the Apocrypha.

> "One of the great values of the Apocrypha for the Christians was the fact that it bridged the gap between the end of prophecy and the writing of the NT books, furnishing valuable historical, political, and religious information which would otherwise have been difficult to obtain." (R. K. Harrison, "Apocrypha," *The Zondervan Encyclopedia of the Bible*, M. C. Tenney, ed., 5 vols. [Grand Rapids, MI: Zondervan, 2009], s. v. Apocrypha).

Reasons for Rejecting the Apocrypha

While this historical survey raises serious questions about the inclusion of the Apocrypha in the canon of the Old Testament, this inclusion is even more questionable when we consider the theological differences between the apocryphal and the canonical books. It is noteworthy that there are indications in the Apocrypha that at the time of their origin the prophetic gift had ceased. In "The Prayer of Azariah and the Song of the Three Young Men," which is one of the additions to the canonical book of Daniel, it says in verse 15, "and at this time there is no prince, or prophet, or leader."[8] This of course is not in harmony with the biblical record, because there were at least two prophets at the supposed time of the prayer: Daniel at the court of king Nebuchadnezzar and Ezekiel among the exiles.

A description of the condition of Israel in the time of the Maccabees records that "there was great distress in Israel, such as had not been since the time that the prophets ceased to appear among them" (1 Macc 9:27).

In fact, the Prologue to the apocryphal book Ecclesiasticus or Sirach seems to indicate that the threefold canon of the Hebrew Scriptures—"the law and the prophets and the other books of our fathers"—was already in existence. The prophetic voice of the canonical prophets is absent from the apocryphal books.

The immortality of the soul – The Apocrypha, originating between 200 B.C. and A.D. 100, show marked differences with the canonical books in theology and historical truthfulness. For example, the doctrine of the soul in the apocryphal book Wisdom of Solomon is distinctly different from the concept of the soul in the Hebrew Scriptures. In Wisdom 8:19, 20 we find these words supposedly written by Solomon in reference to himself: "As a child I was by nature well endowed, and a good soul fell to my lot; or rather, being good, I entered an undefiled body." This text presents a body-soul dualism that is foreign to the teaching of the Old Testament, which holds that the entire human being is a living soul (see Gen 2:7). The text also implies the preexistence of the soul, a doctrine unknown to the canonical Scriptures. From this text and other passages in the book Wisdom (such as Wisdom 2:23, 3:1; and 9:15) some have derived the doctrine of an immortal soul.

John Collins, giving a Catholic view of the deuterocanonical books, observes that the Hebrew Bible "is notoriously lacking in attestations of immortality and resurrection." He then stresses with obvious approval "the support of the Wisdom of Solomon for the immortality of the soul, an idea that presupposes Greek anthropology and is alien to Hebrew thought." After quoting Wisdom 2:23 and 9:15 in support, he concludes that, "On this point the deuterocanonical book provides an important foundation for the Catholic tradition, which affirms both the resurrection of the body and the immortality of the soul."[9] Collins is correct in observing that the Hebrew Scriptures do not support the doctrine of the immortality of the soul; neither do they support the body-soul dualism of Greek philosophy and Catholic tradition. However, they do teach the doctrine of the resurrection. Jesus made that clear to the Sadducees as recorded in Matthew 22:23-33.

Salvation by works – Another teaching in some of the Apocrypha contrary to that of the Holy Scriptures is their doctrine of atonement. In Tobit 12:8, 9 we find an angel, called Raphael, instructing Tobit and his son Tobias that, "It is better to give alms than to treasure up gold. For almsgiving delivers from death, and it will purge away every sin." This contradicts clearly the biblical teaching that sin is purged away by blood, in type by the blood of the sacrificial animals and ultimately by the blood of Christ in fulfillment of the Old Testament type (Heb 9:22; 1:3). It is Christ, the Lamb of God, who takes away the sin of the world (John 1:29). There are several texts in the apocryphal books Tobit and Sirach focusing on almsgiving as a way to find favor with God. Tobit 4:10 tells us that "charity [almsgiving] delivers from death and keeps you from entering the darkness." According to Sirach 17:22, "A man's almsgiving is like a signet with the Lord." However, most explicit is Sirach 3:30, "Water extinguishes a blazing fire; so almsgiving atones for sin." This is clearly heretical. No amount of almsgiving can atone for sin! Rather, according to Leviticus 17:11, "it is the blood that makes atonement for one's life." And the apostle Peter makes it clear that we were not redeemed with perishable things such as silver or gold—even if all given away as alms— "but with the precious blood of Christ, a lamb without blemish or defect" (1 Pet 1:19).

Other contradictions – There are many other ways in which the teachings and historical narratives of the Apocrypha contradict the teachings and history of the canonical Old Testament. Sirach 46:20, speaking about the prophet Samuel, tells us that, "Even after he had fallen asleep he prophesied and revealed to the king [King Saul] his death, and lifted up his voice out of the earth in prophecy, to blot out the wickedness of the people." This obviously refers to the message given by the witch of Endor to King Saul, a message supposedly coming from Samuel. The clear teaching of the Old Testament is that "the dead know nothing" and that they never "have a part in anything that happens under the sun" (Eccl 9:5, 6). The spirit that communicated with the witch and king Saul was not the spirit of Samuel, but undoubtedly the lying spirit of a fallen angel.

Judith 9:2 ascribes the murder of the Shechemites by Simeon (and Levi, who is not mentioned in Judith) to divine providence in these words: "O Lord God of my father Simeon, to whom thou gavest a sword to take revenge on the strangers who had loosed the girdle of a virgin [Dinah] to defile her, etc." This is in flagrant contradiction to the curse pronounced under inspiration by the patriarch Jacob in Genesis:

Simeon and Levi are brothers; their swords are implements of violence. Let my soul not enter into their council; let not my glory be united with their assembly; because in their anger they slew men, and in their self-will they lamed oxen. Cursed be their anger, for it is fierce; and their wrath, for it is cruel. I will disperse them in Jacob, and scatter them in Israel (Gen 49:5-7).

Historical inaccuracies – Besides such theological contradictions there are also many historical errors in the Apocrypha. The book Judith is riddled with historical inaccuracies. In Judith 1:1 Nebuchadnezzar is said to rule "over the Assyrians in the great city of Nineveh, in the days of Arphaxad, who ruled over the Medes in Ecbatana." Nebuchadnezzar ruled over the Babylonians in the great city of Babylon, not over the Assyrians in the great city of Nineveh. Nineveh had been destroyed by king Nabopolassar, the father of Nebuchadnezzar. Arphaxad, as a ruler of the Medes in the time of Nebuchadnezzar, is unknown to both biblical and secular history. Similar historical errors can be found throughout the book. Bruce Metzger makes the following comment in a footnote: "Some scholars believe that the historical confusion of the book . . . is deliberate, intended to stamp the work unmistakably as fiction."[10] By contrast, the inspired books of the Old Testament give us genuine history, not fictional history. These differences constitute significant reasons why the Apocrypha should not be recognized or accepted as part of the Holy Scriptures of the Old Testament.

> Some of the books of the Apocrypha teach the immortality of the soul and salvation by works.

Conclusion – The preceding discussion of theological aberrations and historical errors in the Apocrypha is by no means exhaustive. The evidence presented in this chapter is sufficient, however, to show the numerous contradictions and discrepancies in the Apocrypha when compared with the theological teachings and historical records in the canonical books of the Old Testament. While there may be valid reasons for studying the Apocrypha or Deuterocanonical books from a historical perspective, there are no justifiable reasons why they should be counted among the God-breathed Scriptures of which the apostle Paul wrote that they "are able to make you wise for salvation through faith in Christ Jesus," and which he deemed "useful for teaching, rebuking, correcting, and training in righteousness" (2 Tim 3:15, 16). They do not belong to the Scriptures of which Jesus said with divine authority: "These are the Scriptures that testify about me" (John 5:39).

Peter M. van Bemmelen

References

[1]Melito, "Fragments No. 4: From the Book of Extracts," in *Ante-Nicene Fathers*, eds. Alexander Roberts and James Donaldson, 10 vols. (Reprint edition, Grand Rapids, MI: William B. Eerdmans Publishing Co., 1951), 8:759.

[2]Henry Denzinger, *The Sources of Catholic Dogma*, trans. Roy J. Deferrari (St. Louis, MO: B. Herder Book Co., 1957), 33, 34.

[3]Augustine, "Letter 28," in *Works of Saint Augustine: A Translation for the 21st Century*, Part 2—Letters, Volume 1: Letters 1-99, trans. and notes Roland Teske; ed. John E. Rotelle (Hyde Park, NY: New City Press, 2001), 92.

[4]Jerome, "Preface to the Books of Samuel and Kings," in *Nicene and Post-Nicene Fathers, Second Series*, eds. Philip Schaff and Henry Wace, 14 vols. (Reprint edition, Grand Rapids, MI: William B. Eerdmans Publishing Co., 1989), 6:490.

[5]Martin Luther, "Prefaces to the Apocrypha," in *Luther's Works*, trans. and ed. E. Theodore Bachmann, 55 vols. (Philadelphia, PA: Muhlenberg Press, 1960), 35:337, n.1.

[6]Bruce M. Metzger, ed., *The Apocrypha of the Old Testament: Revised Standard Version* (New York, NY: Oxford University Press, 1965), xv.

[7]Denzinger, 244, 245.

[8]Metzger, 210.

[9]John J. Collins, "The Apocryphal/Deuterocanonical Books: A Catholic View," in John R. Kohlenberger III, gen. ed., *The Parallel Apocrypha* (New York, NY: Oxford University Press, 1997), xxxiii, xxxiv.

[10]Metzger, 76, note on Judith 1:1.

Take time to study the Bible, the book of books. There never was a time when it was so important that the followers of Christ should study the Bible as now.

YI, May 18, 1893

HOW TO CHOOSE A BIBLE TRANSLATION?

Translation [into a modern language] involves aiming at a moving target, which has accelerated over the centuries. English is developing more quickly today than at any time in its previous history. Some words have ceased to be used; others have changed their meanings. When a translation itself requires translation, it has ceased to serve its original purpose.[1]

While the King James Bible is still one of the most widely used Bibles in the English-speaking world, its language is frequently no longer understood by modern people, particularly young people. The second half of the twentieth century, therefore, has seen a proliferation of modern Bible versions. While most of them have been produced by Protestants scholars, Roman Catholics, who in the past relied on the Douay Bible (published in 1609), have also produced a number of modern translations: *The Knox Translation* (1956), *The Revised Standard Version: Catholic Edition* (1966), *The Jerusalem Bible* (1966), *The New American Bible* (1970–83), *The New Jerusalem Bible* (1985), and *The African Bible* (1999). In contrast to the Protestant Bibles, the Catholic Bibles all include seven additional books, the Apocrypha (Tobit, Judith, Wisdom, Sirach, 1 and 2 Maccabees, and Baruch), as well as some additions to Daniel and Esther. Furthermore, "Canon Law" of the Roman Church requires all Bible versions to include explanatory notes.

> The King James Version is frequently no longer understood by modern people, particularly young people.

While Protestant Bibles generally come without explanatory notes, a number of annotated Bibles and Study Bibles have been produced over the years. The controversial notes in the *Scofield Reference Bible* (1909) have most effectively promoted dispensationalism. Less controversial Study Bibles are *The Thompson Chain Reference Bible* (1908), *The New Oxford Annotated Bible with Apocrypha* (1973), *The Life Application Bible* with 10,000 notes (1991), and *The Archaeological Study Bible* (2005).

Evaluating Bible Translations

There is no substitute for reading the Bible in the original languages. But, when that is not possible, the best way to get as close to the original as possible is to read a number of different translations. The advantage of using various translations is that in this way we can catch a glimpse of the richness a word may have in the original Hebrew or Greek. Furthermore, different translations may provide different solutions to difficult texts.

Bible Translations: The whole Bible has been translated into 429 languages, the New Testament into a further 1,144 languages and portions of the Bible into a further 862 languages, making a total of more than two thousand and four hundred languages. (Bible Society *Record*, Fall 2007, 8).

The proliferation of English versions in the twentieth century has made it necessary to carefully consider which translation one is going to use and for which purpose. Generally, the preface or introduction of a translation will explain the philosophy behind the translation, and it is useful to read it. Below is a brief outline of some of the major criteria by which Bible translations can be evaluated.

The type of translation – First, we need to recognize that there are two basic types of Bible translations: (1) The formal equivalence or literal translation attempts to translate the text word for word as close as possible to the original, e.g., *The King James Version* (KJV 1611), *The Revised Version* (RV 1885), *The Revised Standard Version* (RSV 1952), *The New American Standard Bible* (NASB 1971) or *The English Standard Version* (ESV 2001). (2) The dynamic or functional equivalence translation is not so much concerned with the original wording as with the original meaning and the impact it had on the original readers, e.g., *The New English Bible* (NEB 1970), *The New International Version* (NIV 1978), *The Revised English Bible* (REB 1989), *The Good News Bible* (GNB) or *Today's English Version* (TEV 1976), and *The Contemporary English Version* (CEV 1995).

What is often considered a third type of translation, the paraphrase Bible, is more of a commentary than a translation. It seeks to restate in simplified but related ways the ideas conveyed in the original language, e.g., *The New Testament in Modern English*, by J. B. Phillips (NT, 1958), *The Living Bible* (1971), *The Clear Word* (1996) *The Message* (NT, 1993, OT

2002). For example, Colossians 2:9 "For in Him dwells all the fullness of the Godhead bodily" (NKJV) in *The Message* is expanded to "Everything of God gets expressed in Him, so you can see and hear Him clearly. You don't need a telescope, a microscope, or a horoscope to realize the fullness of Christ, and the emptiness of the universe without Him."

The first two types of translations are generally done by committees; paraphrases are done by one person who is skilled in literary style, but not necessarily in biblical languages. In spite of the fact that functional equivalence translations do not translate word for word, they try to translate every unit of meaning and

> ## No translation is completely without interpretation.

function, whereas a paraphrase does not attempt an exact correspondence in units between the original and the paraphrase. In other words, whereas a paraphrase must render only the general idea of a passage, a functional equivalence translation is bound by more explicit standards of accuracy.

The formal equivalence translation – The advantage of a literal/formal equivalence translation is that it comes closest to the original text and it allows readers familiar with the original languages to see how idioms and rhetorical patterns are rendered. The major weakness of a formal translation is that a word for word translation produces some awkward sentences and can at times be misleading. For example, Genesis 12:19, "Why saidst thou, She is my sister? so I might have taken her to me to wife" (KJV) is literally what the Hebrew says, but it is not good English. In the New Testament the *King James Version* translates Titus 2:13 as "Looking for that blessed hope, and the glorious appearing of the great God and our Saviour Jesus Christ," thereby splitting the terms "God" and "Saviour" and making one refer to the Father and the other to the Son. According to Greek grammar, however, the text should say "Looking for the blessed hope and the appearing of the glory of our great God and Savior, Christ Jesus" (NASB) – showing that Jesus is both our God and our Saviour. Nevertheless, for serious Bible study it is best to select one of the newer formal equivalence translations such as *The Revised Standard Version*, the *New King James Version*, or The *New American Standard Version*.

The dynamic equivalence translation – An advantage of the dynamic/ functional equivalence translation is that it is easier to understand. Its major weakness is that it involves more interpretation by the translators as indicated by the variant translations of many Bible passages. For example, the time period in Daniel 8:14 in Hebrew is literally 2,300 "evenings mornings" rather than "days." The NIV has "2,300 evenings and mornings" the TEV, however, translates it as "1,150 days," based on the interpretation that these are evening and morning sacrifices (i.e., 2,300 evening and morning offerings require 1,150 days). Yet, the KJV translation "days" is equally an interpretation (i.e., an evening and a morning equals one day), albeit one that is supported by other texts, such as Genesis 1:5, 8, 13, etc.

> Most of the Greek manuscripts were found in monasteries, libraries, or ancient churches in Egypt, the Middle East, and in Europe. Codex Vaticanus (fourth century), thought to be the oldest (nearly) complete copy of the Greek Bible in existence, is believed to have reached Rome in 1483, during the Council of Florence, as a gift from the Byzantine Emperor Giovanni VIII to Pope Eugenio IV. Some manuscripts were found in the most unlikely places. More than fifty New Testament papyrus fragments, for example, were found in the ancient rubbish heaps of Oxyrhynchus in Egypt. Constantine von Tischendorf found about forty pages of Codex Sinaiticus (fourth century) in a trash bin in the convent of St. Catherine at the foot of Mount Sinai.

When giving Bible studies with a dynamic equivalence translation, care needs to be taken that the translation does not undermine the Bible study. For example, the NIV or CEV will not be helpful when the sanctuary truth is studied in the book of Hebrews because they use the incorrect term "Most Holy Place," in Hebrews 9:8, 12, and 25, instead of "sanctuary," which is used by the REB and NEB.

Whichever translation is used, we need to keep in mind that no translation is completely without interpretation. Therefore, we need to understand the strengths and weaknesses of each translation.

The underlying text – A second criterion concerns the underlying text from which the translation is made. The first complete English Bible, the Wycliffe Bible (c. 1380), was a translation of the Latin Vulgate; an early fifth-century version of the Bible in Latin. The Vulgate became the standard Bible of Roman Catholicism. During the Counter-Reformation the Vulgate was reaffirmed by the Council of Trent as the sole, authorized Latin text of the Bible. The Douay-Rheims Bible and the Ronald Knox translation were made from the Vulgate. In other words, they are translations of a translation.

The New Testament of the standard Protestant Bibles from Tyndale to the King James Bible were all based on the Received Text (*Textus Receptus*), which goes back to the Dutch scholar Erasmus (1466–1536), who published the first Greek New Testament in 1516. When Erasmus prepared his first edition of the Greek New Testament in 1515, he had only six manuscripts available to him, and since the last verses of Revelation were missing, he retranslated them from Latin into Greek. Today, there are over 5,000 Greek New Testament manuscript fragments attested, and many of the earliest papyri came to light only in the last hundred years.

The same is true of many Old Testament manuscripts. Until the discovery of biblical texts from the fifth century A.D. in the Cairo Geniza[2] in the latter half of the nineteenth century, the oldest Hebrew Old Testament manuscripts were copied about a millennium after Christ. With the discovery of the Nash Papyrus[3] in 1902 and the Dead Sea Scrolls in the beginning of 1947, Old Testament scholars finally obtained manuscripts containing parts of the Hebrew Old Testament that date from the time before Christ.

The primary value in these finds is that we have a much broader and better textual basis than the translators of the KJV had at their disposal. And although the age of a manuscript does not necessarily correspond to its accuracy, manuscripts that are a thousand years older than what was previously available must be taken into account. Most modern versions take advantage of the newly discovered Old and New Testament manuscripts.

The translator(s) – Another factor to consider is the competence of the translator(s). Just because someone publishes a translation of the Bible does not mean that the translator is competent for the task. In general, it is best to use translations done by committees rather than individuals.

Also, all translations reflect the presuppositions of the translators. These presuppositions may conform to a specific faith persuasion (e.g., Jewish, Catholic, Evangelical-Interdenominational, etc.) or be influenced by the scholarly views of the translators. It is useful to know the faith presupposition of the translator(s), not in order to determine whether or not to avoid the translation but to be able to use it knowledgeably. Even though one may not agree with another religion or denomination, it may still be useful to read a translation done for that specific faith persuasion.

The intended audience – Some Bible translations are produced with specific audiences in mind. For example, the TEV made special efforts to be readable by someone whose first language is not English. Similarly, the NEB uses British English, and the NASB American English. J. B. Philips began a paraphrase of the New Testament epistles, later published as *Letters to Young Churches* in 1947, for the youth of his church during the bombings of England in World War II. He continued with other portions of the Bible and with later editions, but his later work became less paraphrased and less focused on a specific generation, especially as he recognized that his version was being more widely used. These are just a few examples showing the effect of the intended audience on a Bible translation. Knowing a translation's intended audience also helps the reader to evaluate its appropriateness in various settings.

Summary – There is no substitute to being able to read the Bible in the original languages. When that is not possible, several translations should be compared with one another to make sure the text says the same in English as in the original languages. In order to evaluate a translation it is helpful to know what type of translation it is, what the underlying text was, who the translators were, and what intended audience they had in mind.

> Several good translations should be compared with one another to make sure the text says the same in English as in the original languages.

For serious Bible study it is best to use a literal translation that comes as close to the original text as possible (RSV, NASB, ESV, NKJV), as well as more dynamic versions that translate more the thoughts than the words of the original text (NIV, NEB, REB). For preaching and teaching in church a version should be used with which the listeners are familiar. For personal and family devotion a good paraphrase may sometimes be used. Paraphrases, however, should be avoided in Sabbath School or in the pulpit.

Finally, there is no "all-purpose best" translation. No single translation can fit all needs. However, understanding the various Bible versions and how and why they were translated is a means of helping one to know how to make the best use of them.

Tarsee Li

References

[1]Alister McGrath, *In the Beginning: The Story of the King James Bible* (Hodder and Stoughton, 2001), 308, 309.

[2]A geniza is a store room in a synagogue.

[3]The Nash Papyrus contains a portion of Deuteronomy 6:4 and dates to about 100 B.C.

Codex Leningradensis (showing parts of Exodus 20) is the oldest complete manuscript of the Hebrew Bible. It is dated to the first decade of the eleventh century A.D.

ARE THERE MISTAKES IN THE BIBLE?

Bible students throughout the centuries have accepted the Scriptures as God's written word of truth, and Seventh-day Adventists today join those who continue to uphold God's word. Their Fundamental Belief number one states that "the Holy Scriptures are the infallible revelation of His will. They are the standard of character, the test of experience, the authoritative revealer of doctrines, and the trustworthy record of God's acts in history."[1] While Seventh-day Adventists support the divine authority and complete reliability of the Bible, they do not claim absolute perfection for the Bible because of their understanding of the nature of inspiration.

Especially since the Enlightenment in the seventeenth century, many biblical scholars have claimed that the Bible contains a variety of mistakes – doctrinal errors, scientific mistakes, contradictions, discrepancies in names and numbers, as well as imprecise language. Before we address these claims we need to understand the nature of Scripture.

Scripture is of divine origin – According to the self-testimony of Scripture, the entire Bible is indeed God-breathed or God-inspired. In the Old Testament, the writers, at times, claim to be recording what the Lord said to them, e.g., "Then the Lord spoke to Moses, saying . . ." (Exod 25:1) or "The word of the Lord came to me, saying . . ." (Ezek 32:1). David said, "The Spirit of the Lord spoke by me, and His word was on my tongue" (2 Sam 23:2). It has been estimated that there are about twenty-six hundred such claims in the Old Testament.

The New Testament confirms the divine inspiration of the Old Testament. Paul wrote, "All Scripture is given by inspiration of God" (2 Tim 3:16). And Peter stated that "prophecy never came by the will of man, but holy men of God spoke as they were moved by the Holy Spirit" (2 Pet 1:21). The same is true, of course, of the New Testament. Although the apostles do not claim inspiration as frequently as did the Old Testament writers, it is clear that they did regard their messages as given by divine authority. Paul, for example, wrote, "These things we also speak, not in words which man's wisdom teaches but which the Holy Spirit teaches" (1 Cor 2:13), and "When you received the word of God which you heard from us, you welcomed it not as the word of men, but as it is in truth, the word of God" (1 Thess 2:13).

Paul also acknowledged the inspiration of other parts of the New Testament. In 1 Timothy 5:18, he quotes from both Testaments as Scripture, "For the Scripture says, 'You shall not muzzle an ox while it treads out the grain,' and, 'The laborer is worthy of his wages.'" The first part of the text is a quote from Deuteronomy 25:4 and the second from Luke 10:7. Similarly, Peter refers to the writings of Paul as Scripture when he says that in Paul's epistles "are some things hard to understand, which untaught and unstable people twist to their own destruction as they do also the rest of the Scriptures" (2 Pet 3:15, 16). In summary, the Bible is clearly of divine origin.

The human element in Scripture – While Scripture was given by divine inspiration, the writers of the biblical books were not simply God's pens but his penmen, i.e., they wrote the sixty-six books in their own characteristic style, language, and thought form under the guidance of the Holy Spirit. All the books of the Bible, therefore, bear the hallmarks of human authorship. Many books carry the name of the author, and the multitude of historical references and literary links with the times and backgrounds in which these books were written

> The word pseudepigraphal refers to those ancient Jewish writings not in the Old Testament canon or in the apocrypha whose authorship is falsly ascribed to a famous person, e.g., Enoch, Abraham, Ezra, etc.

"give the Bible a very human face."[2] Some books, like Kings, Chronicles, and the Gospel of Luke provide evidence of historical research (1 Kgs 22:39, 45; 1 Chron 29:29; Luke 1:1-4); some biblical writers even quoted pagan authors (Acts 17:28) while at least Jude seems to refer to a pseudepigraphal work (Jude 14, 15). Following are some elements of this "human face":

Language – In dealing with biblical statements we need to remember that the Bible writers frequently used non-technical, ordinary, everyday language to describe things. For example, they spoke of sunrise (Num 2:3; Josh 19:12) and sunset (Deut 11:30; Dan 6:14), i.e., they used the language of appearance rather than scientific language. Furthermore, one must not confuse a social convention with a scientific affirmation. The need for technical precision varies according to the situation in which a statement is made. Therefore imprecision cannot be equated with untruthfulness.[3]

Literary devices – The Bible writers also used different literary devices, such as poetry, parables, metaphors, symbols, etc. Many biblical books, particularly in the OT, are historical narratives; others contain legal texts, wisdom sayings, or apocalyptic prophecies. Because different types of literary material require slightly different methods of interpretation, to distinguish these different literary devices in Scripture helps to avoid wrong interpretations.

Ancient customs – Many biblical passages reflect ancient customs, a knowledge of which can be very helpful in interpreting a text. For example, in ancient times it was common to give the same person different names (Edom/Esau; Gideon/Jerubbaal), and different methods were used to count the reigns of kings.[4]

The transmission of biblical manuscript – It is a well known fact that all the biblical autographs, i.e., the original manuscripts of the biblical authors, have been lost. Although the Jews were very careful in copying biblical manuscripts, some minor mistakes have crept into the text in the course of transmitting and copying the Bible manuscripts.[5] Yet, these mistakes are so insignificant that not

In contrast to the verbal inspiration theory, Seventh-day Adventists generally believe in thought inspiration. However, this does not mean that words were not important. Many times the prophets were also given the very words to write. "The Holy Spirit's guidance did not overrule the thinking and the writing process of biblical writers but supervised the process of writing in order to maximize clarity of the ideas and to prevent, if necessary, the distortion of revelation, or changing divine truth into a lie." (F. Canale "Revelation and Inspiration" in *Understanding Scripture*, ed. G. W. Reid [Silver Spring, MD: Biblical Research Institute, 2006], 65.

one honest soul need stumble or get lost over them (1SM 16). "The Lord has preserved this Holy Book," says Ellen White, "by His own miraculous power in its present shape" (1SM 15). Indeed, the Bible is the best transmitted and best preserved document of antiquity. No other ancient book has been so well preserved as the Bible, with some copies going back to just a few years after the original was written.

Nevertheless, there are a number of differences or discrepancies in the extant Hebrew and Greek texts upon which our Bible translations are based. For example, the Old Testament contains a number of numerical discrepancies in referring to the same events or things in the books of Samuel, Kings, and Chronicles. In 2 Samuel 8:4, David is said to have taken

700 horsemen from Hadadezer while in 1 Chronicles 18:3, 4 the figure is given as 7000.[6] According to 1 Kings 4:26, Solomon had 40,000 stalls for horses, but, in 2 Chronicles 9:25, he had only 4000 stalls. In Matthew 27:54, the centurion says, "Truly, this was the Son of God." In Luke 23:47, however, the centurion is quoted as saying, "Truly, this man was righteous."[7] In the book of Acts, Stephen told the Jews that Abraham bought the cave of Machpelah for a sum of money from the sons of Hamor in Shechem (Acts 7:16). According to the book of Genesis, however, Abraham bought the cave from Ephron the Hittite (Gen 23:8), and it was Jacob who bought his plot of land from the sons of Hamor in Shechem (Gen 33:19).[8] Some of these discrepancies may have perfectly good explanations; others may be due to copyists' mistakes or human frailties. Ellen White wrote: "Some look to us gravely and say, 'Don't you think there might have been some mistake in the copyist or in the translators?' This is all probable . . . . All the mistakes will not cause trouble to one soul, or cause any feet to stumble, that would not manufacture difficulties from the plainest revealed truth" (1SM 16). Do such minor discrepancies destroy our confidence in the Bible? No, unless we insist on a verbal inspiration of Scripture, which claims that "all the words and all the verbal relationships are inspired by God."[9] As Seventh-day Adventists we do not hold this view. "It is not the words of the Bible that are inspired, but the men that were inspired. Inspiration acts not on the man's words or his expressions but on the man himself, who, under the influence of the Holy Ghost, is imbued with thoughts" (1SM 21). Ellen White also stated that God "by His Holy Spirit, qualified men and enabled them to do His work. He guided the mind in the selection of what to speak and what to write" (1SM 26; GC v-vi; cf. also 1SM 36, 37; 3SM 51, 52). Nevertheless, we cannot exclude the possibility of discrepancies or a lack of precision in minor details in the text – details that could be left out without changing the overall reliability of the historical records or the veracity of the theological message.

"When reading Scripture we should not expect to find perfect accuracy. The imperfections and inaccuracies we do find there serve us as evidences of its historicity." (F. Canale, *The Cognitive Principle of Christian Theology*, Berrien Springs, MI: Andrews University Lithotech, 2005], 464).

The historical reliability of Scripture – Even when we allow for the possibility of discrepancies, this does not mean that we cannot trust the Bible when it speaks about historical events or scientific facts. The presence of discrepancies in the Bible does not give license to call into question the historicity of the first eleven chapters of Genesis, the patriarchal stories, or the events related in the Prophets and in the Gospels. The Christian faith is a historical faith in the sense that it essentially depends upon what did, in fact, happen (cf. 1 Cor 15:12-22). The historical aspects of Scripture, therefore, cannot be separated from their theological content. In fact, "to remove the historical from the concerns of Scripture is to remove what demonstrates the faithfulness of God,"[10] because God acts in history. From the New Testament we know that Jesus Christ and the Apostles accepted as true the historical events recorded in the Old Testament (Matt 19:4, 5; 24:37; Acts 24:14; Rom. 15:4), because historical events, such as Creation, the Flood, and the Exodus, are part of the salvation history revealed in Scripture.

The infallibility of Scripture – In spite of imperfections and discrepancies in the Bible, Seventh-day Adventists believe that "the Holy Scriptures are the *infallible revelation of [God's] will.*"[11] But what do we mean by this statement?

Within Christianity, the Eastern Orthodox Church believes that the first seven general councils of the church were infallible; Roman Catholics teach that the pope is infallible when he speaks *ex cathedra;* and conservative Protestants accept Scripture as infallible in matters of faith and practice though some take the belief in the infallibility of Scripture further by saying that the original autographs of the Bible must have been completely inerrant in all matters, whether they referred to history, chronology or science, etc.

Seventh-day Adventists believe in the infallibility of Scripture in the sense that

> Seventh-day Adventists believe in the infallibility of Scripture in the sense that God through the prophetic gift made His will known to humanity without error.

God, through the prophetic gift, made His truth and will known to humanity without error. "God's Word is full of precious promises and helpful counsel. It is infallible; for God cannot err" (FLB 27). Infallibility, however, does not mean the Gospel writers cannot differ in the way they recount the words and works of Jesus. Just as witnesses in a court of law will describe the same event somewhat differently, so in the Gospels we have some-times slightly different accounts of the same events. Neither does infallibil-ity mean that the authors of the biblical books were infallible or perfectly understood everything they wrote; nor does it mean they could not use historical or general information in recording God's messages. Yet, despite all the possible discrepancies found in Scripture, the Bible is still the Word of God.

Ellen White and the trustworthiness of Scripture – Ellen White repeatedly stated that the Word of God is "an unerring counselor, and infallible guide" (FE 100) and an "unerring standard" (MH 462). Does this mean she believed the Bible to be inerrant? While Ellen White strongly defended the infallibility of the Bible, she never used the words inerrant or inerrancy. "The Bible," she said, "is not given to us in grand superhuman language. Jesus in order to reach man where he is took humanity. The Bible must be given in the language of men. Everything that is human is imperfect. Different meanings are expressed by the same word; there is not one word for each distinct idea" (1SM 20). Yet, she claimed that the Bible is, nevertheless, characterized by a "simple beauty of language" and an "unerring truthfulness" (YI, May 7, 1884, cf. LHU 127). Ellen White did not deify Scripture: to her God alone is infallible (Letter 10, 1895, in 1SM 37). But she also firmly believed that "His word is true" (Letter 10, 1895 in 1SM 37) and "reliable" (ST, Oct 1, 1894).

How to Deal with Difficult Texts

What do we do when we come across apparent mistakes in the Bible? The biblical writers themselves freely admit that there are in Scripture "some things hard to be understood" (2 Pet 3:16, KJV), and, as we indi-cated above, some discrepancies do exist in the Old and New Testaments. The challenges of such difficult passages in the Bible have been recognized by serious students throughout history. Although many discrepancies and contradictions disappear under open-minded scrutiny, some problems re-main. To frankly admit those difficulties as unanswered questions is some-thing quite different, however, from claiming that Scripture has definitely erred. The latter is a value judgment on Scripture while the former shows an awareness of the limitations of our human understanding and acknowl-edges that humans are not omniscient but dependent upon further infor-mation and the enlightenment of the Holy Spirit in understanding spiritual things (cf. 1 Cor 1: 18-20; 2: 12-14).

Identifying difficulties – In dealing with difficulties in Scripture we must remember, that many so-called mistakes are not the result of God's revelation but are the result of the misinterpretation of human beings. It has been pointed out that "many contradictory opinions in regard to what the Bible teaches do not arise from any obscurity in the book itself, but from blindness and prejudice on the part of interpreters. Men ignore the plain statements of the Bible to follow their own perverted reason" (RH Jan 27, 1885). Thus, often the problem is not with the biblical text but rather with the interpreter.

Some apparent mistakes in some versions of the Bible may be due to a wrong, or misleading, translation of the original words. Ideally one should have a knowledge of the biblical languages in order to be able to study the Bible in Hebrew, Aramaic, and Greek. Because this ideal is generally not the case, one should compare several good translations before drawing any conclusions. Extended paraphrases such as *The Clear Word* or *The Message,* are not translations and should not be used in Bible Study; they may, however, be useful for devotional reading.

Integrity – When we deal with a difficult passage in Scripture we do well to approach it in perfect honesty. God is *"pleased with integrity"* (1 Chron 19:17, NIV). This preference implies, first of all, that we acknowledge a difficulty and do not try to obscure or evade it. An honest person has an open mindset that is receptive toward the message and the content of what is being studied. Furthermore, honesty includes the willingness to use proper methods of investigation. To explain and understand the word of God properly we cannot use methods with secular presuppositions that are based on atheistic premises running counter to God's Word.

> Often the problem is not with the biblical text but with the interpreter.

Deal with difficulties prayerfully – Prayer is no substitute for hard work and thorough study. However, in prayer we confess that we are dependent upon God to understand His Word. It is an expression of humility to acknowledge that God and His Word are greater than our human reason and greater than our current understanding. On our knees we can ask for the leading of the Holy Spirit and gain a new perspective of the biblical text that we would not have if we placed ourselves above the Word of God.

Explain Scripture with Scripture – With God as the ultimate author of Scripture, we can assume a fundamental unity among its various parts.

That assumption is to say that to deal with challenging aspects of Scripture we need to deal with all difficulties scripturally. The best solution to Bible difficulties is still found in the Bible itself. There is no better explanation than explaining Scripture with Scripture. This means that we have to compare Scripture with Scripture, taking into consideration the biblical context and moving from the clear statements of the Bible to those that are less clear. In other words, we shed light from the clear passages of Scripture on those statements that are more difficult to understand.

> On our knees we can gain a new perspective of the biblical text that we would not have if we placed ourselves above the Word of God.

Be patient – While all of the aspects mentioned above can help in dealing with any difficulty in Scripture with confidence, this method will not always produce an easy or swift solution. We have to be determined that, no matter how much time and study and hard thinking it may require, we will patiently work on finding a solution. At the same time, as we wrestle with difficulties in Scripture, we need to focus on the main points and not get lost in the difficulties. And if some problems persistently defy even our hardest efforts to solve them, we should not get discouraged. It is interesting to note that one characteristic of the faithful believers at the end of history is to live patiently (Rev. 14:12). Part of our perseverance is to be able to live with open questions yet to be faithful to God's Word. For God's Word has proved to be reliable and trustworthy.

Summary – Are there mistakes in the Bible? If by mistake we mean that Scripture teaches error or is fallible and historically unreliable, the answer is "No!" The Bible is God's infallible revelation of His truth and will. Many so-called "problems" in the Bible often are not with the biblical text but rather with the interpreter. Furthermore, particularly since the rise of biblical criticism, the historical reliability of the Bible has often been confirmed by new discoveries in archaeology and other sciences. The suggestion that the Bible contains mistakes can easily be misunderstood to mean that God makes mistakes or that He has placed them there, but this is not the case. The discrepancies and imperfections in Scripture are due to human frailties.

Without question, we do find challenging statements and even discrepancies in the Bible. But none of these discrepancies negatively affects the teaching or the historical reliability of Scripture. We can have full confidence that the Bible we have today is God's truth making every willing man and woman wise unto salvation.

Frank M. Hasel

References

[1]"Fundamental Beliefs," *Seventh-day Adventist Yearbook 2007* (Silver Spring, MD: General Conference of Seventh-day Adventists, 2007), 5.

[2]Peter M. van Bemmelen, "Revelation and Inspiration," in *Handbook of Seventh-day Adventist Theology*, ed. Raoul Dederen (Hagerstown, MD: Review and Herald, 2000), 35. See also the box on page 36.

[3]Cf. Noel Weeks, *The Sufficiency of Scripture* (Edinburgh: The Banner of Trust, 1988), 32.

[4]For more than two thousand years Hebrew chronology has been a serious problem for Old Testament scholars. The numbers of one kingdom could not be made to agree with the numbers of the other. After many years of painstaking research into these apparently hopeless contradictions, the Adventist scholar Edwin R. Thiele succeeded in solving this problem in his widely recognized and well accepted book *The Mysterious Numbers of the Hebrew Kings,* third ed. (Grand Rapids, MI: Zondervan, 1983).

[5]Cf. Paul D. Wenger, *A Student's Guide to Textual Criticism of the Bible* (Downers Grove, IL: InterVarsity Press, 2006).

[6]For an explanation of this problem see Gleason L. Archer, *Encyclopedia of Bible Difficulties* (Grand Rapids, MI: Zondervan, 1982), 184.

[7]On this question see the helpful discussion in Archer, 346-356.

[8]For possible explanations see Walter C. Kaiser Jr., Peter H. Davids, F. F. Bruce, and Manfred T. Brauch, *Hard Sayings of the Bible* (Downers Grove, IL: InterVarsity Press, 1996), 521, 522, and Archer, 379-381.

[9]Walter A. Elwell, ed., *Evangelical Dictionary of Theology* (Grand Rapids, MI: Baker Book House, 1984), 1139.

[10]Weeks, 50.

[11]Fundamental Belief No. 1, emphasis added.

IS THE BIBLE HISTORICALLY RELIABLE?

In 1947 a discovery was made that became the most important archaeological discovery of the twentieth century. The story begins in February or March of 1947, when a Bedouin shepherd boy named Muhammed was searching for a lost goat. He tossed a stone into a hole in a cliff on the west side of the Dead Sea, about eight miles south of Jericho. To his surprise he heard the sound of shattering pottery. Investigating, he discovered an amazing sight. On the floor of the cave were several large jars some of which contained leather scrolls, wrapped in linen cloth. Because the jars were carefully sealed, the scrolls had been preserved in excellent condition for nearly nineteen hundred years. They were evidently placed there before the fall of Jerusalem in A.D. 70.

The Value of the Dead Sea Scrolls

Until the discovery of the Qumran scrolls, which date from the third century B.C. to the first century A.D., the oldest Old Testament manuscripts were a fragment of Deuteronomy 6:4 (Nash Papyrus), dated to the first century B.C., a few biblical fragments from the Cairo Geniza (a synagogue storeroom), dating to the fifth century A.D., and the Masoretic texts[1] from the ninth to the eleventh centuries A.D.

The oldest existing complete Hebrew manuscript of the Old Testament, the Leningrad Codex (see p. 31), comes from the first decade of the eleventh century A.D. The great importance of the Dead Sea Scrolls, therefore, lies in the fact that the earliest scrolls date back to only about two hundred years after the last book of the Old Testament was completed.

Thanks to the Dead Sea Scrolls, we now have a complete manuscript of the Hebrew text of the book of Isaiah and fragments of most of the other biblical books that are more than one thousand years older than the manuscript previously known to exist.

The significance of this discovery has to do with the detailed closeness of the Isaiah scroll (c. 125 B.C.) to the Masoretic Text of Isaiah one thousand years later. It demonstrates the unusual accuracy of the copyists of the Scripture over a thousand-year period. When the Masoretic text was compared with the Qumran texts, they were found to be almost identical.

Even though the two copies of Isaiah discovered in Qumran Cave 1 near the Dead Sea in 1947 were a thousand years earlier than the oldest dated manuscript previously known (A.D. 980), they proved to be word for word identical with our standard Hebrew Bible in more than 95 percent of the text. The 5 percent of variation consisted chiefly of obvious slips of the pen and variations of spelling. Even those Dead Sea fragments of Deuteronomy and Samuel which point to a different manuscript family from that which underlies our received Hebrew text do not indicate any differences in doctrine or teaching. They do not affect the message of revelation in the slightest.[2]

Thus we can know that our present Old Testament text, based on the Masoretic text, is practically identical with the Hebrew text in use at the time of Jesus. There is, therefore, no reason to doubt that what the authors of the Old Testament wrote is substantially the same as what we have in our Bibles today.

> The great importance of the Dead Sea Scrolls lies in the fact that they are more than one thousand years older than the oldest manuscript we had before 1948.

No other ancient writings comparable to the Old Testament have been transmitted so accurately, mainly because the Jewish scribes and the Masoretes treated God's Word with the greatest imaginable reverence. They devised a complicated system of counting the verses, words, and letters of the text to safeguard against any scribal slips. Any scroll not measuring up to these rules was buried or burned.

The Transmission of the New Testament

All of the New Testament books were written during the second half of the first century: Galatians and the two letters to the Thessalonians, around A.D. 50, and John's Gospel and the book of Revelation, ca. A.D. 90 -100.

As with the Old Testament, all of the New Testament autographs have been lost. However, because the New Testament books were the most frequently copied and widely circulated books in antiquity, we have today more than five thousand known Greek manuscripts of the New Testament.

No other book in antiquity even begins to approach such a large number of extant manuscripts. In comparison, "the *Iliad* by Homer is second with only 643 manuscripts that still survive. The first complete preserved text of Homer dates from the 13th century."[3]

For Caesar's *Gallic War* (composed between 58 and 50 B.C.) there are several extant MSS, but only nine or ten are good, and the oldest is some 900 years later than Caesar's day. Of the 142 books of the Roman history of Livy (59 B.C. - A.D. 17), only 35 survive; these are known to us from not more than twenty MSS of any consequence, only one of which, and that containing fragments of Book II-VI, is as old as the fourth century.[4]

The Manuscripts of the New Testament – The earliest manuscript among the more than five thousand known Greek manuscripts of the New Testament is a small fragment of papyrus (called P52) from around A.D. 130, containing portions of John 18:31-33 and 37-38 (see p. 320).

The Chester Beatty papyri (named after their original owner) come from the second and third centuries and consist of papyri containing portions of all four Gospels and Acts, almost all of Paul's epistles, the book of Hebrews and Revelation 9-17. From the same time period we have the Bodmer papyri (also named after their owner) that contain the Gospels of Luke and John, and the letters to Jude and 1 and 2 Peter. These papyri all come from Egypt, where the dry climate helped to preserve them.

The most complete New Testament manuscripts, written on vellum (parchment), come from the fourth century: (1) Codex Sinaiticus (ℵ), discovered by Constantine von Tischendorf in St. Catherine's Monastery (at the foot of Mount Sinai), comes from

> Today we have more than 5,000 known Greek manuscripts of the New Testament.

the middle of the fourth century and contains the entire Greek New Testament. (2) Codex Vaticanus (B), from the Vatican Library, is dated slightly earlier than Sinaiticus and contains the New Testament up to Hebrews 9:14. On textual grounds Codex Vaticanus is considered the most valuable of all existing New Testament manuscripts. Three other important manuscripts are Codex Alexandrinus, Codex Beza, and Codex Ephraemi from the fifth century.

In addition to the approximately thirty-two hundred manuscripts, which are continuous text manuscripts, we have another 2,200 lectionary manuscripts. Lectionaries are "manuscripts in which the text of the New Testament books is divided into separate pericopes [sections], arranged according to their sequence as lessons appointed for the church year."[5] While a few of these lectionaries go back to the fourth century, the majority were written after the eighth century.

New Testament Textual Criticism – We have seen that there is no body of literature in history that enjoys such a wealth of ancient manuscripts as the New Testament. Yet this very fact produces its own problems. The more manuscripts, the greater the textual variations created by scribal mistakes. If a scribe was listening to a dictation, he could make mistakes with words that sounded alike; if he was copying from a manuscript before him, he could mistake one word for another that looked like it. Or his eyes could jump from one word to another occurrence of the same word or to another word that had the same ending, and thus a portion of the text could be left out or written twice. Textual critics seek to reconstruct as closely as possible the original wording of the biblical text.

The English classical scholar Sir Frederic Kenyon stated: "It is reassuring at the end to find that the general result of all these discoveries and all this study is to strengthen the proof of the authenticity of the Scriptures, and our conviction that we have in our hands, in substantial integrity, the veritable Word of God."[6] It should also be clearly stated that in spite of the many variant readings in the manuscripts, none of them affect any point of Christian faith and practice.

The Evidence from Archaeology

While archaeology cannot prove the spiritual truths of the Bible, it can illuminate and clarify the historical circumstances of numerous passages and thereby validate the historicity of many of the events recorded in Scripture. Among the most important discoveries of archaeology that support the historical reliability of Scripture are the following:

1. The Hammurabi Stele (ca. 1700 B.C.) was found by French archaeologists in the winter of 1901-1902 at Susa, the biblical Shushan (Dan 8:2), and is now exhibited in the Louvre in Paris. It contains about 280 laws, many of which are strikingly similar to the Mosaic laws:

Hammurabi #14

If a citizen kidnaps and sells a member of another citizen's household into slavery, then the sentence is death.

Exodus 21:16
He who kidnaps a man, whether he sells him or he is found in his possession, shall surely be put to death.

Hammurabi # 196 and 197
If a citizen blinds an eye of an official, then his eye is to be blinded. If one citizen breaks a bone of another, then his own bone is to be broken.

Exodus 21:24
Eye for eye, tooth for tooth, hand for hand, foot for foot.

The discovery of the Hammurabi Stele and other ancient law codes disposed of the old critical view that the laws of the Pentateuch could not have come from the time of Moses.

2. The Merneptah Stele (ca. 1200 B.C.) was found by Sir Flinders Petrie in the mortuary temple at Thebes and published in 1897. It is today exhibited in Cairo. The stele celebrates Pharaoh Merneptah's (1213-1203) victory over rebellious forces in his Asiatic possessions. It contains the earliest reference to the people of Israel in the ancient world.

3. The Moabite Stone (ca. 850 B.C.) is exhibited in the Louvre. In 1868, an Arab Sheikh, at Diban, showed the German missionary, F. Klein, an inscribed slab that was 3 feet 10 inches high, 2 feet wide and 10 inches thick. German and French officials showed interest in the stone. A French orientalist, Ch. Clermont-Ganneau, was able to obtain a squeeze, i.e., a fac-

"Archaeology can help verify certain historical events that have taken place in the past, but archaeology can only go so far in that archaeology can perhaps demonstrate the truth of some historical event, but it certainly cannot verify the truth of the miraculous. So we get to a point where we have to accept the message of the Bible on faith and we can't depend on archaeology for that" (Bryant Wood cited in Randall Price, *The Stones Cry Out* [Eugene, OR: Harvest House Publishers, 1997], 343).

simile impression, of the inscription. This was fortunate because the Arabs, realizing that they had something valuable, broke it into pieces. The fragments were then carried away to bless their grain. Not all the pieces have been recovered, but the inscription has been restored. It recounts the story of the Moabite king Mesha's rebellion against the king of Israel. It supplements the account of Israel's relations with Moab as recorded in 2 Kings 3.

Moabite Stone
Omri, ruler of Israel, invaded Moab year after year because Chemosh, the divine patron of Moab, was angry with his people. When the son of Omri succeeded him during my reign, he bragged: "I too will invade Moab." However, I defeated the son of Omri and drove Israel out of our land forever. Omri and his son ruled the Madaba plains for forty years.

2 Kings 3:4, 5
Now Mesha king of Moab was a sheep breeder, and he regularly paid the king of Israel one hundred thousand lambs and the wool of one hundred thousand rams. But it happened, when Ahab died, that the king of Moab rebelled against the king of Israel.

4. The Black Obelisk of Shalmaneser III (ca. 840 B.C.) was discovered in 1846 by A. H. Layard at Nimrud. It is exhibited in the British Museum. It shows the Israelite king Jehu paying tribute to the Assyrian king and provides extrabiblical evidence for the domination of Assyria over Israel as well as the existence of Jehu as king of Israel. "Also, anoint Jehu son of Nimshi king over Israel, and anoint Elisha son of Shaphat from Abel Meholah to succeed you as prophet" (1 Kings 19:16).

5. The Taylor Prism (ca. 690 B.C.) is in the British Museum. It was found at Nineveh and contains the military campaigns of Sennacherib (705-681), king of Assyria. The best known passage describes Sennacherib's unsuccessful siege of Jerusalem in the days of Hezekiah, as recorded in 2 Kings 19 and Isaiah 36 and 37. The Assyrian account tacitly agrees with the biblical account by making no claim that Jerusalem was taken. The six-sided hexagonal clay prism says, "[Hezekiah] I made a prisoner in Jerusalem, his royal residence, like a bird in a cage." According to 2 Kings 19:35, 36 Sennacherib was unable to capture Jerusalem because "the angel of the LORD went out, and struck 185,000 in the camp of the Assyrians. . . . So Sennacherib king of Assyria departed and returned *home*, and lived at Nineveh."

6. The Tel Dan Stele (9th or 8th century B.C.) is a black basalt stele erected by an Aramaean king in northernmost Israel, containing an Aramaic inscription to commemorate his victory over the ancient Israelites. Only portions of the inscription remain, but clearly legible is the phrase "house of David" (1 Sam 20:16). Joram son of Ahab (2 Kings 8:16) also appears in the inscription. This is the first time that the name "David" has been recognized at any archaeological site. Like the Moabite Stone, the Tel Dan Stele seems typical of a memorial intended as a sort of military propaganda, which boasts of Hazael's or his son's victories.

7. The Babylonian Chronicles (6th century B.C.) are clay tablets that present a concise account of major internal events in Babylonia. They describe the fall of Nineveh in 612 B.C. (Zeph 2:13, 15), the battle of Carchemish and the submission of Judah, in 605 B.C. (2 Kings 24:7; Dan 1:2), the capture of Jerusalem in 597 B.C. (2 Kings 24:10-17), and the fall of Babylon to the Persians in 539 B.C. (Isa 45:1; Dan 5:30). In connection with the fall of Babylon, the chronicles refer to Belshazzar (Dan 5:1), who was coregent with his father Nabonidus, the last king of Babylon.

The Tel Dan Stele

8. The Pontius Pilate Inscription (first century A.D.) was found in 1961 in the theatre of Caesarea Maritima, the city of Pilate's residence in Palestine. Among the few lines still legible are the words "Pontius Pilate Prefect of Judea." The inscription is the first archaeological evidence for Pilate, before whom Jesus was tried and condemned to death (Matt 27:11-26).

9. Politarch inscriptions – Critics of the New Testament claimed that Luke was mistaken in calling the chief magistrates in Thessalonica "politarchs" (Acts 17:6), a title not found in extant classical literature. In the latter half of the nineteenth century, a number of inscriptions using this term have been found in Macedonian towns, including Thessalonica.

Apart from these major finds of which there are quite a few more, there have been many smaller finds, such as rings and seals, that have confirmed the historical reliability of Scripture. William F. Albright, probably the greatest archaeologist of the twentieth century, whose theological position in the 1920s was one of "extreme radicalism," came to appreciate the historical value of Scripture and wrote in 1956, "There can be no doubt that archaeology has confirmed the substantial historicity of the Old Testament tradition."[7] The same is true of the New Testament. Concerning Luke, the historian of the New Testament, F. F. Bruce wrote, "Our respect for Luke's [historical] reliability continues to grow as our knowledge of this field increases."[8]

The Evidence from Prophecy

The purpose of prophecy is not to satisfy men's curiosity about the future, but to reveal important facts about God's nature – His foreknowledge, His control over all the nations, and His plans for the people of God. In addition, fulfilled prophecies are an important evidence for the inspiration and trustworthiness of God's Word. The two prophecies explained below are representative of the many prophecies found in the Old and New Testaments.

Daniel 2 – The book of Daniel was written in the sixth century B.C., but its prophecies provide evidence for the fact that history is under God's control. Daniel interprets the image in chapter 2 as four successive world empires, beginning with Babylon as the first empire (2:38). The fourth empire would be followed by many smaller kingdoms or nations, symbolized by the ten toes (2:41-43). These nations would continue until God's kingdom, symbolized by the rock "cut out without human hands" smashing the image to bits (2:34), would be established on the earth (2:44).

This prophecy found a remarkable fulfilment in history. Babylon was succeeded by three other world empires, Medo-Persia, Greece, and Rome, and Rome was divided up into many smaller kingdoms that still exist in Europe and around the Mediterranean Sea. The only part of the prophecy still unfulfilled is the arrival of the kingdom of God.

Micah 5:1 – According to the prophecy in Micah 5:1, the Messiah would be born in Bethlehem. The Gospels tell us that although the parents of Jesus lived in Nazareth, because of a census in the Roman Empire, Joseph and Mary had to travel to Bethlehem, Joseph's ancestral home town, where Jesus was born (Luke 2:4-7).

Conclusion

While the Bible is self-authenticating, i.e., the books of Scripture themselves testify to their God-inspired truth, the manuscript evidence, as well as the archaeological and prophetic evidence, confirms the reliability of Scripture.The Dead Sea Scrolls and other manuscript finds have demonstrated the textual reliability of the Bible; and the many archaeological discoveries support the historical reliability of Scripture. While archaeology cannot prove that the Bible is true, it does confirm the historical background of the Bible. "What biblical archaeology offers to us is the widening of the environment against which we may see the Bible and its world. The canvas is now larger and the context wider."[9] Finally, the fulfilment of Bible prophecies confirms the Bible's claim that "prophecy never came by the will of man, but holy men of God spoke *as they were* moved by the Holy Spirit. (2 Peter 1:21, NKJ)

Gerhard Pfandl

References

[1]The Masoretes (A.D. 500 - 1000) were Jewish scholars who added the vowel points to the Hebrew consonantal text.

[2]Gleason A. Archer, *A Survey of the Old Testament* (Chicago, IL: Moody Press, 1974), 25.

[3]Charles Leach, Our Bible. *How We Got It* (Chicago, IL: Moody Press, n.d.), 145.

[4]F. F. Bruce, *The Book and the Parchments*, revised edition (London: Marshall and Pickering, 1991), 170.

[5]Ibid., 163.

[6]Sir Frederic Kenyon, *The Story of the Bible* (Grand Rapids, MI: Wm.B. Eerdmans, 1967), 113.

[7]William F. Albright, *Archaeology and the Religion of Israel* (Baltimore, MD: John Hopkins, 1956), 176.

[8]F. F. Bruce, *The New Testament Documents* (London: Inter-Varsity Fellowship, 1960), 91.

[9]Edgar Jones, *Discoveries and Documents* (London, Epworth Press, 1974), 4.

WHO WROTE THE BOOKS OF THE PENTATEUCH?

The word "Pentateuch" is the scholarly name for the five books of Moses: Genesis, Exodus, Leviticus, Numbers, and Deuteronomy. The name is derived from two Greek words, which simply translated mean "five books." Unfortunately, there is no specific biblical statement that unequivocally states who authored the Pentateuch. However, Jewish and early Christian traditions both attributed the Pentateuch to Moses. The first-century Jewish historian Josephus, for example, speaking of the books of the Old Testament says, "Five belong to Moses, which contain his laws, and the traditions of the origin of mankind till his death."[1]

The liberal or historical-critical view – While Jews and Christians until the nineteenth century believed that Moses was the author of the Pentateuch, historical-critical scholars for the past two hundred years have taught that the books of the Pentateuch were compiled from a number of different sources. For example, because of a number of so-called "doublets," i.e., two different accounts of the same story in the Pentateuch (e.g., two creation accounts in Genesis 1 and 2), they believe that whenever we find doublets of the same story in the Pentateuch they were written by two different writers.

These scholars believe that different authors of the books of the Pentateuch used different names for God. Hence they refer to one author as the Yahwist because he used the name Yahweh (Gen 2:5; 7:1). He supposedly wrote in the ninth century B.C. Another author is called the Elohist, because he used the name Elohim (Gen 1:1; 6:2); he wrote a hundred years after the Yahwist, it is claimed. The book of Deuteronomy is attributed to a writer in the time of Josiah (seventh century B.C.) and much of Leviticus and other "priestly material" is thought to have been written by priests of the temple in Jerusalem in the sixth and fifth centuries B.C. There is by no means agreement among these scholars as to who wrote what and when, and many different hypotheses have been developed over time.[2]

These hypotheses have repeatedly been shown to be largely speculative and out of harmony with what we know about ancient Near Eastern literature. Many Christians, therefore, continue to hold to the Mosaic authorship of the Pentateuch.[3] As we will show below, the biblical evidence supports this view.

The witness of the Pentateuch itself – Within the Pentateuch, the *only* individual who is said to have written anything for future use, besides God Himself (Exod 34:1), was Moses (Exod 24:4; 34:28; Num 17:2, 3; Deut 31:9; 31:22). In addition, God commanded Moses to write information in a book (Exod 17:14). Thus, toward the end of the Israelite wanderings the "Book of the Law" was available for reference, warning, and direction (Deut 28:61; 29:20, 21; 30:10, 31:26).

That the first five books of the Bible belong together, as a unit, is clear within the books themselves. The book of Genesis starts at creation and ends with Joseph, its last hero, dead and buried in Egypt (Gen 50:26). This turn of events is shocking, given the multiple promises made to Abraham that he and his seed would inherit Canaan (e.g., Gen 13:15; 15:18; 17:8). No ancient Near Eastern reader would have been happy to find their hero buried and abandoned in a foreign land, much less when the story line promised the reader and their ancestors their own homeland. Such an unfulfilled ending demands the question, "What happened next?" The Exodus event is the partial an-

---

That Moses was preeminently prepared to author a work such as the Pentateuch is witnessed by the following qualifications:

(a) Education: "At the court of Pharaoh, Moses received the highest civil and military training" (PP 245; Acts 7:22). This undoubtedly included the skill of writing.

(b) Tradition: He received the traditions of the early Hebrew history, and while tending the sheep in Midian he wrote the book of Genesis under the inspiration of the Holy Spirit (PP 251).

(c) Geographical familiarity: Moses possessed an intimate knowledge of the climate and geography of Egypt and Sinai as displayed in the Pentateuch.

(d) Motivation: As the founder of the nation of Israel, he had a great incentive to provide the nation with concrete moral and religious foundations.

(e) Time: Forty long years of wandering in the Sinai wilderness provided ample opportunity to write the Pentateuch.

---

swer to the questions of Genesis. On the other hand, the book of Exodus provides its own drama with the spectacular bonding of the Israelites to Yahweh by the Mount Sinai covenant. Yet Exodus does not conclude the story of Joseph's bones, which were carried out of Egypt with the Israelites (Exod 13:19), and, additionally, the book of Exodus creates its own questions regarding Israelite worship. In the last section of the book, Exodus describes the assembly of the Israelite tabernacle, but the reader is told few details about the worship of Yahweh, which the stories of the book of Exodus imply (consider the problem of the golden calf and the subsequent punishment, Exod 32). Without the fuller details of Leviticus one might be confused as to why the golden calf did not fit within the Israelite system of worship. In addition, when the Exodus account ends the "glory of the LORD" and the tent of meeting is left in the wilderness (Exod 40:34-38).

Leviticus picks up the story where the book of Exodus leaves it, in the wilderness, at the tent of meeting, and spends most of its chapters explaining the holiness and duties of the priests in the worship of Yahweh. The book of Numbers finds the Israelites still in the wilderness and Moses in the tent of meeting (Num 1:1). Much of Numbers recounts this journey, interspersed with ceremonial issues (e.g., Num 29–30), which one would expect arose while on the journey, ending with preparatory issues regarding appropriating and properly living in the Promised Land. All said, at the end of the book of Numbers, the Israelites are camped in Moab across from Jericho, which lies at the edge of the Promised Land. From this vantage point, Moses' sermon (Deuteronomy) is most appropriate: a repeating of their story, a plea for faithfulness, and a final farewell. While he preached his Deuteronomic sermon, one can almost visualize Moses with the scroll of the Pentateuch in one hand and his other hand outstretched, pleading for faithfulness from the Israelites.

With the addition of some details in the book of Joshua, the story of the Israelites (i.e., leaving their homeland, serving as slaves in a foreign country, saved by a mighty Exodus from Egypt, bonded to God by the covenantal experience, wandering in the wilderness, and claiming their homeland), begun in the Pentateuch, is complete. Even the question of what happened to the bones of Joseph is settled (Josh 24:32). No part of this Israelite story, nor any book of the Pentateuch, could be left out without affecting the sense and completeness of the overall story of Israel's origins.

Thus, the most likely reason that the Pentateuch is divided into five books is its topical and historical settings and not a variety of authors. In its totality it is one story by one main author. That the writer largely ignored the issue of authorship implies that everyone knew who the author was when the work was completed. Indeed, had the work been a forgery, then the false claims would certainly have been clearly produced.

The witness of the book of Joshua – One of the strongest evidences that Moses is the author of the books of the Pentateuch is suggested by the omnipresence of Moses in the book of Joshua. Over fifty times in its twenty-four chapters the book of Joshua connects Moses with the commandments or law of the LORD (Josh 1:1, 3, 5, 7, 13-15, 17; 3:7; 4:10, 12, 14; 8:31-33, 35; 9:24, etc.). After the death of Moses God said to Joshua:

> Only be strong and very courageous; be careful to do according to all the law which Moses My servant commanded you; do not turn from it to the right or to the left, so that you may have success wherever you go. This book of the law shall not depart from your mouth, but you shall meditate on it day and night, so that you may be careful to do according to all that is written in it, for then you will make your way prosperous, and then you will have success. (Josh 1:7, 8)

Among other things, these verses suggest that Joshua had ready access to the "Book of the Law," which means that what Moses had written was for Joshua's (and future leaders') ready reference. The command that the words were not to depart from his mouth (Josh 1:8) obviously means that he was to study continuously the writings of Moses as a guide for His decisions as leader and teacher of Israel.

No part of the Israelite story, nor any book of the Pentateuch, could be left out, without affecting the sense and completeness of the overall story of Israel's origins.

In the books Exodus, Numbers, and Deuteronomy, which show Moses leading Israel, Joshua is present to witness the contribution of Moses to Israelite law (Exod 24:13; Num 27:22, 23; Deut 34:9). If there was any doubt as to Moses' contribution, Joshua, after the death of Moses, could have provided the clarifying details. Yet with the many references to Moses in the book of Joshua, the reader is struck only by the unanimity of the book of Joshua's appeal to Moses as the writer of the law.

So the most knowledgeable expert about the writings and authorship issues of the Pentateuch was Joshua, an eyewitness to many of the events described in the Pentateuch as they occurred and the one whom God challenged to study carefully the Pentateuch. The book of Joshua is also the book with the largest number of references to Moses and the Pentateuch.

The witness of the rest of the Old Testament – The emphasis on the Mosaic authorship of the Pentateuch is continued in the rest of the Old Testament. The editorial voice of Judges ties the commandments of God to the writings of Moses. God used the surrounding nations "for testing Israel, to find out if they would obey the commandments of the LORD, which He had commanded their fathers through Moses" (Judg 3:4).

> The disciples and the early Christian church followed the lead of Jesus, noting Moses as the author of the Pentateuch.

The writer of Judges saw Moses as the only writer who provided "commandments of the LORD" and whose work was authoritative enough for God to use as a test. Such sentiments are also found in Kings and in the other books of the Old Testament (1 Kgs 2:3; 2 Kgs 14:6; 21:8; Ezra 6:18; Neh 13:1; Dan 9:11; Mal 4:4). Again, it cannot be over-emphasized that no other writer, other than Moses, is tied to the books of the Pentateuch.

The witness of Jesus and the disciples – Jesus plainly connected Moses with the Law. By New Testament times, the Jews had divided the Old Testament into three major sections: the Law (i.e., Pentateuch), the Prophets, and the Writings. Jesus acknowledged these divisions: "Now He said to them [the disciples], 'These are My words which I spoke to you while I was still with you, that all things which are written about Me in the Law of Moses and the Prophets and the Psalms (the first book of the Writings) must be fulfilled'" (Luke 24:44). On another occasion, to an astonished audience, Jesus said, "Did not Moses give you the Law, and yet none of you carries out the Law?" (John 7:19). In addition, Jesus quoted from four of the Pentateuchal books, while making reference to Moses as their author (Mark 12:26; Exod 3:6; Mark 1:44; Lev 14:1-32; John 6:31, 32; Num 11:8; Mark 12:19-26; Deut 25:5).

The disciples and the early Christian church followed the lead of Jesus, noting Moses as the author of the Pentateuchal books (Luke 2:22; John

1:45; Acts 3:22; 13:39; 28:23; Rom 10:5, etc.). There is no hint from them that any other writer is known for the Pentateuch. For a discussion of who wrote Deuteronomy 34 see page 185.

Summary – The Pentateuch implies that Moses was its author. In addition, Joshua, who was a witness to the Exodus and the events following it, gives credit to Moses for what was written in the Pentateuch. The rest of the Old Testament follows Joshua's lead. Jesus Himself and His disciples also credit the authorship of the Pentateuch to Moses. Therefore, the conclusion that must be reached, using the biblical materials as our guide, is that Moses was the author of the Pentateuch.

David Merling

References

[1]Josephus *Against Apion* 1:39.

[2]A useful summery of the various theories is given by Josh McDowell, *The New Evidence That Demands a Verdict* (Nashville, TN: Thomas Nelson Publishers, 1999), 391–454.

[3]Modern biblical scholars who defend the Mosaic authorship of the Pentateuch include: Kenneth A. Mathews, *Genesis 1:11:26*, The New American Commentary (Nashville, TN: Broadman & Holman, 1995), 24; and Bruce K. Waltke with Cathi J. Fredericks, *Genesis: A Commentary* (Grand Rapids, MI: Zondervan, 2001), 21–29.

Mt. Sinai

DID ISAIAH WRITE THE PROPHETIC BOOK OF ISAIAH?

Until the last two hundred years or so, both Jews and Christians would have thought that the answer to the question posed in the title of this chapter was self-evident and simple. Yes, of course, Isaiah wrote the Old Testament prophetic book that bears his name, and there was no reason to think otherwise. After all, the church and the synagogue had both held this view for many centuries. Also, the superscription in Isaiah 1:1 seems to refer to the entire book with the title, "The vision of Isaiah. . . ." Additionally, New Testament writers repeatedly quote from the book of Isaiah and attribute it to the prophet by name (e.g., Matt 3:3; 4:14-16).

However, with the rise of biblical criticism in the seventeenth and eighteenth centuries, Isaiah, along with the Pentateuch and Daniel (as well as other parts of the Bible), came under increasing scrutiny, and revisionist theories were put forward that stood in stark contrast to traditional beliefs. Regarding Isaiah, most scholars who were committed to the higher-critical approach concluded that, due to factors which will be discussed below, the prophet Isaiah could not have been responsible for the entire prophetic book that bears his name and that his authorship did not extend past chapter 39. Chapters 40-66 were attributed to an anonymous individual living around the time of Cyrus' conquest of Babylon in 539 B.C. Since this person is anonymous and his prophecies were attached to those of Isaiah, he was labeled "Deutero-Isaiah" (Second Isaiah).

Pressing this line of argument still further, a number of critical scholars suggested that chapters 56-66 may have come from an even later hand, and this person was dubbed "Trito-Isaiah" (Third Isaiah). Moreover, noticing that certain references, which they considered to be telltale indicators of the so-called Deutero-Isaiah (such as the prophecies of Babylon's destruction in Isaiah 46 and 47), were also found in chapters 1-39, certain scholars began attributing less and less of chapters 1-39 to the prophet Isaiah with the result that, at least in the minds of these critical scholars, the prophet Isaiah is credited with an ever-dwindling amount of material in the book that bears his name.

Objections to Isaiah's authorship – There are several questions that should be addressed in connection with the aforementioned description.

First, what are some objections that are raised against Isaiah himself being the author of the book that bears his name? Second, what response might be given to these objections? Finally, what are some positive evidences that favor Isaiah as the composer of the entirety of this prophetic book? We turn to these in order.

As to the objections against Isaiah as author, the following evidence is usually set forth. First, the time span presupposed by the book seems impossibly long to incorporate into the life span of the prophet Isaiah. Chapters 1-39 refer to a number of events that took place during the life of Isaiah, whose ministry extended from about 740 to 690 B.C. For example, the Syro-Ephraimite War of about 733 B.C. (Isa 7:1), Sargon's conquest of Ashdod in 711 B.C. (Isa 20:1), and Sennacherib's attack on Judah in 701 B.C. (Isa 36:1) all occurred during Isaiah's ministry. By contrast, the references to the rebuilding of Jerusalem and its temple (Isa 44:28) and to the exodus from Babylon (Isa 48:20) allude to events that took place a couple of hundred years later, long after Isaiah's death.

> Today, critical scholars credit the prophet Isaiah with an ever-dwindling amount of material in the book that bears his name.

A second objection is connected with the first. The subject matter of Isaiah 40-66 is different from that of chapters 1-39. Isaiah 1-39 has as a major concern the threat posed to Judah and Jerusalem by the military might of the Assyrian Empire, a threat which was very real and present during Isaiah's ministry in the second half of the eighth-century B.C. However, in the later chapters, the Assyrian threat is in the past and the focus is on God's rescue of His people and their return to their land from exile, an event that took place following Cyrus' overthrow of Babylon in 539 B.C. How could Isaiah have described events and conditions that would occur nearly two hundred years later?

A third objection points to the different vocabulary and style between the two sections of the book. Words such as "woe" and "judgment," common in chapters 1-39, are infrequent in chapters 40-66. Moreover, terms such as "sing for joy" and "cry aloud," characteristic of chapters 40-66, are rare in chapters 1-39. As to style, while chapters 1-39 include historical narrative (most of Isa 7 and 36-39) and prophetic symbolic action (Isa 20), chapters 40-66 consist almost exclusively of poetic prophecy.

A final objection, one that is insurmountable in the minds of many critical scholars, is the fact that Cyrus of Persia is mentioned by name twice in the so-called Deutero-Isaiah section of the book (Isa 44:28; 45:1). Since Isaiah likely died sometime around 690 B.C. and Cyrus was not born until about 580 B.C., over 100 years later, and was not a prominent leader till many years after that, critical scholars declare that the prophet Isaiah could not have referred to Cyrus by name as anointed by the Lord to defeat Babylon and restore the people of God to their own land.

Responses to objections – What should be said in response to these objections to Isaiah's authorship of the entire prophetic book? Regarding the first objection, it is certainly true that the time span in view in the latter chapters of the book stretches beyond the lifetime of the prophet. Some events that are alluded to, such as the return from Babylonian exile, clearly occurred long after his death. For those who believe either that there is no God, that God doesn't know the future or that even if He does, He does not reveal it to humans, this presents indisputable proof that Isaiah could not have written the entire book, because no one could guess the future with such amazing accuracy.

However, for those who believe in divine foreknowledge and who affirm the biblical teaching that God at times reveals the future to His faithful servants and inspires them to record the revelation for posterity, such an objection is not compelling. This is especially so in light of other displays of foreknowledge in Scripture. Jeremiah prophesied that the Babylonian exile would last for 70 years before God would bring His people home (Jer 29:10); Daniel announced the rise and fall of nations (Dan 2, 7, 8), even specifying some kingdoms by name (Dan 8:20, 21); and Jesus predicted that the temple would be so thoroughly demolished that one stone would not be left on another (Matt 24:2). Even so, Isaiah, speaking by prophetic revelation, anticipated certain events that would transpire long after his death.

As for the different subject matter in chapters 40-66, it is true that these chapters deal with different themes and concepts than the earlier chapters, focusing to some degree on events connected with the Babylonian exile and the return of God's people to their homeland. However, it should not be thought strange that Isaiah should speak of various concepts and themes during a lengthy ministry of some fifty years. One should not expect him to have merely a single focus.

To those who point out that the exile and return were still in the dim future in Isaiah's time and who query how the prophet could describe these matters, it should be noted that the earlier chapters of Isaiah anticipate the coming danger from Babylon, placing the Babylonians first in the section of oracles against the nations (Isa 13-23) and concluding the entire section of chapters 1-39 with a warning of the exile that is to befall the people (Isa 39:6, 7). Perhaps in these ways Isaiah is indicating his recognition that ultimately the Babylonians will prove the greater threat to God's people than the Assyrians who receive more attention in chapters 1-39.

> **Isaiah, speaking by prophetic revelation, anticipated certain events that would transpire long after his death.**

Concerning the objection of the different vocabulary and style used in chapters 40-66, it is true that these chapters are different both in the vocabulary and the style employed when compared with the first half of the book. One can sense this difference even when reading the book in an English translation. However, it does not necessarily follow that such a feature is inconsistent with Isaiah as author. It should not be surprising that the different subject matter and themes of these chapters would make use of a different vocabulary and style, for the latter is related to the former.

Furthermore, it is only to be expected that a towering prophetic genius, such as Isaiah, would be capable of using a wide vocabulary and various styles and genres. Just as modern authors, such as C. S. Lewis, could write books as diverse as *Mere Christianity* and *The Chronicles of Narnia*, using different literary genres and a wide ranging vocabulary, so biblical prophets, especially those of Isaiah's erudition, were not limited to a single style or a narrow range of vocabulary.

Regarding the fact that Cyrus is mentioned by name over 100 years prior to his birth, it is correct to say that this is an unusual feature of Scripture. However, unusual is not the same as unprecedented, for Scripture tells of an unnamed prophet who confronts Jeroboam while the latter is offering a sacrifice at his idolatrous shrine at Bethel, and the anonymous prophet names Josiah (1 Kgs 13:2) as the one who will eventually desecrate this illegitimate place of worship. The confrontation with Jeroboam occurred about 930 B.C., while Josiah was not born until around 650 B.C., some 280 years later.

Evidences for the unity and single authorship of the book – Having addressed the objections to Isaiah as author of the prophecy that bears his name, we turn to some positive evidences of the unity and single authorship of the prophetic book. First, there is no textual evidence that suggests that the book of Isaiah ever existed as anything other than a unified whole. Though we do not possess an abundant number of Old Testament manuscripts, as is the case with the New Testament, the ones we do have support the unity of the entire book. For example, the single most famous manuscript among the Dead Sea Scrolls is the book of Isaiah, dating from pre-Christian times, and it gives no suggestion of a break between Isaiah chapters 39 and 40. Thus, any theory advocating that the latter chapters of Isaiah came from a later time and a different author has no textual support whatsoever.

A second evidence is found in the unifying features discernible in the entire book that infers the single authorship of the whole document. Many features could be catalogued, but one worth noting is the use of the phrase "the Holy One of Israel" to refer to God. Though it is used only thirty-one times in the Old Testament as a whole, twenty-five of these instances are in Isaiah, making it a somewhat distinctive feature of the book. Interestingly, these twenty-five appearances are nearly evenly distributed among the portions of the book that are considered to come from different authors, with twelve occurrences in chapters 1-39 and thirteen in chapters 40-66. Thus, this somewhat distinctive phrase serves to integrate the entire book.

> "Both parts of Isaiah [1-39 and 40-66] have in common an unusual number of the same unique attributes of God, specific designations for the Jewish people, the same special formulas of prophecy, similar words of consolation and rebuke, similar expressions on the future of Zion and Jerusalem, and the ingathering of the exiles, the same forms for emotions of joy and gladness, failure and destruction – all this points to a common and single mentality" (Rachel Margalioth, *The Indivisible Isaiah* [New York: Sura Institute for Research, 1964], 41).

A third evidence was the tendency among the Israelite community to attribute even the smallest prophetic document to the originating prophet. For example, the twenty-one verses that compose the prophecy of Obadiah, though very small in size, were not attached to another prophetic book but were credited to the prophet himself. Conversely, when a section of a prophetic book was thought to have come from someone other than the prophet, as was the case with Jeremiah 52, it was clearly stated (Jer 51:64). In light of this practice, it would be highly unusual for the last twenty-seven chapters of Isaiah, containing some of the most eloquent, beautiful and treasured passages in the entire Old Testament, to have come from a prophet whose name was lost and to simply be attached to another prophetic book as if they had come from that prophet. Thus, the practice of those involved in collecting the prophetic books supports the view that the entire document came from the prophet himself.

Yet a fourth evidence is found in the support offered by the repeated New Testament references to verses from both parts of Isaiah, attributing these passages to the prophet himself. A number of references could be mentioned, because Isaiah was a favorite among the writers of the New Testament documents. However, one especially telling passage is from John 12:38-41, which quotes from both Isaiah and the so-called Deutero-Isaiah. John 12:38 quotes Isaiah 53:1, while John 12:40 cites Isaiah 6:10. Notably, both are credited to the prophet Isaiah himself. It is clear that the New Testament authors considered Isaiah as the author of the prophetic book that bears his name, including the latter chapters of the book often considered to have come from someone else.

Conclusion – Though some scholars have abandoned the view held for many centuries by both Jews and Christians that the prophet Isaiah was the author of the entire book that bears his name, there are persuasive reasons not to embrace their position. Adequate answers can be offered to the objections made against the authorship of Isaiah, while a number of evidences can be set forth in favor of the unity and single authorship of the entire book. The historic position that the whole book should be attributed to the prophet himself can be maintained by thoughtful believers who take Scripture seriously and who affirm that God foretells the future through His prophetic servants.

Gregory A. King

DID THE PROPHET DANIEL WRITE THE BOOK OF DANIEL?

The authorship of the book of Daniel has been debated for centuries. Two basic views have been held by biblical scholars. Some believe that the book was written by the prophet Daniel in the sixth century B.C., as the book itself claims. Others teach that the book was written by an unknown Jew in the second century, during the so-called Maccabean era. The second view, therefore, is often called the Maccabean hypothesis.

To identify the writer of the book of Daniel is crucial because the interpretation and validity of the prophecies of the book depend on the identification of the author. If Daniel in the sixth century wrote the book then it contains real prophecies. If an unknown Jew wrote the book in the second century, its prophecies are not prophecies at all, but history written in the form of prophecy after the event prophesied had already occurred.

> If Daniel in the sixth century wrote the book then it contains real prophecies. If an unknown Jew wrote the book in the second century its prophecies are only history disguised as prophecy.

Sixth-century origin – Scholars who defend Danielic authorship maintain that the book was written and put together in stages by the prophet Daniel himself around 530 B.C. in Babylon. The focus of the book was to proclaim God's Sovereignty from an international perspective and encourage His children to follow faithfully the Lord knowing that He is in control of history. God cares, and He is the ultimate and highest Judge because all human beings are accountable to Him. Daniel presents a sequence of four world empires, the first coming of the Messiah, the rise and activities of the Antichrist (the little horn), the persecution of the saints, the heavenly Judgment, and finally the establishment of the eternal kingdom of God. The culmination of this apocalyptic book lies in the hopeful prediction of a resurrection at the end of time. This view may be designated as the Persian (or Exilic) hypothesis.

Second-century origin – The traditional dating of the book of Daniel to the sixth century B.C. by Jews and Christians was challenged from the end of the eighteenth century onward by the so-called Maccabean hypothesis, and this view prevails today among historical-critical scholars. The first critic who put the origin of Daniel in the second century B.C. was the neo-Platonist philosopher Porphyry (ca. A.D. 234–305). In the twelfth book of his work *Against the Christians* he argued that Daniel was written by an individual living in Judea during the time of persecution by the Syrian king Antiochus IV Epiphanes (175–163 B.C.), because it described these events too accurately for prophecy. In his commentary on the book of Daniel, the Church Father Jerome (ca. 348–420) addressed Porphyry's arguments and defended the authorship of Daniel. Porphyry's publications were later destroyed, and his view on the book of Daniel survived only because Jerome mentioned it.

According to the Maccabean hypothesis, an unknown author in the second century wrote the book and used the pseudonym "Daniel" to add authority to his manuscript. He recounted past history in the form of prophecy, and he genuinely prophesied only the events described in Daniel 11:40–12:2 with the resurrection expected in his time, which the author believed to be the time of the end. But this "genuine "prophecy failed, because what he predicted never happened. According to historical-critical scholarship, the writer made several historical mistakes because he was not well acquainted with the history of Babylon and Medo-Persia. He was only correct when he dealt with the history of his own time, the time of the Seleucids and Ptolemies. Thus, the Maccabean thesis claims that the book of Daniel was written in Judea around 165 B.C., in a time of deep crisis when King Antiochus IV Epiphanes desecrated Jerusalem's temple (167 B.C.) and brutally persecuted the Jews for their religious convictions. The purpose of the book, it is claimed, was to guide the Jews in their faithfulness to God and in their revolt against the tyrannical oppressive reign of this Greek king.

Evidence for the Sixth-Century Origin of the Book

The following points will demonstrate the problem with the historical-critical view and document that there are in fact many arguments in favor of the sixth-century-B.C. origin of the book. Some of these points are:

1. The historical trustworthiness and reliability of the book – Contrary to the claims of many critics, there is a striking accuracy in the detailed accounts of historical events in Daniel, which are so precise in comparison to the known extra-biblical materials, that the conclusion is unequivocal: the author had to be an eyewitness who experienced these events and therefore could provide historically precise accounts. Primary sources definitely demonstrate that the author knew things that were unknown in the second century B.C. but recently rediscovered by archaeologists. A few examples must suffice to prove the point: (a) In Daniel 4 Nebuchadnezzar is mentioned as the proud builder of Babylon. This knowledge about his building activity was lost (it is never mentioned by the ancient historians Herodotus, Ctesias, Strabo, or Plinius) but has been confirmed by modern excavations of Babylon. Some inscriptions resemble the biblical account of Daniel 4 so closely (e.g., the Grotefend Cylinder) that R. H. Pfeiffer admitted, "We shall presumably never know how our author learned that the new Babylon was the creation of Nebuchadnezzar (4:30), as the excavations have proved";[1] (b) Belshazzar's existence was disputed by scholars until the end of nineteenth century.

> Primary sources demonstrate that the author knew things that were unknown in the second century B.C. but rediscovered in modern times.

Then it was found that he was not only the firstborn son of Nabonidus but that his father made him coregent and "entrusted him the [Babylonian] kingdom."[2] Belshazzar, therefore, correctly offered Daniel the third position of authority in his kingdom (i.e., after Nabonidus and himself; see Dan 5:7, 16, 29); (c) The Nabonidus Chronicle confirms that Nabonidus, the last Babylonian king, was not in Babylon when it fell to the Persians in 539 B.C.

> In the month of Tashritu, when Cyrus attacked the army of Akkad in Opis on the Tigris, the inhabitants of Akkad revolted, but he (*Nabonidus*) massacred the confused inhabitants. The 14th day, Sippar was seized without battle. Nabonidus fled. The 16th day, Gobryas (*Ugbaru*), the governor of Gutium and the army of Cyrus entered Babylon without battle. Afterwards Nabonidus was arrested in Babylon when he returned (there).[3]

R. P. Dougherty strongly affirms the historicity of the book of Daniel: "Of all the non-Babylonian records dealing with the situation at the close of the Neo-Babylonian empire, the fifth chapter of Daniel ranks next to cuneiform literature in accuracy so far as outstanding events are concerned. "[4]

Only one historical problem, the identification of Darius the Mede, remains in the book of Daniel. It has not yet been satisfactorily solved because of the lack of adequate historical background material. William Shea's hypothesis of identifying this figure with Gubaru/Ugbaru/ Gobryas, general of Cyrus' army who conquered Babylon in October 539, is the best option in the current debate.[5]

2. The language of the book – Historical-critical scholars have claimed that the language of Daniel indicates a second-century origin. However, linguistic comparisons of Daniel's Hebrew with Qumran Hebrew manuscripts (second century B.C.) speak in favor of the Persian hypothesis, because Daniel's Hebrew is not close to the Hebrew of the Qumran literature. Also the Persian loanwords in Daniel are Old Persian words indicating their antiquity; their meaning is sometimes hard to discern or even lost. In addition, the Aramaic of Daniel belongs to the official or Imperial Aramaic (ca. 600–330 B.C.) and not to the second-century Aramaic. Gleason Archer explains that "the Genesis Apocryphon furnishes very powerful evidence that the Aramaic of Daniel comes from a considerably earlier period than the second century B.C."[6]

There are only three Greek words in Daniel, and they all designate the names of musical instruments (Dan 3:5, 7, 10, 15). This is not very surprising in view of the fact that Greek trade was going on all over the ancient Near East from the eighth century onwards. Also Greeks were employed in Babylon in the time of Nebuchadnezzar as soldiers in his army, and they could have brought these musical instruments with them. If the book had been written in the middle of the second century, as the Maccabean hypothesis claims, then the document should teem with Greek words because at that time it was the predominant language in the East, and Greek culture was prevalent in the Middle East.

3. Daniel's four empires – The Maccabean hypothesis claims that the four world empires in Daniel are Babylon, Media, Persia, and Greece. However, the proper sequence of the four world empires is Babylon, Medo-Persia, Greece, and Rome. This can be documented by the following facts: (a) In 550 B.C., the Persian king Cyrus defeated the Median king Astyages and formed one kingdom known as Medo-Persia, which means that, at the time of the fall of Babylon in 539 B.C., Medo-Persia was already a united empire; (b) the symbolism employed in the book describing the Medo-Persia kingdom indicates that it was counted as one kingdom and not two – the silver part of the statue has two arms (Dan 2:32); the bear representing the same power has two unequal sides (Dan 7:5); and the ram, identified as Medo-Persia, has two different horns (Dan 8:3, 20); (c) Daniel clearly identifies the first three empires as Babylon, Medo-Persia (one united kingdom!), and Greece (Dan 2:38; 5:28; 6:8, 12, 15; 8:20, 21). As far as the biblical text is concerned, the book makes no separation between the Median and Persian empires. Rome is the fourth empire since it succeeded the Grecian Empire in history.

4. The time element in the book of Daniel – The scope of the book goes far beyond Maccabean times, namely, to the time of the end. It means that the sequence of the four successive kingdoms does not end in the Maccabean time. The book predicts the first (Dan 9) and the second coming of Jesus (Dan 2 and 7) with the resurrection at the end of time as the climax of the book (Dan 12:2, 13). The message of Daniel is centered on God and His eternal kingdom in the future.

5. The tone in the book of Daniel – The atmosphere of the book of Daniel does not correspond to or fit the situation of the Maccabean revolt. The prophet Daniel has a very reverent attitude towards Nebuchadnezzar and Darius the Mede (Dan 2:37, 38; 6:21). He works for them in very high government positions and is loyal to them. He speaks with great respect and dignity even to the wicked King Belshazzar (Dan 5:22–24). Nebuchadnezzar himself acts very reverently toward Daniel, even bows down before him (Dan 2:46–48); and according to chapter 4, Nebuchadnezzar reports his conversion story and praises the true High God (Dan 4:34, 37). Even though in the prophetic part

> "The arguments for the Maccabean dating of Daniel can hardly be said to be convincing. Such a period of composition is in any event absolutely precluded by the evidence from Qumran, . . . because there would have been insufficient time for Maccabean compositions to be circulated, venerated, and accepted as canonical Scripture by a Maccabean sect" (R. K. Harrison, *Introduction to the Old Testament* [Grand Rapids, MI: W.B. Eerdmans, 1969], 1127).

of the book, the faithful are persecuted and suffer, they never are encouraged to organize a revolt against their rulers and oppressors. It is a picture rather of passive resistance. This stands in sharp contrast to the Maccabean revolt against king Antiochus IV Epiphanes in the second century. J. J. Collins rightly argues that "the court-tales in chapters 1-6 were not written in Maccabean times. It is not even possible to isolate a single verse which betrays an editorial insertion from that period."[7]

6. The evidence from the Qumran Manuscripts – The Dead Sea Scroll manuscripts speak persuasively in favor of the Persian hypothesis. Daniel is called a prophet, and his book was extensively used in Qumran. Eight manuscripts of Daniel were found there in three caves (1Q, 4Q, and 6Q); they date from 125 B.C. to A.D. 50. This means that this community of faith highly respected and widely used the book of Daniel. It is quoted along with other books such as Moses, Samuel, Isaiah, Ezekiel, Amos, and the Psalms. This would have been highly unusual if the book had been written only in the middle of the second century, only two decades prior to the use of this document by the Qumran community. This period of time is far too short for the book to have been written, copied, and widely read, which would have been necessary for it to gain such great popularity and authority.

7. The dating of the visions – The manner of dating the visions in the book of Daniel corresponds closely to the dating used in the books of Jeremiah, Ezekiel, and Haggai (sixth century), but not to the book of Malachi (fifth century). The practice of putting a date to the visions in the book of Daniel (2:1; 7:1; 8:1; 9:1; 10:1) is similar to the prophets closely connected with the Babylonian exile. Jeremiah marked eight visions (1:2, 3; 25:1; 28:1; 32:1; 36:1; 41:1; 45:1; 46:1, 2), and others he described by certain events (21:1; 24:2; 26:1; 27:1; 33:1; 38:1, 7; 39:15; 40:1; 47:1). The book of Ezekiel has 12 visions with a specific date (1:1, 2; 8:1; 20:1; 24:1; 29:1, 17; 30:20; 31:1; 32:1, 17; 33:21; 40:1). The small book of Haggai, written in 520 B.C., contains five visions, and all are dated (1:1; 1:15; 2:1; 2:10; 2:20). The book of Malachi (ca. 425 B.C.) comprises several visions, but none is dated! The same is true of the apocalyptic literature of the second century B.C. and later. The book of Daniel is, in this respect, closer to the exilic prophets than to the Jewish apocryphal or pseudepigraphical works in which visions are not dated.

8. The testimony of the book of Daniel – The book presents itself as a work from the sixth century B.C., in the Babylonian-Persian setting, and clearly states that Daniel is its author (7:1; 12:4, 9). Daniel is directly mentioned as the author of several chapters that are written in the first-person (7:2, 4, 6, etc.; 8:1, 2; 9:2-4, 20-23; 10:2, 7, 10, 15-19; 12:5, 7, 8). That he also refers to himself in the third person (1:6; 2:14; 5:29; 6:1-4, 28; 7:1; 10:1) is no contradiction, because even some ancient extra-biblical documents were written in this style (for example, Xenophon's *Anabasis*, or Gaius Julius Caesar's *Gallic War*).

9. The testimony of Jesus Christ – In the New Testament, Jesus speaks highly of Daniel (Matt 24:15). He calls him a prophet and connects the prophecy about "the abomination of desolation" (Dan 9:27) to the future fall of Jerusalem in the year A.D. 70 (see Matt 24:16; Mark 13:14; Luke 21:20, 21). Jesus takes Daniel as a historical figure of the sixth century and explains that the focus of the book goes far beyond the Maccabean times!

Conclusion – The Maccabean hypothesis has serious weaknesses and is not convincing. To deny that God knows the end from the beginning (Isa 46:10) and is able to accurately predict the flow of history before it happens is in direct opposition to the biblical assertions that God revealed the future to Daniel (Dan 2:19-23; 7:1, 2; 8:1, 2). The existence of genuine predictive prophecies and God's foreknowledge of historical events are the interpretative keys that unlock the meaning of Daniel.

Objections raised by historical-critical scholars and problems related to a sixth-century authorship of the book can be adequately explained. The author of the book of Daniel is the prophet Daniel himself.

Jiří Moskala

References

[1]Robert H. Pfeiffer, *Introduction to the Old Testament* (New York, London: Harper & Brothers, 1941), 758, 759.

[2]James B. Pritchard, ed., "Verse Account of Nabonidus," in *Ancient Near Eastern Texts Relating to the Old Testament,* third ed. (Princeton, NJ: Princeton University Press, 1969), 312–315.

[3]Idem, "Nabonidus Chronicle," in *Ancient Near Eastern Texts Relating to the Old Testament,* 306.

[4]Raymond P. Dougherty, *Nabonidus and Belshazzar: A Study of the Closing Events of the Neo-Babylonian Empire* (New Haven, CT: Yale University Press, 1929), 216.

[5]William H. Shea, "Darius the Mede: An Update" in *Andrews University Seminary Studies* 20 (1982): 229–247.

[6]Gleason L. Archer, Jr., "The Aramaic of the 'Genesis Apocryphon' Compared with the Aramaic of Daniel," in *New Perspectives on the Old Testament,* ed. J. B. Paine (Waco, TX: Word Books, 1970), 169.

[7]John J. Collins, *The Apocalyptic Vision of the Book of Daniel.* Harvard Semitic Monographs 16 (Missoula, MT: Scholars Press, 1977), 11.

WHY ARE THERE FOUR GOSPELS?

Those who come to believe in Jesus as Savior will be delighted to find in the Bible many documents about him. The New Testament includes four Gospels—Matthew, Mark, Luke, and John—and twenty-three other documents that bear witness to Jesus. Within these documents are the earliest stories about Jesus' earthly ministry (e.g. 1 Cor 11:23-26; 15:1-11), profound reflections on His identity (Phil 2:1-11; Col 1:15-20; Heb 1:1-4), prophecies of His return (e.g. 1 Thess 4:13-18; Rev 19:11-16), visions and messages from the risen and resurrected Christ (e.g. Acts 18:9, 10; Rev 1:9–3:22), and much more. Moreover, read from a Christian point of view, the Old Testament documents also bear witness to Jesus (John 5:39). Believers will learn to treasure this complete witness of the Bible to Jesus.

Only four Gospels – Christians will always come back to the Gospels as the most complete accounts of Jesus' life and ministry. And, in studying them, an important question will emerge: Why are there four Gospels? The question, interestingly, takes two divergent forms: 1) Why are there only four Gospels and not many more? 2) Why are there four Gospels and not just one?

Especially in recent years, the question has been asked, *Why are there only four Gospels and not many more?* Many recent writers argue that a considerable diversity of thinking about Jesus existed among early Christians, which resulted in a wide variety of "Gospels." In the process of forming the canon of the New Testament, these other "Gospels" were inappropriately screened out, leaving a bland orthodoxy. This type of thinking has been popularized by Dan Brown's novel, *The Da Vinci Code*.[1]

Indeed, there are many documents that lay claim to the title "Gospel." Most of these were written long after the four canonical Gospels and bear little resemblance to them. The list of works that claim to recount at least part of Jesus' earthly life and ministry and that may have been composed in the first two centuries after Christ is much smaller.

The Gospel of Judas – One of these, the Gospel of Judas, was written in the Coptic language. The manuscript was discovered in Egypt in the 1970s and is currently in over one thousand pieces with many gaps. The document itself is dated to around AD 300, though it may be a translation of a mid-second century document. If so, that still places it well beyond the time frame of the four canonical Gospels, with which it contrasts sharply in content. The Gospel of Judas is laced with false teaching about God, Creation, and the relationship of the body and soul. The idea that such a document could provide Christians a valid, alternative source for understanding the life and ministry of Jesus is simply wrong.

The Gospel of Thomas – In fact, of all these "Gospels," there is only one document commonly regarded by scholars as possibly preserving authentic information about Jesus not contained in the canonical Gospels: The Gospel of Thomas, another Coptic document, discovered in Egypt in 1945. It consists of a collection of some 114 sayings attributed to Jesus, most of which have parallels in the canonical Gospels. These are offered with little narrative framework. Like the Gospel of Judas, the Gospel of Thomas is clearly a Gnostic document, presenting Jesus as a revealer of secret wisdom and advocating distinctive, Gnostic theology (which regarded the material world as evil and taught secret knowledge as the path to salvation). It was likely composed well into the second century and is dependent upon the canonical documents of the New Testament.[2]

Christopher Tuckett offers a restrained assessment:

> For the most part, the Gospels provide our main source of any knowledge about Jesus. The value of the noncanonical Gospels in this respect is probably mostly negligible. Rather than giving any information about Jesus himself, these texts witness to the ideas of their writers and the communities that preserved them. Many are gnostic texts from a period after the time of Jesus and reflect gnostic ideas read back onto the lips of Jesus.[3]

So why should we not add to the four Gospels? Because only in these four do we possess authentic testimony to the life and ministry of Jesus.

Why not just one Gospel? – Down through the centuries of Christian history, the more usual way to ask our title question has been, *So why are there four Gospels and not just one?* Early on, Christians felt some strain in the fact that four authoritative Gospels were circulating. After all, the four versions of the story of Jesus do not wholly agree on the details of His life. Some of these differences are relatively minor. For example, each Gospel gives a different version of the inscription attached to Jesus' Cross (Matt 27:37, "This is Jesus, the King of the Jews"; Mark 15:26, "The King of the Jews"; Luke 23:38, "This is the King of the Jews"; John 19:19, "Jesus of

Nazareth, the King of the Jews"). And Mark and Luke contain a story about Jesus' healing of a single demoniac (Mark 5:1-20; Luke 8:26-39), while Matthew has Jesus restoring two demoniacs to sanity (Matt 8:28–9:1). An extreme position would require absolute agreement, discounting the testimony of the Gospels because they do not agree in such cases. Such a standard may be dismissed as too stringent and failing to discern the underlying unity of the fourfold testimony to Jesus.

Other differences, though, are more complex. One only need read the accounts of the post-Resurrection appearances of Jesus (Matthew 28; Mark 16; Luke 24; John 20–21) to understand that often the four accounts are not easily harmonized. While there is everywhere a unity in basic convictions about Jesus, there is also a rich diversity in the way His life, ministry, and death are treated.

Would it not be better—in service of a clear, coherent witness to Jesus—to have a single, authoritative Gospel rather than four accounts that exhibit so many differences? Two notable early Christians thought so. Marcion, who died around AD 160, wished to distinguish between the God of the Christian faith and the Creator, the God of Judaism and the Old Testament. So Marcion rejected Matthew, Mark, and John as too Jewish. He preferred Luke, but only in a highly-edited form in which material he regarded as tainted was removed in order to restore the original Gospel. Relying on a faulty understanding of Romans 2:15-16, Marcion argued that there should be only one Gospel, his condensed version of Luke. Another early Christian, Tatian, around AD 170 compiled a single narrative or Gospel harmony out of the four. The resulting document, known as the *Diatessaron* ("through [the] four"), was widely popular and even supplanted the four Gospels in some geographical areas.

> Only in the four Gospels do we possess authentic testimony to the life and ministry of Jesus.

The witness to one Gospel – In spite of the differences among the four Gospels, Christians have come to acknowledge their inspiration and unity. While separate accounts, they bear witness to one gospel; so they were labeled, "The Gospel According to . . ." Two valuable, biblical statements concerning the composition of the Gospels help us understand why early Christians reached these conclusions. The first is Luke 1:1-4:

Inasmuch as many have taken in hand to set in order a narrative of those things which have been fulfilled among us, ² just as those who from the beginning were eyewitnesses and ministers of the word delivered them to us, ³ it seemed good to me also, having had perfect understanding of all things from the very first, to write to you an orderly account, most excellent Theophilus, ⁴ that you may know the certainty of those things in which you were instructed. (NKJV)

Luke tells us that in his time there were in circulation multiple, written accounts of the life and ministry of Jesus ("those things which have been fulfilled among us") that sought to preserve the testimony of "eyewitnesses and ministers of the word." These were people who had experienced the ministry of Jesus and had come to an inspired understanding of it. The writers of these accounts had done their work faithfully since they had performed it in the same spirit and motivation ("just as," v. 2) demonstrated by the "eyewitnesses and ministers of the word."[4]

> Christians acknowledge the inspiration and unity of all four Gospels included in the Bible, in spite of the differences among them.

While others have faithfully recorded their accounts, Luke feels impelled to craft his own narrative based on his careful investigation and motivated by his desire to write an "orderly account." He hopes that his narrative will have a specific impact on Theophilus and his other readers—that they will "know the certainty" (v. 4) about Jesus. Luke is not interested in his readers simply knowing the historical facts (Theophilus seems to already have been "instructed" about these). His desire is that they will understand the profound meaning of them.

The purpose of the Gospels – Luke's desire for his readers is in harmony with that expressed in a second, important biblical statement about the composition of the Gospels, John 20:30, 31:

And truly Jesus did many other signs in the presence of His disciples, which are not written in this book; ³¹ but these are written that you may believe that Jesus is the Christ, the Son of God, and that believing you may have life in His name. (NKJV)

John, too, is interested that his readers move beyond a simple understanding of historical facts. He wishes them to come to a saving knowledge of Jesus, to "believe that Jesus is the Messiah, the Son of God."

John's statement contains another important point: He acknowledges that he has left much out in the writing of his Gospel, that he operated on a principle of selectivity in crafting his account. The point is expanded in John 21:25, "And there are also many other things that Jesus did; which if they were written one by one, I suppose that even the whole world itself could not contain the books that would be written. Amen." (NKJV)

Principles for the study of the Gospels – These important, biblical statements (Luke 1:1-4; John 20:30, 31; 21:25) suggest four significant principles that should guide our study of the Gospels: (1) They are historically reliable witnesses to the life and ministry of Jesus, though we should not read the Gospels with an expectation that we will find exact uniformity in matters of detail and implied chronology. (2) Because the Gospels were written to witness to the fact that Jesus is the Messiah, rather than as detailed biographies of Jesus, our emphasis should be on appreciating the distinctive witness each Gospel offers to a broad, shared understanding of the meaning of the events of Jesus' life and ministry. (3) Similarly, since the Gospel authors—motivated by their desire to communicate the meanings they saw in the history— selected from a much larger body of materials in composing their accounts, we should not expect them all to record exactly the same events. These biblical state-

> As we read the Gospels, we should expect to be drawn to faith in Jesus as Savior.

ments, then, prepare us for a good deal of variety in the canonical Gospels and to appreciate the unique witness of each to the one, true gospel message about Jesus (Gal 1:6-9; Eph 4:4-6). (4) In line with their stated purpose, as we read the Gospels, we should expect to be drawn to faith in Jesus as Savior.

Summary – These biblical statements and the principles that we may deduce from them suggest a most profound answer to the question, "Why do we have four Gospels and not just one?": We have four not just one because they provide an independent historical witness to Jesus' life which would not be as well substantiated if we had just one. For example, were it not for John's Gospel we might suppose that Jesus' ministry lasted only about a year rather than three years. Also, they offer different perspectives on Jesus, offered to different audiences (Jews and Gentiles). Four different historical portraits of Jesus provide a fuller understanding of him than just one. According to Scripture "by the mouth of two or three witnesses every word may be established" (Deut 19:15; Matt 18:16). We have a better opportunity for a complete and well-rounded understanding of Jesus by reading and treasuring all four Gospels.

In reflecting on the complexities of our question, "Why do we have four Gospels?", Christians should feel blessed that we possess four different and authoritative narratives of the life and teachings of Jesus, each written from a different perspective and with a different audience in view. While some may wish for more "Gospels" and others still desire a single narrative, we would do well to study the four great inspired witnesses to Jesus, the Gospels of Matthew, Mark, Luke and John, in the context of the wider biblical revelation.

John K. McVay

References

[1]Dan Brown, *The Da Vinci Code: A Novel* (New York: Doubleday, 2003), 233, 234.

[2]See the helpful analysis by Darrell L. Bock and Daniel B. Wallace, *Dethroning Jesus: Exposing Popular Culture's Quest to Unseat the Biblical Christ* (Nashville, TN: Thomas Nelson, 2007), 105-130.

[3]Christopher Tuckett, "Gospel, Gospels," in *Eerdmans Dictionary of the Bible*, ed. David Noel Freedman (Grand Rapids, MI: Eerdmans, 2000), 523.

[4]Luke knows only of accounts of the life and ministry of Jesus that reflect the gospel message that he discloses in his own account, that Jesus Christ, the Son of God, became a human being and died to save humankind. He seems unaware of the existence of any alternative accounts that would offer a radically different understanding of Jesus' life and ministry.

HOW DO SEVENTH-DAY ADVENTISTS INTERPRET DANIEL AND REVELATION?

Seventh-day Adventists use the historical-grammatical approach for the interpretation of Scripture. This approach, which accepts Scripture as the authoritative Word of God, takes the self-testimony and the claims of the Bible seriously and exegetes the text carefully.

The books of Daniel and Revelation have occasioned a greater variety of interpretations than any other books in the Bible. It is the purpose of this chapter to provide an outline of the major systems of interpretation used for understanding these books and to summarize the Adventist understanding of the prophecies of Daniel and Revelation.

Schools of Interpretation

The Historicist School – This is the oldest school of interpretation and until the nineteenth century it was the dominant one. It can be traced back to some of the church fathers such as Irenaeus, Hippolytus, and Jerome.

The historical-grammatical approach, also called the historical-biblical method, acknowledges the self-testimony of the Bible that God revealed His truths to the biblical authors and inspired them to share His messages in the Scriptures (2 Tim 3:16; 1 Pet 1:10-12; 2 Pet 1:19-21). It takes the historical background and the literary features of the text seriously and exegetes it accordingly.

Historicists believe in the divine inspiration of the books of Daniel and Revelation. They believe that the book of Daniel was written by the prophet Daniel in the sixth century B.C. and that its main prophecies cover the period from the Babylonian Empire to the second coming of Christ. They believe that the apostle John wrote the book of Revelation and that its prophecies cover the period from John's day to the end of the millennium. They generally see the antichrist—portrayed under the symbols of Daniel's little horn, and

John's first beast in Revelation 13, as the papacy. Seventh-day Adventists use the historicist method in interpreting Daniel and Revelation.

The Historic-Preterist School – The historical roots of preterism go back to the time of the Counter-Reformation. When the Protestant Reformers identified the papacy with the prophesied antichrist in the books of Daniel and Revelation, the Spanish Jesuit Luis de Alcazar (1554-1613) claimed that these prophecies were already fulfilled in the time of the Roman Empire. Thus, the papacy could not be the antichrist.

Interpreters of the historic-preterist school consider the book of Daniel as a revelation from God but generally limit the fulfillment of its prophecies to the time period that runs from the time of Daniel in the sixth century B.C. to the first coming of Christ. They apply the book of Revelation to the beginning of the Christian era. They view the antichrist, therefore, as a persecuting Roman emperor in the past.

The Historical-Critical or Modern-Preterist School – The roots of this school of interpretation go back to Porphyry, a philosopher in the third century A.D., who taught that the book of Daniel was written by an unknown Jew in the second century B.C. Daniel's prophecies, therefore, are *vaticinia ex eventu* (Latin for "prophecies written after the event"). This view was revived in the age of the Enlightenment and Rationalism in the seventeenth and eighteenth centuries. Modern preterists see the book of Daniel as a reflection of the political and religious situation of the Jewish people under the Syrian king Antiochus IV Epiphanes, who persecuted the Jews. Not accepting the existence of true prophecies, modern preterists believe that the prophecies of the book of Revelation refer to historical events in the time of the Roman Empire, especially in the first century.

> Seventh-day Adventists use the historicist method in interpreting Daniel and Revelation.

The Futurist-Dispensational School – One of the defenders of the papacy against the Reformers' identification of the pope with the antichrist was the Spanish Jesuit Francisco Ribera (1537-1591), who applied most of the prophecies in the books of Daniel and Revelation to the future.

Futurist-dispensationalist interpreters, like historicists and historic preterists, accept Daniel's authorship of the book in the sixth century B.C., but unlike historicists, they generally do not apply the figure of the antichrist to the papacy or another power in the past. Rather, they expect that a personal antichrist will appear in the time of the end and continue in power for three and a half years and fulfill what is said of the little horn in Daniel and of the beast-antichrist in the book of Revelation.

The Idealist School – This is a fairly modern system of interpretation. It does not attempt to find specific historical fulfillments of the prophecies in the books Daniel and Revelation, but simply takes these prophecies as depicting the spiritual conflict between Christ and Satan in all ages. Fulfillment of the prophecies is, therefore, seen either "as entirely spiritual or as recurrent, finding representative expressions in historical events throughout the age, rather than in one-time, specific fulfillments."[1] Thus the antichrist in the time of John was the Roman Empire as a representative of all antichristian governments throughout history.

The Eclectic School – The eclectic approach, a modified version of the idealist approach, usually combines some elements from all the above-mentioned schools of interpretation. Some elements in the books Daniel and Revelation are clearly future (the resurrection and the Second Coming, at least); others are seen as having been fulfilled in the past (e.g., most of the prophecies of Daniel and the messages to the seven churches in Rev 1-3); and some prophecies symbolically portray events throughout history, though most eclectic commentators will not identify specific historical events. The basic problem with this approach is to determine which elements belong to which category.

When we compare the various schools of interpretations, taking note of the fact that the specific angelic interpretations in the book of Daniel are along historicist lines (Dan 8:20, 21), we come to the conclusion that historicism is the only method that satisfies all the data.

The Year-Day Principle

The year-day principle, in which one day in prophecy is counted as one year in history, constitutes the backbone of the historicist interpretation of apocalyptic prophecy. During the nineteenth century, modern preterism and futurism replaced historicism, and with this change the year-day principle fell into disrepute. Today, Seventh-day Adventists

> Since the visions in Daniel and Revelation are largely symbolic the time periods should also be seen as symbolic.

are the only major Christian church still using historicism and the year-day principle.

The biblical evidence – The main points in support of the year-day principle from Scripture can be summarized as follows:

1. Since the visions in Daniel and Revelation are largely symbolic, with a number of different beasts representing important historical empires (Dan 7:3-7; 8:3-5, 20, 21; Rev 13:1, 11), the time periods (Dan 7:25; 8:14, Rev 12:6, 14; 13:5) should also be seen as symbolic.

2. The fact that the visions in the book of Daniel deal with the rise and fall of known empires in history that existed for hundreds of years indicates that the prophetic time periods must also cover long time periods.

3. In Daniel 7 the four beasts that together account for a reign of at least one thousand years are followed by the little horn power. It is the focus of the vision since it is most directly in opposition to God. Three and a half literal years for the struggle between the little horn and the Most High are out of proportion to the comprehensive scope of salvation history portrayed in this vision. The same applies to Revelation 12:6 and 14 in which the one thousand and two hundred and sixty days or three and a half time cover most of the history between the First and Second Advents.

4. The peculiar, distinctive way in which the time periods are ex-

> As early as the third century BC, the 70 weeks of Daniel 9 were understood to be 70 "weeks of years," i.e., 70 x 7 = 490 years. The LXX (the Greek translation of the Hebrew Scriptures in the 3rd century BC), in translating the Hebrew for "weeks" in Dan 7:25-27, inserted the additional phrase "of years," providing the first published example of what would later be called the "year-day principle." Not until enough centuries had passed to make such long ages of prophecy comprehensible, were the longer prophecies of 1290 days, 1335 days, and 2300 days understood as years. Thus Rabbi Nahawendi in the early ninth century AD was the first to recognize the year-day principle as operative in the 1290 and 2300 days. (Jerry Moon, "The Year-Day Principle and the 2300 Days," http://www.sdanet.org/atissue/end/yearday.htm, accessed Nov. 2, 2009).

pressed indicates that they should not be taken literally. According to the context, the expressions "time, times, and half a time" (Dan 7:25; 12:7; Rev 12:14), "forty-two months" (Rev 11:2; 13:5), and "one thousand two hundred and sixty days" (Rev 11:3; 12:6) all apply to the same time period, but the natural expression "three years and six months" is not used once.

> The Holy Spirit seems, in a manner, to exhaust all the phrases by which the interval could be expressed, excluding always that one form which would be used of course in ordinary writing, and is used invariably in Scripture on other occasions, to denote the literal period. This variation is most significant if we accept the year-day principle, but quite inexplicable on the other view[2]

5. The prophecies in Daniel 7-8, and 10-12 lead up to the "time of the end" (8:17; 11:35, 40; 12:4, 9), which is followed by the resurrection (12:2) and the setting up of God's everlasting kingdom (7:27). Considering the more than twenty-five hundred years since the sixth century B.C., literal time periods of only 3 ½ to 6 ½ years are not capable of reaching anywhere near the time of the end. These prophetic time periods, therefore, should be seen as symbolic, standing for long periods of actual time.

6. In Numbers 14:34 and Ezekiel 4:6 God deliberately used the day for a year principle as a teaching device. And the 70-week time prophecy in Daniel 9:24-27 met its fulfillment at the exact time if we use the year-day principle to interpret it. Many interpreters, who in other apocalyptic texts do not use the year-day principle, recognize that the 70 weeks are in fact "weeks of years" reaching from the Persian period to the time of Christ. Thus, the pragmatic test in Daniel 9 confirms the validity of the year-day principle.

7. The reason why the year-day principle is applied to some prophecies in the apocalyptic writings (such as the 70 weeks of Dan 9:24-27) and not to others (such as the 70 years of Dan 9:2) is well explained by the concept of "miniature symbolization."[3] According to this concept, the year-day principle is applicable only to those symbolic prophecies in which its main entity (person, animal, or horn) is a representation of a larger reality (nation, kingdom, or power). Thus, in apocalyptic settings, both the main entity and the time involved have to be interpreted on a larger scale. The time element has to be viewed from a year-day perspective.

Outline of the Seventh-day Adventist Interpretation of Daniel

Today, the Seventh-day Adventist Church is the largest church that still uses the historicist principle of interpretation as did all the Reformers. Accordingly, Seventh-day Adventists understand the four empires of Daniel 2 and 7 to represent the kingdoms of Babylon, Medo-Persia, Greece, and Rome. They identify the stone in Daniel 2 as the Second Coming and the little horn in Daniel 7 as a symbol for the papacy. On the basis of the year-day principle,[4] they see the 1260 days in 7:25 as representing the 1260-year time period from 538 to 1798[5] and the changing of "times and laws" as referring to the change of the fourth commandment from Sabbath to Sunday.

> All the prophecies of Daniel cover essentially the same ground from the time of the ancient kingdoms of Babylon and Medo-Persia to the Second Advent.

In Daniel 8, the ram and the goat are symbols for Medo-Persia and Greece (vv. 20, 21) and the little horn is again identified with the papacy. Daniel 8:1-14 describes the last and most important symbolic vision in the book. In what follows, from 8:15 until the end of the book, the angelic interpreter explains in detail and in non-symbolic language different aspects of the vision; e.g., in Daniel 9 the angel explains that the 2300 days in Daniel 8:14 begin at the same time as the 70 weeks in 9:24, namely at 457 B.C.[6] The focus of the prophecy in 9:24-27 is Jesus Christ who fulfilled it during His life here on earth. Seventh-day Adventists understand the cleansing of the sanctuary in 8:14, which began in 1844 at the end of the 2300 years, as a reference to the pre-Advent judgment going on in heaven now. The last vision of the book in chapters 10-12, like the sanctuary vision in chapter 8, begins in the days of the Medo-Persian kingdom and reaches to the time of the end (12:4).

Summary – All the prophecies of Daniel cover essentially the same ground from the time of the ancient kingdoms of Babylon and Medo-Persia to the Second Advent:

a. Daniel 2   Babylon to Second Advent (stone kingdom)
b. Daniel 7   Babylon to Second Advent (kingdom given to the saints)

c. Daniel 8 & 9   Medo-Persia to Second Advent (little horn is broken)

d. Daniel 10-12   Medo-Persia to Second Advent (resurrection)

Each vision has its special focus, and later visions enlarge upon and provide further explanations for earlier visions. The book of Daniel clearly shows that the principle of recapitulation, according to which each vision covers approximately the same historical era but focuses on different aspects of the events depicted, is a valid principle of prophetic interpretation.

Gerhard Pfandl

The Book of Revelation

Although the Book of Revelation contains apocalyptic prophecy, it begins and ends like a letter (Revelation 1-3 and 22:6-20). One is almost reminded of a Pauline epistle. Yet there are also differences from other letters: (1) the messages in Revelation 2 and 3 are coming directly from Jesus, not from a human author; (2) the entire Apocalypse, not just the seven messages, is addressed to the seven churches.

The letter frame of the book resembles somewhat more classical prophecy than apocalyptic prophecy. Classical prophecy is found in the major and minor prophets of the Old Testament. It contains straightforward predictions that are normally conditional and at times may have more than one fulfillment. By contrast, apocalyptic prophecy uses extensive symbolism; frequently it contains visions and dreams and has a cosmic sweep as well as a strong eschatological emphasis. Apocalyptic prophecy also contains striking contrasts

> Apocalyptic prophecy is not conditional in nature and does not contain more than one fulfillment.

such as the seal of God and the mark of the beast, the marriage supper of God and the birds' supper of humans, and the woman and the harlot. Most importantly, apocalyptic prophecy is not conditional in nature and has only one fulfillment.

That the letter frame of Revelation may be closer to classical prophecy is evident from the vocabulary. Revelation 1-3 and 22:6-20 have fewer symbols and must frequently be interpreted literally. Here are two examples: whereas Jesus appears throughout the apocalyptic part of the book as the "lamb" (28 times), the name most often used for Jesus in Revelation, this word is not found in the letter frame. On the other hand, the term *ekklesia* (church) is found only in the letter frame of the Apocalypse and not at all in the apocalyptic part of the book. There the church appears as the woman clothed with the sun, as the bride, and as the 144,000.

Despite the differences between the letter frame and the apocalyptic part of Revelation, the two are integrally related. The messages to the seven churches point forward to and anticipate the rest of the book.

The Interpretation of Revelation

In the interpretation of the book, the interpreter must take note of:

1.   **The Old and New Testament background of the book** – The book of Revelation is the climax of both the Old and the New Testament. Thus, one needs to have a good knowledge of the Bible in order to understand Revelation. Although Revelation does not contain a single quoted verse from the Old or New Testament, the book is filled with allusions especially to the Old Testament but also to the New Testament. For instance, the background of Revelation 4 is Ezekiel 1 and 10, and the background of Revelation 6 is Zechariah 1 and Matthew 24.

> Although Revelation does not contain a single quoted verse from the Old or New Testaments, the book is filled with allusions, especially to the Old Testament.

2.   **The symbolism of the book** – Generally speaking, we should interpret the Bible literally. Jesus' approach to Scripture, as well as that of the apostles', points to a literal interpretation. However, in Revelation the symbolic understanding is predominant. This may be indicated in Revelation 1:1 by the word *semaino* ("signify" [KJV]; "make known" [NIV]), which points to Jesus as "symbolizing" the book of Revelation to John. We should carefully study the indicators in the text in order to notice when a shift from the symbolic to the literal understanding takes place. For instance, the comparison of the sun with sackcloth and the falling of the stars with the falling of the figs from the fig tree in the sixth seal (Rev 6:12, 13) in-

dicates that the author switches from a symbolic to a literal depiction of events.

3. **The historical nature of the prophecies** – The book of Revelation seems also to demand the historicist approach mentioned above in connection with the interpretation of the book of Daniel. In Revelation 12 a woman, the church, gives birth to the Messiah, the Messiah is taken to heaven, Satan persecutes the woman, and finally Satan makes war against the remnant of her offspring. Revelation 13 further describes this final war. The vision ends with a depiction of Christ's second coming (Rev 14:14-20). Thus the center of the book clearly points out that the book refers to events at the beginning of the first century A.D., runs through historical times, and ends with the final consummation. The time periods in the Apocalypse further underline this view. The 1260 days, 42 months, or three and a half times refer back to Daniel 7 and 12 and must be interpreted according to the year-day-principle as covering more than a millennium, an extensive period of time, which has already passed by.

4. **The principle of recapitulation** – In the book of Daniel we have four visions that cover basically the same historical period but each from a different perspective and with different emphases. The book of Revelation resembles the book of Daniel in using this principle of recapitulation or repetition. For example, the seven seals, the seven trumpets, and the vision of the satanic trinity in Revelation 12-14 all describe events beginning in the first century A.D. and reaching to the final consummation.

Outline of the Seventh-day Adventist Interpretation of Revelation

After the general introduction to the book (Rev 1:1-8) John describes a vision of Jesus that forms the introduction (1:9-20) to the seven letters (ch. 2-3). There is a clear-cut end to this first set of "sevens" in Revelation 3:22. A new section begins with Revelation 4:1, although 3:21 already prepares the way for it. In Revelation 4:1 John is told, "Come up here [to heaven], and I will show you what must take place after these things."

The vision of the six seals (Rev 4-8:1) focuses on the time period from the first century A.D. to the final consummation. It begins with the slaughtered Lamb, the crucified Christ, who appears before God the Father, and with events on earth in the first century A.D. The sixth seal takes us to the cosmic signs of the time of the end, the Second Coming and the redeemed in heaven (6:12-7:17), and the seventh seal to the time beyond (8:1). The seven trumpets (8:2-11:18) contain the time period of 1260 days (11:2,

3) equaling 1260 years, according to the year-day principle. This time period covers most of church history and takes us to the time of the end. Revelation 12-14 again covers the time period from the time of Jesus (12:5) to the Second Advent and the harvest of the earth (14:14-20). Thus, these visions are a clear case of the principle of recapitulation.

While the first part of Revelation (1-14) is primarily historical, dealing with events from the time of John to the end of the world's history, the second part of Revelation deals only with final events (15-22). This part begins with the seven last plagues, which are still future from our present perspective (Rev 15-16). Chapters 17-19 are a more detailed description of the sixth and seventh plagues shown to John by one of the angels carrying bowls. They portray the fall of Babylon, first as harlot (ch. 17) and then as the great city (ch. 18), before they depict the marriage supper of the Lamb and the supper of the birds (ch. 19) in connection with Armageddon. Revelation 20 follows the Second Coming, describing the Millennium and the executive judgment before finally revealing a new heaven and a new earth with a New Jerusalem and God's immediate presence.

"It was Victorinus of Pettau (d. ca. 304) who introduced the principle of recapitulation in Revelation that has been followed with some modification by subsequent interpreters. . . . The application of the recapitulative principle can be very helpful to the interpreter of Revelation. Information and insight obtained from clear passages may unlock the theological meaning of parallel difficult ones. For instance, Revelation 7 may be the clue for understanding chapters 10-11, particularly with regard to the two witnesses. Also, one can notice that the seven trumpets and the seven-bowl-plagues series are deliberately parallel in terms of their language and content" (R. Stefanovic, *Revelation of Jesus Christ* [Berrien Springs, MI: Andrews University Press, 2002], 28).

The book's focus – The many symbolic and sometimes disturbing images must not distract from the main focus of the book. Revelation is a book about God the Father and Jesus Christ. It is the Revelation of Jesus Christ (Rev 1:1). Therefore, we should interpret it in a Christ-centered way. The book is also a book about the bride of the Lamb, the church and the remnant. The message to the church must be heard.

The book makes an immense eschatological contribution, furnishing detailed information about end-time events. It portrays the great Controversy theme in a way that no other biblical book does.

Ekkehardt Mueller

References

[1]Steve Gregg, *Revelation: Four Views* (Nashville, TN: Thomas Nelson, 1997), 3.

[2]Thomas R. Birks, *First Elements of Sacred Prophecy* (London: William E. Painter, 1843), 352.

[3]See Alberto R. Timm, "The Miniature Symbolization and the Year-day Principle of Prophetic Interpretation," *Andrews University Seminary Studies* 42 (Spring 2004): 149-167.

[4]Among the smaller churches that still use the year-day principle are the Church of God (Seventh-day) with ca. 125,000 members and the Advent Christian Church with ca. 25,000 members.

[5]In A.D. 538, the Ostrogoths abandoned the siege of Rome, and the bishop of Rome, released from Arian control, was free to exercise the prerogatives of Justinian's decree of 533. Exactly 1260 years later (1798), at the command of Napoleon, Berthier, with a French army, entered Rome, proclaimed the political rule of the papacy at an end and took the pope prisoner, carrying him off to France, where he died in exile.

[6]The text says that the 70 weeks are cut off from a longer time period. In view of the connections between Daniel 8 and 9, the 70 weeks are cut off from the longer period of the 2300 evenings and mornings in Daniel 8:14.

When the books of Daniel and Revelation are better understood, believers will have an entirely different religious experience.

TM 114

WHY WERE SOME PROPHECIES IN
THE OLD TESTAMENT NOT FULFILLED?

Every reader of the Old Testament has come across prophecies that were not fulfilled in their original Old Testament context, nor in the New Testament. One example is the description of the future glory of Jerusalem after the exile as described in Isaiah 60–66. Compared to the humble beginnings of Jerusalem in the time of Sheshbazzar, after the return from the Babylonian exile in 537 B.C., or during Ezra and Nehemiah's time nearly a hundred years later, the prophetic descriptions in Isaiah appear to be quite different – much more fundamental and majestic. Other examples of this type of biblical prophecy can be found in Ezekiel 40–48, involving the description of a future temple. This temple never became a reality. While there are hundreds of fulfilled prophecies in the Old Testament, some prophecies were—apparently—never fulfilled. How does this harmonize with the New Testament statement found in 2 Peter 1:19: "And we have the word of the prophets made more certain, and you will do well to pay attention to it, as to a light shining in a dark place, until the day dawns and the morning star rises in your hearts." Will not the true prophet (and thus his/her prophecy) be confirmed when his/her prophecies are fulfilled, as can be so aptly seen in the narrative of Micaiah and the prophets of Baal before Jehoshaphat and Ahab (1 Kgs 22)?

In order to understand this apparent tension, we will first look at the nature of biblical prophecy, in general, followed by a concise introduction to conditional prophecy. The final section will deal with the relationship between Old Testament prophecy and the Messianic kingdom to which the Old Testament writers were looking forward.

The nature of biblical prophecy – The prophetic texts of the Old Testament are much more comprehensive and wide-ranging than our twenty-first-century concept of prophecy. The modern understanding of a prophet focuses almost exclusively on the element of predicting the future. In the Old Testament, however, not all the prophets spoke about future events or eschatological happenings. For example, most of the book of the prophet Haggai is built around the reconstruction of the temple. The prophet challenges and encourages the people to rebuild the temple; there are only a few references to the future of Israel and the glory of the reconstructed temple (Hag 2:6-9, 22).

The Pentateuch contains a very helpful definition of a prophet (Heb. *nabi'*) – a prophet is somebody who speaks on behalf of God to His people or to the world in general (Deut 18:18-20; also 1 Kgs 22:14); he is the Lord's mouthpiece. One can find similar terms and concepts in the surrounding religions although it appears that biblical prophecy was more comprehensive than its extra-biblical counterpart. The prophetic word for the world and God's people did not always involve predictions concerning the future. Most of the Old Testament prophets spent a lot of time talking about social justice, the lack of ethics (e.g., Amos 2:6-16; 4:1-3; Isa 1:2-20; 5:1-30; Jer 5; 7; etc.), and religious formalism (Isa 58; Jer 2; 11; Ezek 14; Hos 2; 5; Amos 4:4-13; etc.). To speak on behalf of God without being called and empowered by Him was considered a grave sin. False prophets, therefore, were to be killed (Deut 18:20).

> The fulfillment of the divine word, spoken through the prophet, was one of the important indicators of true prophecy.

The fulfillment of the divine word, spoken through the prophet, was one of the important indicators of true prophecy (see Deut 18:21, 22; Jer 28:9; Ezek 13:6; 33:33), albeit not the only one. And it is precisely here that the issue of unfulfilled prophecy comes in. Considering the biblical standard for evaluating prophets, does not the mere fact that some of the prophecies included in the book of Isaiah (or of any other prophet for that matter) were not fulfilled disqualify the prophet from being an authentic, divinely called, mouthpiece of God? The biblical concept of conditional prophecy provides a solution to this critical issue.

Conditional prophecy – The principle of conditional prophecy is well explained by the prophet Jeremiah. In Jeremiah 18 God instructs the prophet to visit the potter down the road. Jeremiah visits the potter's workshop and observes the molding, shaping, and reshaping that characterize the work of a potter. It is precisely this action of molding and reshaping that God utilizes to explain the principle of conditionality in biblical prophecy, focusing upon the human element and response involved in human history.

The instant I speak concerning a nation and concerning a kingdom, to pluck up, to pull down, and to destroy it, if that nation against whom I have spoken turns from its evil, I will relent of the disaster that I thought to bring upon it. Or at another moment I might speak concerning a nation or concerning a kingdom to build up or to plant it; if it does evil in My sight so that it does not obey My voice, then I will relent concerning the good with which I said I would benefit it (Jer 18:7-10; NKJV).

Thus, the fulfillment of a prophecy is, to a certain degree, dependent upon a particular human response. The best example of this principle can be found in the book of Jonah. The divine message that Jonah communicated to the people of Nineveh was clear and left no margin for renegotiation: "Yet forty days, and Nineveh shall be overthrown!" (Jonah 3:4; NKJV). However, the Ninevites repented (Jonah 3:6-9), and after 40 days Nineveh still stood. This lack of fulfillment also explains, at least partly,

> Apocalyptic prophecies, particularly apocalyptic time prophecies, are always unconditional.

the strong reaction of the prophet Jonah in this matter (Jonah 4:1). After all, fulfillment of prophecy was one important indicator to distinguish a true prophet from a false prophet. How would he stand before the Ninevites (and perhaps even before his own people) if the Word of the Lord, which he proclaimed, was not fulfilled? Another example for a conditional prophecy is the revoking of the pronouncement of Hezekiah's imminent death found in Isaiah 38:1-22 in which God, through the prophet Isaiah, first tells Hezekiah that he will die, but then adds another fifteen years to the king's life because of Hezekiah's earnest entreaties.

It should be noted, however, that not all prophecy is conditional. General prophecy concerned with individuals or a particular people (e.g., Israel) can contain conditional elements that are dependent on the human response in a particular historical setting. Apocalyptic prophecies, on the other hand, particularly apocalyptic time prophecies are always unconditional. These prophecies deal with the history of humanity and the final advent of the kingdom of God. They are not dependent on human responses; they will be fulfilled no matter how human beings respond.

Conditional prophecy involving individual lives or corporal entities underlines the important theological concept of human freedom. God did not create robots and, although He is sovereign, in His acts and designs, He accommodates human responses in His prophetic master plan.

Prophecy and the Messianic Kingdom – The basis for the special relationship between the Lord and His people Israel was the covenant that was solemnly established on Mount Sinai (Exod 19-24). However, this particular covenant was based upon earlier divine promises (and conditions) given to the patriarchs (Gen 12:1-3; 15:5, 13-16; 17:1-8; 26:1-6, 24; 28:10-15; etc.). While Israel was primarily a faith community, it was also a political/national entity that received important covenant promises (Deut 26-28). These promises were dependent on Israel's faithfulness. Many of these promises were connected to the land of Canaan — the Promised Land. Yet, the covenant stipulations did not include only blessings but also curses in case Israel did not remain faithful.

> "The children of Israel were to occupy all the territory which God appointed them. Those nations that rejected the worship and service of the true God were to be dispossessed. But it was God's purpose that by the revelation of His character through Israel men should be drawn unto Him. To all the world the gospel invitation was to be given. Through the teaching of the sacrificial service Christ was to be uplifted before the nations, and all who would look unto Him should live. All who, like Rahab the Canaanite, and Ruth the Moabitess, turned from idolatry to the worship of the true God, were to unite themselves with His chosen people. As the numbers of Israel increased they were to enlarge their borders, until their kingdom should embrace the world." (COL 290)

Sadly, the history of Israel after the conquest during the period of the Judges and the United and Divided monarchy is a history of rebellion, religious apostasy, short periods of reformation, and continued spiritual (and political) decline. At the end of the eighth century B.C., the northern kingdom, known as Israel, disappeared—destroyed by the Neo-Assyrian conquerors. Less than one hundred and fifty years later the same fate befell Jerusalem—this time at the hands of the Babylonians. During all this time God sent prophets with calls for repentance and religious, social, and political reform. However, these reforms were short-lived and limited. The prophetic messages of these prophets often included messages of hope and the promise of a future restoration (see Isa 27; 32:1-8; 40; 44:1-5, 24-

28; 48:12-19; 49:8-26; etc.). Generally, these promises were conditional on a whole-hearted return of the nation to God. Some of these promises involved the inclusion of other nations among the covenant remnant (Amos 9:11, 12; Isa 56:6-8), the centrality and power of Zion and Jerusalem (Mic 4:1-13; Isa 2:1-4; Zech 8:20-23), and the establishment of the Messianic kingdom here on earth as outlined in Isaiah 60-66. This Messianic kingdom would still have included sinners, the birth of children, and the death of old people (see chapter on Isa 65:20).

Unfortunately, Israel did not live up to the conditions included in the prophetic messages. The postexilic community, therefore, did not fully experience the blessings of the Messianic kingdom which included the coming and the death of a universal Messiah, the resurrection, the destruction of the wicked (Isa 25:8; 26:19; Zech 12), and, finally, the establishment of the universal reign of God (Zech 14). Comparatively few Israelites returned from the exile when given the opportunity (Ezra 2:64). Only a few put their heart into the rebuilding of the temple, so that God had to raise up the prophets Haggai and Zechariah to encourage the remnant in this project (Ezra 5:1, 2; 6:13-18). Only a few were attentive to Scripture around the time of Jesus, awaiting the biblical Messiah as portrayed in Scripture rather than a popular Messiah, who would drive out the Romans. As a result, many (although not all) of the promises for the returning Jews were not fulfilled due to the fact that the conditions stipulated by God were not met. These prophecies, however, were to be fulfilled in principle, though not in detail, on a larger scale in the future.

> The failure of Israel made impossible the fulfillment of these prophecies according to the original intent. Nevertheless the purposes of Jehovah will move forward to their complete fulfillment (see PK 705, 706) . . . the purposes of God instead of being accomplished through Israel, the chosen nation, will be accomplished through the Christian church.[1]

Summary – God spoke in biblical times through prophets. These prophets addressed religious and social issues, admonished people to more faithfulness, and at times made predictions for the future. One major element to distinguish between true and false prophets concerned the fulfillment of their prophecies, a concept firmly established in the biblical text. However, many prophecies, concerned with a particular historical context, involved conditions that required a response from the human participants of the covenant. Obedience and disobedience were key elements in these conditional prophecies as were rebellion and repentance. A very helpful biblical narrative that illustrates the principle of conditional prophecy is Jonah's mission to Nineveh.

While some of the writings of the prophets contain sections describing the future Messianic kingdom to be established after the return from the Babylonian exile, these promises were also conditional, dependent on Israel's obedience. Due to the lack of true obedience these prophecies were not or were only partly fulfilled in postexilic Israel. Unlike general prophecy, apocalyptic prophecy is not characterized by conditional elements, since it expresses God's sovereign design to save and to judge the world.

God's Word still stands firm (Isa 40:8) and will accomplish its purpose (Isa 55:11). The conditional elements of biblical prophecy helps us to see a sovereign God who foremost is interested in the salvation of an estranged humanity and respects the free will of human beings. It is this same God who sent His Son in the "fullness of time" (Gal 4:4) and who will also make certain that the prophetic timetable will be fulfilled in due time.

Gerald A. Klingbeil

References

[1] F. D. Nichol, ed., *Seventh-day Adventist Bible Commentary*, revised, 7 vols. (Washington, D.C.: Review and Herald, 1977), 4:332.

Know the Bible in your mind
Keep it in your heart
Live it in your life
Share it with the world.

Bible Society Record

WHY DO CHRISTIAN SCHOLARS INTERPRET SCRIPTURE IN SO MANY DIFFERENT WAYS?

Due to several factors, the interpretation of the Bible is a challenging task. Written over a period of about sixteen hundred years, spanning quite a variety of cultures and traditions, the gaps between the biblical documents and the interpreter today are formidable. There are time, culture, and language gaps that have to be bridged in order to understand not only what the writer meant in his time but also to grasp the timeless message for today's world and concerns.

Some basic reasons – An obvious reason for different interpretations of a text is the fact that some texts are ambiguous and therefore difficult to understand. Another factor is that, at times, different methods are used in interpreting a text. Every interpreter endeavors to understand Scripture on the basis of his or her worldview, pre-knowledge, and personal experience, largely depending on the educational training he or she has received. "Interpreters don't come to the Bible as blank books. We come with vested interests, commitments, ideas about what can and can't happen, and ideas of what should and shouldn't happen. Sometimes our personal and national histories contribute to the bias."[1]

When it comes to the scholarly world, the non-scholar asks with bewilderment why two scholars who have been equally trained in theology and exegesis come up with different interpretations of one and the same text. Not a few people get discouraged and conclude that Scripture is obscure and ambiguous. The Catholic Church seeks to eliminate this ambiguity by decreeing that an authentic interpretation of the word of God can be done only by the teaching office of the Church. However, there are numerous scholars even within the Catholic tradition who, through their varied interpretations, prove this claim to be wrong and show how futile it is to declare one teacher or teaching office to be authoritative over all the others.

Important aspects to consider – In order to understand why there are so many different interpretations of biblical texts within the Christian church, several aspects need to be considered:

1. Development of Thinking – The understanding of biblical texts is first of all dependent on one's basic philosophy of life, on how one thinks. In this regard, one's upbringing is important. When love and obedience toward God have been put into a child's heart, when the Bible has been granted authority and the power to guide in the lives of those who have been instrumental in the development of character in childhood and adolescence, the grown-up individual will more likely be willing to trust the biblical data and message as well. At the core of one's thinking and critical to the task of interpreting the Bible is the interpreter's view of God. This view is shaped by several factors: observing others who claim to believe in God; trusting relationships with those on whom one is dependent, such as parents or close relatives; and the influence of pastors and teachers who reveal a certain view of God.

> At the core of one's thinking and critical to the task of interpreting the Bible is the interpreter's view of God.

The effect of Christian education in church and school where a biblical, or not so biblical, view of God is being portrayed and taught should not be underestimated. Personal experience plays another defining role, from having to endure suffering, pain, and loss to committing sin and dealing with a bad conscience.

When it comes to scholarly research, much depends on the theological training one has received. Some may even experience a "second conversion" from uncritical faith to acceptance of a more critical view of the Bible. Professors of theology have much influence on their students and may lead them either to a higher-critical view of the Bible or to a new confidence in the trustworthiness of the word of God. Naturally this will affect the way the interpretation of biblical texts is being conducted.

2. Selective reading of the Bible – It is common knowledge that not all information received by our brains is being processed according to its significance but is selected and filtered. In the selection process, we decide to pay attention to those stimuli that are either the strongest or the ones we have been expecting.

In biblical interpretation this selective perception would mean that the interpreter is prone to pay most attention to that which he or she has been expecting all along or which has the strongest impact. Biblical texts are so rich and deep in their meaning that it takes an extra effort to dig into them in such a way as to explore them to the fullest. It is more likely that we have difficulties perceiving everything that is to be perceived and select instead that which we would like to see manifested in a particular text.

This selective perception more often than not leads to divergent interpretations of Scripture. Undoubtedly, it takes humility and effort to integrate new knowledge or clearer truth into one's existing thought frames, and there may be emotional reasons that can hinder a person from accepting new truth. In extreme cases we are talking about a closed mind that is not willing or flexible enough to look at a biblical text with fresh eyes and probe deep enough in order to receive new knowledge through proper exegesis. There is no human being on this earth who is completely unbiased. Therefore openness and willingness to receive new light in the interpretation of Scripture is essential to responsible exegesis of the biblical text.

Another form of reading the Bible selectively is to cherish one's own philosophical or theological hobbyhorse that hinders one's ability to interpret the Bible in an adequate and balanced manner, overemphasizing one point or interpretation at the expense of other points.

3. Presuppositions – As indicated above, "a key factor in the process of interpreting Scripture is the interpreter's horizon or preunderstanding – one's world view, presuppositions, and personal predilections."[2] This means that the interpreter of Scripture has to address the issue of his or her own premises in approaching the text. Apart from a naturally subjective approach to the text that cannot be avoided, but which has to be balanced and finally overruled by the objective information that is visible in the text, there are far more serious philosophical presuppositions that influence an interpretation of a given passage in Scripture.

For example, if critical assumptions[3] rule out that the Creation accounts of Genesis 1 and 2 are a factual rendering of what happened within the first seven days of this world's history or deny that the nation of Israel ever existed the way the Old Testament reports it, then the interpretation of Bible passages that deal with these events will be quite different from the exegesis of someone who believes that these events and developments indeed took place in history. Apart from the fact that this critical approach makes the human interpreter the arbiter of truth, the denial of the authority of Scripture in describing historical events consequently leads to doubts concerning the truthfulness and reliability of all Scripture. The basic claim of the Bible to be divine truth does not allow for selecting one text and pronouncing it trustworthy while abandoning another as unreliable on the basis of historical information, the reliability of which we may not even be able to prove.

The development of critical presuppositions has led to the establishment of various schools of interpretation to which scholars adhere. Each of these schools forms a system of thought that provides the framework within which a biblical text is interpreted. Historical criticism is comprised of subcategories, such as source criticism, form criticism, redaction criticism, literary criticism, etc., and the interpretation of prophetic texts is carried out under the premises of either preterism, futurism, idealism, or historicism. Other scholars, including most Seventh-day Adventist scholars, have adopted the grammatical-historical approach of the Reformers that leaves the biblical text intact and takes into account the self-explanatory character of Scripture.[4]

According to Ernst Troeltsch (*On Historical and Dogmatic Method in Theology* [1898]), "the historical method of thought and explanation has three principles: (1) **The principle of criticism** or methodological doubt, which implies that history only achieves probability. Religious tradition must also be subjected to criticism; (2) **The principle of analogy** makes criticism possible. Present experience and occurrence become the criteria of probability in the past. This 'almighty power' of analogy implies that all events are in principle similar. (3) **The principle of correlation** (or mutual interdependence) implies that all historical phenomena are so interrelated that a change in one phenomenon necessitates a change in the causes leading to it and in the effects it has. Historical explanation rests on this chain of cause and effect. The third principle rules out miracles and salvation history" (Edgar Krentz, *The Historical-Critical Method* [Philadelphia: Fortress Press, 1975], 55).

4. *Preconditions and Predispositions* – Apart from presuppositions that are philosophical in nature, there are certain preconditions and predispositions by which scholars may feel pressured. These can be expectations from colleagues, church authorities, and employing organizations or institutions. Reputation in the scholarly world, in general, and in the field of expertise, in particular, is essential not only to remain a respected member of the scholarly community but also at times to remain in office or employment. Political correctness becomes an issue not taken lightly by most scholars, and the obligation a scholar feels towards his or her own church tradition may strongly influence the process and outcome of interpretations. A classic example is

the interpretation and application of texts that speak about the weekly Sabbath. While scholars who adhere to the Sunday tradition use biblical texts to support their church's claims that Jesus and the apostles changed the day of rest from Sabbath to Sunday, others who hold to the keeping of the seventh-day Sabbath will interpret the same texts quite differently.

A unified interpretation of Scripture – The question then remains as to what can be done to make sure that the interpretation of Scripture is true and consistent with its intended meaning. How can divergent interpretations be avoided? In answering these questions several aspects have to be considered.

1. First of all, confidence in the inspired word of God will lead to an interpretation that honors the claim of the text to be of divine origin.

2. Critical reflection on the development of one's own thinking is necessary. It takes a conscious effort to evaluate one's own viewpoint whether it is in harmony with the position of one's parents and teachers or in deliberate contrast to it.

> Presuppositions of the historical-grammatical method of interpretation: (1) The Bible is the inspired Word of God; it transcends its cultural background to serve as God's Word for all cultural, racial, and situational contexts in all ages. (2) Scripture, as an indivisible blend of the divine and human, is an authentic, reliable record of history and God's acts in history. (3) Human reason is subject to the Bible, not equal to or above it. (4) The Bible can be understood only with the help of the Holy Spirit. ("Methods of Bible Study" in G. W. Reid, ed., *Understanding Scripture* [Silver Spring, MD: Biblical Research Institute, 2006], 330, 331).

3. The interpretational process requires openness of mind and a willingness to listen to others. The inquisitive scholar should not only look forward to the known but should be open to fresh thoughts that the text contains. The text itself must be the arbiter of its own interpretation and should not be subordinated to preconceived ideas, traditions or agendas that are foreign to the text and to biblical thinking.

4. A balanced, biblical view of God is needed for an interpretation that will do justice to the revelation of that same God in Scripture. God can be perceived only through the acceptance of His own revelation.

5. The interpreter needs to make an informed and honest decision as to which hermeneutical approach is to be accepted. A proven approach has been grammatical-historical exegesis that pays attention to the language of the original text and to its literary and cultural context. This approach gives the Bible its full weight of authority and demonstrates its unity and clarity. This information should not be hidden from the public, because no interpreter should pretend to embrace a certain philosophy concerning biblical interpretation when quite the opposite is true. It is a matter of integrity and academic fairness to reveal one's own position.

6. The interpreter should endeavor not to succumb to the pressures of interpretative trends in the scholarly world or to the demands of political correctness when it comes to interpreting the Bible. Truth is not necessarily embraced by the majority, and it may be important to stand alone courageously without regard to one's career or tenure.

7. The interpretative approach adopted should be one that preserves the divine authority of Scripture and safeguards an exegesis that does justice to the intention of the text and its author. The interpretation should not only preserve the uniqueness of the Bible but also make careful use of exegetical tools, such as linguistic, literary, historical, and theological analyses. Moreover, this approach should take into account the predispositions of the original reader, respecting the reading conventions of that time and the worldview expected of his or her readers.

The Holy Spirit and the interpreter – The divine authorship of the Bible and the assurance that the Holy Spirit will guide the interpretation process should be humbly acknowledged. "The Holy Spirit illumines the mind by removing the barrier to a positive judgment and welcoming the truth of God's Word. The same type of illumination operates in the process of interpretation and application."[5] There can be no doubt that sinful attitudes prove to be an obstacle to the unbiased and fair treatment of the biblical text and, even more so, to the application of its truth claims.[6] Character traits that are detrimental to an open and honest dealing with Scripture must be submitted to the Holy Spirit, who through His regenerating power can change attitudes of pride and doubt into ones of humble subordination to the divine Author and His communication in the biblical text. In fact, an act of transformation and renewal is necessary (2 Cor 4:6) in order for the Holy Spirit to unfold biblical truth to the interpreter. "An interpreter who sets himself against this transformation, e.g., by claiming some sort of 'neutrality' falls into existential contradiction of the revelation that he wishes to interpret and understand."[7]

The Holy Spirit will work best with an attitude of receptivity, an open mind, and a teachable spirit. Furthermore, the adequate use of exegetical tools and the willingness to accept and obey the instructions of Scripture is essential. When such a model of interpretation is followed, the divergence of interpretations among Christian scholars will diminish.

Winfried Vogel

References

[1]Jerry Camery-Hoggatt, *Reading the Good Book Well: A Guide to Biblical Interpretation* (Nashville, TN: Abingdon, 2007), 25.

[2]William J. Larkin, Jr., *Culture and Biblical Hermeneutics* (Grand Rapids, MI: Baker, 1988), 97.

[3]Historical-critical philosophy means in essence that historical information outside of the biblical text determines its truth content.

[4]The hallmark motto of the Reformation was *"scriptura sui ipsius interpres"* – Scripture is its own interpreter.

[5]Larkin, 289.

[6]Frank M. Hasel, "Presuppositions in the Interpretation of Scripture" in *Understanding Scripture: An Adventist Approach,* ed. G. W. Reid (Silver Spring, MD: Biblical Research Institute, 2005), 30-33.

[7]Gerhard Maier, *Biblical Hermeneutics* (Wheaton, IL: Crossway, 1994), 56, 57.

The many contradictory opinions in regard to what the Bible teaches do not arise from any obscurity in the book itself, but from blindness and prejudice on the part of interpreters.

CSW23

OLD TESTAMENT
TEXTS

DOES GENESIS TEACH THAT THE EARTH EXISTED IN AN UNFORMED STATE PRIOR TO THE CREATION WEEK?

In the beginning God created the heavens and the earth. And the earth was formless and void, and darkness was over the surface of the deep, and the Spirit of God was moving over the surface of the waters. Genesis 1:1, 2.

Much ink has been spilled over the meaning of the first two verses in the Bible. The first sentence "In the beginning God created the heavens and the earth" has been seen as: (1) a summary or title to what follows in the chapter; (2) the creation of this earth with life on it millions or billions of years before the seven-day Creation week; (3) the creation of the universe, including the earth in its raw state, long before the seven-day Creation week 6,000-10,000 years ago; (4) the creation of the universe on day one of the seven-day Creation week; (5) the first part of day one of the seven-day Creation week long after the creation of the universe. The first three views require that the earth existed in an unformed state prior to the seven-day Creation week.

"In the beginning" – A possible interpretation of the Hebrew word *bereshit* is to translate the first word in the Bible as "In the beginning when . . ."[1] The *New Revised Standard Bible*, for example, translates Genesis 1:1, 2 as "In the beginning when God created the heavens and the earth, the earth was a formless void. . . ." Similar translations are found in several modern Bible versions, e.g., *Moffatt's* translation, *The New Jewish Publication Society Bible* (NJPS), NEB, and NAB. According to such a reading, the universe, or this earth in an unformed state, depending on how the expression "heaven and earth" is understood, already existed when God began the Creation week. Genesis 1:1, therefore, would not describe a creation out of nothing (*creatio ex nihilo*) but rather could open the door to the idea that God and matter existed eternally side by side. The first act of Creation would have been the creation of light in verse 3, not the creation of "heaven and earth." While this is a possible interpretation, there is no compelling grammatical reason to adopt the modern reading found in some translations.

The traditional rendering of verse one is "in the beginning God created the heavens and the earth."[2] This translation is found in the ancient versions (Greek Septuagint and Theodotion, the Samaritan Pentateuch, the Syriac Bible, the Latin Vulgate) and in most modern versions, e. g., NKJV, RSV, NASB, NIV. While this translation upholds creation out of nothing, it does not exclude the possibility that this creation event took place a long time prior to the seven-day Creation week of Genesis 1.

"The heavens and the earth" – The expression "the heavens and the earth"[3] or "heaven and earth" appears about forty times in the Bible; five times we find the term "earth and heaven" and another four times the expression "heaven of heavens" is used (1 Kgs 8:27; 2 Chron 2:6; 6:18; Neh 9:6), which some interpret as a term for the universe. About a third of the texts refer to the creation of heaven and earth (Gen 1:1; 2:1, 4; Exod 20:11; 31:17; Ps 115:15; 121:2; etc.); six texts declare that God is the possessor of heaven and earth (Gen 14:19, 22; 1 Chron 29:11; Matt 11:25; Luke 10:21; Acts 17:24). In Haggai the Lord promises that He will shake heaven and earth (2:6, 21) and, according to Joel 3:16, the Lord's roar from Zion will make heaven and earth tremble. Jesus affirms that heaven and earth will pass away (Matt 24:35; Mark 13:31; Luke 21:33), and Isaiah (65:17; 66:22) and Peter (2 Pet 3:13) are looking forward to the "new heavens and the new earth" that the Lord will create.

The term "heaven and earth" is generally understood as a merism (a statement of opposites to indicate totality, like "day and night," meaning "all the time"), representing "the organized universe in which humankind lives."[4] Thus Genesis 1:1 is interpreted either as a title for what follows, or as a reference to the creation of the universe billions of years ago. Others, interpret the phrase in a more restricted sense to mean the solar system[5] while some restrict it even further to this earth and the atmospheric heav-

> "When we closely examine Gen 1, especially such words as 'in the beginning' and 'heaven and earth,' contextually and linguistically, we can say that the creation narrative is talking only about our world and is silent about the creation of the entire universe, as we understand the universe today" (F. O. Regalado, "The Creation Account in Genesis 1: Our World Only or the Universe?" *Journal of the Adventist Theological Society* 13/2 [Autumn 2002]: 120).

en surrounding it. W. H. Shea, for example, says:

> An examination of those occurrences [where "heaven and earth" is used in the Creation account] shows that the word 'heavens' does not focus upon the universe, but rather upon the atmospheric heavens that surround this earth. . . . Thus the focus of the use of the phrase 'heavens and the earth' in Genesis 1 is upon this earth, not the universe or the starry heavens. This shows the geocentric emphasis of this Creation account."[6]

In Isaiah 65:17 God says, "For behold, I create new heavens and a new earth," and in Revelation 21:1 John sees "a new heaven and a new earth" that replace the old, sinful "heaven and earth." There is no suggestion anywhere in Scripture that the whole universe is being replaced. Peter says, "But the day of the Lord will come like a thief, in which the heavens will pass away with a roar and the elements will be destroyed with intense heat, and the earth and its works will be burned up" (2 Pet 3:10). Peter is not saying that the universe will be burned up, but only that that which has been infested with sin will be renewed. While this verse does not prove that there is no time gap between Genesis 1:1 and 1:2, if "heavens and earth" in verse 1 are not a reference to the universe but to this planet and its surroundings, then there is less of a necessity to see a time gap.[7]

"And the earth was formless and void" – The Hebrew phrase *tohu wa-bohu* (formless and void) consists of two nouns joined by "and." *Tohu* which appears a number of times by itself can mean "nothingness," "empty" (Isa 29:21), or "nowhere" (Job 6:18). It is used to refer to the "vanity" of idols (1 Sam 12:21), to the "insignificance" of the nations in God's eyes (Isa 40:17), and to the "empty pleas" in court (Isa 59:4, RSV). The second word *bohu* appears only twice in the rest of Scripture, each time with *tohu*

> The phrase *tohu wa-bohu* refers to the unorganized state of the earth before the divine Word brought order into it.

(Isa 34:11; Jer 4:23), referring both times to the desolation and emptiness of the land as a result of God's judgment. In Genesis 1, in the context of Creation, the phrase *tohu wa-bohu* refers to the unorganized state of the earth before the divine Word brought order to it.

Interpretations

1. Genesis 1:1 as a Title – If verse 1 is a summary or title, then we are not told when God created the unformed matter of the earth or if He created matter at all; matter may have existed from eternity, a view that the rest of Scripture denies (Ps 33:6; Rom 4:17; Heb 11:1). According to this view, the state of the earth as "formless and void," in verse 2, the beginning of the *Creation* account, is viewed as a "mystery."[8]

2. The Ruin-Restoration Theory – Some Christians believe that Genesis 1:1 refers to the creation of this physical world and all life upon it at a moment of time long before the seven days of Creation week but that an appalling cataclysm obliterated every trace of life upon it and reduced its surface to a state that might be described as "without form, and void." This view is taught by the *Scofield Reference Bible.*

After Charles Darwin published his book *The Origin of Species,* in 1859, many Christians thought they found in this interpretation the means of harmonizing the Mosaic account of creation with the idea that the earth had passed through long ages of geological change, as advocated by the theory of evolution. According to this view, sin, suffering, and death existed millions of years before the creation of Adam and Eve. The Bible, however, clearly says that death came into the world only as a result of Adam's sin after the seven-day Creation week (Rom 5:12).

> "The theory that God did not create matter when He brought the world into existence is without foundation. In the formation of our world, God was not indebted to pre-existing matter" (8T 258).

3. The "Passive Gap" Theory – This view understands Genesis 1:1 as a reference to the creation of the universe, including the earth in its raw state, billions of years ago. Several thousand years ago the Holy Spirit hovered above the waters and the seven-day Creation took place. This has been a long-standing view in the Seventh-day Adventist Church. Contrary to the Ruin-Restoration theory of the *Scofield Bible,* Adventists do not believe that life existed on earth prior to Genesis 1. Only non-fossil bearing rock can be billions of years old.

4. Creation of the Universe on Day One – This view sees the creation of everything in the universe, including Lucifer and the angels, on Day One of the seven-day Creation week several thousand years ago. This view is propagated by the Institute for Creation Research and the Answers-in-Genesis Organization. However, according to Job 38:4-7, other created beings already existed when the foundations of the world were laid. Furthermore, the Adventist understanding of the great controversy[9] between Christ and Satan (Rev 12:7, 8) presupposes the existence of Satan and the angels prior to the creation of the earth.

5. The Traditional Creation Theory – This view, held by Luther and Calvin and many Christians since, understands Genesis 1:1 to be part of the first day of the Creation week. Thus verse two describes the condition of the earth immediately after the creation of "heaven and earth" (our planetary system) and before the creation of light. The fourth commandment says, "In six days the LORD made the heavens and the earth, the sea and all that is in them" (Exod 20:11; 31:17; Acts 4:24; 14:15). According to the traditional Creation theory, the phrase "all that is in them" includes the raw material of the heavens and the earth.

Two Possible Views in the SDA Church

In reading Genesis we must remember that Moses was not writing a scientific report. He used the language of appearance. He described the Creation process as it would have appeared to an observer standing somewhere in space watching God creating the world.

In regard to the question, "Does Genesis teach that the earth existed in an unformed state prior to the Creation week?" the Seventh-day Adventist Encyclopedia says:

SDAs have always affirmed belief in creation *ex nihilo*—that God was not indebted to previously existing matter when He brought the earth into existence. They have generally taken it for granted that it was on the first day of Creation week that He brought into existence the matter that composed the earth and that He proceeded immediately with the work of the six days. However, almost from the first, some SDAs have allowed that the Genesis account can be understood to mean that God spoke into existence the substance of the earth sometime prior to the events of the six literal days of creation.[10]

Thus, the first chapter in Genesis allows for both the passive gap theory or the traditional Creation theory. It is one of the greatest chapters in the

Bible, introducing us to the awesome power of the creator God and telling us that we are His creatures. It provides the basis for all that follows, and, as such, it deserves our careful study.

Gerhard Pfandl

References

[1]In this case *b*ᵉ*reshit* is treated as a noun in the construct state and verse 1 is seen as a dependent, temporal clause.

[2]This view takes *b*ᵉ*reshit* as a noun in the absolute state and the first sentence as an independent clause.

[3]The Hebrew word *shamayim* (heavens), though a plural word, is frequently translated as a singular noun.

[4]Bruce K. Waltke, *Genesis* (Grand Rapids, MI: Zondervan, 2001), 59. The Jewish scholar U. Cassuto, however, says, "This view is incorrect. The concept of the unity of the world was unknown among the Israelites till a later period, and then the appropriate term for it was immediately coined" (*From Adam to Noah* [Jerusalem: Magnes Press, 1978], 20).

[5]Adam Clarke, *The Holy Bible*, 6 vols. (New York, NY: Abingdon-Cokesbury Press, n.d.), 1:30.

[6]William H. Shea, "Creation," *Handbook of Seventh-Day Adventist Theology*, ed., Raoul Dederen (Hagerstown, MD : Review and Herald, 2000), 420.

[7]In this case, the rocks, like the trees and Adam and Eve, would have been created with apparent age.

[8]Bruce K. Waltke, "The Creation Account of Genesis 1:1-3, Part IV," *Bibliotheca Sacra* (1975), 338.

[9]See Ellen G. White, *Spiritual Gifts,* 4 vols. (Washington, D.C.: Review and Herald, 1945), 3:36-38.

[10]"Creation" in *The Seventh-day Adventist Encyclopedia, ed.* Don F. Neufeld (Hagerstown, MD: Review and Herald, 1976), 357.

WHAT WAS THE LIGHT CREATED ON THE FIRST DAY OF THE CREATION WEEK?

Then God said, "Let there be light"; and there was light. Genesis 1:3.

Although no human observer was present during the first five days of the Creation week, we have the inspired record of "Moses, the historian of creation" (GC v), who wrote down what was shown to him in vision.

The sequence of days was counted from the very beginning of the Creation week (Gen 1:5, 8, 13, 19, 23, 31; 2:2, 3), and the phrase "and there was evening, and there was morning" (Gen 1:5, 8, 13, 19, 23, 31) was applied to each of the first six days.[1] Therefore, the logic of the question is clear: If light was created on the first day (Gen 1:4) and the sun was made only on the fourth day (Gen 1:14), what was the light of the first day? This apparent discrepancy or even contradiction has led Bible scholars to propose several solutions to this puzzling phenomenon of the Creation process. Among all the suggested interpretations, two are worthy of closer consideration.

God's presence was the light – The first view states that God's presence was the light of the first day. In Psalm 104, which is a poetic hymn describing each of the seven days of Creation in the same sequence as the Genesis Creation account (Gen 1:1–2:4a), the light of the first day is associated with the glory of God who wrapped Himself "with light as with a cloak" (v. 2). The Lord is the light (Ps 27:1; 1 John 1:5), therefore His presence brings light; the light comes forth from Him. Similarly, God's presence was the source of light during the Exodus from Egypt (Exod 13:21), as well during at the Red Sea experience, in which the Lord was light to Israel and darkness to the Egyptian army at the same time (Exod 14:19, 20).

The idea of light having existence independent of the sun is attested to in Revelation (21:23; 22:5), in which God Himself is the light. Ancient rabbinic sources also mentioned that the light of the first Creation day was the splendor of the divine presence.[2] Although according to the biblical view the sun is a source of light, God Himself is the ultimate source of light (Isa 60:19, 20).

The light on the first day was sunlight – The second view says that on the first day of Creation, God created the solar system (this would explain the evening-morning cycle from the first day), but that the sun was not yet put to its intended purpose in relationship to the earth. This would mean that on the fourth day God did not create the sun and moon, but rather appointed them to govern the day and the night, to separate light from darkness, and to mark seasons and days and years (Gen 1:14, 18). Thus, the sun and moon were in existence from day one but visible on the surface of the earth only on and after the fourth day. It may be that the water above the earth (mentioned on the second day of Creation, v. 7) or heavy clouds (Job 38:9) could have covered our planet which prevented the sun from being seen on the earth. According to this view, on the fourth day the watery envelope or cloud cover would have disappeared.

> Ancient rabbinic sources mentioned that the light of the first Creation day was the splendor of the divine presence.

Genesis 1:14 can be translated as a purpose clause: "Let the lights . . . be (appointed) to separate the day from the night." This translation assumes that the luminaries were already in the firmament. It is important to note that the statement in Genesis 1:16 that God made two lights may be rendered as "had made," implying that they were created before the fourth day of Creation. According to Hebrew grammar, such a translation is a legitimate possibility.[3]

There is a possibility of combining the two proposed solutions, because they could be complementary. God's presence may have been the principle source of light for the first three days, but this light could also have included light from the sun (the solar system being here from the first day). However, from the fourth day on the focus was directed on light coming forth from the astronomical bodies as we know them today.

"He made the stars also" – To include the stars in the creation of the sun and moon on day four would imply the creation of at least the visible universe at that time. In view of our understanding of the great controversy, this is hardly likely.

The words "He made" and "also" in "He made the stars also" were supplied by the translators; they are not in the Hebrew text. Verse 16 can be translated as follows: "And God made the two great lights; the greater light to rule the day, the lesser light to rule the night with the stars."[4] Thus, the starry heaven could have been created long before the Creation week.

According to Job 38:7, "the morning stars sang together, and all the sons of God shouted for joy" at the creation of the earth. If "the morning stars" represent here angels and are understood as a personification of the starry heaven, then this text would support the existence of the angels and stars prior to the Creation week.

Creation and worship – The creation of light made possible the counting of time and so the succession of days began. Consequently, on the first day God ordered time for this planet. In addition, on the fourth day God appointed sun and moon to mark the seasons and other time units, including time for worship.

In contrast to the sun and moon deities of pagan pantheons, the Creation account states that God created only nameless luminaries, the bigger light and the lesser light. Thus He built a wall against the infiltration of sun and moon worship among God's followers. This anti-mythological element stresses that God is in control, He is the Creator of light and its ultimate source. Light and time depend on Him. He alone needs to be praised, for He is the Creator God.

Jiří Moskala

References

[1] The author of the Genesis Creation account wrote from an earthly (not from a cosmic) viewpoint. Shea rightly asserts: "The Creation acts were revealed and recorded as if they had passed before an observer positioned upon the earth, not outside of its system. That point of view makes some elements in the narrative more understandable" (W. H. Shea, "Creation," in *Handbook of Seventh-day Adventist Theology* [Hagerstown, MD: Review and Herald, 2000], 420).

[2] Talmud, *Genesis Rabba* 3:4.

[3] See *Gesenius' Hebrew Grammar*, edited by Emil Kautsch and A. E. Cowley, Second English Edition (Oxford: Clarendon Press, 1910), 348.

[4] Colin L. House, "Some Notes on Translating in Genesis 1:16," *Andrews University Seminary Studies* 25.3 (1987): 247.

WERE THE CREATION DAYS 24-HOUR DAYS OR INDEFINITE PERIODS OF TIME?

"God called the light "day," and the darkness he called "night." And there was evening, and there was morning—the first day." Genesis 1:5.

The Creation days have been understood in different ways. Some interpret them as symbolic days; others as a poetic description or an evolutionary account of God's creative activity; again others see it as a revelation of God and take the days as literal days. In order to determine which interpretation is correct, one must closely investigate the term *yom* (day) in the Creation account (Gen 1:1–2:4) because only the context can shed light on the issue.[1]

Genesis 1 as a genealogy – The immediate context of the Creation story suggests that it is a genealogy or history (Gen 2:4); it is not mythology, a prediction, a metaphor, a parable, poetry, or a hymn. A genealogy is a historic account with real meaning, e.g., water in the Creation story is water; vegetation is vegetation; animals are animals; and days are days. This observation is significant when one discovers that the literary structure of the whole book of Genesis is divided into ten genealogies (Gen 2:4; 5:1; 6:9; 10:1; 11:10; 11:27; 25:12; 25:19; 36:1; 37:2). If the genealogies of Adam, Noah, Abraham, Isaac, Jacob, and Joseph are literal, and these persons are historical, it suggests that the genealogy of the heavens and the earth should be interpreted in the same way. One must be consistent; either all genealogies are literal or none are.

The Creation days – The word "day" in the Creation week consistently occurs in the singular (in verse 14b, days have a different function). Furthermore, it is significant that the word "day" in Genesis 1 always appears as a plain noun without prepositions, suffixes, or other particles. On the other hand, a Creation day is always accompanied by a numeral, "the first day," "the second day," etc. When the Bible, in a historical account, uses the word day in combination with a numeral, it consistently refers to a regular day, e.g., "on the first day," "on the second day," etc. (Num 7:12-78; 29:1-35).

The unique phrase "and there was evening, and there was morning," always precedes the particular Creation day (Gen 1:5, 8, 13, 19, 23, 31). This expression provides a temporal boundary that implies the existence of a day consisting of a 24-hour period.

Other scriptural texts interpret the seven Creation days in a literal way, as well. For example, the fourth commandment contains the phrase, "For in six days God created the heavens and the earth and on the seventh day he rested" (Exod 20:9); and in Exodus 31:17 the Israelites were told to keep the Sabbath "for in six days the Lord made the heavens and the earth, and on the seventh day he abstained from work and rested." In both texts human beings are admonished to follow God's example and rest on the seventh day.

Scholarly opinions – Gerhard von Rad stresses: "The seven days are unquestionably to be understood as actual days and a unique, unrepeatable lapse of time in the world."[2] T. E. Fretheim agrees and says, "Other possibilities for understanding *day* (symbolic; sequential but not consecutive; liturgical) are less likely. Efforts to understand *day* in terms of, say, evolutionary periods, betray too much of an interest in harmonization."[3] Gordon Wenham concurs: "There can be little doubt that here day has its basic sense of a 24-hour period."[4] And James Barr aptly states: "So far as I know there is no professor of Hebrew or Old Testament at any world-class university who does not believe that the writer(s) of *Genesis 1-11* intended to convey to their readers the idea that creation took place in a series of six days which were the same as the days of 24 hours we now experience."[5]

> When the Bible, in a historical account, uses the word day in combination with a numeral, it consistently refers to a regular day.

The days of Creation were seven literal consecutive days – The biblical teaching of a seven-day Creation week is a unique account that has no parallel in any extra-biblical creation stories in ancient Near Eastern literature. The teaching that the Creator God made everything in seven days is built into the very fabric of the Creation order. To remove it means a gross distortion of the doctrine of Creation.

There are several good reasons for taking the days of Creation as identical to our week as we know it. The fivefold evidence associated with the term day in Genesis 1 (singular in form, always connected with a numeral, standing as a plain noun without a preposition or any other kind of constructions, preceded by a temporal phrase, and tied to divine rest) points unequivocally to one conclusion: the author of the book of Genesis intended to say that the day of the Creation week is a regular day consisting of a twenty-four hour period and cannot be interpreted figuratively. It is the only time-cycle that is not derived from natural astronomic phenomena and must be understood as consisting of seven literal, historical, factual, consecutive, and contiguous days. Genesis 1 provides the only evidence we have for the origin of our seven-day week. The author's purpose was to provide an account of what actually happened during the Creation week. The theology and history of the Creation account fit together; they are complementary and do not contradict each other.

> "The rhythmic boundary phrase 'and there was evening and there was morning' provides a definition of the creation 'day.' The creation 'day' consists of 'evening' and 'morning' and is thus a literal 'day.' . . . It cannot be made to mean anything else" (G. F. Hasel, "The 'Days' of Creation in Genesis 1," in J. T. Baldwin, ed., *Creation, Catastrophe & Calvary* [Hagerstown, MD: Review and Herald, 2000], 60).

Jiří Moskala

References

[1]For a comprehensive discussion of these issues, see Gerhard F. Hasel, "The 'Days' of Creation in Genesis 1: Literal 'Days' or Figurative 'Periods/Epochs' of Time," in *Creation, Catastrophe and Calvary*, ed. John Templeton Baldwin (Hagerstown, MD: Review and Herald, 2000), 40-68.

[2]Gerhard von Rad, *Genesis: A Commentary*, trans. John Marks (Philadelphia, PA: Westminster, 1972), 65.

[3]Terence E. Fretheim, "Were the Days of Creation Twenty-Four Hours Long? YES," in *The Genesis Debate: Persistent Questions About Creation and the Flood*, ed., Ronald Youngblood (Nashville, TN: Nelson, 1990), 12-34.

[4]Gordon J. Wenham, *Genesis 1-15*, Word Bible Commentary, 52 vols. (Waco, TX: Word, 1987), 1:19.

[5]James Barr, Personal letter to D. C. K. Watson, April 23, 1984, published in the *Newsletter* of the Creation Science Council of Ontario, 3/4 (1990-91).

ARE THERE TWO CONTRADICTORY ACCOUNTS OF CREATION IN GENESIS 1 AND 2?

This is the account of the heavens and the earth when they were created, in the day that the LORD God made earth and heaven. ⁵ Now no shrub of the field was yet in the earth, and no plant of the field had yet sprouted, for the LORD God had not sent rain upon the earth; and there was no man to cultivate the ground. ⁶ But a mist used to rise from the earth and water the whole surface of the ground. Genesis 2:4-6.

One of the challenges to the integrity of the Bible's account of Creation is the claim that the first two chapters of Genesis offer two conflicting accounts of Creation, because the two chapters use different names for God (Elohim vs. Yahweh). There are also various discrepancies, such as that chapter 1 has plants being created on the third day, while in chapter 2, they are created after human beings. Neither chapter, it is claimed, was written by Moses.

Ancient writing customs – The presence of two versions of a story within the same literary piece was not uncommon in ancient times. There was in the ancient Near East a literary convention of telling the story of the origin of humankind in doublet form. Like Genesis 1 and 2, the Sumerian story, *Enki and Ninmah,* describes the creation of humankind in two parallel parts. A similar structure can also be seen in the Atrahasis epic.

The Creation story of Genesis 1 ends in 2:4, not in 1:31. Chapter and verse divisions were inserted much later and often divide the text in an arbitrary fashion. Many modern English versions, therefore, indicate the actual break by placing a gap or a heading between 2:4a and 2:4b, right in the middle of the verse!

Vegetation in Genesis 1 and 2 – The first point chapter 2 makes is that there were four things that did *not yet* exist after God had completed the earth and the heavens—the shrub of the field, the plant of the field, the man to till the soil, and rain. Are these things, especially the plants and man, somehow different from those mentioned in Chapter 1? If so, how and why did these things come into existence?

The shrub of the field – In Genesis 1:12 it says, "And the earth brought forth vegetation [*deshe'*], plants yielding seed [*'eseb mazrya' zera'*] after their kind, and trees bearing fruit [*'etz 'oseh peri*], with seed in them, after their kind. . . ." Genesis 2:5, on the other hand, reads that prior to man's creation there was no shrub of the field (*siach hassadeh*), and no plant of the field (*'eseb hassadeh*) "had yet sprung up."

Most scholars assume that the words and phrases for plants or vegetation used in Genesis 1:12 and 2:5 carry the same meaning. A close reading of the text, however, reveals that the botanical terms of Genesis 1:12 and 2:5 do not have an identical meaning. The word *siach* appears only four times in the Hebrew Bible (Gen 2:5, 21:15 and Job 30:4, 7), while the full expression *siach hassadeh* is unique, appearing only in Genesis 2:5. The contexts of both Genesis 21:15 and Job 30:4, 7 make it clear that the *siach* is a xerophyte, that is, a plant adapted to dry or desert environments. As such, it is most likely a spiny or thorny plant. This understanding of the *siach* receives support from Genesis 3:18 in which the expression "plant of the field [*'eseb hassadeh*]" is coupled with "thorns and thistles." "Thorns and thistles" was apparently intended as a parallel expression for the earlier "shrub of the field [*siach hassadeh*]." These spiny plants are not the type of plant that a farmer of the ancient Near East would deliberately cultivate in his garden, nor were these plants likely included among the species when God planted

Thomas L. Thompson, who supports a late multiple authorship of Genesis, nevertheless questions the traditional use of the "double" Creation story as suitable support for the theory He writes, "This time-worn effort to relate parallel traditions and units of traditions, which has been a fundamental first step into the history of the traditions, needs to be radically questioned. We have neither the number nor the variety of tale-types in the Bible with which one might reasonably analyze their interrelatedness. Moreover, the existence of doublets is definitely not a criterion with which we can demonstrate a separateness in the traditions or in the complex sources of traditions. Doublet and triplet stories can and do exist within the same traditions." (*The Origin Tradition of Ancient Israel* [Sheffield, England: Sheffield Academic Press, 1987], 59).

God planted the garden east in Eden, filling it with all sorts of "trees that were pleasing to the eye and good for food" (Gen 2:8, 9). Thus, one of the plants that did *not yet* exist as we begin the narrative of Genesis 2:4b, was the thorny xerophytes – the agriculturist's bane. What is the point the author is trying to make here, then? To better understand, we first go on to the next plant that was *not yet* – the "plant of the field."

The plant of the field – While the other botanical term in Genesis 2, *ᶜeseb* (plant) is fairly common in the Hebrew text, it appears in the full expression *ᶜeseb hassadeh* ("plant of the field") in Genesis only in 2:5 and 3:18. In Genesis 3:18 "plants of the field" are specifically designated as the food Adam will have to eat as a result of his sin and that they come about directly by man's "painful toil" and by the "sweat of [his] brow." In other words, "plants of the field" are those plants that are specifically produced by the labor by which man was burdened *because of his fall into sin*. As U. Cassuto points out, "these species did not exist, or were not found in the form known to us until after Adam's transgression, and it was in consequence of his fall that they came into the world and received their present form."[1]

The fact that Genesis 3:19 explicitly states that these plants were used to make bread would indicate that the expression "plants of the field" specifically refers to the well-known grains of the Middle East that are used to make bread – that is, wheat , barley and other grains. In the Middle East, the growing of these bread grains requires the "tilling of the ground," another feature of these plants that

> Genesis 2 is setting the stage for what comes later in Genesis 3.

is specifically mentioned in Genesis. Thus the two botanical terms "shrub of the field" and "plant of the field" encompass not the entire plant kingdom but rather that part of the plant kingdom that the cultivator is particularly concerned with – annual cultivants and intrusives.

No man to till the ground – Again, some scholars have assumed that Genesis 2:5b contradicts chapter 1, because, while the first chapter depicts the creation of man on day six, Genesis 2:5b seems to imply that God had not yet made man after "the earth and heavens were made." However, this is again an over-simplified reading of the text that ignores the critical modifier "to till the ground."

It is important to note that the man who was created in Genesis 1:26-30 was not intended to work the ground. Rather, he was to "rule over the fish of the seas and the birds of the air and over every other living creature that moves on the ground." Further, he was given "every seed-bearing plant on the face of the earth and every tree that has fruit with seed in it" for food. Nothing is said of deriving food from "working the ground."

A man who "works the ground" does not come into view until *after* Adam's fall. Then, *because of his sin*, Adam is told, "cursed is the ground because of you; through painful toil you will eat of it [the ground] all the days of your life" (Gen 1:17b). Thus, like the "plant of the field" of Genesis 2:5, the "man to work the ground" does not come into existence until *after* the Fall as a direct result of sin. Genesis 2:5b, therefore, is not saying that no man yet existed after God had made the earth and heavens. Rather, it is saying that no *sinful* man (i.e. one who must work the ground for food) yet existed. Such a man would not exist until after the Fall, an event that is not discussed until the next chapter (chapter 3). Genesis 2, thus, is setting the stage for what comes later in Genesis 3.

Rain – The final thing that Genesis 2:5b indicates did not yet exist after God finished the earth and the heavens is rain. Following the same pattern that has clearly been set for the three previous categories, it is logical to assume that rain does not make its appearance until *after* the entrance of sin. This is, indeed, the case. However, unlike the first three items, which appear immediately after man's fall, rain is not mentioned until Genesis 7:4, 12, at the commencement of the Flood, although the context clearly indicates that rain, too, comes as a consequence of the entrance of sin into the world.

> Rain makes its entrance into the world, not as a water source for agriculture but as an agent of God's judgment.

Although the thorny shrubs, cultivated plants, and the act of cultivation were immediate judgments brought upon human beings for their sin, they were permitted to continue living. The final judgment of rain comes only after the condition of the antediluvians worsens to the point that God regrets giving them this second chance and determines to terminate the race. Rain makes its entrance into the world, not as a water source for agriculture but as an agent of God's judgment.

Summary – A close reading of the text suggests that chapter 2 does not offer a Creation account that contradicts chapter 1. Rather, the point of Genesis 2:4-9 is to explain the origin of four things that were not part of the original creation described in chapter one: (1) thorns; (2) agriculture; (3) cultivation/irrigation; (4) rain. Chapter 2 informs the reader that each of these things was introduced as a direct result of the entrance of sin. Thorns, plants requiring cultivation, and a human race that must work the ground for its food are introduced in Genesis 3:17, 18 as curses or judgments immediately after the Fall. Although rain is not mentioned until the Flood, it, too, comes as a curse—a judgment against humanity's sin. Thus, rather, than a contradiction of chapter 1, these early verses in Chapter 2 actually serve as a bridge between the perfect creation of Chapter 1 and the introduction of sin into the world in Chapter 3.

Randall W. Younker

References

[1]U. Cassuto, *The Documentary Hypothesis*, trans. I Abrahams (Jerusalem: Magnes, 1961), 102.

I can see how it might be possible for a man to look down upon the earth and be an atheist, but I cannot conceive how he could look up into the heavens and say there is no God.

Abraham Lincoln

CAN WE KNOW WHERE THE GARDEN OF EDEN WAS LOCATED BASED ON THE NAMES OF RIVERS?

Now a river flowed out of Eden to water the garden; and from there it divided and became four rivers. The name of the first is Pishon; it flows around the whole land of Havilah, where there is gold. And the gold of that land is good; the bdellium and the onyx stone are there. And the name of the second river is Gihon; it flows around the whole land of Cush. And the name of the third river is Tigris; it flows east of Assyria. And the fourth river is the Euphrates. Genesis 2:10-14.

This passage is part of the Creation story in Genesis 2. While textual matters do not seem to present difficulties in this passage, a literal reading of the text presents formidable difficulties for a modern location. First, the current Tigris and Euphrates Rivers have no common source but start from different sources in the Armenian mountains. Second, the biblical teaching of a historical global Flood would have involved major changes in the crust of the earth, rendering our present landscape nothing like that of the pre-Flood world.[1] Thus, it is not possible to locate the Garden of Eden today.

> The biblical teaching of a historical global Flood would have involved major changes in the crust of the earth, rendering our present landscape nothing like that of the pre-Flood world.

The intent of the passage is to describe the beauties, rivers, and good life of a blissful home in Eden. The current river names (Tigris and Euphrates) may reflect the practice of borrowing beloved original river names to describe present geographical places. Many countries have a city named Paris after the original in France, and New York is named after York, England. This practice may help to explain the naming of the Tigris and Euphrates after pre-Flood rivers.

While the Bible does not explicitly describe what happened to the Garden of Eden and the tree of life, the tree of life is described as now being in heaven (Rev 22:2), ready to provide food for saved human beings. This

> "When the tide of iniquity overspread the world, and the wickedness of men determined their destruction by a flood of waters, the hand that had planted Eden withdrew it from the earth. But in the final restitution, when there shall be 'a new heaven and a new earth' (Revelation 21:1), it is to be restored more gloriously adorned than at the beginning," (PP 62).

knowledge leads to the conclusion that the Garden of Eden and the tree of life were taken to heaven before the Flood to save them from destruction.

John T. Baldwin and Erno Gyeresi

References

[1]See Ellen G. White, *Patriarchs and Prophets* (Mountain View, CA: Pacific Press, 1958), 107, 108. On the significance of the undoing of the world by the Flood see, Richard M. Davidson, "The Genesis Flood Narrative: Crucial Issues in the Current Debate," *Andrews University Seminary Studies* 42.1 (Spring 2004): 49-78.

We are dependent on the Bible for a knowledge of the early history of our world.

MM 89

WHY DIDN'T ADAM AND EVE DIE IMMEDIATELY?

And the LORD God commanded the man, saying, "From any tree of the garden you may eat freely; but from the tree of the knowledge of good and evil you shall not eat, for in the day that you eat from it you shall surely die." Genesis 2:16, 17.

Because Adam and Eve did not die on the exact day that they ate of the forbidden fruit, it is sometimes claimed that since one day is with the Lord as a thousand years (2 Pet 3:8) and Adam lived less than a thousand years (Gen 5:5), Adam, therefore, did die within that one-thousand-year long "day." Another common explanation is that Adam and Eve *began* to die immediately. A third view is that the death penalty was commuted because God promised a Savior in Genesis 3:15. However, a correct understanding of the Hebrew expressions in the passage points to another possibility.

> The Hebrew for "in the day that" can refer to a moment, a day, or some other unspecified time.

On Day Six of the Creation week, God placed Adam in the Garden of Eden and told him that he could freely eat of every tree in the garden except one – the tree of the knowledge of good and evil. Before Adam and Eve "could be rendered eternally secure" (CC 13), their loyalty had to be tested. The warning given was clear and straightforward, "in the day that you eat of it you shall surely die."

The meaning of "in the day that" – In Hebrew, the expression "in the day that" occurs five other times in Genesis (2:4; 3:5; 5:1, 2; 21:8). A comparison of different translations of these verses reveals that it is variously translated as "in the day that," "when," "as soon as," etc., depending on the context. One reason for the different translations is that the Hebrew for "in the day that" (*b⁰yom* + infinitive) is frequently imprecise as to the exact point or period of time referred to. It may be a moment, a day, or some other unspecified time. A similar use of *b⁰yom* occurs in Genesis 30:33, in which the expression *b⁰yom machar* (literally, "in a day of tomorrow") means "at a future time," referring to an unspecified time in the future, not to a specific day. Therefore, unless the context indicates otherwise, the expression *b*ᵉ*yom* + infinitive simply means "when."[1] Although the translation "in the day that" seems literal, it misleads the English reader into thinking that it refers to a specific "day." Rather, a translation that does not use the word "day," such as, "when," "as soon as," "whenever," etc., captures better the intent of the Hebrew.

The meaning of "you shall surely die" – In Hebrew, "surely" is expressed by an infinitive absolute of "to die." It reinforces the "notion of certainty."[2] In Genesis 2:17, its function is to highlight the certainty of death, not the time of death.

An interesting parallel to Genesis 2:17 in 1 Kings 2 may help to explain this. According to 1 Kings 2:36-46, Solomon placed Shimei under house arrest, with a stern warning that contains grammatical parallels to Genesis 2:17, "For it will happen on the day you go out [*b*ᵉ*yom* + infinitive] and cross over the brook Kidron, you will know for certain [infinitive + finite verb] that you shall surely die [infinitive + finite verb]; your blood shall be on your own head" (1 Kgs 2:37; cf. v. 42).

> The Hebrew may be appropriately rendered, "As soon as you eat of it, you are surely destined to die."

Three years later, two of Shimei's servants ran away. Shimei went to Gath and brought them back home. Sometime after Shimei's return, Solomon was told about the incident and had Shimei arrested and executed. Though it is not stated how long it took for all this to transpire, such a series of events would normally entail a number of days, which means that Shimei's execution did not occur on the day of his departure. Therefore, Solomon's words of warning in v. 37 ("On the day that . . . thou shalt know for certain that thou shalt surely die") did not mean that Shimei would "surely die" on the day of his departure. Instead, Solomon's words emphasized the certainty of Shimei's death penalty rather than the time of its execution. That is, as soon as he violated his agreement, Shimei was destined to die, even if his execution did not take place on that very day.

God's words were true – God's words in Genesis 2:17 did not mean that Adam's death would occur on the day he ate the forbidden fruit but rather that the moment he ate of it his death would be certain. The Hebrew may be appropriately rendered, "As soon as you eat of it, you are surely destined to die." That is why the serpent's counter-claim was not that Adam and Eve would *not* die "on that day," but that they would "surely not die" (Gen 3:4). As it turned out, Genesis 2:17 was, in fact, fulfilled. Adam and Eve were expelled from Eden and did die. Although the serpent's words were partially true (i.e., their eyes were opened, knowing both good and evil, Gen 3:5, 22), God's words were not partially, but completely, true.

The death of Adam and Eve testifies to the reality that "the wages of sin *is* death" (Rom 6:23). Nevertheless, "as in Adam all die, even so in Christ shall all be made alive" (1 Cor 15:22).

Tarsee Li

References

[1]See L. J. Coppes "*ywm*," in *Theological Wordbook of the Old Testament*, ed. R. Laird Harris, *et. al.* 2 vols. (Chicago, IL: Moody Press, 1980), 1:370, 371.
[2]Bruce K. Waltke and M. O'Connor, *An Introduction to Biblical Hebrew Syntax* (Winona Lake, IN: Eisenbrauns, 1990), 584; see also the full discussion, 584-588.

We need the authentic history of the origin of the earth, of the fall of the covering cherub, and of the introduction of sin into our world. Without the Bible, we should be bewildered by false theories.

MM 89

IS GENESIS 3:15 A MESSIANIC PROPHECY?

And I will put enmity between you and the woman, and between your seed and her seed; He shall bruise you on the head, and you shall bruise him on the heel. Genesis 3:15.

For centuries of Christian interpretation, Genesis 3:15 has been given a wide divergence of literal and symbolic interpretations. Some interpret this text merely as a description of the conflict between humans and snakes. Others claim that it is a fictional story to explain the human fear of snakes and why snakes crawl and eat dust. Catholic interpreters read Mary, the mother of Jesus, and the virgin birth into this text, insisting that she is superior to other humans. As far as we know Martin Luther was the first to call Genesis 3:15 the *protoevangelium*, i.e., "the first gospel promise."[1]

The Messianic Seed – The Hebrew term *zerac* "seed," together with the expression "generations of" (*tolᵉdoth*), forms the organizing fabric of the book of Genesis. Genesis documents the search for the family lineage chosen to produce the Messianic Seed promised in 3:15. This lineage of the Messiah goes from Adam and Eve to Seth to Noah to Abraham to Isaac to Jacob and to Judah. Judah became the ancestor of King David, the progenitor of Jesus, the Son of David (Gen 49:8-12; Luke 3:23-34). Abraham and Sarah were promised a royal dynasty (Gen 17:6, 16). This promise was repeated to Jacob (Gen 35:11). Many Messianic royal psalms echo Genesis 3:15 (Pss 2; 72; 89:4, 20, 24-29, 36; 110:1).

The first biblical Messianic commentary of Genesis 3:15 is Eve's exclamation at the birth of Cain: "I have gotten a man from the LORD" (KJV). Allusions made to the Seed of Genesis 3:15 by other major seed passages (e.g. Gen 4:25; 15:13-16; Isaiah 53) show a similar and consistent pattern of understanding of the Messianic implication of the Seed. Interestingly, Genesis 22:17, 18; 24:60; Numbers 23-24; and 2 Samuel 7:12-15 exhibit similar movements from the collective plural to the single individual. This is a key characteristic of Messianic texts. Consequently, the New Testament refers to the collective seed (Rom 16:20; Gal 3:29; and Rev 12:17) and narrows it down to the specific singular individual Seed in the person of Jesus

Christ (Gal 3:16, 19), who overcame the serpent identified specifically as Satan or the Devil (Rev 12:9).

From the collective plural to the single individual – The narrowing movement from the collective plural seed, *zera^c*, to the single individual representative Seed is the major Messianic indicator in the text. This narrowing occurs on both sides of the enmity that began between the serpent (singular) and the woman (singular) [15b]. The enmity multiplies to engulf the entire seed of the serpent (collective) and the seed of the woman (collective) [15c] and then narrows down to culminate in the serpent (singular) and the representative Seed of the woman (singular) [15d, e]. The *zera^c* "seed" of Genesis 3:15 is neither exclusively singular nor exclusively plural. The drama of the enmity in Genesis 3:15 unfolds in stages.

> The narrowing movement from the collective plural seed to the single individual representative Seed is the major Messianic indicator in the text.

Genesis 3:15 can be translated and divided up as follows:

15a   And I [*God*] will put [*divinely-instigate*] enmity

15b   between you [*Satan, singular*] and the woman [*Eve, singular*];

15c   and between your seed [*collective plural, i.e. all followers of Satan*] and her seed [*collective plural, i.e. all human beings who follow righteousness*];

15d   He [*singular individual representative Seed of the woman*] shall crush [*ultimately annihilate along with followers*] you [*Satan, singular*] on the head,

15e   And you [*Satan, singular*] shall crush Him [*Christ, singular*]at the heel."

The conjunction "and" at the beginning of the last phrase (15e) corroborates the shift from the collective seed of the serpent to the singular serpent himself.

The hostility between the serpent and the woman continues for generations. Therefore, Genesis 3:15 must be prophetic and eschatological. This enmity culminates in the fatal clash between Satan and Christ in which Satan and his cohorts are ultimately vanquished. Christ, the special Seed of the woman is a servant-like Redeemer, gracious Savior, and High Priest because He was offering His life as a sacrifice in lieu of Satan's lethal attack on Him. It is as if Christ stepped on the serpent's head with His bare heels voluntarily and vicariously. This is Messianic!

Not only the Hebrew of Genesis 3:15 but also the early translations of this text confirm the idea of a narrowing from the collective to the singular. The most important textual support comes from the Greek Old Testament (*Septuagint*), which follows the Hebrew text in Genesis 3:15 to the extent that it intentionally violates Greek grammar by using a masculine pronoun (*autos*) to refer to the neuter noun for seed (*sperma*) in order to favor a Messianic reading of this text. This is not a coincidence or a mere oversight! The Messianic narrowing phenomenon is also evident in the Aramaic translations, the Syriac Peshitta, in Old Latin manuscripts from Europe and North Africa, and the Vulgate.

> "I do find the fullness of meaning [of Gen 3:15] in some as-yet-unspecified member of the human race who would destroy the satanic serpent, thus playing a key role in God's redemptive plan. In that sense, the passage is indeed the first enunciation of the good news" (W. S. LaSor, "Prophecy, Inspiration, and Sensus Plenior," *Tyndale Bulletin* 29 [1978], 56, 57).

Interpretation – Based on the grammatical, textual, and scriptural evidence, we can justifiably see Genesis 3:15 as a Messianic prophecy that God intentionally placed at the beginning of Scripture. It is the seedbed of all Messianic prophecies, even though the Messianic idea was historically not fully developed, exemplified, and demonstrated until later revelations. It was fulfilled in the life and death of Jesus Christ and will culminate in the final annihilation of Satan, the extinction of all evil, the vindication of God, the redemption for all God's followers, and the establishment of the Messianic Kingdom of God.

Conclusion – There is enough grammatical, syntactical, textual, structural, and scriptural evidence for one to conclude that Genesis 3:15 is a Messianic prophecy. Though brief at that early stage in human history, it continues to be the watershed text upon which other Messianic texts build. The narrowing movement from collective seed to singular Seed in the verse is the best proof of its Messianic intent. If the Bible is its best interpreter, then Genesis 3:15 is a Messianic prophecy.

Afolarin Olutunde Ojewole

References

[1]Ojewole, Afolarin Olutunde, "The Seed in Genesis 3:15: An Exegetical and Intertextual Study." (Ph.D. dissertation, Andrews University, 2002).

WHERE TO LOOK IN THE BIBLE

When God seems far away, read Psalm 139.
When sorrowful, read John 14; Psalm 46.
When men fail you, read Psalm 27.
When you have sinned, read Psalm 51; I John 1.
When you worry, read Matthew 6:19-34; Psalm 43.
When in sickness, read Psalm 41.
When in danger, read Psalm 91.
When you have the blues, read Psalm 34.
When you are discouraged, read Isaiah 40.
When you are lonely or fearful, read Psalm 23.
When you forget your blessings, read Psalm 103.
When you want courage, read Joshua 1:1-9.
When the world seems bigger than God, read Psalm 90.
When you want rest and peace, read Matthew 11:25-30.
When you want assurance, read Romans 8.
When looking for joy, read Colossians 3.
When you leave home to travel, read Psalm 121.
When you grow bitter or critical, read I Corinthians 13.
When you think of investments, read Mark 10:17-31.
Some rules of conduct? read Romans 12.
Why not follow Psalm 119:11?

WHERE DID CAIN GET HIS WIFE?

And Cain had relations with his wife and she conceived, and gave birth to Enoch. Genesis 4:17.

The mention of Cain's wife seems to create a problem. Where did she suddenly come from? The earliest inhabitants of earth obviously had no other choice but to marry their brothers and sisters. This custom raises the question whether God intended incest from the beginning in order for the earliest human beings to carry out His instruction to be "fruitful and multiply and fill the earth" (Gen 1:28).

Marriage between close relatives – Adam and Eve did indeed have other sons and daughters (Gen 5:4) the latter of which Cain and Abel must have married.[1] This practice was inevitable in the second generation. In the third generation, marriage could have taken place between first cousins and by the fourth generation through second cousins. Since Adam and Eve came

> The earliest inhabitants of earth had no other choice but to marry their brothers and sisters.

perfect from the Creator's hand, the danger of birth defects through inbreeding at this stage of human history did not exist, despite the entrance of sin.

Even a long time after the Flood, we find that Abraham married his half-sister Sarah. During the sojourn when the children of Israel were in Egypt, it was common in the Egyptian royal family for marriages to take place among siblings. For example, in the time of Moses, during the eighteenth dynasty, Hatshepsut married her half-brother Thutmose II. Among the Israelites, we find that Moses' father Amram married a young aunt, his father's sister, Jochebed (Exod 6:20). Such marriages were viewed very differently in those ancient cultures.

However, after God called Israel out of Egypt and set them apart as a holy nation of priests (Exod 19:6; Lev 19:2), Israel received laws governing all forms of incest (Lev 18:7-17; 20:11, 12, 14, 17, 20, 21; Deut 22:30; 27:20,

22, 23). While in Egypt such practices were common; the Israelites in their new land were to avoid these customs of pagan societies. Leviticus 18:6 prohibits sexual relationships with close relatives such as a mother, father, stepmother, sister, brother, half-brother, granddaughter, daughter-in-law, son-in-law, aunt, uncle, or a brother's wife. What had once been permitted out of necessity was now forbidden. As a holy nation they were called to a high standard of moral living that would distinguish them from the nations around them. The specific sexual prohibitions must be viewed in terms of the conditions that prevailed in the ancient Near East at that time. The worship of the various fertility goddesses among the nations made "the abandonment of one's body to various sensual pleasures a religious obligation."[2] By contrast, the Israelites were to consecrate themselves to Yahweh and reflect His holiness to the nations around them (Exod 19:2; Isa 49:6).

Conclusion – While at the beginning of human history marriage among relatives was a necessity, by the time Israel became a nation sexual relations between close relatives was prohibited. The reason for this prohibition was primarily because of their special status as God's holy people but also because the danger of genetic damage increased as the effects of sin became more pronounced. This danger was not present immediately after the Creation. God had created all things perfect. While today the risk of genetic damage is extremely high, the early generations of human beings did not face the same biological risks.

Michael G. Hasel

References

[1]"We must assume that Cain's wife was one of Adam's 'other daughters' (Gen 5:4). Later sibling marriage was unnecessary, and it was soundly denounced in Mosaic tradition (e.g., Lev 18:9)" (K. A. Matthews, *Genesis 1-11:26*, The American Commentary [n.p.: Broadman and Holman, 2002).

[2]A. Noordtzij, *Leviticus*, Bible Student's Commentary (Grand Rapids, MI: Zondervan, 1982), 181.

WHO WERE THE "SONS OF GOD" AND THE "DAUGHTERS OF MEN"?

The Nephilim were on the earth in those days, and also afterward, when the sons of God came in to the daughters of men, and they bore *children* to them. Those were the mighty men that were of old, the men of renown. Genesis 6:4.

Genesis 6:4 raises a number of questions, primarily in regard to the identity of the various people mentioned in the text: Who are the *Nephilim*? Who are the "sons of God" and the "daughters of men?" Who are the "mighty men, the men of renown?"And what is the relationship between these various groups?

The passage in Genesis 6:1-8 is preceded by the genealogy of Adam (5:1-32) and followed by the genealogy of Noah (6:9, 10) and the story of the Flood (6:13-8:22). It provides the reason for God's judgment upon the earth in form of the Flood. The increase in numbers was matched by an outbreak of immorality. "The LORD saw that the wickedness of man was great on the earth and that every intent of the thoughts of his heart was only evil continually" (6:5). And the marriages between the daughters of men and the sons of God seem to have contributed in some way to this moral decline.

The Identity of the Nephilim

The origin and meaning of the word *Nephilim* is uncertain. If the word goes back to the Hebrew word *pala'*, meaning "be extraordinary," the *Nephilim* are simply "extraordinary men." If the term is derived from the Hebrew word *naphal,* the meaning of which is "to fall," the Nephilim may have been morally fallen men or those who fell upon others, i.e., invaders or hostile, violent men. There is one other reference to *Nephilim* in the Bible. Long after the Flood, in Numbers 13:33, ten of the spies sent into Canaan by Moses report, "And there we saw the *Nephilim* (the sons of Anak, who come from the *Nephilim*); and we seemed to ourselves like grasshoppers, and so we seemed to them" (ESV). This later reference to the *Nephilim* tells

135

us that they were (or were perceived to be) physically large and, therefore, unlikely to be overcome in war. It is not clear whether the Nephilim in Numbers 13 were descendants of the antediluvian Nephilim or whether the spies simply appealed to these figures from the past to win their case.

> The interpretation of the "sons of God" as angels is not possible in view of Jesus' statement that angels do not marry (Matt 22:30).

The KJV translation "giants" follows the Septuagint and other ancient versions, which were probably influenced by the report of the spies.

Although many commentators identify the *Nephilim* in Genesis 6 with "the mighty men," "the men of renown," at the end of verse 4, the text does not say so. The *Nephilim* are not the offspring of the marital union between the sons of God and the daughters of men; rather they lived "in those days," i.e., in the antediluvian period, when the sons of God had sexual relations with the daughters of men from which came the mighty men of renown. All we know about the Nephilim is that they were tall and powerful people, possibly violent men, who lived before the Flood.

The identity of the "Sons of God"

The "sons of God" as angels – Some interpreters, following an ancient Jewish tradition, have concluded from the references to the "sons of God" in Job 1:6, 2:1 and 38:7 that these beings must be supernatural, possibly fallen angels. In this interpretation, the "daughters of men" would be human females who had offspring resulting from sexual relations with these supernatural beings. Their offspring were semi-supernatural persons of great power. However, this theory clashes with Jesus' declaration that angels do not marry (Matt 22:30). Sons of God can also refer to human beings; e.g., in Luke 3:38, Adam is called a "son of God" and in Psalm 82:6 human beings are called "sons of the Most High." In addition, if God's displeasure in Genesis 6:3 is provoked by the intercourse described in Genesis 6:2, it would seem odd that human beings were punished for the sin of angels. The Flood is God's punishment on humanity, not on angels.

The "sons of God" as royal despots – A second theory holds that the "sons of God" are royal despots who engage in polygamy by taking as many wives as they wanted. This is supported by the references to kings as "sons of God" in 2 Samuel 7:14, and 1 Chronicles 28:6. In addition, those who administer justice are sometimes referred to by the Hebrew word for God, 'Elohim (e.g., Exod 22:8). In this interpretation, the "daughters of men" would be women of non-royal birth who were taken into the harems of the despotic kings. Their offspring became mighty men of war.

Against this view is the fact that nowhere in this passage is there a reference to kingship. Furthermore, although individual kings in the Old Testament are sometimes referred to as a "son of God" (see Ps 2:7), there is no evidence in the Bible or in the ancient Near East for a group of kings being given this title.

> "'The sons of God saw the daughters of men that they were fair.' The children of Seth, attracted by the beauty of the daughters of Cain's descendants, displeased the Lord by intermarrying with them. Many of the worshipers of God were beguiled into sin by the allurements that were now constantly before them, and they lost their peculiar, holy character." (PP 81)

The "sons of God" as descendants of Seth – A final interpretation of this text suggests that the "sons of God" were the righteous and God-fearing descendants of Seth, and the "daughters of men" were the corrupt and impious descendants of Cain. The practice of referring to the righteous (directly or indirectly) as "sons of God" is evidenced elsewhere in the Bible (e.g., Deut 14:1; Isa 43:6; Mal 2:10; etc.). According to this view, the Sethites, abandoning their spiritual principles, intermarried with the Cainites (perhaps even polygamously) and had offspring who became men of renown.

This last view interprets "sons of God" in a sense consistent with Old Testament usage, without suggesting angelic marriage.

Donn W. Leatherman

HOW COULD EVERY SPECIES BE PRESERVED ON THE ARK? WHAT ABOUT THE DINOSAURS?

You shall take with you of every clean animal by sevens, a male and his female; and of the animals that are not clean two, a male and his female. Genesis 7:2.

Some people have questioned the historicity of a worldwide flood because, among other things, they cannot imagine that Noah's ark could have housed all the different species of animals in existence today. Therefore, they believe that only a local flood, somewhere in the Near East, is described in Genesis 7-9. The text, however, is clear, the Flood was worldwide and all the different species of land animals God had created were saved in the ark.

The size of the ark – First, one must realize the tremendous size of Noah's ark, as indicated by the biblical data. According to Genesis 6:15, the ark was 300 cubits long, fifty cubits wide, thirty cubits high, and contained three decks. Assuming the length of a cubit as 17.5 inches (it could have been longer, but this is widely recognized as the length of the standard cubit for Egyptians and Israelites), the dimensions of the ark were 437.5 feet (ca. 133 m) long, 72.92 feet (ca. 22 m) wide, and 43.75 feet (ca. 13 m) high. John Whitcomb and Henry Morris calculate that this would provide a total deck area of approximately 95,700 square feet (8,891 m²), total volume of 1,396,000 cubic feet (39,530 m³), and gross tonnage of 13,960 tons.[1] This size would place the ark well within the category of modern ships today.

Second, although the biblical text indicates that Noah was to take representatives of every air-breathing terrestrial creature into the ark, "to keep seed alive on the face of all the earth" (Gen 7:2, 3), it is not correct to assume that all the present species (in the modern technical taxonomical sense of the word) that are alive today were represented in the ark. Genesis 2:19 implies that at the time of Creation there were far fewer kinds of large animals ("beasts of the field") and birds than today, since Adam was able to observe and name each one individually on the sixth day of Creation before the creation of Eve. Such was no doubt also the case with the other

138

smaller terrestrial creatures that Adam did not name on the sixth day. By the time of the Flood each basic "kind" (Hebrew *min*) of animal created by God may have diversified somewhat into various sub-groupings, but still would not have approached the almost endless species and sub-species of terrestrial creatures that have developed today as different strains from the basic kinds at Creation.[2] Given these basic restrictions, recent calculations[3] indicate there would be more than sufficient room for the basic kinds of animals created by God in the beginning to be housed in the ark, along with the food for their sustenance.

> Given these basic restrictions, recent calculations indicate there would be more than sufficient room for the basic kinds of animals created by God in the beginning to be housed in the ark, along with the food for their sustenance.

What about the dinosaurs? – Although there is no specific Hebrew word that can be translated as "dinosaur," the biblical Creation account does indicate that God created *tanninim* "great sea creatures" (Gen 1:21) and every *beʰemah,* "powerful animal" (Gen 1:24), that could, well have included what we today call dinosaurs. Each type of animal made by God would have been preserved on the ark (Gen 9:10), but the larger ones might have been represented by young animals who were still small in size.

Along with the animals that God made at Creation, there also seem to have existed some varieties of large, ferocious animals that were not specifically created by God, but came into existence as a result of changes occurring after the Fall and perhaps even through direct manipulation by Satan. Genesis 3:15 points to the ongoing work on earth of the "serpent," Satan, from the time of the Fall, and Genesis 3:18 depicts the results of the enemy's work in the plant world, with the appearance of thorns and thistles. Similar corruption of animal types also seems implied in Genesis 6:12, in which God observes that "all flesh [which in light of Genesis 6:17 and 7:21 includes animals as well as humans] had corrupted their way on the earth." This corruption led to *chamas* "violence," a strong Hebrew word often implying cruel, vicious, violence involving bloodshed. These corrupt animals that God did not create, no doubt including some dinosaurs, would not have been represented in the ark, but would have perished in the Flood.[4]

Ellen White's insights – All these points, hinted at in the biblical text, are made more explicit by Ellen White. She notes that God "never made a thorn, a thistle, or a tare. These are Satan's work, the result of degeneration, introduced by him among the precious things" (6T 186). "All tares are sown by the evil one. Every noxious herb is of his sowing, and by his ingenious methods of amalgamation he has corrupted the earth with tares" (2SM 288). Similarly, regarding the animals, she writes: "Every species [i.e., Genesis 1 'kind', not the technical 'species' of modern taxonomy] of animal which God had created were preserved in the ark. The confused species which God did not create, which were the result of amalgamation, were destroyed by the flood" (3SG 75). She may have been referring to the dinosaurs (among other animals) when she states what had been revealed to her: "I was shown that very large, powerful animals existed before the flood which do not now exist" (3SG 92). "There were [sic] a class of very large animals which perished at the flood. God knew that the strength of man would decrease, and these mammoth animals could not be controlled by feeble man" (4aSG 121). While it is not possible to be absolutely certain that these inspired statements from Scripture and Ellen White refer specifically to the dinosaurs, there seems to be no compelling reason to exclude dinosaurs from these descriptions.[5]

> "There were a class of very large animals which perished at the flood. God knew that the strength of man would decrease, and these mammoth animals could not be controlled by feeble man" (4aSG 121).

Richard M. Davidson

References

[1]John Whitcomb and Henry Morris, *The Genesis Flood: The Biblical Record and Its Scientific Implications* (Philadelphia, PA: Presbyterian and Reformed Publishing Company, 1961), 10, 11.

[2]A. Rahel Davidson Schafer, "The 'Kinds' of Genesis 1: What is the Meaning of *Min*?" *Journal of the Adventist Theological Society* 14/1 (Spring 2003): 86-100.

[3]John Woodmorappe, *Noah's Ark: A Feasibility Study* (Santee, CA: Institute for

Creation Research, 1996).

[4]The ancient Near Eastern parallel flood story found in the Eridu Genesis (written in Sumerian about 1600 B.C.), may also allude to the fact that the large, violent animals, such as the dinosaurs, were not created by God and were not preserved on the ark. The Eridu Genesis indicates that only the "small animals that come up from the earth" were created by the deity and preserved on the ark (Thorkild Jacobsen, "The Eridu Genesis," *Journal of Biblical Literature* 100/4 [1981]: 515, 525).

[5]On dinosaurs and the ark, see Paul S. Taylor, *The Great Dinosaur Mystery and the Bible* (Denver, CO: Accent Books, 1987); Elaine Kennedy, *Dinosaurs: Where Did They Come From and Where Did They Go?* (Boise, ID: Pacific Press, 2006); David C. Read, *Dinosaurs an Adventist View* (2009).

Chronology of the Flood in Genesis

Genesis 7:7-9	Noah entered the ark.	2/10/600
Genesis 7:10, 11	It began to rain	2/17/600
Genesis 7:12	It rained for 40 days	3/27/600
Genesis 7:24	Water prevailed for 110 more days	7/17/600
Genesis 8:4	Ark came to rest on Mount Ararat	7/17/600
Genesis 8:5	Mountains became visible	10/1/600
Genesis 8:6, 7	After 40 days, a raven is released	11/11/600
Genesis 8:8	A dove is released the first time	11/18/600 (PP 105)
Genesis 8:10	Seven days later, the dove is released the second time	11/25/600
Genesis 8:12	Seven days later, the dove is released the third time	12/2/600
Genesis 8:13	Noah saw the earth was dry	1/1/601
Genesis 8: 14-16	Noah left the ark	2/27/601

Note: According to Genesis 7:11, 24 and 8:3, 4, the five months of the Flood comprised 150 days; thus one month had 30 days.

WAS THE FLOOD GLOBAL?

And the water prevailed more and more upon the earth, so that all the high mountains everywhere under the heavens were covered. The water prevailed fifteen cubits higher, and the mountains were covered. Genesis 7:19, 20.

The traditional interpretation of Genesis 6-9 affirms the global extent of the Genesis Flood, but in recent times various limited-flood theories have been suggested that narrow its scope to a particular geographical location in Mesopotamia, the Black Sea, or elsewhere. Limited-flood theories rest primarily on scientific arguments that set forth seemingly difficult geological problems for a global flood. These arguments generally assume uniformity in the history of the earth's geology. However, numerous recent scientific studies provide a growing body of evidence for diluvial catastrophism (catastrophic changes through a flood) instead of uniformitarianism.[1]

> Uniformitarianism is the concept that geological processes occur by the action of natural laws that are always the same, and by processes that can be observed today.

Evidence for a global Flood – Only the traditional understanding of Genesis 6-9 as depicting a global Flood does full justice to all the biblical data. Many lines of biblical evidence converge in affirming the global extent of the Flood: (1) all the major themes in Genesis 1-11 (Creation, Fall, plan of redemption, spread of sin) are universal in scope and call for a matching universal judgment in the Flood; (2) the genealogical lines from both Adam (Gen 4:17-26; 5:1-31) and Noah (Gen 10:1-32; 11:1-9) are exclusive in nature, indicating that as Adam was the father of all pre-Flood humanity, so Noah was father of all post-Flood humanity, thus clearly implying that all humanity on the globe outside of the ark perished in the Flood; (3) the same inclusive divine blessing "Be fruitful and multiply" is given to both Adam and Noah (Gen 1:28; 9:1), indicating that Noah is a "new Adam," re-populating the world as did the first Adam; (4) God's covenant and rainbow sign (Gen 9:9-18) are linked with the extent of the Flood; if there had been only a local flood, then the covenant would be only a limited covenant; (5) the viability of God's promise (Gen 9:15; cf. Isa 54:9) is at stake in the worldwide extent of the Flood; if only a local flood occurred, then God has broken His promise every time another local flood has happened; (6) the universality of the Flood is underscored by the enormous size of the ark (Gen 6:14, 15) and the stated necessity for saving all the species of animals and plants in the ark (Gen 6:16-21; 7:2, 3); a massive ark filled with representatives of humanity and all non-aquatic animal/plant species would be unnecessary if this were only a local flood; Noah and his family and the animals could have simply escaped to another region of the earth; (7) the covering of "all the high mountains" of the pre-Flood Earth (which were not as high as today's post-Flood uplifted mountain ranges) by at least

> If the Flood had been only a local flood, Noah and his family could have simply escaped to another region of the earth.

15 cubits (Gen 7:19, 20) could not involve simply a local flood, since water seeks its own level across the surface of the globe; (8) the long duration of the Flood (Noah in the ark over a year, Gen 7:11-8:14) makes sense only with a global Flood; (9) the New Testament passages concerning the Flood all employ universal language (e.g., "swept them *all* away" [Matt 24:39]; "destroyed them *all*," [Luke 17:27]; "he did not spare the ancient *world*. . . when he brought a flood upon the *world* of the ungodly" [2 Pet 2:5]; Noah "condemned the *world*" [Heb 11:7]); and (10) the New Testament Flood typology assumes and *depends upon* the global extent of the Flood to theologically argue for an imminent global judgment by fire [2 Pet 3:6-7].

Flood terminology – Among the most important biblical evidences for a global Flood are numerous universal terms or expressions in Genesis 6-9, indicating the global scope of the Flood[2]: (1) the Hebrew word *mabbul* ("Flood/Deluge"), occurring twelve times in Genesis (Gen 6:17; 7:6, 7, 10, 17; 9:11 [2 times], 15, 28; 10:1, 32; 11:10) and once in Psalm 29:10, is in the Old Testament reserved exclusively for reference to the Genesis Flood, thus setting the Genesis Flood apart from all local floods and giving it a global context; (2) "the Earth" (Gen 6:12, 13, 17), without any limiting descriptor, harks back to the same expression in the global Creation (Gen 1:1, 2, 10); (3) "the face of all the Earth" (Gen 7:3; 8:9) echoes the same phrase in the global context of Creation (Gen 1:29); (4) "face of the ground" (7:4, 22, 23; 8:8), in parallel with "face of all the Earth" (8:9), links with its usage in the context of global Creation (Gen 2:6); (5) "all flesh" (13 times in Gen 6-9) is accompanied by additional phrases that recall the global Creation of animals and man (Gen 1:24, 30; 2:7): e.g., "in which is the breath of life" (Gen 6:17 and 7:15), "all in whose nostrils was the breath of the spirit of life" (Gen 7:21, 22); (6) "every living thing" of all flesh (Gen 6:19; 9:16) and the similar expression "all living things that I have made" (Gen 7:4), the latter specifically referring back to Creation; (7) "all existence [*kol hayqum*]" (Gen 7:4, 23) is one of the most inclusive terms available to the Hebrew writer to express totality of life; (8) "all on the dry land" (Gen 7:22) indicates the global extent of the Flood, but clarifies that this world-wide destruction is limited to terrestrial creatures; (9) "under the whole heaven" (Gen 7:19) a phrase that is always universal elsewhere in Scripture (see e.g., Exod. 17:14; Deut 4:19), in contrast with the word "heaven" alone which can have a local meaning (e.g., 1 Kings 18:45); and (10) "all the fountains of the Great Deep [*tᵉhom*]" (Gen 7:11; 8:2), harks back to the same expression "Deep" or world-ocean (*tᵉhom*) in Gen 1:2.

The many links with the global creation in Genesis 1, 2 show that the Flood is an eschatological, step-by-step, global "uncreation," followed by a step-by-step global "re-creation." It is difficult to imagine how the biblical writer could have used any more forceful expressions than these to indicate the global extent of the Genesis Flood.

Richard M. Davidson

References

[1]See especially the summaries of this evidence by Harold G. Coffin, Robert H. Brown, and L. James Gibson, *Origin by Design*, revised edition (Hagerstown, MD: Review and Herald, 2005); Henry Morris and John Whitcomb, *The Genesis Flood: The Biblical Record and Its Scientific Implications* (Philadelphia, PA: Presbyterian and Reformed Publishing Company, 1961); and Ariel Roth, *Origins: Linking Science and Scripture* (Hagerstown, MD: Review and Herald, 1998).

[2]See Richard M. Davidson, "The Genesis Flood Narrative: Crucial Issues in the Current Debate," *Andrews University Seminary Studies* 42.1 (2004): 49-77.

DID THE LORD REALLY HARDEN PHARAOH'S HEART?

The LORD said to Moses, "When you go back to Egypt, see that you perform before Pharaoh all the wonders which I have put in your power; but I will harden his heart, so that he will not let the people go." Exodus 4:21.

What has troubled some readers of Scripture is the fact that, after God said He would harden Pharaoh's heart so that he would not let the people of Israel go, God brings the ten plagues upon Egypt because Pharaoh did what God said He would make him do. Was Pharaoh predestined by God to play this role, or is he responsible for his behavior and thus guilty of rebellion against God?

The theme of Pharaoh's hardening occurs several times between Exodus 3 and 14. It is described in the following ways:

a. God predicts that He will harden Pharaoh's heart: Exodus 4:21; 7:3
b. Pharaoh's heart was hardened without identifying the agent: Exodus 7:13, 14, 22; 8:19; 9:7, 35
c. Pharaoh hardened his own heart: Exodus 8:15, 32; 9:34
d. God hardened Pharaoh's heart: Exodus 9:12; 10:1, 20, 27; 11:10; 14:4, 8, 17

As early as Exodus 3:19, God predicted "that the king of Egypt will not permit you to go, except under compulsion." When Moses returned to Egypt to do what God had asked him to do, God told him that He "will harden his [Pharaoh's] heart so that he will not let the people go" (4:21). This prediction is reiterated in 7:3.

Pharaoh and the ten plagues – In the first incident, even before God issued the first plague on Pharaoh and Egypt, the biblical text indicates Pharaoh's resistance toward God when he called for his magicians to do their "secret arts" (Exod 7:12). When God showed His sovereignty and power through Moses and Aaron, "Pharaoh's heart became hard (*chazaq*) and he did not listen to them, just as the LORD had predicted" (7:13, NEB). The Hebrew word *chazaq* indicates an attitude that is unyielding and firm.

Because he relied upon the magicians of Egypt, "Pharaoh's heart was hardened" (7:22).

During the second plague, Pharaoh for the first time asked Moses and Aaron to entreat God to help him and his people (Exod 8:8); but after the help occurred (8:10), "he hardened his heart and did not listen to them" (8:15). It was Pharaoh himself who hardened his heart. During the third plague, the magicians (8:18) freely admitted in front of Pharaoh that "this is the finger of God" (8:19); yet "Pharaoh's heart was hardened and he did not listen to them." Similarly during the next two plagues, Pharaoh continued hardening his heart (8:32), and it remained hardened (9:7).

It is only after the seventh hardening, during the sixth plague of boils, that we read "the Lord hardened Pharaoh's heart" (Exod 9:12). While several servants of Pharaoh believed God had saved their lives (9:20), Pharaoh did "not yet fear the Lord God" (9:30). After the devastating hail storm, "he sinned again and hardened his heart" (9:34).

> In the Bible, God is often described as doing that which He does not prevent.

The text makes clear that the hardening of his heart was his sin and that he disobeyed God. God is not responsible for the hardening. Thus, "Pharaoh's heart was hardened, and he did not let the sons of Israel go" (9:35). The use of two descriptions of the hardening of Pharaoh's heart in close succession underscores the growing extent of the problem. It is then, that we read in Exodus 10:1 that God said, "I have hardened his heart," because in the Bible God is often described as doing that which He does not prevent. However, the fact that God permits something does not mean that He necessarily causes it.

Before the eighth plague begins, the individual responsibility of Pharaoh is pointed out again in the question that Moses and Aaron pose: "Thus says the Lord, the God of the Hebrews, 'How long will *you refuse to humble yourself* before Me? For if *you refuse* to let My people go, behold, tomorrow I will bring locusts into your territory" (Exod 10:3, 4, emphasis added). Pharaoh, despite admitting that he has sinned, still refused to let the Israelites go. God's forgiveness (10:16, 17) did not lead him to repentance. Instead Pharaoh remained stubborn and so we read again that "the Lord hardened Pharaoh's heart" (10:20), i.e., God allowed Pharaoh to oppose Him. What condescension of the Almighty! The story illustrates the intricate connection between man's free will and God's sovereignty.

Before the tenth plague started, God told Moses that "Pharaoh will not listen to you" (Exod 11:9). This prediction indicates that Pharaoh willfully decided as he did. In the next verse, however, we read that "the Lord hardened Pharaoh's heart, and he did not let the sons of Israel go out of his land" (11:10). At the end of the Exodus story, we read: "With a powerful hand the Lord brought us out of Egypt, from the house of slavery. It came about, when Pharaoh was stubborn about letting us go, that the Lord killed every firstborn in the land of Egypt" (13:14, 15). This passage indicates that the hardening of Pharaoh's heart did not occur contrary to his own free choice.

> "God had declared concerning Pharaoh, 'I will harden his heart, that he shall not let the people go.' Exodus 4:21. There was no exercise of supernatural power to harden the heart of the king. God gave to Pharaoh the most striking evidence of divine power, but the monarch stubbornly refused to heed the light. Every display of infinite power rejected by him, rendered him the more determined in his rebellion" (PP 268).

Conclusion – God's predictions are not necessarily His decrees. God was responsible for the process of sending the plagues, and Pharaoh was responsible for his unrepentance. Just as the sunlight melts wax and hardens clay, the same revelation of God's power led the servants of Pharaoh to obedience (Exod 9:20) but hardened Pharaoh's heart.

Frank M. Hasel

If we would study the Bible diligently and prayerfully every day, we should every day see some beautiful truth in a new, clear, and forcible light.

CG 511

WHY DID GOD SAY THE PATRIARCHS DID NOT KNOW HIM UNDER THE NAME OF YAHWEH?

I appeared to Abraham, Isaac, and Jacob, as God Almighty, but by My name, LORD [Yahweh], I did not make Myself known to them. Exodus 6:3.

A cursory reading of Exodus 6:3 might suggest that the name "Yahweh" (LORD) was unfamiliar to the patriarchs. Did Abraham, Isaac, and Jacob not know Yahweh?

The name Yahweh in the Pentateuch – The book of Genesis, with its 143 occurrences of the name "Yahweh," implies that the Patriarchs did know the name Yahweh. The name is used by human beings as early as in Genesis 4:1, 26. It frequently occurs in the patriarchal narratives. God identified Himself by the phrase "I am Yahweh" to Abraham (15:7) and to Jacob (28:13), each time promising the land to them and their descendants.

In the book of Exodus, the name "Yahweh" occurs again in 3:15 when God instructed Moses to say "Yahweh, the God of your fathers, the God of Abraham, the God of Isaac, and the God of Jacob, has sent me to you." Clearly, Yahweh is identified as the God of the fathers. So, how is Exodus 6:3 to be understood?

God's character revealed – A close reading of the verse in its immediate context leads to a better understanding of Exodus 6:3. First, we need to remember that biblical names do have meaning. God's many names—from 'Adonai to Yahweh—portray His multifaceted and great character. Two of His names appear in Exodus 6:3; and the associations with these names explain the apparent mystery of this verse. Exodus 6:3 is not about a revelation of a new name, it is about what God does and which name fits His doings.

The first half of the verse states that God appeared to the patriarchs as "'El Shaddai" or "God Almighty." This name was clearly known to the patriarchs, for God revealed Himself to them as 'El Shaddai (Gen 17:1; 35:11; cf. 28:3; 43:14; 48:3). This name refers to God's power. The book of Exodus obviously connects this characteristic of God with the patriarchal period. The same mighty God of the patriarchs is the God of the people of Israel.

148

The second half of Exodus 6:3 states that God did not make Himself known as Yahweh to the patriarchs. "Yahweh" is more than a simple name; it is a program, the promised assurance that the One, who is with, and for, His people, has turned to them and engages in their salvation (6:5-8). Certainly Yahweh was God to the patriarchs and established His covenant with them, but the experience of the compassionate and redeeming God, the deliverance of an entire nation and the fulfillment of the promise of the land, was left to the people of Israel as they came out of Egypt. The patriarch's experience of the covenant was not complete insofar as they were not able to take possession of the land.

Knowing Yahweh – Furthermore, Exodus 6:3 does not say that the name "Yahweh" was foreign to the patriarchs, rather that it was not "known," i.e., known through experience. The Hebrew verb for "to know" has connotations beyond intellectual knowledge. It also describes existential knowledge, often the intimate relationship between covenant and marital partners (e.g., in Gen 4:1, KJV).

Knowing the name Yahweh means to experience Him as Yahweh. This is explicit in such passages as Jeremiah 16:21, "This time I will make

> By the Exodus experience the Israelites will came to know God in a way that the patriarchs did not.

them know my power and my might; and they shall know that my name is Yahweh" (cf. Isa 52:6; Exod 7:5; and the negative in Exod 5:2). Often the context of those passages in which Yahweh is known or makes Himself known is judgment (Exod 6:3; Isa 19:21; Ezek 20:5, 9; 35:11; 38:23; Pss 9:16; 48:3; 76:1-3). Since judgment and salvation belong together (see Isa 19:21, 22), the "knowing of Yahweh" involves knowing Him as judge who brings salvation or judgment.

Exodus 6:3 declares that the significance of God's name is now to be fully understood. "Yahweh" signifies the covenant keeping God who will save His people. By the Exodus experience the Israelites will come to know God in a way that the patriarchs did not.

Conclusion – Exodus 6:2-8 stands in continuity with the patriarchal history. Constant references to the patriarchs in the first chapters of Exodus establish a close connection to the past. It would be strange to present now a contrast between the names by which God was known.

The same "God Almighty" ('El Shaddai) is going to reveal Himself now as the one He has pledged to be, the God who is with His people, who honors the terms of the covenant, and gives them the Promised Land. The following paraphrase captures the thought of Exodus 6:3: "I appeared to Abraham, Isaac, and Jacob in my capacity as 'El Shaddai (who makes covenantal promises). But I was not the object of (full) covenantal knowledge to them as conveyed by my capacity as Yahweh (who fulfills covenantal promises)."

Martin Pröbstle

Names of God

In Hebrew:

God	– El (Exod 15:2; Num 12:13)
	– Elohim (Gen 1:1, 3; 9:6)
	– Eloha (Deut 32:17. Job 3:4)
Jehovah (KJV)	– Yahweh (Exod 6:3; Isa 12:2)
LORD	– Yah (Exod 15:2; Ps 77:12)
Lord	– Adonai (Ps 57:9; Dan 9:7)
Most High	– Elyon (Gen 14:18; Ps 91:1)
Holy One	– Qadosh (Ps 71:22; 89:18)
LORD God	– Yahweh Elohim (Gen 2:4, 5)
Almighty	– Shadday (Job 13:3; Ps 68:15)
God Almighty	– El Shadday (Gen 17:1; Exod 6:3)
God of gods	– Elohey HaElohim (Deut 10:17)
Lord of lords	– Adoney Ha'Adonim (Deut 10:17; Ps 136:3)
Father	– Ab (Ps 89:26; Jer 3:4)
Judge	– Shaphat (Gen 18:25; Judg 11:27)
Redeemer	– Goel (Job 19:25; Ps 19:14)

Savior	– Moshia (Isa 43:3; 49:26
Deliverer	– Mᵉphalt (2 Sam 22:2; Ps 40:17)
Shield	– Magen (Gen 15:1; Ps 3:4
Strength	– Eyaluth (Ps 22:19)
God of Seeing	– El roi (Gen 16:13)
LORD of Hosts	–Yahweh Tsebaoth (1 Sam 4:4; Jer 11:20)
Rock	– Tsur (Ps 19:14; Isa 26:4)

In Greek:

God	– Theos (Matt 3:9; Mark1 :1)
Lord	– Kyrios (Matt 2:19; Luke 1:38)
Godhead	– Theotes (Col 2:9)
	– Theios (Acts 17:29)
	– Theiotes (Rom 1:20)
Most High	– Hypsistos (Mark 5:7; Luke 8:28)
Savior	– Soter (Luke 1:47, John 4:42
Father	– Pater (Matt 6:6; John 5:17)

HOW DID TWO MILLION OR MORE ISRAELITES CROSS THE RED SEA IN ONE NIGHT?

Then Moses stretched out his hand over the sea; and the LORD swept the sea back by a strong east wind all night, and turned the sea into dry land, so the waters were divided. And the sons of Israel went through the midst of the sea on the dry land, and the waters were like a wall to them on their right hand and on their left. Exodus 14:21, 22.

The issues surrounding this passage are these: (1) How could the large number of Israelites with their flocks have been organized enough to cross the sea quickly? (2) Would not the time required for this crossing have been much longer than the few hours of one night which the text describes? and (3) Could not the Egyptian chariots have caught up with slow moving Israelites on foot?

The number of Israelites – Numbers 1:46; 26:51 and Exodus 12:37 consistently portray the Israelites as numbering about 600,000 men. With women and children that number could be estimated at around 2,000,000 people. It is true that the Hebrew term 'eleph ("thousand" in Num 1:21, 23, 25, 27, etc.) may mean clan or family in some contexts (Judg 6:15; 1 Sam 10:19, NKJV); however, this meaning does not appear to be the intention in Numbers 1 and 26. For one thing, 'eleph, "thousand" is not the only designation used, the additional figures of "hundreds" and "fifties" are employed in conjunction with 'eleph (e.g., the tribe of Gad numbered 45,650, Num 1:25). Second, in each case, the numbers from all the tribes are totaled and the numbers consistently add up to over 600,000. Finally, the offering of a half shekel is requested from all males and the total adds up to exactly half of the number found in Numbers 1.[1]

Important Considerations

There are other assumptions that need further attention. For one thing, many might imagine that the Israelites were an unorganized group of men, women, and children who were moving out of Egypt in a rather haphazard manner with their flocks and herds. When the threat of the Egyptian army becomes evident, the disorganization becomes even more intense. Finally, some assume that the passage through the sea was very narrow and would have required a nearly single-file advance that would have indeed taken several days. These assumptions, however, are not supported by the biblical account.

The crossing was a miracle – First, we must remember that throughout the Old Testament this crossing is recognized as a miraculous event made possible by the intervention of God. As the Egyptian army approached, the Israelites "became very frightened" and "cried out to the Lord" (Exod 4:13). The Lord reassured Moses, and the pillar of fire, or "Angel of the Lord," moved behind them, separating Israel from the Egyptians all night as the sea was parted and was prepared for their crossing. Even though the Egyptians were equipped for swift action, the cloud prevented such action against Israel. This intervention allowed the Israelites the necessary time to begin the crossing. As the last of the Israelites crossed, the cloud remained behind Israel and followed them into the sea so that the Egyptians also entered. It was in the morning that "the LORD looked down on the army of the Egyptians through the pillar of fire and cloud and brought the army of the Egyptians into confusion" (Exod 14:24).

> # The crossing of the Red Sea was a miracle.

The site of the crossing – The location of the crossing is probably not through the Gulf of Aqaba to Saudi Arabia. Recent studies have shown the crossing to be into the Sinai region. [2] Ellen G. White wrote, "The Hebrews were encamped beside the sea, whose waters presented a seemingly impassible barrier before them, while on the south a rugged mountain obstructed further progress" (PP 283, 284). Some have interpreted the Hebrew *yam suph* as Sea of Reeds instead of Red Sea. Based on the lexicographical evidence and recent geographical research, archaeologists have located the crossing through a chain of lakes, known as the Bitter Lakes, in the Isthmus of Suez. The water levels in these lakes and the Red Sea would have been much higher in ancient times than they are today. However, there are no mountains anywhere in this area. The only possible location that fits both the biblical description and the Ellen G. White statement, must place the crossing at the northern tip of the Gulf of Suez where the mountain Jebel 'Ataqa reaches down to the gulf.

The manner of the crossing – Exodus 13:18 states that God led the Israelites "around by the way of the wilderness to the Red Sea; and the sons of Israel went up in martial array from the land of Egypt." The key phrase "in martial array" indicates that this exodus was an organized march in military formation. The Hebrew verb for "in martial array" derives from the number five and could be translated "and the sons of Israel went up *in fives*"; that is, the people were divided into five major divisions. The Bible does not indicate the size of these divisions or the way in which they were organized, but it is important to remember that Moses, who was a prince of Egypt and destined to be its next king, was militarily trained and would have known how to organize a large group in military formation. It is interesting that the very same term is used in Joshua 1:14 and 4:12 to describe the organization just before Israel crosses the Jordan River into the Promised Land. This organization meant that Israel did not walk from Egypt or through the sea in single file or in a haphazard manner.

The Bible also does not indicate how wide the area of dry land was. Two million Israelites, divided into five divisions, the Israelites may have stood 600 abreast which would have been less than half a mile wide. Thus each of the five divisions of about four hundred thousand people (c. 600 abreast and 670 deep) could have occupied less than four miles in length, having added another mile for flocks and herds. If the opening in the sea was a mile wide, it would have allowed an even wider advance. Even so, given that the rate of walking would not have exceeded more than thirty minutes for one mile and given that the width of the sea at that location was about ten miles, the crossing could have been accomplished within 5-6 hours or in one night.

Michael G. Hasel

References

[1]For a more detailed discussion, see John J. Davis, *Biblical Numerology* (Grand Rapids, MI: Baker, 1968), 58-91. The view of a large numbers of Israelites in the Exodus is also supported by Ellen G. White (PP 281).

[2]James K. Hoffmeier, *Israel in Egypt: The Evidence for the Authenticity of the Exodus Tradition* (New York, NY: Oxford University Press, 1997), 208, 209.

DOES THE LORD REALLY CHANGE HIS MIND?

So the LORD changed His mind about the harm which He said He would do to His people. Exodus 32:14.

The idea of God repenting does not seem to be compatible with the idea of an unchanging, everlasting God (Mal 3:6) whose designs are laid out from before the foundation of the world (Isa 51:16). Exodus 32:14 is one of a number of texts that apparently points to God changing his mind and going back on a decision. For example, God repented of having created man (Gen 6:6); of having made Saul king (1 Sam 15:11); and of thinking to destroy Jerusalem after David's census (2 Sam 24:16).

The golden-calf episode – Exodus 32:14 serves as the climax in a dialogue between God and Moses on Mount Sinai. After Moses had been on the mountain longer than expected, the people of Israel distanced themselves from their leader (32:1) and in a spiritual sense returned to Egypt by worshipping the golden calf (32:4-6). Thus, they deliberately broke the covenant and forgot the solemn promises they had made to God a short while before (19:8; 24:3). God revealed to Moses on top of the mountain the ensuing scenes of image worship at the foot of the mountain (34:7-9) and announced His decision to destroy Israel. At the same time, God intended to remain faithful to Moses and make him "a great nation" (34:10).

Moses the intercessor – This invitation to Moses to make him a great nation echoes the covenant promises to Abraham and the patriarchs and is identical to it in its wording (Gen 12:2; 17:20; 18:18; 21:18; 46:3). It turned the conclusion of the discourse between God and Moses into a test of faith for the latter, inviting him to start all over again with a new and not so stubborn people; but at the same time it probed Moses' identification with the people of Israel who were apostatizing at the foot of the mountain. In response, Moses offered a number of reasons for Israel's continued existence (Exod 32:11-13), going so far as offering himself in lieu of the people (32:32), an assertion that marks him as one of the greatest Messianic types in the Old Testament. It is the fact that God has found a true intercessor who is ready to die for His people, and not Moses' argumentative ability, that convinces the Lord to go back on His decision in verse 14.

The meaning of "repent" – Most modern translations draw on a linguistic analysis of the crucial verb in the sentence and render it with phrases such as "changed his mind" (*NRSV*), "relented" (*NIV*), or "renounced" (*JPS*). The Hebrew word *nacham,* according to the grammatical form used in this verse, can have the meaning "to be sorry, have compassion, suffer grief, relent, etc." It can refer to the processing of feelings related to a personal loss, often through receiving comfort given by God (Isa 40:1; 49:13) or by humans (Gen 24:67; 37:35). In a few texts it refers to human repentance (Job 42:6; Jer 31:19).

Reasons for God's "repentance" – In about a third of the 31 occurrences in the Old Testament in which the Hebrew word *nacham* is used in reference to God,[1] He changed His mind in response to human activity. In Genesis 6:6 it is the wickedness of humankind that necessitates God's changing His plan and bringing about the Flood (Gen 6:5). In 1 Samuel 15:11 it is the fact that Saul has turned his back on God that requires a change in God's actions and results in Samuel's search for a new king. Yet, in the same chapter, God's immutability is particularly emphasized (v. 29). God also can relent from executing judgment, based on human repentance, as can be seen in Jonah's experience in Nineveh (Jonah 3:9, 10; 4:2). Another factor that results in God's changing His mind is human intercession, as the detention of the destroying angel above Jerusalem shows (2 Sam 24:17); this is also the case in Exodus 32:14 in which Moses intercedes for Israel.

> God never repents in the human sense of the term, i.e., because He has committed a mistake or a moral transgression.

The conditionality of God's judgments – The concept that God's decisions are at times dependent on human repentance is perhaps most thoroughly developed in Jeremiah 18:5-10 in which God changes His mind toward nations, depending on the human response. It is important to note that the theological keyword that normally characterizes human repentance (*shub,* "repent, return, turn back, go back"; e.g., Ezek 14:6) is never applied to God in these contexts. Thus, God never repents in the human sense of the term, i.e., because He has committed a mistake or a moral transgression although God can turn (*shub*) toward the repentant (Zech 1:3) and His anger can turn away (*shub*) from a person (Hos 14:4).

The difference between human and divine repentance – The Bible sometimes speaks anthropomorphically, i.e., it refers to God in human terms, but in using these terms one should keep in mind that the connotations may not necessarily be identical. While human repentance is always preceded by sin, God's changing His mind can be preceded by human sin, human repentance, or human intercession. The consequence of human repentance is a change of character and means moving into a new direction towards God; whereas God's changing His mind leads to a renewed integration of the human element into His overall plan of salvation. "God's repentance is not like man's repentance. 'The Strength of Israel will not lie nor repent: for He is not a man, that He should repent.' Man's repentance implies a change of mind. God's repentance implies a change of circumstances and relations" (PP 630).

> "Man's repentance implies a change of mind. God's repentance implies a change of circumstances and relations" (PP 630).

Martin G. Klingbeil

References

[1]Gen 6:6, 7; Exod 32:12, 14; Num 23:19; Judg 2:18; 1 Sam 15:11, 29 (2x); 2 Sam 24:16; 1 Chron 21:15; Pss 106:45; 110:4; Jer 4:28; 15:6; 18:8, 10; 20:16; 26:3, 13, 19; 42:10; Ezek 24:14; Joel 2:13, 14; Amos 7:3, 6; Jonah 3:9, 10; 4:2; Zech 8:14.

God desires man to exercise his reasoning powers; and the study of the Bible will strengthen and elevate the mind as no other study can.

CSA 47

ARE THE LAWS REGARDING CLEAN AND UNCLEAN ANIMALS STILL RELEVANT?

The LORD spoke again to Moses and to Aaron, saying to them, "Speak to the sons of Israel, saying, 'These are the creatures which you may eat from all the animals that are on the earth.'" Leviticus 11:1, 2.

Two main objections are given against the observance of the Mosaic dietary laws regarding clean and unclean food: (1) choosing only the uncleanness of animals and neglecting other uncleanness laws, e.g., the uncleanness of women (Lev 12) is arbitrary; and (2) it is claimed that the New Testament explicitly abolishes the laws of clean and unclean dietary regulations. Thus, many Christians believe that they are under no obligation to observe these food regulations.

The uncleanness of animals – In response to these objections a number of reasons exist to demonstrate the continuing validity of the dietary instructions:[1]

1. The principal rationale behind the distinction between clean and unclean food is that God is holy and He calls His people to holiness (Lev 11:45; 1 Pet 1:15, 16).

2. A comparative study of different kinds of uncleanness in the Pentateuch indicates that the impurity of animals is of a unique category. The two basic categories of uncleanness can be differentiated in the following ways:

   a. The type of uncleanness of unclean animals is permanent, natural, hereditary, non-cultic, and thus universal (Gen 7:2, 3; Lev 11:1-47; 20:25, 26; Deut 14:3-21), while the other kind of uncleanness is acquired, temporary, and ceremonial (Lev 5:1-13; 11:24-40; 12:1-8; 13:1-46; 15:1-33; 16:26-28; etc.).

   b. The impurity of unclean animals is not contagious. Animals cannot cause or transmit uncleanness. No living unclean animal belongs to the six sources of contagious uncleanness: carcasses, corpses, various skin diseases, mildew, and sexual discharges (blood or semen).

   c. Touching or carrying an unclean animal does not result in exclusion from social or religious activities, such as visiting the temple or worshiping in the sanctuary.

d. There is no provision for making unclean animals clean. There is no remedy for the removal of this type of uncleanness; it is impossible to cleanse it or cure it.

e. There is no penalty for disobedience against these food prescriptions. However, the absence of a penalty does not mean that they are to be taken lightly. These prescriptions belong to the category of sins that could not be atoned for by rituals in the sanctuary.

f. These dietary laws are not related to the Old Testament earthly sanctuary services or to the visible presence of the Lord (the *Shekinah*) among God's people.

g. The origin of these dietary laws is pre-Mosaic (Gen 7:2, 3) and thus much older than the laws concerning other kinds of uncleanness.

h. The dietary regulations in the Pentateuch are also applicable to the stranger and sojourner (Heb. *ger*). From the whole corpus of uncleanness in Leviticus 11–15, only the dietary laws are applicable to the sojourner via the law of hunting, which was binding on the Israelites as well as on strangers (Lev 17:13; see also Gen 9:4; Lev 7:17, 18).

3. The strong call to holiness in Leviticus is in harmony with Peter's powerful admonition to holiness for Christians. Peter's reason for being holy (1 Pet 1:15, 16) is derived from the passage dealing with the Mosaic dietary laws (Lev 11:44, 45).

> The dietary laws are much older than the laws concerning other kinds of uncleanness (Gen 7:2, 3).

4. The close connection between dietary prohibitions, warnings against idolatry, and the prohibition against all immoral behavior (all three are called an abomination [Heb. *to'ebah*] Lev 18:22; Deut 7:25; Ezra 9:1) is an indication that these are moral issues that continue in the New Testament era (see Acts 15:20; Ezek 33:25, 26).

5. The Mosaic laws form a mosaic, i.e., a complete, coherent picture. We cannot throw away certain laws simply because they are present in the Pentateuch, e.g., laws against idolatry, prostitution, homosexuality, or incest. The two greatest commandments are also taken from the same source (Deut 6:5; Lev 19:18)!

6. The health aspect must be taken seriously, even though the issue is not only health but also holiness.

7. Unclean food legislation is not abrogated in the New Testament.

There is nothing typological or symbolic in the nature of the clean and unclean food regulations that would point to Jesus as their ultimate fulfillment. On the other hand, ordinances related to the ceremonial system lost their validity with the arrival of the reality that they foreshadowed (Dan 9:27; Eph 2:15).

The New Testament and unclean meat – In order to correctly interpret New Testament passages dealing with food instructions, one must differentiate between two Greek words: *akathartos*, "unclean," reflects the Old Testament teaching, and *koinos*, "common, polluted," points to the specific rabbinical concept adopted sometime during the intertestamental period and known as defilement by association. It was believed that if something clean touched something even potentially unclean it would become *koinos*, i.e., defiled.

Seen from this perspective, Mark 7:18, 19[2] does not speak about eating unclean food but about eating with defiled hands. Christ contrasts the tradition of the elders with the biblical law and underlines the difference between spiritual and physical defilement. Danger to the purity of the mind/heart is more important than what goes into the stomach.

> Mark 7 does not speak about eating unclean food but about eating with defiled hands.

Peter in Acts 10:14 felt he could not eat of the animals, because even the clean animals became polluted by association with the unclean animals (not a biblical but a rabbinic teaching). God asked Peter to stop calling clean animals *koinos*, i.e., defiled by association with the unclean animals. This meant that he (a Jew) had to stop considering himself unclean by associating with Gentiles (see Acts 10:28; 11:12).

Confirmation of the validity of the Mosaic dietary laws may be seen in Acts 15, through the prohibition of eating blood. It is highly significant that the four issues decided at the Jerusalem Council (Acts 15:20, 29) are found in the same sequence in Leviticus 17-18, and all of them are applied to the alien sojourner (see Lev 17:8, 10, 12, 13, 15; 18:26): (1) food offered to idols (Lev 17:3-9); (2) prohibition of blood (Lev 17:10–14); (3) abstaining from the meat of strangled animals (Lev 17:15, 16); and (4) abstaining from sexual immorality (Lev 18:1–30). In light of Leviticus 17:10–14, these apostolic decrees implicitly include the clean and unclean food legislation (see especially Lev 17:13).

In Romans 14 and 1 Corinthians 8:10, Paul explains that meat offered to idols is not polluted because of its contact with idols. Association of the food with idols changes nothing, because the idol is nothing. For this reason, he declares that no food is defiled (*koinos*) in itself (Rom 14:14). Note that Paul does not use the word unclean (*akathartos*).

Conclusion – It is not arbitrary to take seriously the uncleanness of food, because it is in a different category. No text in the New Testament, when taken in its context, supports the idea that the clean-unclean food regulations have been abolished. Such a position is not tenable or verifiable.

Christians do not earn salvation or gain God's favor because they observe dietary principles. Doing so is simply an expression of faithfulness to God. By not consuming things our Lord prohibited, humans exercise deep respect for their holy Creator. In this way our tables become silent witnesses for allegiance to our Creator God. Taking seriously His revelation is a celebration of God's gift of creation.

Jiří Moskala

> "It is historically unimaginable to an increasing number of New Testament scholars that Jesus taught against the Torah's dietary laws." (David J. Rudolph, "Jesus and the Food Laws: A Reassessment of Mark 7:19b," *The Evangelical Quarterly* 74. 4 [2002]: 293).

> "The break which Jesus brings is not demonstrated in relationship to the fundamental Old Testament doctrine, but in contrast to the formalism of the scribes and Pharisees of his time." (René Péter-Contesse, *Levitique 1–16, Commentaire de l'Ancien Testament*, 3a [Geneva: Editions Labor& Fides, 1993], 178.

References

[1]For a detailed study, see Jiří Moskala, *The Laws of Clean and Unclean Animals in Leviticus 11: Their Nature, Theology, and Rationale. An Intertextual Study*, Adventist Theological Society Dissertation Series, vol. 4 (Berrien Springs, MI: Adventist Theological Society, 2000); see also Gerhard F. Hasel, "Clean and Unclean Meats in Leviticus 11: Still Relevant?" *Journal of the Adventist Theological Society*

2.2 (1991): 91-125.
  [2]See the article on Mark 7:19 in this volume.

The Old Testament Sanctuary

In the work of christ for our redemption, symbolized by the sanctuary service, "mercy and truth are met together, righteousness and peace have kissed each other." (Ps 85:10).

FLB 194

WHAT WAS THE ROLE OF THE SCAPEGOAT?

And Aaron shall cast lots upon the two goats, one lot for the LORD and the other lot for Azazel [scapegoat, NASB, KJV, NIV]. And Aaron shall present the goat on which the lot fell the LORD, and offer it as a sin offering; but the goat on which the lot fell for Azazel shall be presented alive before the LORD to make atonement over it, that it may be sent away into the wilderness to Azazel. Leviticus 16:8-10; RSV.

Seventh-day Adventists have been accused of making Satan their vicarious sin- bearer and savior because they believe that the scapegoat in Leviticus 16 represents Satan. By contrast, many Christians hold that the scapegoat represents Christ as truly as does the slain goat.

The Leviticus 16 ritual – In Leviticus 16, the Israelite community is to provide two male goats, each of which is to function in a ritual of purification on the Day of Atonement (v. 5). To determine which goat is used for each ritual, the high priest uses lots, implying that the Lord makes the selection. Then the lots are placed on the two goats as labels for distinguishing between them (v. 8). The goat receiving the lot "belonging to the Lord" is the Lord's goat, which is to be sacrificed as a purification offering (the so-called "sin offering," v. 9) for purging physical ritual impurities and sins from the sanctuary (cf. vv. 15-19, 25). The other goat, which receives the lot "belonging to Azazel" (ʿAzaʾzel), is to be presented before the Lord. But instead of being sacrificed *to* the Lord, this live goat is to be sent *away* from the Lord to Azazel in the wilderness (v. 10). "Atonement" is made *on* the live goat (v. 10) in the sense that it bears the moral faults of the Israelites away from their camp after the high priest has transferred these evils to the goat through confession while pressing both his hands on its head (vv. 20-22).

Different views concerning Azazel – The main question is: Who is Azazel, and what does his goat represent? Numerous attempts to explain the meaning of the name "Azazel" on the basis of etymology have failed. The common translation of Azazel as "scapegoat"—the goat that goes away or escapes *(ʿez-ʾazel)*—is certainly incorrect and should be abandoned be-

162

cause it makes no sense in Leviticus 16:10. There the goat belonging to Azazel is sent to Azazel, but if you read "scapegoat" for Azazel, the goat belonging to the goat is sent to the goat.

Various scholars have interpreted "Azazel" as a desolate place, as an idea of "removal," or as a deity. A prominent Jewish view is to regard Azazel as a demon (e.g., 1 Enoch 9:6; 10:4, 5, 8, *Apocalypse of Abraham*; for association of wild goats, goat-demons, and demons with uninhabited regions, compare Lev 17:7; Isa 13:21; 34:14; Luke 11:24; Rev 18:2). In harmony with the concept that Azazel is a demon, some Christians (including Seventh-day Adventists) see in the live goat a representation of Satan, the chief demon and arch-enemy of God. But other Christians object that such an approach makes Satan our sin-bearer and prefer to interpret the so-called "scapegoat" as a symbol of Christ, who bore human sins and suffered outside the city (Heb 13:12, 13—but v. 11 shows that this passage does not concern the "scapegoat").

The goat for Azazel is not sacrificed – The key to the identification of "Azazel" is found in Leviticus 16:8-10 in which one goat belongs to the Lord and the other

> "The Lord's goat belonged to the Lord and was offered to the Lord, but it also represented the one who died for human sin: Christ (Heb. 13:11-13), who is the Lord (John 8:58; 10:30). If there is this tight a connection between the Lord and his goat, we must consider the possibility that the goat belonging to Azazel and sent to him also represents him" (Roy Gane, *Leviticus*, The NIV Application Commentary [Grand Rapids, MI: Zondervan, 2004], 290).

belongs to Azazel. Azazel is clearly the proper name of a personal being, other than the Lord, who is capable of owning a goat. However, the live goat is not a sacrifice to Azazel. Rather, this "tote-goat" serves as a "garbage truck" in a non-sacrificial purification ritual of elimination (see v. 5, but not to be translated "sin offering" in this case) to send Israelite sins away to Azazel's territory in the wilderness. Dumping such a load of toxic waste in someone's "yard" is a singularly unfriendly gesture. So the Lord, who commanded this ritual, must view Azazel as the originator of the sins of Israel; these sins are, therefore, returned to their source. This would make sense if Azazel is Satan, who originated sin and tempts people (Gen 3; Rev 12:9), and then maliciously accuses them even when they are forgiven (Rev 12:10; compare Deut 19:16-21 where the accuser receives the punishment).

Christ alone is our sin-bearer – The goat that belongs to the Lord is sacrificed to Him. But on a higher level of symbolism (or "typology") that points beyond the Israelite ritual system, this goat represents the Lord, i.e., Christ, who died for human sin (John 1:29; Heb 13:11-13). So on this higher level, it would make sense that the live goat, banished to Azazel's wilderness territory, also represents Azazel, i.e., Satan as the one who bears *his part* in the sins of God's people and who ends up with responsibility as the mastermind behind their offenses. Sin comes back on the one who causes it, and he is sent to where he belongs.

> **Satan is not our sin-bearer, Christ is.**

This accomplishes a kind of atonement (Lev. 16:10) for God's people in the basic sense of reconciling them to God by purging from their midst the sinner (Satan) who has obstructed their divine-human relationship (compare Num 25:7, 8, 13). There is no substitution in this atonement in contrast to the atonement that Christ provides by taking our place: bearing all of our blame when we accept His sacrifice on our behalf. Satan will die for his own part in our sins; Christ alone is our vicarious sin-bearer.

Conclusion – On the Day of Atonement, Azazel's live goat bore sins of the Israelites away from their camp in order to purify their community by returning these evils to their demonic source. Similarly, God's people will ultimately be freed from temptation and malicious false testimony (compare Rev 20:1-3) when Satan will receive his blame and punishment for using these strategies against them.[1]

Roy E. Gane

References

[1]For further reading, see Roy Gane, *Leviticus, Numbers,* NIV Application Commentary; (Grand Rapids, MI: Zondervan, 2004), 273-277, 288-291; Roy Gane, *Altar Call* (Berrien Springs, MI: Diadem, 1999), 247-255.

DOES LEVITICUS 18:22 CONDEMN HOMOSEXUALITY?

You shall not lie with a male as one lies with a female; it is an abomination. Leviticus 18:22.

In contemporary society homosexuality is not only viewed by many as acceptable but is also strongly advocated by the media and social rights groups. Does the Bible allow or condemn homosexual practices? Does Leviticus 18:22 and other passages indicate a biblical position on this issue?

The biblical view of homosexuality – Leviticus 20:13 reiterates the prohibition against homosexuality with more detail and a penalty directly attached: "If there is a man who lies with a male as those who lie with a woman, both of them have committed a detestable act; they shall surely be put to death. Their blood-guiltiness is upon them." The word translated "male" (*zakar*) is clearly "male" rather than the more generic "man" or "mankind," as some modern versions translate, denoting all members of this gender regardless of age, and clearly implying consensual male-male intercourse, not just homosexual rape.

The absolute nature of this biblical prohibition contrasts sharply with the more tolerant attitudes toward homosexuality found elsewhere in the ancient Near East. While the legislation is considered from a man's perspective, the prohibition of lesbian relationships is implicit in the general Levitical injunction against following the abominable practices of the Egyptians or Canaanites and other nations (Lev 18:3, 24-28, 30). Likewise, the homosexual abuse of children (pedophilia) is indirectly covered, as *zakar* means "male," not just "grown man." Homosexuality is "an abomination" that carries the death penalty (Lev 18:22; 20:13) and is on a par with bestiality, which violates the principle that human sexuality is to be shared only with other human beings (Lev 18:23; 20:15, 16). The prohibition appears within the same legal framework that covers incest, adultery, and bestiality.

The wider context of Leviticus 18 points to departures from God's ideal for human sexuality. From the time of Creation, God created man and woman for each other, represented by the metaphor "one flesh," and intended that they be fruitful and multiply (Gen 1:26-28; 2:23, 24). This relationship was to be permanent, monogamous, heterosexual, and between human beings. The prohibitions in Leviticus 18 reinforce the boundaries set up in Genesis 1-3. Thus homosexuality both disrupts and violates the created order set in motion by God. To surrender one's self sexually by assuming the role of the opposite sex, as in a homosexual or lesbian relationship, is a desecration of the divine order of Creation because sexuality is an essential feature of human existence and personhood (Gen 1:27).

Homosexuality is rebellion against God – Ultimately, God Himself is in view: "I am the LORD your God" (Lev 18:1, 4, 5, 6, 30). For a man to have sexual intercourse with another man, as though the latter were not a male but a female, is nothing short of a rebellion against the way God made human beings to function as sexual beings. Not only is the divine design of heterosexuality and the created order violated, the holy nature of God as Creator and Redeemer is insulted: "For I am the LORD your God. . . . Be holy, for I am holy" (Lev 20:26; cf. 11:44; 19:2; 21:8). Thus God stands apart morally from the gods of the nations and the morally defiling practices that their worship includes. Because God is holy, the sexual distortions described in Leviticus 18 (including homosexuality) are morally defiling and God-rejecting in their very nature (Lev 18:1, 4, 5, 6, 22, 24-30). God's holy character influences one's moral values and choices even in matters of sexuality (cf. Rom 1:21-27).

> Homosexuality both disrupts and violates the created order set into motion by God.

Homosexuality is an abomination – References in the context of Leviticus 18 to "the land of Egypt," "land of Canaan" (v. 3), "all the nations" (v. 24), "the native" and "the alien who sojourns among you" (v. 26) affirm that the abominations listed together with homosexuality cut across the grain of natural and moral principles that are transcultural and transtemporal, i.e., universal and timeless (Lev 18:2, 24-30). The inherently degrading character of these acts destabilizes the community, morally defiles the individual (whether victim, perpetrator, or consenting participant), is exploitive of other persons (their bodies, self-identity, standing in the community or family, and purity before God), and maligns the holy character of God. Such is true for every culture and all times. God, self, and society are each in view. It is no wonder then that the underlying characterization of homosexual practice from the divine perspective is "abomination."

Homosexual intercourse is the only forbidden sexual act in the entire Pentateuch to which the word "abomination" *(toᶜebah)* is specifically attached. In Acts 15 the categories of prohibitions imposed upon Gentile Christians—"to abstain from food sacrificed to idols, from blood, from meat of strangled animals and from sexual immorality"—follow those listed in Leviticus 17, 18. Therefore, *porneia* the Greek word for sexual immorality in Acts 15:20, 29 includes homosexuality, as does the related verb *ekporneuo* in Jude 7. The New Testament explicitly condemns male homosexuality (Rom 1:27; 1 Cor 6:9; 1 Tim 1:10), and lesbianism (Rom 1:26).

> Divine power is ever available to enable human beings to live above their sinful tendencies and natures.

Homosexual tendencies and homosexual practices – While only a few biblical texts speak of homoerotic activity, those that do mention it express unqualified disapproval. There are no loopholes or exception clauses that might allow for the acceptance of homosexual practices under some circumstances. It is important to note, however, that Leviticus does not address homosexual tendencies; it condemns homosexual *practice* (which would include homosexual lifestyle).

The biblical view of human nature assumes that after the fall all humans have a sinful nature or orientation. Through no fault of their own, whether the result of heredity or environmental factors, people are afflicted with overpowering tendencies toward all sorts of evil: heterosexual promiscuity, alcoholism, gluttony, violence, impurity, sensuality, suicide, anger, arrogance, etc. (Gal 5:19-21). Homoerotic tendencies are to be expected. But so are proper personal moral orientation, moral choice, and moral restraint. As moral beings, human beings are called to restrain their immoral obsessions. Thoughts are to be kept pure and sexual temptations arising from one's fallen nature or orientation are to be resisted—both heterosexual and homosexual. Divine power is ever available to enable human beings to live above their sinful tendencies and natures (Gal 5:16-24). First-century Christians experienced such power over homosexual tendencies: "and that is what some of you were [including homosexuals, see v. 9]; but you were washed, but you were sanctified, but you were justified in the name of the Lord Jesus Christ and in the Spirit of our God" (1 Cor 6:11). There is hope for redemption from destructive lifestyles. Such is implied in Leviticus 18:22 and 20:13 where an already redeemed people are now being called to live their new holy identity through the sanctifying power of their holy God (Lev 20:7, 8; 21:8; 22:32, 33).

Larry L. Lichtenwalter

Qumran cave 4 where more than 15,000 fragments from over 200 books were found.

WHY IS THE REASON GIVEN FOR SABBATH KEEPING IN DEUTERONOMY 5 DIFFERENT FROM THAT GIVEN IN EXODUS 20?

Remember the Sabbath day, to keep it holy. . . . For *in* six days the LORD made the heavens and the earth, the sea, and all that *is* in them, and rested the seventh day. Exodus 20:8-11.

Observe the Sabbath day to keep it holy. . . . you shall remember that you were a slave in the land of Egypt, and the LORD your God brought you out of there by a mighty hand and by an outstretched arm; therefore the LORD your God commanded you to observe the Sabbath day. Deuteronomy 5:12-15.

How do we explain the differences between the Sabbath command-ments in Exodus 20:8-11 and Deuteronomy 5:12-15? Exodus 20 gives Cre-ation as the reason for keeping the Sabbath while Deuteronomy states that deliverance from slavery is the reason for the Sabbath. Do these texts con-tradict each other? Which text gives the correct reason? What does this mean for keeping the seventh-day Sabbath today?

A Comparison – The following comparison contains a fairly literal trans-lation of the Sabbath commandments in Exodus 20:8-11 and Deuteronomy 5:12-15. Similarities that appear in exactly the same places are underlined. Those similarities found in different places within the two passages are printed in bold.

Exodus 20	Deuteronomy 5
[8] **Remember** the Sabbath day to keep it holy.	[12] Observe the Sabbath day to keep it holy, as the LORD your God com-manded you.
[9] Six days you shall labor and do all your work,	[13] Six days you shall labor and do all your work,
[10] but the seventh day is a Sabbath of the LORD your God; *in it* you	[14] but the seventh day is a Sabbath of the LORD your God; *in it* you

Exodus 20	Deuteronomy 5
shall not do any work, you or your son or your daughter, *your male or your female servant* or your cattle or your sojourner who stays with you.	*shall* not do any work, you or your son or your daughter, *your male or your female servant* or your cattle or your sojourner who stays with you.
[11] For in six days the LORD made the heavens and the _earth_, the sea and all that is in them, and rested on the seventh day; <u>therefore</u> the LORD blessed _the Sabbath day_ and made it holy.	[15] And **you shall remember** that you were a slave in the _land_ of Egypt, and the LORD your God brought you out of there by a mighty hand and by an outstretched arm; <u>therefore</u> the LORD your God commanded you to observe _the Sabbath day_.

There is a high degree of correspondence in the first three verses of both lists but not in the last verses which contain the reasons for observing the Sabbath. Whereas Exodus focuses on Creation, Deuteronomy stresses deliverance from Egypt and thus redemption. Theologically, the two concepts are complementary and point to the rich theological meaning of the Sabbath. Both commandments share a common outline:

1. First command:	Remember / keep the Sabbath holy	(Exod 20:8; Deut 5:12)
2. Second command:	To work six days	(Exod 20:9; Deut 5:13)
3. Third command:	Not to work on the seventh day	(Exod 20:10; Deut 5:14)
4. Reasons:	Creation / Salvation	(Exod 20:11; Deut 5:16)

The major difference between the two forms of the Sabbath commandment is the reason provided for keeping it holy. Yet the call to keep the Sabbath remains the same. In both cases the element of remembering and looking back at the great things, which the Lord has done, is present.

Additions in Deuteronomy 5 – The Sabbath commandment in Deuteronomy 5 contains the phrases "as Yahweh your God commanded you" and "therefore Yahweh your God commanded you." Such phrases are not limited to the Sabbath commandment. They are repeated in the next commandment to honor father and mother (Deut 5:16), as well as in Deuteronomy 5:33, which is outside of the Decalogue but still in the same context. Whereas the singular "you" is used in the Ten Commandments, in

Deuteronomy 5:33 the plural "you" is used. A similar formula occurs in Deuteronomy 6:1, 17, 20, 25.

In Deuteronomy, Moses is speaking to Israel; he reminds them of God's mighty acts in delivering them from Egypt, and, in the process, he reiterates the Ten Commandments, as well as other commandments and admonitions. While reciting the Decalogue, he inserts the words "as/therefore Yahweh your God has commanded you" (5:12, 15), emphasizing that the Ten Commandments are of divine origin. Exodus 20:1 says, "Then God spoke all these words, saying . . . ." In Deuteronomy 5:4, 5 Moses tells the children of

> In Exodus we find the Ten Commandments as proclaimed by the Lord whereas in Deuteronomy Moses is applying the commandments to the experience of the Israelites.

Israel what God said. In other words, in Exodus we find the Ten Commandments as proclaimed by the Lord (Exod 20:18-23; Deut 9:10), whereas in Deuteronomy Moses is applying the commandments to the experience of the Israelites.

Reasons for the additions – While Moses repeated the Ten Commandments, he apparently commented on them in several places. These comments are minor and do not alter the meaning or authority of God's law. Only the reason for keeping the seventh day differs. According to Deuteronomy 18:15, Moses was a prophet, i.e., he made these comments on the Decalogue under inspiration, providing additional insights into the will and character of God.

Deuteronomy 5:22 refers back to the Sinai experience when God spoke to Israel and when the Decalogue was written on tables of stone. At Sinai the origin of the Sabbath was given. The phrase "and he added no more" stresses that the content of the Decalogue was complete and that it had "'canonical' authority."[1] No other commandments were part of it. But the repetition of the Decalogue by Moses in Deuteronomy 5 is still in agreement with the version proclaimed by the Lord himself. Deuteronomy 5:22 contains a historical gap without being incorrect or untruthful,[2] because "according to Exodus 19-34 the tablets containing the decalogue were not delivered to Moses until after he had mediated between Yahweh and the people and had received the additional covenant commandments, cf. Exod 24:12; 32:15f.; Deut 9:7ff."[3] This also means that the text cannot be pressed to denote that the precise wording of Deuteronomy 5:6-21 must have been the text contained on the tables of stone or that there is a contradiction between Deuteronomy 5:22 and Exodus 24:12; 31:18.

Effects of these additions – What effects do these additions have on the Decalogue? We have already noted that the phrases "as/therefore Yahweh your God commanded you" stress the divine origin of the Decalogue. Because this phrase is repeated in the fifth commandment, it ties together the commandments to keep the Sabbath and to honor one's parents. In both of them the relational aspect is strongly emphasized. Furthermore, the first table of the law, containing commandments focusing on humanity's relationship with God, and the second table of the law, containing commandments stressing interpersonal relationships, are linked. The interpersonal-relationship concept is enhanced by the specific emphasis on male and female servants, twice found in 5:14 and elaborated on in verse 15, in which Israel's liberation from slavery is referred to.

> In Deuteronomy the Sabbath commandment is in a special way connected to the first commandment. By keeping the Sabbath we accept Yahweh as the only God and Lord and reject all other gods and idols.

In Deuteronomy 5:15 "the land of Egypt" appears. The same expression is found in verse 6, in the introduction to the Ten Commandments.[4] In addition, the verb "to bring out," the divine name "Yahweh your God," and the term "slave" occur in both verses. In Deuteronomy, the Sabbath commandment is in a special way connected to the first commandment. By keeping the Sabbath we accept Yahweh as the only God and Lord and reject all other gods and idols. At the same time, we enjoy liberation and salvation.

Deuteronomy 5:14 contains the addition "your ox and your donkey." Instead of talking about animals in general only, Moses seems to mention ox and donkey deliberately. Ox and donkey are found in the same order in Deuteronomy 5:21, the tenth commandment. Thus, the Sabbath commandment and the commandment not to covet are associated. Whoever has found rest in the Lord on the Sabbath day, also has found rest from coveting material goods, especially those that belong to one's neighbor. "Verses 6-11 describe one's duties to Yahweh and verses 16-21 deal with relationships among humans. By dealing with both these topics simultaneously, the Deuteronomic Sabbath commandment forms a bridge between these two sections."[5]

Conclusion – The Sabbath commandment in Deuteronomy agrees with the one found in Exodus 20 that the Sabbath should be kept holy and that after six days of labor on the specific seventh day, the Sabbath, humanity should rest. There are some differences with regard to the reasons given. Moses in repeating the Sabbath commandment has—under inspiration—made some additions, which, in a specific way, link the Sabbath commandment to the rest of the Ten Commandments to the effect that the Decalogue culminates in the Sabbath commandment.[6] This has also been recognized by a number of non-Adventist scholars. For example, R. D. Nelson says, "Deuteronomy's distinctive formulation of the Ten Commandments increases the importance of the Sabbath."[7] Thus, the Sabbath commandment is not only referring to Creation but also to salvation. We keep the Sabbath because God has created us and has saved us.

Ekkehardt Mueller

References

[1]Richard D. Nelson, *Deuteronomy: A Commentary*, The Old Testament Library (Louisville, KY: Westminister John Knox Press, 2002), 84.

[2]In many parts of Scripture summaries of events are employed that do not point to every little detail. See, e.g., Genesis 6:19 and 7:2, 3; John 20:30, 31; 21:25.

[3]A. D. H. Mayes, *Deuteronomy*, The New Century Bible Commentary (Grand Rapids, MI: Wm. B. Eerdmans Publishing Company, 1979), 172.

[4]See also, Exodus 20:2.

[5]Nelson, 82.

[6]In a similar way, Jesus does this in Matthew 5 in the Sermon on the Mount.

[7]Nelson, 81, 82.

HOW CAN THE STATEMENT "THERE SHALL BE NO POOR AMONG YOU" BE RECONCILED WITH "FOR THE POOR WILL NEVER CEASE TO BE IN THE LAND"?

However, there will be no poor among you, since the LORD will surely bless you in the land which the LORD your God is giving you as an inheritance to possess. . . . For the poor will never cease to be in the land; therefore I command you, saying, 'You shall freely open your hand to your brother, to your needy and poor in your land.' Deuteronomy 15:4, 11.

The historical context of this passage is the latter part of the 40 years of Israel's sojourn in the wilderness. They have arrived at the launching point for the crossing of the Jordan River where Moses addresses the nation in what may be thought of as three great farewell sermons. These sermons serve as a review of the experiences of the 40 years since Israel left Egypt; they summarize what God has done for them and appeal for a renewal of the covenant.

The Sabbatical year – Deuteronomy 15 is the middle portion of the second and longest sermon (chapters 4:44–26:19). This sermon focuses on the Ten Commandments and the Mosaic laws. That is, it is restating many of the laws already given at Sinai, because they are the legal terms or stipulations of the covenant into which Israel had entered and then broken.

The laws referred to in chapter 15 form a portion of the law for the safeguarding of individual rights, including the poor. Every member of society was important, irrespective of wealth, poverty, or any other social distinctions. Thus it gives guidelines for the year of release (the sabbatical year) and for the treatment of Hebrew slaves. (For some of the original laws see Exod 22:22; 23:10, 11, and Lev 25.)

It is interesting to note that there are several Hebrew words for "poor" in the Old Testament. The word used in this passage is *'ebyon* from the root *'abah* "to be willing, to wish for," which usually refers to the needy poor. The term frequently also includes the concept of the oppressed or wretched. Another word *'ani* refers more specifically to the oppressed poor and is used more frequently in the Old Testament, often with *'ebyon*.

Let there be no poor among you – There is considerable difference of opinion on how to translate the first part of verse 4. Keil and Delitzsch insist that the first verb[1] has the meaning that there is no need to remit a debt to foreigners in the seventh year but to make sure that there are no poor among their people.[2] The Jerusalem Bible renders the statement as "Let there be no poor among you then." Similarly the NIV, "However, there should be no poor among you . . ." These appear to preserve the sense of the text better than the RSV, which says, "But there will be no poor among you. . . ." If the statement is taken as a command, it is an instruction as to what should be attempted. Thus the statement of verse 11 that the poor will always be with them is recognition of reality, without diminishing the goal to be upheld. The verse then seems to mean, "Try to have no poor among you."

> "In placing among them the helpless and the poor, to be dependent upon their care, Christ tests His professed followers. By our love and service for His needy children we prove the genuineness of our love for Him. To neglect them is to declare ourselves false disciples, strangers to Christ and His love" (MH 205).

One of the ways that this ideal is to be attempted is by following the instruction of verses 1-3, that is, to remit debt during the sabbatical seventh year. This would take pressure off the poor regardless of the manner in which this ideal was applied. Some, like Gerhard von Rad, have claimed that the instruction is to forgive the debt, or to cancel it completely.[3] Most recent commentators think it means simply to relax or remit the debt during the year (when little income would be received) but that the indebtedness would return after the seventh year.[4]

If the instruction of verse 4 means to endeavor to have no poor among you, or is stated as an ideal to be constantly aimed for, there is no problem or contradiction with the statement of verse 11. Even though God's blessing was so great and His enablement so significant, yet the reality of poverty would remain. There would always be poor among them. This is not only a prediction of the human reality but an appeal for nation and individuals to respond with benevolence. Thus the verses may be paraphrased as "strive to have no poor among you, because the LORD will bless you with plenty to enable you to reflect His grace. Yet, in fact, the opportunity to show grace will always be with you since there will always be some poor people around you." A similar view sees verse 4 as a conditional promise. *If* you follow *all* the instruction in generous sharing (vv. 8, 9), *then* there will be no poor among you. But (implied), I know that will not happen.

An invitation to generosity – This passage is an invitation to generosity and kindness to the poor. Strive to have no poor among you, and yet there will always be some. It was in this sense that Jesus referred to the passage in Matthew 26:11, "For the poor you have with you always; but you do not always have Me." In those days and also today, there will be opportunities for God's people to demonstrate their trust in God and their closeness to His pattern of unselfish giving to all who have need.

> Even though God's blessing was so great and His enablement so significant, yet the reality of poverty was to remain.

Lloyd Willis

References

[1]A jussive – a Hebrew grammatical form that translates a verb with "let. . . ."

[2]C. F. Keil and F. Delitzsch, *Commentary on the Old Testament in Ten Volumes*, vol. III: *The Pentateuch* (Grand Rapids, MI: Eerdmans, 1870), 370.

[3]Gerhard von Rad, *Deuteronomy*, The Old Testament Library, trans. Dorothea Barton (Philadelphia, PA: Westminster, 1966), 106.

[4]Keil and Delitzsch, 369; J. Ridderbos, *Deuteronomy*, Bible Student's Commentary (Grand Rapids, MI: Zondervan, 1984), 180; P.C. Craigie, *The Book of Deuteronomy*, New International Commentary on the Old Testament (Grand Rapids, MI: Eerdmans, 1976), 236.

WHY DID GOD ORDER THE ISRAELITES TO "UTTERLY DESTROY" THE CANAANITE NATIONS, INCLUDING WOMEN AND CHILDREN?

In the cities of these peoples that the LORD your God is giving you as an inheritance, you shall not leave alive anything that breathes. But you shall utterly destroy them, the Hittite and the Amorite, the Canaanite and the Perizzite, the Hivite and the Jebusite, as the LORD your God has commanded you. Deuteronomy 20:16, 17

Several issues have been raised regarding the destruction of the nations by Israel during the conquest. The first is ethical. Why did God instruct Israel to destroy men, women, and children, as well as cattle and everything that breathes? The second has to do with the character of God. How does this action relate to a loving God who notices when a sparrow falls and who sent His Son to die for all humanity? Does the Old Testament portray a God of vengeance while the New Testament portrays a God of love and grace? Finally, why did God use Israel to exact these actions against the Canaanites?

Divine love and justice – Several general observations are in order as we look at these passages. First, God's principle of love cannot be understood apart from justice. Love without justice cannot exist. A God who is not just becomes no better than the capricious man-made gods of the surrounding nations. Second, God in His omnipotence understands the motives of the heart. Although God is longsuffering with humanity, there comes a time when justice must prevail and sin must be eradicated. This act of divine justice occurred at the Flood (Gen-6-9) and will take place again at the end of time when the wicked are destroyed (Rev 21-22). In both cases, God, in His justice and in love for His faithful, roots out evil so that humanity can live peacefully with one another and with their Creator.

A time of probation – The instructions found in Deuteronomy 20 are part of the laws of warfare outlined in this chapter. They constitute the instructions of God to Israel as they are about to enter into the Promised Land. These instructions must be understood within the context of that event in history and within the broader history of the Canaanites.

177

For more than two hundred years, from the time Abraham left Haran until Jacob entered Egypt, the patriarchs and their families were God's witnesses among the Canaanites, but the inhabitants of Canaan refused to accept the God of Abraham, Isaac, and Jacob. Thus, the destruction of the Canaanites is the outcome of their choice to reject God and their descent into "every evil" and the inherent result that comes from living apart from God. It had been predicted through Abraham that his descendants would be exiled and oppressed for four hundred years before God would lead them out of Egypt. The reason for the long delay is explained in Genesis 15:13-16: "for the iniquity of the Amorite [Canaanite] is not yet complete." Other translations read, "had not yet reached their full measure." In other words, God waited for centuries while the Canaanite nations slowly filled up their own cups of destruction by their behavior. Ultimately God's justice demanded that the outcome of their choices would result in self-destruction. The destruction of the nations in Canaan was not a precipitous act of vengeance; it was the final result of a gracious and loving God who provided every opportunity for them to change their ways (see Balaam in Numbers 22), but who, in the end, could not tolerate their wickedness.[1]

> Although God is longsuffering with humanity, there comes a time when justice must prevail and sin must be eradicated.

The extent of their degradation becomes clear from Canaanite texts describing worship practices that included child-sacrifices and sacred prostitution.[2] The decisions they made affected so-called innocent lives. Even women and children were affected by the depth of evil. It was not God's will that such atrocities continue. It was not because the Israelites were superior that He brought them into Canaan, it was "because of the wickedness of these nations" (Deut 9:5) that the Canaanites would be dispossessed. For that reason Deuteronomy 20 and similar texts clearly indicate that Israel was specifically to destroy all the altars, sacred pillars, Asherim, and graven images "in order that they may not teach you to do according to all their detestable things which they have done for their gods" (Deut 20:18).

The role of Israel – If divine retribution was God's plan, it still does not explain why He used the Israelites to destroy the nations before them. A broader contextual analysis indicates that it was never God's intention to use the Israelites as the primary agent of destruction. In Exodus 23 God set out His plan for the conquest, "But if you will *truly obey his [angel] voice and do all that I say*, then I will be an enemy to your enemies and an adversary to your adversaries. For My angel will go before you and bring you in to *the land of* the Amorites, the Hittites, the Perizzites, the Canaanites, the Hivites and the Jebusites; and I will completely destroy them" (Exod 23:22, 23).

The text clearly indicates that if Israel obeyed and did all that God said, God would do the rest. He would destroy their enemies. Their responsibility was to demolish the Amorite gods and "break their sacred stones to pieces" (Exod 23:24). Deuteronomy 1:30 reaffirms that "The LORD your God who goes before you will himself fight on your behalf, just as He did for you in Egypt before your eyes." This is precisely what God had done in the past. When the children of Israel complained to Moses at the Red Sea, Moses responded, "Stand firm and you will see the deliverance the LORD will bring you today . . . The LORD will fight for you, you need only to be still" (Ex 14:13, 14 NIV). Indeed, Deuteronomy 7:18-22, referring to the Red Sea experience, gives precisely the same promise: "But do not be afraid of them; remember well what the LORD your God did to Pharaoh and to all Egypt. . . . The LORD your God will do the same to all the peoples you now fear. Moreover, the LORD your God will send the hornet among them until even the survivors who hide from you have perished." God was going to drive out these nations "little by little" (v. 22). This was God's ideal plan for Israel.

> God dedicated the Canaanite nations and their gods to destruction because they had violently and persistently opposed Him.

Yahweh's War – But did not God instruct Israel to "utterly destroy" them in these passages? The term that is translated here "utterly destroy" is the Hebrew term *cherem*. It means "curse" or "that which stands under ban" or "that which is dedicated to destruction."[3] God had dedicated these nations and their gods to destruction because they had violently and persistently opposed Him. Although some scholars have interpreted this destruction as a "Holy War" it was more precisely a "Yahweh War" in the sense that God himself was the one fighting against the forces of evil and working out divine retribution. Israel was to place these nations and their belongings under a ban, meaning that they were to give them over to God for judgment. They were to be completely separated from them. Israel was to take no spoils. They were to make no covenant with them. They were not to intermarry with the enemies of God in order to prevent being influenced by their wicked ways. Instead, Israel was to work with God, their supreme Leader in the theocracy, to bring about His will.

Israel's choice – In the end, even though God's ideal plan was for Israel to be still in order to see the deliverance of the Lord, God worked with Israel. They chose to be the conquerors themselves and to militarily slay those whom they would dispossess. Once they inherited the land, they did not completely conquer it so that the Canaanite still occupied many cities and territories (Josh 13:2-5; Judg 1:19-35). But God worked with Israel's choices and accompanied them even when they took matters into their own hands. Even so, at the end of his life, Joshua could say, "And the Amorite and the Perizzite and the Canaanite and the Hittite and the Girgashite, the Hivite and the Jebusite. Thus I gave them into your hand . . . *but* not by your sword or your bow. And I gave you a land on which you had not labored, and cities which you had not built, and you have lived in them; you are eating of vineyards and olive groves which you did not plant" (Josh 24:11-13).

Michael G. Hasel

References

[1] On the iniquity of the Canaanites, see PP 492.

[2] John Day, "Canaan, Religion of" in *The Anchor Bible Dictionary*, ed. David N. Freedman, 6 vols. (New York, NY: Doubleday, 1992), 1:834, 835.

[3] On the term *cherem*, see Michael G. Hasel, *Military Practice and Polemic: Israel's Laws of Warfare in Near Eastern Perspective* (Berrien Springs, MI: Andrews University Press, 2005), 26-28.

IS DIVORCE AND REMARRIAGE PERMITTED IN THE OLD TESTAMENT?

"When a man takes a wife and marries her, and it happens that she finds no favor in his eyes because he has found some indecency in her, and he writes her a certificate of divorce and puts it in her hand and sends her out from his house, [2] and she leaves his house and goes and becomes another man's wife, [3] and if the latter husband turns against her and writes her a certificate of divorce and puts it in her hand and sends her out of his house . . . [4] then her former husband who sent her away is not allowed to take her again to be his wife, since she has been defiled; for that is an abomination before the LORD. Deuteronomy 24:1-4.

In Deuteronomy 24:1-4, as in the rest of the Old Testament, divorce is tolerated, conceded, permitted, but not commanded, commended, or approved by divine legislation. Most modern versions properly represent the Hebrew grammar of this case law: Verses 1-3 constitute the *description* of conditions (introduced by "if"), while the actual *legislation* is found only in verse 4a (introduced by "then he may not. . ."). This legislation forbids the woman's former husband to take her back to be his wife under the circumstances described in verses 1-3. The implication is clear -- God, while tolerating it, is in no wise legislating divorce in this passage.

Reasons for divorce – Deuteronomy 24:1 describes, it does not legislate, the circumstance of divorce, in which a husband is no longer able to love his wife because he has found in her some *ʿerwat dabar* (literally, "nakedness of a thing"). This apparently refers to some type of serious, shameful, and disgraceful conduct of indecent exposure on the part of his wife, probably associated with sexual activity, but less than actual illicit sexual intercourse, which would have received the death penalty (Deut 22:22).

Although verses 1-3 indicate that divorce on grounds less than illicit sexual intercourse was tolerated and not punished in ancient Israel, within the legislation of verse 4 a very rare Hebrew grammatical form[1] provides an internal indicator that such a divorce does not meet with divine approval. When the husband divorced his wife, and she was forced to marry someone else, according to the literal translation of verse 4 "she has been caused to defile herself." This terminology of a woman "defiling herself" is the same used elsewhere in the Pentateuch for adultery (Num 5:13, 14, 20)[2], although here it is not punished as such because the blame is placed upon the first husband and not the wife. Thus according to Deuteronomy 24:4, divorce of a woman on grounds less than illicit sexual intercourse causes the woman to "defile herself," i.e., commit what is tantamount to adultery when she marries again. Jesus in His Sermon on the Mount makes explicit the nuance already implicit in Deuteronomy 24:4, "whoever divorces his wife for any reason except sexual immorality *causes her to commit adultery*; and whoever marries a woman who is divorced commits adultery" (Matt 5:32).

> Divorce in the Old Testament is tolerated, conceded, permitted, but not commanded, commended, or approved by divine legislation.

Deuteronomy 24:4 also sheds light on Jesus' "exception clause" in Matthew 5:32 (and 19:9), "whoever divorces his wife for any reason *except sexual immorality [porneia]. . . .*" The exception clause is not found in the parallel accounts in Mark (10:11-12) and Luke (16:18), since these Gospels, like Deuteronomy 24:4, do not take into account the situations of adultery, or other illicit sexual intercourse, the penalty for which in the Mosaic law was being "cut off" or put to death (Lev 18:29; 20:10; Deut 22:22). It was assumed in Deuteronomy 24 and in all three Synoptic Gospels that the death penalty or being "cut off" from the congregation meant a *de facto* dissolution of the marriage. All three Gospel writers teach that marriage is indissoluble for all offences short of adultery and other illicit sexual intercourse. What is implicit in Mark and Luke is made explicit in Matthew. Matthew apparently preserves the original intent of Jesus for readers after A.D. 30 when the death penalty for adultery was abolished in Judaism.[3]

The goal of the legislation was to protect a woman's personhood – The key to the overall purpose of the legislation in Deuteronomy 24:1-4 is found in its placement within the larger context of Deuteronomic law. Studies have shown that Deuteronomy 12-26 presents an amplification of the Decalogue, moving in order through each of the Ten Commandments. The legislation of Deuteronomy 24:1-4 is not placed within the section of

Deuteronomy amplifying the seventh commandment, as one might expect, but within the section dealing with theft – the eighth commandment. Seen in its larger context in the book of Deuteronomy, this passage constitutes legislation with an ultimate goal to protect women from being robbed of their personhood, their dignity, and their self-respect. It prevents men from treating women as chattel, mere property to be swapped back and forth at will. A woman's dignity and value as an individual is preserved.

Divorce was tolerated because of the hardness of men's hearts – The potentially abusive and male-dominated practices in the Old Testament such as divorce must be understood along the same lines as other institutions, like slavery, which God regulated by means of legislation but did not totally abolish in the social life of Israel. "Because of "the hardness of their hearts" God temporarily allowed certain situations to continue while making it very clear in Genesis 1-3 and in the context of the laws themselves that "from the beginning it was not so" (Matt 19:8). By providing an internal indicator of divine disapproval of divorce, the legislation in Deuteronomy 24:4 harks back to God's Edenic ideal for permanency in marriage (Gen 2:24).

> Divorce must be understood along the same lines as other Old Testament institutions, like slavery, which God regulated by means of legislation but did not totally abolish.

God reveals His great patience and condescension in meeting Israel where she is and yet calling her up to a higher standard. Overarching this illustrative case law of the Mosaic code stands the broad principles of the Decalogue, the full application of which to the area of sexuality would lead an enlightened Israel back toward the Edenic ideal. In its tolerance of, but self-expressed disapproval of inequalities afforded women due to the hardness of men's hearts, Deuteronomy 24:1-4 points toward the day when such inequalities will be resolved by a return to the Edenic pattern for marriage. Such a day was proclaimed by Jesus in His teaching on divorce (Matt 5:32 and 19:8-9)!

Richard M. Davidson

References

[1]*Hothpael* or passive reflexive of *tame'*.

[2]Among the Jews, therefore, the followers of Shammai identified "nakedness of a thing" as adultery; the followers of Hillel concluded that the two words refer to two different grounds for divorce – "nakedness" or adultery and "a matter" which could mean any matter which displeased the husband.

[3]See the Babylonian Talmud *Sanhedrin* 41a.

Pottery jars from Qumran. The Dead Sea Scrolls were hidden in such jars just before the destruction of Jerusalem in A.D. 70 and discovered in 1948.

HOW COULD MOSES HAVE WRITTEN IN ADVANCE ABOUT HIS OWN DEATH?

So Moses the servant of the LORD died there in the land of Moab, according to the word of the LORD. And He buried him in the valley in the land of Moab, opposite Beth-peor; but no man knows his burial place to this day. Although Moses was one hundred and twenty years old when he died, his eye was not dim, nor his vigor abated. So the sons of Israel wept for Moses in the plains of Moab thirty days; then the days of weeping *and* mourning for Moses came to an end. Deuteronomy 34:5-8.

Even though it is not unusual for a literary work such as the Pentateuch to conclude with the death of its leading figure (see the same feature in Joshua 24:29, 30), this very feature creates a problem concerning the issue of authorship. For centuries, many Jews and Christians have assumed that Moses wrote the first five books of the Bible.[1] Yet how can Moses have written in advance about his own death?

A historical appendix – In responding to this question, several points should be kept in mind. First, the position that Moses is the author of the Pentateuch does not demand that he wrote the account of his own death in advance. Though this position was evidently held by Josephus, who stated that Moses "wrote in the holy books that he died, which was done out of fear, lest they (the Israelites) should venture to say that, because of his extraordinary virtue, he went to God,"[2] evidence from elsewhere in Scripture reveals that claims that a certain prophet or apostle was the author of a given biblical document does not demand that every single portion of the document came from that person's hand. For instance, the next-to-last chapter of Jeremiah concludes with the words, "Thus far are the words of Jeremiah" (Jer 51:64), indicating that the concluding chapter of Jeremiah was written by someone else. Proverbs, which three times alludes to Solomon as author of the book (Prov. 1:1; 10:1; 25:1), credits Agur and Lemuel with the last two chapters. As the Gospel of John comes to an end, there is a brief note by the community of faith (notice the use of "we" in John 21:24), vouching for the trustworthiness of the account. In none of these cases does the inclusion of a historical appendix or other concluding verses by another person change the identity of the document's primary author any more than a later postscript added by an editor to a contemporary autobiography after the author's death would negate that person as the author.

Evidences of Mosaic authorship – A second point to keep in mind is that there are a number of references to the writing activity of Moses sprinkled throughout the Pentateuch. Exodus 24:4 states, "And Moses wrote down all the words of the Lord." Deuteronomy 31:9 asserts, "So Moses wrote down this law." And Numbers 33:2 indicates that Moses kept something of a travel diary as Israel journeyed in the wilderness. There is ample evidence indicating that Moses was closely involved in writing the material that came to compose the first five books of the Bible.

A third point worth noting is that Jesus apparently considered Moses the author of the earliest part of Scripture. In John 5:46, He declares, "For if you believed Moses, you would believe Me; for he wrote of Me." This perspective of Jesus is a fact that should be taken into account by those who are dismissive of the view that Moses authored the Pentateuch.

> The inclusion of a historical appendix by another person does not change the identity of the document's primary author.

A fourth point to be made is that a number of internal evidences support the position that Moses wrote the Pentateuch. These evidences include the eyewitness details that would be expected from an actual participant in the events described therein (see Exod 15:27), the thoroughgoing acquaintance with Egypt that is on display, the fact that a greater percentage of Egyptian words is used here than elsewhere in the Old Testament, and the fact that the flora and fauna referred to are found in Egypt and in the Sinai peninsula. These features are what one would expect from Moses, who was raised and educated in Egypt and who also spent many years in the desert.

A final point to make is that recent years have witnessed increasing appreciation for the unity of the Pentateuch and its careful literary artistry. Whereas a previous generation of biblical scholars tended to divide the first five books of Scripture into their supposed literary sources,[3] this view has been strongly challenged by both conservative and liberal scholars with cogent and compelling arguments given in favor of a single author behind most of the material of the Pentateuch. In light of these arguments, there is good reason to affirm the traditional position and identify this single author as Moses with perhaps Joshua or another leader responsible for the account of his death in Deuteronomy 34.

Gregory A. King

References

[1]See the chapter "Who wrote the Books of the Pentateuch?" by D. Merling in this volume.
[2]Flavius Josephus *Antiquities of the Jews* 8.48.
[3]See the chapter by D. Merling.

The pyramid of Khafre and the Sphinx. (ca 2500 B.C.). Both were already more than 1000 years old when Israel and Moses left Egypt.

DID JOSHUA REALLY CONQUER
THE WHOLE LAND OF CANAAN?

So Joshua took the whole land, according to all that the LORD had spoken to Moses, and Joshua gave it for an inheritance to Israel according to their divisions by their tribes. Thus the land had rest from war. Joshua 11:23.

Joshua 11:23 concludes the account of conquests by the united Israelite army under the command of Joshua, saying that "Joshua took the whole land" and gave it to the Israelite tribes for their inheritance and "the land had rest from war" (compare Josh 21:43-45, which says that "the Lord gave Israel all the land"). According to Judges 1, however, it was necessary for the Israelite tribes to fight the inhabitants of Canaan in various places after the death of Joshua (e.g., Judg 1:1-3, 9-17), and pockets of non-Israelites remained in the land:

Manasseh did not take possession of Beth-shean and its villages, or Taanach and its villages, or the inhabitants of Dor and its villages, or the inhabitants of Ibleam and its villages, or the inhabitants of Megiddo and its villages; so the Canaanites persisted in living in that land" (Judg 1:27; cf. 29-33).

Judges 1, where the Israelite tribes must continue the effort of possessing the land of Canaan, appears to contradict Joshua 11 and 21, which claim that the job of conquest was finished.

Reasons for the Canaanite remnants in the land – According to Joshua 11 and 21, the united army of Israelites under Joshua broke the back of military opposition to their permanent residence in the land of Canaan. These passages do not say that the army under Joshua totally drove out or exterminated all the inhabitants of the land as God commanded them to do (Num 33:50-53; Deut 7:1, 2, 16; 20:16, 17). These campaigns were disabling raids, not territorial conquests with instant Hebrew occupation. For example, Joshua 11:22 acknowledges that even an exceptional pocket of Anakim (or giants) remained in Gaza, which the tribe of Judah later took (Judg 1:18).

Indeed, God had said that He would clear the nations of Canaan away from the Israelites little by little for a practical reason: so that (dangerous) wild beasts would not multiply too quickly in a land depleted of inhabitants (Deut 7:22). Therefore, it was clearly up to the individual tribes to progressively remove the inhabitants of the land over a period of time after the united army finished its work and was disbanded. This continuation is what Judges 1 describes. However, because the tribes did not adequately complete the commission that God gave them, they suffered ongoing resistance and negative religious influences from the non-Israelites they left in the land (compare Num 33:55, 56 with Judg 2:2, 3, 20-23; 3:1-6).

A two-phase conquest – Joshua and Judges speak of two phases in the process of conquering the land. The first phase of military defeat of the Canaanite strongholds

> "The book of Joshua simply records the Hebrew entry into Canaan, their base camp at Gilgal by the Jordan, their initial raids (without occupation!) against local rulers and subjects in south and north Canaan, followed by localized occupation (a) north from Gilgal as far as Shechem and Tirzah and (b) south to Hebron/Debir, and very little more. This is *not* the sweeping, instant conquest-with-occupation that some hasty scholars would foist upon the text of Joshua, without any factual justification." (K. A. Kitchen, *On the Reliability of the Old Testament* [Grand Rapids, MI: Wm. B. Eerdmans, 2003], 163).

was successfully completed under Joshua. The second phase of completely clearing out the inhabitants of Canaan was accomplished only partially by the armies of the individual tribes. Joshua did not leave a job too difficult for them, but because they failed to decisively follow it through to completion, the strength of the enemy grew and the Israelites again were faced with a formidable opposition (Judg 1). So the conquest was partially undone.

Thus, there is no real contradiction between Joshua and Judges. Joshua and his united army conquered Canaan by defeating its armies. However, the Israelite tribes let inhabitants of the land remain without destroying them or driving them out so that these non-Israelites were able to fight again.[1]

Roy E. Gane

References

[1]See Roy Gane, *God's Faulty Heroes* (Hagerstown, MD: Review and Herald, 1996), 17-35.

The Philistines

The name "Philistines" is recognizable in several languages. In Hebrew they are known as the P[e]lishtim, which translated into English as Philistines. In the Egyptian sources they are listed among the Sea Peoples. They are best known for their part in the invasion of Egypt by the Sea Peoples, who were vanquished by Pharaoh Rameses III (c. 1183–1152 B.C.) in a land and sea battle in the Delta. Detailed scenes of this fighting are shown on the north exterior wall of the temple of Rameses III at Medinet Habu, opposite Luxor.

The origin of the Philistines is still not certain. The Bible states that the Philistines came from Caphtor (Deut 2:23; Jer 47:4; Amos 9:7), which is generally regarded as Crete. The name of the Cherethites has been equated with Cretans. The Cherethites were apparently a Philistine subgroup who lived in the Negeb not far from Ziklag, David's home among the Philistines (cf. 1 Sam 30:14). The Cherethites and the Pelethites were among David's bodyguards, along with 600 Gittites (men from Gath) (cf. 2 Sam 15:19; 20:7, 23; 1 Chron 18:17).

Warfare between Israel and the Philistines is reported in 1 Samuel 4:1 at Aphek. The Philistines won that round and captured the ark of the covenant (1 Sam 4:17), which they returned after seven months because the Lord sent plagues upon them (1 Sam 5:1–6:21). Later, when Samuel had become leader, the Philistines attacked Israel at Mizpah, but God gave the victory to Israel. On this occasion Samuel set up a memorial stone and named it Ebenezer ("Stone of Help," 7:12). The Philistines did not invade Israel again during the lifetime of Samuel, and Israel recovered cities that had been taken by the Philistines (1 Sam 7:14). (Adapted from W. E. Elwell and B. J. Beitzel, *Baker Encyclopedia of the Bible* 2 vols. [Grand Rapids, MI: Baker Book House, 1988], 2:1680-1682).

WAS GOD TELLING SAMUEL TO LIE?

But Samuel said, "How can I go? When Saul hears of it, he will kill me." And the LORD said, "Take a heifer with you, and say, 'I have come to sacrifice to the LORD.'" 1 Samuel 16:2.

When people of the Bible resort to deceptions, which make a person believe as truth what is not true (Genesis 12:10-20), or they lie with the intention to deceive (Acts 5:1-6) or they evade the truth through prevarication (Exod 1:15-22), we rightly ascribe such a behavior to human finiteness and sin. But when faced with 1 Samuel 16:1, 2, the stakes are infinitely higher. There Samuel is told that God has rejected Saul and that Samuel should go and anoint David as king. Samuel, however, is afraid that Saul will kill him. In response God says to Samuel, "Take a heifer with you, and say, 'I have come to sacrifice to the LORD.'"

How strange! Is God telling Samuel to protect his life by deceiving the king or his patrolmen? How can this same God expect truthfulness (Gen 17:1), if He teaches His prophet to lie?

Suggested solutions to such dilemmas – When dealing with such dilemmas some have concluded that: (1) the prohibition against lying or deceiving is not an absolute standard in the Bible; lying is rather considered an "acceptable and generally praiseworthy means for a weaker party to succeed against a stronger power. . . . God, too, can legitimately encourage prevarication when operating on behalf of an underdog;"[1] (2) lying to a liar is condoned. So lying to Laban is "indirectly justified" (Gen 30:1-43);[2] (3) higher norms transcend lower norms without abolishing them. So the duty to save life is greater than the duty to be truthful (e.g., Josh 2:5);[3] and (4) divine deception is acceptable if it serves a higher end.[4]

But can such conclusions be drawn from the Biblical text?

God and integrity – The testimony of Scripture about God's character challenges the above opinions. In Numbers we read, "God is not man, that he should lie" (Num 23:19). Just a few verses before the episode under consideration, Samuel declares, "The Glory of Israel will not lie" (1 Sam 15:29; see also Ps 89:35, Titus 1:2, and Heb 6:18). Truthfulness characterizes the very nature of God's being and His way of acting.

The prohibition against lying is an absolute standard of conduct for humans as well. Truth cannot suffer manipulation. God expects truthfulness in the very core of human beings (Ps 51:6), and in their actions (Exod 20:16, Rev 14:5). Without it human life and destiny are in ultimate jeopardy (Lev 19:11, Prov 12:22, Rev 21:8, 27; 22:15). Consequently, the interpretation of the text in 1 Samuel 16:1, 2 requires us to safeguard God's reputation as a Being of integrity and honesty, expecting the same requirement for humans.

> Truthfulness characterizes the very nature of God's being and His way of acting.

Concealment of truth – The context of 1 Samuel 16 shows the miserable state into which Saul placed himself and his kingdom. Ever since God rejected him as king of Israel (1 Samuel 16:1), even Samuel could not feel safe from the king's unpredictable rage. So God responded to Samuel's fear by reminding him that his trip to Bethlehem need not worry him that much. First, priests did go from place to place offering sacrifices, followed by a special feast at which the elders of the place were honored guests. In the case of Bethlehem, the invitation of Jesse and his sons would be nothing unusual. Besides, due to his position as a levitical judge, Samuel could travel even outside of his regular priestly jurisdiction, especially when the sacrifice of a heifer was needed to atone for an unsolved murder in a rural region. This might explain the fear with which the town's elders met Samuel: "Do you come peaceably?" And he said, "Peaceably" (1 Sam 16:4, 5). Moreover, while sacrifice and the feast that followed it were public events, the anointing happened disconnected from the sacrifice and feasting, in a more private setting. So it happened for Saul's anointing (1 Sam 9:22-10:8), and also in David's case, who was anointed "in the midst of his brothers" (1 Sam 16:13). No aspect of the public events could identify Samuel's ministry in Bethlehem as an anointing ceremony, nor was the taking of a heifer with him connected with the anointing.

God's advice to His frightened servant ("Say, I have come to sacrifice") belongs to a different moral category than deception, lying, or prevarication. Keil and Delitzsch comment:

> There was no untruth in this, for Samuel was really about to go to a sacrificial festival, and was to invite Jesse's family to it, and then anoint the one whom Jehovah should point out to him as the cho-

sen one. It was simply a concealment of an unrelated detail of his mission. God has rejected Saul and hence he was not privy to the theocratic dimension of the kingdom of Israel.[5]

Lesson from 1 Samuel 16 – First Samuel 16:1, 2 teaches several lessons:

1. God teaches Samuel how to be a careful custodian of truth. It is only the cynic, says Bonhoeffer, who claims to speak the truth at all times and in all places *to all men in the same way.* "Every utterance lives and has its home in a particular environment. The word in the family is different from the word in business or in public. The word which has come to life in the warmth of personal relationship is frozen to death in the cold air of public existence."[6] Samuel cannot speak in the same way to Saul as he does to David. But in what way should the word be different?

> Even life itself should not be purchased with the price of falsehood.

2. God does not teach Samuel to lie. The difference between his word spoken to David and to Saul is not the difference between a truth and a lie. If asked about his purpose, Samuel would not have lied by disclosing only the sacrifice aspect of his visit. Samuel's reply would have been strictly true. He did

> offer a sacrifice; and it does not appear that he could have done the work which God had designed unless he had offered this sacrifice, and called the elders of the people together and thus called Jesse's sons. But he did not tell the principal design of his coming; had he done so, it would have produced only evil and no good: and though no man, in any circumstance, should ever tell a lie, yet, in all circumstances he is not obliged to tell the whole truth, though in every circumstance he must tell nothing but the truth, and in every case so tell the truth that the hearer shall not believe a lie by it.[7]

This is not the same as telling a half-truth.

3. Concealment of truth is not lying, and on some occasions it may be a duty. Walter Kaiser explains, in the case of Samuel,

> only what was true was presented to Saul. As for Samuel's ultimate intention, nothing is affirmed or denied, and nothing incited Saul's

mind to probe concerning what have been Samuel's ultimate motives for coming to Bethlehem at this time. Had such question been raised an altogether different problem would have confronted Samuel, and he would have to avoid either affirming or denying what those purposes were or face the wrath of Saul in his disclosure.[8]

4. The example of Jesus is instructive here. On more than one occasion Jesus escaped from His enemies (John 8:59; 12:36), and more than once He refrained from answering (Mark 14:61; 15:5; Luke 23:9). There is a time to keep silent, and a time to speak, says the wise man (Eccl 3:7) and no one is obligated to give an answer to every question asked. Yet Jesus was not deceptive either in speech or in silence (1 Pet 2:22). To his disciples He prudently replied on one occasion: "I have yet many things to say to you, but you cannot bear them now" (John 16:12).

"Even life itself should not be purchased with the price of falsehood," insists Ellen G. White.

> By a word or a nod the martyrs might have denied the truth and saved their lives. By consenting to cast a single grain of incense upon the idol altar they might have been saved from the rack, the scaffold, or the cross. But they refused to be false in word or deed, though life was the boon they would receive by doing so. . . . Their lives were ennobled and elevated in the sight of God because they stood firmly for the truth under the most aggravated circumstances (4T 336).

In describing those who have been redeemed from mankind as first fruits for God and the Lamb, John the revelator underscores that in their mouths no lie was found, for they are spotless" (Rev 14:5). "The path of obedience is the only path that leads to heaven" (Te 60).

Miroslav M. Kiš

References

[1]O. Horn Prouser, "The Truth About Women and Lying," *Journal for the Study of the Old Testament* 61 (1994) :15.

[2]Richard A. Freund, *Understanding Jewish Ethics,* 2 vols. (Lewiston, NY: Edwin Mellen, 1990), 1:81.

[3]Norman L. Geisler, *Ethics: Alternatives and Issues* (Grand Rapids, MI: Zondervan, 1971), 114-136.

[4]Lee Basham, "Why God Lied to me," Journal *of Religious Ethics* 30.2 (2002): 231-249.

[5]C.F. Keil and F. Dellitzsch, *1 Samuel,* Biblical Commentary on the Old Testament (Grand Rapids, MI: Eerdmans, 1960), 167, 168.

[6]Dietrich Bonhoeffer, *Ethics* (New York, NY: Macmillan, 1975), 367.

[7]Adam Clarke, *A Commentary and Critical Notes* (Nashville, TN: Abingdon, 1938), 257, 258.

[8]Walter C. Kaiser, *Toward Old Testament Ethics* (Grand Rapids, MI: Zondervan, 1983), 225, 226.

Prayers Found in the Bible

Abraham's prayer for Sodom	Gen 18:22, 33	Prayer for forgiveness	51; 130
Jacob's prayer at Penuel	Gen 32:9-12	Prayer of thanksgiving	65; 111; 136
Moses' prayer for Israel	Exod 32:31, 32	Prayer for help	66; 69; 88; 102;
Aaron's blessing	Num 6:24-26		140; 143
Moses' plea for sinful Israel	Num 14:13-19	Hezekiah's prayer for healing	Isa 38:10-20
Joshua's prayer after Ai	Josh 7:7-9	Jeremiah's complaint	Jer 20:7-18
Gideon's prayer for signs	Judg 6:36-39	Daniel's prayer of thanks	Dan 2:20-23
Hanna's prayer for a son	1 Sam 1:11	Daniel's prayer for Jerusalem	Dan 9:4-19
David's prayer of thanks	2 Sam 7:11-29	Jonah's prayer	Jonah 2:2-9
Solomon's prayer for wisdom	1 Kgs 3:6-9	Habakkuk's prayer	Hab 3:2-19
Solomon's dedication prayer	1 Kgs 8:23-61		
Elijah's prayer on Mt. Carmel	1 Kgs 18:36, 37	Mary's thanksgiving	Luke 1:46-55
Hezekiah's prayer for help	2 Kgs 19:15-19	Simon's prayer	Luke 2:29, 32
David's prayer for Solomon	1 Chron 29:10	Steven's prayer	Acts 7:59, 60
Ezra's confession of sin	Ezra 9:6-15	**Prayers of Jesus:**	
Nehemiah's prayer for Judah	Neh 1:5-11	Lord's Prayer	Matt 6:9-13
The people's confession of sin	Neh 9:5-37	In Gethsemane	Matt 26:36-44
Job's confession	Job 42:1-6	From the cross	Matt 27:46
Prayers in the Psalms:		At the raising of Lazarus	John 11:41, 42
Evening prayer	4	Facing death	John 12:27, 28
Morning prayer	5	The high-priestly prayer	John 17:1-25
The shepherd's prayer	3	**Doxologies:**	
Praise and worship	67; 92; 95-98;		Rom 16:25-27
	100; 145-150		1 Cor 13:14
			Eph 3:20, 21
Prayer for guidance	25		Heb 13:20, 21
Prayer for deliverance	40; 116		1 Pet 5:10, 11
Longing for God	27; 42; 63; 84		Jude 24, 25

DID THE MEDIUM AT EN-DOR REALLY BRING FORTH SAMUEL?

And the king said to her, "Do not be afraid; but what do you see?" And the woman said to Saul, "I see a divine being coming up out of the earth." And he said to her, "What is his form?" And she said, "An old man is coming up, and he is wrapped with a robe." And Saul knew that it was Samuel, and he bowed with his face to the ground and did homage. 1 Samuel 28:13, 14.

The narrative in 1 Samuel 28 is used by supporters of the immortal-soul theory to argue that Samuel appeared and spoke after his death, and therefore all humans are conscious after death. Historically the chapter has had two major interpretations:

1. The Prophet Samuel Really Appeared

This view appears first in the apocryphal book of Sirach 46:16-20 (c. 180 B.C.). Some saw Samuel as a disembodied soul, but Augustine (354-430) and others thought Samuel arrived as a resuscitated whole person, with a body like Jesus' resurrection body or Moses' body at Jesus' transfiguration.[1] So the belief that Samuel really appeared does not require a belief that he was only a disembodied soul or that all people are only disembodied souls after death.

Yet the argument that Samuel really appeared raises serious problems: Could mediumship really disturb the rest of God's faithful prophet? Would God send a prophetic message through a medium – a condemned source (Deut 18:10; Lev 20:6) – especially while refusing Saul guidance via approved methods (1 Sam 28:6)? Some see the medium as a fine example of women's ministry, "offering spiritual guidance and insight,"[2] but that interpretation would set a dangerous precedent of expecting divine wisdom through mediums today (See 1 Tim 4:1; 2 Thess 2:8-11).

2. Samuel Was Impersonated by a Demon

Tertullian (A.D. 155-220) and other Church Fathers taught that a demon or Satan impersonated Samuel so as to deceive Saul. This second view best fits the text.

We know from Scripture that Saul was vulnerable to the demonic (1 Sam 16:14-16, 23; 18:10; 19:9). Samuel warned him against the "sin of divination" or witchcraft (Heb. *qesem*, 1 Sam 15:23), yet Saul asked the medium to divine (Heb. *qasam,* 1 Sam 28:8); the word *qasam* is usually used in connection with pagan diviners (Num 22:7; Josh 13:22; 1 Sam 6:2).

Pagan practices at En-Dor – En-Dor was likely a Canaanite, not an Israelite, settlement (Josh 17:11-13), and recent archaeological discoveries show that the Canaanite religion involved ancestor worship, using rituals very similar to the one the woman performed for Saul. A Ugaritic tablet describes a ritual for conjuring up dead ancestors, including the recently deceased king, to bless the current king.[3] These ancestors, "the dead and deified kings of Ugarit,"[4] were believed to become divine beings in the underworld and so were called *'Elohim* — exactly the same word Saul's medium uses for the "gods" (KJV) she says are ascending from the ground (1 Sam 28:13).

> A demon or Satan impersonated Samuel so as to deceive Saul.

Many commentators miss that in Hebrew the medium uses the word *'Elohim* in the plural (matched by a plural participle, "they are ascending," 1 Sam 28:13). This plural construction is how polytheists speak (cf 4:8; 17:43), envisioning various gods. Saul misses her plural and focuses on Samuel: 'What does he look like?' The woman then copies his singular: 'An old man is coming up' (singular participle, 28:14). She tells Saul what he wants to hear, afraid because he has removed her fellow occult practitioners (28:3). The apparition she conjures up uses Yahweh's name seven times, but saying "Lord, Lord" does not prove anything; polytheists were tolerant of mixed religions (cf. Exod 32:4, 5).

The woman feeds Saul, earning approval from many commentators for kindness, yet the writer describes her killing the animal not with the verb "to butcher" (*tabach,* cf. 1 Sam 25:11), but "to slaughter for sacrifice" (*zabach*).[5] She performs a "cultic ritual slaughter."[6] Israel's past apostasy included eating sacrifices to the dead: they "ate and bowed down before these *'Elohim*" (Num 25:1-3; Ps 106:28), with disastrous results. So her seeming kindness actually leads Saul into an act of pagan worship. This may explain why at first he did not want to eat (28:23).

Saul's punishment is increased – This supposed "Samuel" massively increases Saul's punishment for old sins that were already dealt with. Saul's unauthorized sacrifice (1 Sam 13:10-14) and spoil-taking (15:13-35) had been punished by removing his kingship, but now "Samuel" adds that Saul will be given to the Philistines, as will Israel's army, and that tomorrow Saul and his sons will be "with me" (28:19). No new offences are mentioned (28:18), so why would God in fairness add to Saul's punishment? The message sounds calculated to burden Saul with guilt and fear, crushing any possible hope or repentance. The next day Saul commits suicide (31:4, 5). Does that message match God's character? Even the toughest divine rebukes imply a gospel of grace and hope through repentance.

> "God permitted the devil, to answer the design, to put on Samuel's shape, that those who would not *receive the love of the truth* might be *given up to strong delusions and believe a lie.* . . . That the devil, by the divine permission, should be able to personate Samuel is not strange, since he can *transform himself into an angel of light!* nor is it strange that he should be permitted to do it upon this occasion, that Saul might be driven to despair, by enquiring of the devil, since he would not, in a right manner, enquire of the Lord, by which he might have had comfort." (Matthew Henry's Bible Commentary on 1 Samuel 28:7-14 [online edition] http://blueletterbible.org)

Suspiciously, too, this "Samuel" quotes Samuel's words but never rebukes Saul for the "sin of divination" that the real Samuel warned about (1 Sam 15:23; cf. 28:8) and which proved a fatal sin for Saul (1 Chron 10:13, 14).

Inaccurate predictions – The woman's prediction also contains inaccuracies. Saul was not handed over to the Philistines, but committed suicide; and his body, though taken, was recovered by the inhabitants of Jabesh-Gilead (1 Sam 31:12, 13). Also, not all of Saul's sons died the next day; a few chapters later "Ish-Bosheth son of Saul" appears (2 Sam 2:8-10). By contrast, the real Samuel spoke Yahweh's word accurately (1 Sam 3:19-21).

Also, this "Samuel" said Saul and his sons would be "with me" (1 Sam 28:19); but where? What view of the afterlife puts a godless king and a godly prophet in the same place? Not the traditional teaching of heaven and hell; nor the consistent New Testament description of the grave and of heaven and hell. The medium would answer: in Sheol, the underworld where all souls go. Yet her worldview is not that of the Bible.

Neither Saul nor the woman saw the real Samuel – Some object that the text says "Saul knew that it was Samuel" (1 Sam 28:14, NIV). Yet Saul lay face-down, seeing nothing and relying on the medium's description. The word "know" (*yada*ᶜ) is used of perceptions (KJV, "perceived") or beliefs that can be wrong: e.g. in 1 Sam 4:6 the Philistines' *yada*ᶜ that a god has come into the Israelite camp, but it is in fact the ark.

What of the description that "the woman saw Samuel" (1 Sam 28:12)? No doubt she did envision Samuel but that does not prove he was there. The narrator reports that some Israelites "saw" from their point of view that "Saul and his sons were dead" (31:7), but in fact not all his sons died: the narrator himself carefully specifies how many (31:6). In a similar way the narrator seems to report from the woman's point

> # Only the Creator has the power to raise the dead.

of view what "Samuel said" to Saul (28:15, 16). Narrating a character's viewpoint is a common technique involving "the language of appearance."[7] The same technique is used to describe the Philistine god Dagon as a person: "and look, Dagon was fallen on his face" (5:4). Dagon is of course a lifeless stone idol, but the narrator imitates a Philistine point of view. The narrator's description of what the woman and Saul perceived is a technique of subtle suspense writing, letting readers feel the power of the deception until the many textual "warning lights" make us go back and read more carefully about how Saul was finally brought down.

Conclusion – According to Scripture, only the Creator has the power to raise the dead (John 11:25), and God was certainly not responding to the bidding of the medium of En-Dor, who was under the divine edict of death for practicing sorcery (Lev 20:27). The scene in 1 Samuel 28 dramatically depicts a Canaanite séance where a medium promises 'gods rising' from the underworld, but a demon impersonates Samuel to deceive Saul into feeling hopelessly guilty and giving up on Yahweh and on life. The devil is in the details.

Grenville J. R. Kent

References

[1]See Jude 9. Moses and Elijah were called "men" not spirits in Luke 9:28-33.

[2]John Goldingay, *Old Testament Theology,* 2 vols: (Downers Grove, IL: Inter-Varsity Press, 2003), 1:604.

[3]M. Dietrich, O. Lorenz, and J. Sammartin, eds., *Die Keilalphabetischen Texte aus Ugarit* (Neukirchen-Vluyn: Neukirchener Verlag, 1976), 1.161. See also Bill T. Arnold, "Religion in Ancient Israel," in David W. Baker and Bill T. Arnold (eds.), *The Face of Old Testament Studies: A Survey of Contemporary Approaches* (Grand Rapids, MI: Apollos, 1999), 415.

[4]Ibid., 1.39:5.

[5]F. Brown, S. Driver and C. Briggs, *The Brown-Driver-Briggs Hebrew and English Lexicon* (Peabody, MA: Hendrickson Publishers, 1999 [1906]), 257.

[6]J. Milgrom, "Profane Slaughter and a Formulaic Key to the Composition of Deuteronomy," *Hebrew Union College Annual* 47 (1976):1, 2; see also Pamela Tamarkin Reis, "Eating the Blood: Saul and the Witch of Endor," *Journal for the Study of the Old Testament* 73 (1997): 16.

[7]Basil F.C. Atkinson, *Life and Immortality: An Examination of the Nature and Meaning of Life and Death as They Are Revealed in the Scriptures* (Taunton, MA: Self-published; printed by Goodman and Sons, n.d.), 33.

The Canaanites in the Old Testament

Just as "Canaan" designated the whole western Palestinian area, so "Canaanite" described its pre-Israelite inhabitants without specifying race. Of the peoples who lived in Palestine the Amorites first appeared in the 2nd millennium B.C. as immigrants from Mesopotamia. Several Old Testament references seem to equate Amorite territory and the land of Canaan (Gen 12:5, 6; 15:18–21; 48:22), a tradition reflected in the 18th-century B.C. Alalakh tablets, which depicted "Amurru" as part of Syria-Palestine. The Tell el-Amarna texts (14th–13th centuries B.C.) indicate that the Amurru kingdom of the Lebanon region was monopolizing coastal trade and commerce, so references to the two peoples (Amorites and Canaanites) together in Moses' time and throughout the Late Bronze Age (c. 1550-1200 B.C.) are not surprising. The Israelite conquest of Palestine broke the power of many Canaanite and Amorite city-states, while the rise of a Philistine confederacy on the southern Palestinian coast restricted further the range of specifically Canaanite territory. (Adapted from W. E. Elwell and B. J. Beitzel, (1988). *Baker Encyclopedia of the Bible* [Grand Rapids, MI: Baker Book House, 1988], 406).

WHO INCITED DAVID TO TAKE A CENSUS OF ISRAEL?

Now again the anger of the LORD burned against Israel, and it incited David against them to say, "Go, number Israel and Judah." 2 Samuel 24:1.

Then Satan stood up against Israel and moved David to number Israel. 1 Chronicles 21:1.

The two accounts of David's census are often cited as the classic example of contradictions in parallel biblical passages. Why does the writer of Chronicles say that Satan moved David to number Israel when according to 2 Samuel it was God who incited David to do it? And why was it wrong to take a census?

Census taking in Israel – Census taking in Israel was not inherently evil. At the beginning of the forty-year wandering in the desert God said to Moses, "Take a census of all the congregation of the sons of Israel, by their families, by their fathers' households, according to the number of names, every male, head by head from twenty years old and upward" (Num 1:2, 3); and at the end of the wilderness wandering Moses was told to do the same (26:2). The second census revealed that the total of Israel's armed forces was less than it had been forty years earlier. At the same time, the census provided a useful basis for the distribution of the conquered land of Canaan.

David's reason for taking a census – If census taking was not wrong per se, why was Israel punished so severely when David took a census? According to 1 Chronicles 21:14 seventy thousand men died as a result of David's action. The answer is found in the chapters immediately preceding 1 Chronicles 21. These chapters record David's triumphs over his enemies. There we are told that David defeated the Philistines, the Moabites, the Ammonites, and the Syrians (chaps. 18-20). Flushed with success, David, it seems, grew too big in his own eyes; wanting to increase his army he needed to take a census. However, Joab, the commander-in-chief of David's army, realized this action was not wise and tried to dissuade David, "Why does my lord seek to do this thing? Why will he bring guilt upon Israel?" he asked (21:3). But David would not listen; "it was pride and ambition that prompted this action of the king" (PK 747). In spite of the fact that God gave David a final warning through the lips of Joab, the king was not to be deterred. God, therefore, was displeased with David and punished Israel.

Who incited David to take the census? – The originator of the census can be identified by referring to God's *permissive* will in the affairs of this world. We need to remember that according to Hebrew thinking, whatever God permits He commits. For example, God permitted Satan to afflict Job (Job 1:12); He allowed the hardening of Pharaoh's heart (Exod 7:13, 22; 8:15) but is said to have done so Himself (9:12; 10:1); He allowed

> Satan was responsible for *inciting* David to take the census.

the choice of Saul as king of Israel, though He knew Saul would fail. In the two parallel accounts in 2 Samuel 24 and 1 Chronicles 21, we see that (1) David was responsible in the sense that he *chose* to displease God by having the census; (2) Satan, the adversary of God and His people, was responsible for *inciting* David to take the census; and (3) God was responsible in that he *permitted* Satan to incite David and He *allowed* David to follow his ambition.

Conclusion – The two passages when viewed against the larger context of Scripture do not contradict but supplement each other; both accounts are true. In Hebrew thinking, what God permits He does; the freedom He gave Satan to incite David into sin and the freedom He gave David to choose to sin is ultimately attributed to God. God does not impel or instigate sinners to do evil, but He allows them to choose evil.

Samuel Koranteng-Pipim

The Bible is not too sacred and sublime to be opened daily and studied diligently.

AH 189

202

ARAUNAH OR ORNAN?

When the angel stretched out his hand toward Jerusalem to destroy it, the LORD relented from the calamity, and said to the angel who destroyed the people, "It is enough! Now relax your hand!" And the angel of the LORD was by the threshing floor of Araunah the Jebusite. 2 Samuel 24:16.

And God sent an angel to Jerusalem to destroy it; but as he was about to destroy *it*, the LORD saw and was sorry over the calamity, and said to the destroying angel, "It is enough; now relax your hand." And the angel of the LORD was standing by the threshing floor of Ornan the Jebusite. 1 Chronicles 21:15.

When David sinned by taking a census, God was displeased and sent a plague upon Israel in which seventy thousand people died. When the destroying angel came to Jerusalem, God relented and the angel who was destroying the people stopped at a Jebusite threshing floor. Because the books of Samuel and Chronicles give two different names for the owner of the threshing floor, the question is: At whose threshing floor did the angel stop? Was the Jebusite's name Araunah or Ornan?

The custom of two names – The question at whose threshing floor the

The name Araunah has been explained as the Hittite word for "freeman" or "noble." Others believe it derives from the Hurrian word for "lord." In 2 Samuel 24:16 the name is preceded by the definitive article and verse 23 can be translated as referring to "King Araunah." Hence "it has been conjectured that he was the last king of Jebusite Jerusalem" (J. D. Douglas, ed., The *Illustrated Bible Dictionary*, 3 vols. [Leicester, England: Inter-Varsity Press, 1980], s.v. "Araunah").

angel of the Lord appeared requires some analysis. Two names are given in the accounts, "Araunah the Jebusite" and "Ornan the Jebusite." First, we find many people in the Old Testament who were known by two different names – Abram/Abraham, Jacob/Israel, Jethro/Reuel, Joram/Jehoram, Joash/Jehoash, Jehoiachin/Jeconiah, etc. The same is true of personal names in ancient Egypt and Mesopotamia, e. g., the Assyrian king Tiglath-Pileser (2 Kgs 15:29) is called Pul in 1 Chronicles 5:26. At times, a second name was given when there was a change in one's personality, function, experience, or circumstances, e.g., Jacob ("supplanter") became Israel ("he perseveres with God") after his encounter with God at the Jabbok (Gen 32:28). Second, we need not be surprised that Araunah could be the same as Ornan. The original Hebrew alphabet consisted of consonants only; and the consonants for both names are almost the same – 'rn and 'rnn. Vowel signs were not introduced into the written text until almost a thousand years after Malachi, the last book of the Old Testament. The vowels and the endings may have been due simply to variants in pronunciation at the time the accounts were recorded. Both names are linguistically related and come from the same Hebrew root.

Samuel Koranteng-Pipim

As an educating power the Bible is of more value than the writings of all the philosophers of all ages. In its wide range of style and subjects there is something to interest and instruct every mind, to ennoble every interest. The light of revelation shines undimmed into the distant past, where human annals cast not a ray of light.

CSA 69

DID AHAZIAH BECOME KING IN THE TWELFTH OR ELEVENTH YEAR OF JORAM?

In the twelfth year of Joram the son of Ahab king of Israel, Ahaziah the son of Jehoram king of Judah began to reign. 2 Kings 8:25.

Now in the eleventh year of Joram, the son of Ahab, Ahaziah became king over Judah. 2 Kings 9:29.

The chronology of the kings during the divided monarchy can appear rather confusing at first. When trying to harmonize the apparently conflicting data, the following points need to be taken into consideration: (1) the reckoning for the beginning of a king's reign in Israel is given in relation to the reign of a king of Judah and vice versa, as can be seen from the two verses above; (2) the length of a king's reign can be affected by the custom of coregency, i.e., a king could appoint his son to be co-ruler long before he himself died; and (3) the use of the accession-year versus the non-accession-year system results in differences of one year depending on which system was used by which scribe and during which period.

> In the accession year system, the year in which a king came to the throne was not counted as the first year of a king's reign. His first year began on the first day of the New Year. Thus, depending on the time when the previous king died, an accession year could be as long as 11 months or as short as a few days or weeks. In the non-accession-year system the year in which a king came to the throne was counted as his first year. Israel mainly used the non-accession-year system while Judah employed the accession-year reckoning, except for a short period between Jehoram and Joash. (Cf. Edwin R. Thiele, *The Mysterious Numbers of the Hebrew Kings*, New Revised Edition [Grand Rapids, MI: Zondervan, 1983], 59).

Some interpreters of the Bible simply say that the difference between the twelfth and eleventh year is due to a scribal error and that the two cannot be reconciled. Others, who take the reliability of the Bible seriously, take into consideration that in Israel (2 Kgs 8:25) the non-accession-year reckoning was used while in Judah (2 Kgs 9:29) the reign of kings was based on the accession-year system, resulting in the difference of one year. Both 2 Kings 8:29 and 9:25 are correct in that they reflect different scribal traditions.

Martin G. Klingbeil

Kings of Ancient Israel and Judah

Israel			Judah		
B.C.			**B.C.**		
931-910	Jeroboam I	— 1 Kgs 12:20	931-913	Rehoboam	— 1 Kgs 12:1
910-909	Nadab	— 1 Kgs 15:25	913-911	Abijah	— 1 Kgs 15:1
909-886	Baasha	— 1 Kgs 15:33	911-870	Asa	— 1 Kgs 15:9
886-885	Elah	— 1 Kgs 16:8			
885	Zimri	— 1 Kgs 16:15			
885-874	Omri	— 1 Kgs 16:21			
874-853	Ahab	— 1 Kgs 16:29	870-848	Jehoshaphat	— 1 Kgs 22:41
853-852	Ahaziah	— 1 Kgs 22:51	848-841	Jehoram	— 2 Kgs 8:16
852-841	Joram	— 2 Kgs 1:17	841	Ahaziah	— 2 Kgs 8:25
841-814	Jehu	— 2 Kgs 9:3	841-835	Athaiahn (Queen)	— 2 Kgs 11:1
814-798	Jehoahaz	— 2 Kgs 13:1	835-796	Joash	— 2 Kgs 12:1
798-782	Jehoash	— 2 Kgs 13:10	796-767	Amaziah	— 2 Kgs 14:1
782-753	Jeroboam II	— 2 Kgs 14:23	767-740	Azariah (Uzziah)	— 2 Kgs 15:1
753	Zechariah	— 2 Kgs 15:8	740-732	Jotham	— 2 Kgs 15:32
752	Shallum	— 2 Kgs 15:13			
752-742	Menahem	— 2 Kgs 15:17			
742-740	Pekahiah	— 2 Kgs 15:23			
740-732	Pekah	— 2 Kgs 15:27	732-716	Ahaz	— 2 Kgs 16:1
732-722	Hoshea	— 2 Kgs 15:1	716-687	Hezekiah	— 2 Kgs 18:1
End of Israel—beginning of			687-643	Manasseh	— 2 Kgs 21:1
the Assyrian exile			643-641	Amon	— 2 Kgs 21:19
			641-609	Josiah	— 2 Kgs 22:1
			609	Jehoahaz	— 2 Kgs 23:1
			609-598	Jehoiakim	— 2 Kgs 23:36
			598	Jehoiachin	— 2 Kgs 24:8
			597-586	Zedekiah	— 2 Kgs 24:18
			Fall of Jerusalem—beginning		
			of the Babylonian exile		

HOW OLD WAS JEHOIACHIN WHEN HE BECAME KING?

Jehoiachin was eighteen years old when he became king, and he reigned three months in Jerusalem; and his mother's name *was* Nehushta the daughter of Elnathan of Jerusalem. 2 Kings 24:8.

Jehoiachin was eight years old when he became king, and he reigned three months and ten days in Jerusalem, and he did evil in the sight of the LORD. 2 Chronicles 36:9.

Both 2 Kings 24:8 and 2 Chronicles 36:9 tell the story of Jehoiachin's brief reign and his subsequent captivity in Babylon in an abbreviated and formulaic way. The formula is well known in biblical historiographical literature (e.g., 2 Kgs 18:2; 21:1; 22:1; etc.) and involves the age of the king at the beginning of his reign, the length of his reign, and the place where he reigned. Additionally, 2 Kings provides the name and origin of the king's mother.

However, while 2 Kings 24:8 gives Jehoiachin's age as eighteen, the parallel text in 2 Chronicles 36:9 states that he was only eight years. Evidently, there seems to be a contradiction in the biblical accounts. Extra-biblical data from the court of king Nebuchadnezzar, dated to the year 592 B.C., five years after the second fall of Jerusalem in 597 B.C., mention rations for King Jehoiachin of Judah and his five sons.[1] The contradiction between an eight-year-old Jehoiachin, who reigned three months in 597, and a father of five in 592 (having reached 13 years of age) is apparent.

A possible textual corruption – To solve this tension most commentators have suggested a scribal error in 2 Chronicles 36:9.[2] In this context it is important to remember that in Hebrew numbers are not represented by numerical signs but are written as individual words. For example, a literal translation of 2 Kings 24:8 should be "son of eight [and] ten year" whereas 2 Chronicles 36:9 would be "son of eight years." If the scribal-error solution is accepted, one would have to explain not *one* change but *two*, since 2 Chronicles 36:9 misses the Hebrew word for "ten," as well as the plural form of "years," whereas 2 Kings only includes the singular form of "year."

A proposed solution – However, there is another possible solution to this dilemma that does not propose a textual corruption but rather posits a coregency of Jehoiachin with his father Jehoiakim.[3] Based upon Thiele's basic premise of chronological reconstruction, the possibility of two distinct events in the life of Jehoiachin should be considered. According to this proposal, 2 Chronicles 36:9 describes the beginning of Jehoiachin's coregency with his father Jehoiakim, in the first full year of his father's reign in 608 BC, whereas 2 Kings 24:8 describes the beginning of his sole regency at the end of 598 BC, after his father's death. The difference in the duration of Jehoiachin's reign ("three months" *versus* "three months and ten days") could be explained in terms of a rough (or general) *versus* a more specific time reckoning. Taking all data into consideration this contextual explanation seems to be superior to the text-critical solution.

> "In some nations it was at certain periods quite the regular procedure for kings still ruling in the prime of their power to appoint their son as coregent. . . . In working out a correct chronology for a nation, the coregencies are of vital importance. Unless the coregencies are known, years that were overlapping might be made consecutive, causing the history of the nation to be stretched out beyond the actual years" (E. R. Thiele, *The Mysterious Numbers of the Hebrew Kings*, [Grand Rapids, MI: Zondervan, 1983], 46, 47).

Gerald A. Klingbeil

References

[1] J. B. Pritchard, ed., *Ancient Near Eastern Texts*, third edition (Princeton, NJ: Princeton University Press, 1968), 308.

[2] This proposal is also made by the critical textual notes in the *Biblia Hebraica Stuttgartensia*, which indicate that some manuscripts of the LXX, with the exception of Codex Vaticanus, translate here the Greek term for "eighteen."

[3] The following is based upon McFall's convincing and carefully argued reconstruction of the historical and biblical data, Leslie McFall, "Some Missing Coregencies in Thiele's Chronology," *Andrews University Seminary Studies* 30.1 (1992): 35-58.

DOES PROVERBS 8 REFER TO CHRIST?

The LORD possessed me at the beginning of His way, before His works of old. From everlasting I was established, from the beginning, from the earliest times of the earth. When there were no depths I was brought forth. Proverbs 8:22-24.

Throughout Christian history interpreters have identified wisdom in Proverbs 8 with Christ; but does this text really refer to the pre-incarnate Christ, or is wisdom here only a personification of a divine attribute?

Personification in Proverbs – The personification of the divine attribute of wisdom as a woman begins in chapter one: "Wisdom calls aloud outside; she raises her voice in the open squares" (1:20). In chapter three we are told "She is more precious than rubies' and "all her paths are peace" (3:15, 17). In chapter seven she is called a "sister" (7:4), and in chapter eight wisdom lives together with prudence, another personification (8:12). Personified wisdom is also the topic in Proverbs 9:1-5 in which she is compared to the woman Folly (Prov 9:13-18), the counterpart of the personification of wisdom. Her character is described as "loud, undisciplined and without knowledge" (v. 13).

The parallelism between the two women Wisdom and Folly is striking: (1) both have a house at the highest point of the city (Prov 9:3, 14); (2) both invite seekers to their homes (9:4, 16); (3) both offer food and water in their homes (9:5, 17); (4) both offer something more than a meal (9:11, 18). The important difference between the two is in the offer. Wisdom offers life; Folly, personified as a cult prostitute, robs men of their lives – her guests end up in the depth of Sheol (9:18). The two women represent two ways of life, two ways of living and dying. Neither of them refers to an actual person.

The Origin of Wisdom – In Proverbs 8 wisdom is also described as if it were a person. She is metaphorically described as God's "craftman" (8:30), suggesting that she was involved in the creation of the universe. By describing wisdom as a person, a very strong connection is made between her and God. Her origin is located in God Himself: "The Lord possessed [Hebrew qānah] me at the beginning of His ways" (v. 22), which the NIV translates as "The Lord brought me forth as the first of his works" (8:22). The verb *qānah*, translated "to possess" or "to bring forth," can be rendered in English as "he acquired, conceived, created me." The basic meaning of *qānah* seems to be "to possess" (Prov 4:5-7). One can acquire or possess something in different ways. One of them is through begetting (e.g., Gen 4:1). In Proverbs, the context seems to suggest the idea of conception. The phrase "at the beginning of his ways" indicates that, when God began to create, wisdom was already there.

> The two women Wisdom and Folly represent two ways of life, two ways of living and dying. Neither of them refers to an actual person.

"From everlasting I was established [*nasak*, "to pour out]" (Prov 8:23). The phrase "from everlasting" indicates that the action expressed by the verb took place in perpetuity, i.e. continuing forever. In that sense, the translation "from/since eternity" would be appropriate. In any case, contextually the phrase is referring to what was taking place before Creation. Although it may be possible to translate the verb *nasak* "to establish" (e.g., Ps 2:6), this usage is highly unlikely. If that translation were to be accepted it would state that God appointed wisdom from eternity, before the world began, to some specific function. We are not informed concerning the nature of that appointment. However, it is also possible that the Hebrew word is sakak, "to weave," rather than nasak "to establish."[1] The psalmist used that word to describe the process of gestation in his mother's womb (Ps 139:13). In that case Proverbs 8:23 would be describing the eternal process of gestation of wisdom within the Divine Being. It would be metaphorically describing divine wisdom as growing like an embryo within the mother. Wisdom is personified in Proverbs, but it is fundamentally a divine attribute; it belongs to God's being and is hidden within Him.

In verse 24, "when there were no depths I was brought forth," God's wisdom is described as coming into existence through birth; yet it was always part of God's being. The language employed throughout this passage is highly metaphorical, but the message is clear: Before God began His creative work, wisdom was already part of His being; but when God began to create, wisdom "was born" into the world. In other words, everything that came into existence was first conceived in God's mind. The implication is that through God's power wisdom took the concrete form of the realities that we observe today. Therefore, when we explore the natural world we are analyzing God's wisdom, because that wisdom determined not only the physical structure of the created world but also its functions.

In Proverbs 2:6, "For the LORD gives wisdom, from his mouth come knowledge and understanding," wisdom is identified as God speaking; wisdom proceeds from "His mouth"; wisdom is identified *as God's own activity,* not as an entity different from God.

Christ and Wisdom – In the early centuries of Christian history, Proverbs 8 was one of the most popular Old Testament passages utilized by the Church Fathers to refer to Christ.

Many have equated wisdom in this chapter with Jesus Christ. But because wisdom, as used in Proverbs, refers to a divine attribute, it is unlikely that in 8:22-31 it designates the pre-incarnated Christ. The New Testament stresses the religious significance of wisdom by referring to Christ as God's wisdom. Paul wrote: "Christ the power of God, and the wisdom of God" (1 Cor 1:24). While in the Old Testament divine wisdom was, to some extent, accessible through the created world, in the New Testament God's wisdom is revealed in the Person and work of our Lord. In Him "are hidden all the treasures of wisdom and knowledge" (Col 2:3). He in Himself is the

> Only by extracting Proverbs 8:22-31 from its surrounding context could anyone mistake the description of wisdom as a literal description of an actual existing person. The meaning of the passage is not that God literally procreated (or created, LXX) someone called Wisdom before he created anything else. The meaning is that God "had" wisdom and established it as foundational to the created order before he actually made anything in our physical universe. Proverbs 8:22-31 is essentially a more elaborate statement of Proverbs 3:19, 20 using the literary device of personification. (Robert M. Bowman, Jr., *Proverbs, Personification, and Christ,* http://www.forananswer.org/Top_JW/Bowman_prov8.htm. [accessed March 27, 2010].

wisdom of God. In this case wisdom is not a personified divine attribute but God Himself in human flesh. This wonderful wisdom was "God's secret wisdom, a wisdom that has been hidden and that God destined for our glory before time began" (1 Cor 2:7). By becoming flesh He brought life to repentant sinners. Such individuals are "in Christ Jesus, who has become for us wisdom from God—that is, our righteousness, holiness and redemption" (1 Cor 1:30). We appropriate that Wisdom of God in submission to God—in the fear of the Lord.

Conclusion – The most we can say is that the personified attribute of God's wisdom in the Old Testament seems to point, almost like a prophetic type, to the incarnated Wisdom of God in the Person of His Eternal Son. Without Him it is impossible to acquire true salvific wisdom. The most glorious revelation of God's wisdom is now located in the incarnation, death, resurrection, and mediation of our Lord. The revelation of divine wisdom is now uniquely present in a Person and not only in the objects of the natural world.

Ángel Manuel Rodríguez

References

[1]The way the verb is vocalized in Hebrew (*nissakati*) suggests that the verbal root was *nasak*; but there are problems with this verb and this has resulted in different attempts to explain its usage here. The verb means "to pour out," and possibly "anoint" (the pouring out of the oil on the person). It does not mean to "establish" or "appoint." The best contextual solution would be to vocalize it as coming from the verb *sakak* (*nesakkoti*), "to weave, form." For a more detailed discussion of the use of this verb in our passage, leading to the conclusion that *sakak* is the intended meaning, see Michael V. Fox, *Proverbs 1-9: A New Translation with Introduction and Commentary* (New York: Doubleday, 2000), 281.

People are guided to heaven more by footprints than by signposts.

Anonymous

DOES PROVERBS 31 ALLOW THE DRINKING OF ALCOHOLIC BEVERAGES?

Give strong drink to him who is perishing, and wine to him whose life is bitter. Let him drink and forget his poverty, and remember his trouble no more. Proverbs 31:6, 7.

Proverbs 31:6, 7 has long perplexed readers of the Old Testament since it appears not only to condone the use of "strong drink" (*shekar*) and "wine" (*yayin*) but actively to promote it.[1] A superficial reading of the text could give the impression that under certain circumstances it is permissible to drown one's troubles in alcohol.

A mother's counsel – Most scholars divide Proverbs 31 into two sections: Proverbs 31:1-9, which contains the wise counsel of king Lemuel's mother to her royal son, and Proverbs 31:10-31, which includes the hymn of the noble woman, organized as an acrostic poem, i.e., an alphabetic poem in which each verse begins with a different letter of the Hebrew alphabet. The main focus of the chapter, and of the book as a whole, is concerned with practical life choices, mostly presented in a didactic format of instruction.

The first prohibition for the king in verse 3 states that he is not to focus his energy solely on women, a concept easily understood by the ancient Israelites listening to this text, particularly in view of the prevalent practice of acquiring and maintaining a royal harem of wives and concubines. After all, the purpose of kingship was not to serve oneself (by maintaining a large harem), but to serve the people.

The prohibition against wine and strong drink – Neither wine nor strong drink is advisable for kings and rulers because these beverages would impair their remembrance of the law and consequently their ability to establish and execute justice (Prov 31:5). The perversion of justice is one of the major topics in Old Testament theology. Perverted justice or lack of justice is strongly rebuked by the prophets (Isa 1:17, 23; 5:7; Amos 5:7, 12; etc.), particularly when it concerns a king because he is the one who administers justice (2 Sam 8:15). So, anything that may cause him to pervert justice should be shunned by him like the plague, especially when his action will affect the poor, as suggested by Proverbs 31:5. This focus upon those in positions of authority who administer justice seems to be central to this first section of Proverbs 31.

The exception – In verse six the tone suddenly changes from the strong prohibition against wine and strong drink (Prov 31:3, 4) to an order that is quite the opposite, "Give strong drink to him who is perishing" (31:6; NKJV). The contrast is quite pronounced.

> A. No wine (*yayin*)... (31:4a)
>> B. . . . nor strong drink (*shekar*) to kings or leaders (31:4b)
>>> X. Since it will lead to injustice for the needy (31:5)
>> B'. Give (pl.) strong drink (*shekar*). . . (31:6a)
> A'. . . . and wine (*yayin*) to the perishing and bitter (31:6b)

This type of literary device is typical in biblical Hebrew and is called a chiasm, which basically means an inverted structure in which the center is considered to be of major importance.

The text under consideration refers to those who are "perishing" and those whose life is "bitter." Both terms in Hebrew denote a desperate and hopeless situation. The particular form of the Hebrew verb meaning "to perish" (*'abad*) can refer to a nation who has entirely lost all rationality (Deut 32:28) or to people lost in a foreign country (Isa 27:13) or to an animal that has wondered off the track and has gotten lost (1 Sam 9:20), which would ultimately lead to its death. Lions may perish if they do not eat (Job 4:11), as do human beings, though not always for that particular reason (Job 31:19). All of these examples paint a sad picture.

The Jews interpreted the text to refer to people who are being executed. "When one is led out to execution, he is given a goblet of wine containing frankincense, in order to benumb his senses, for it is written, *Give strong drink unto him that is ready to perish, and wine unto the bitter in soul*."[2]

An ironic counsel – "Give strong drink to him who is perishing, And wine to him whose life is bitter." What an ironic statement, considering the fact that the queen mother has just admonished her royal son not to touch wine or strong drink (Prov. 31:3, 4). In light of this categorical prohibition it seems hardly possible that in verse 6 the inspired writer now recommends alcoholic beverages to relieve common pain, stress, and tension. Samuel Bacchiocchi suggests that this imperative should be viewed as a conditional imperative. "The sense would then be, "'[If you are going to give alcoholic beverages to anyone, then] give strong drink to him who is perishing' to relieve him of his misery."[3] In that case verse 6 must be understood as a satirical and ironical statement.

An additional argument for the ironic understanding of the statement can be found in the larger context of the book of Proverbs as a whole. How does the rest of the book view the use of wine and strong drink? Proverbs 20:1 strongly discourages its use, since it makes the person indulging in it unwise, i.e., unfit to distinguish the real life issues and crucial choices of his life. It was already noted that Proverbs 31:4 strongly discourages its use. In Proverbs 4:17 wine is employed in a metaphorical way as a characteristic of the wicked. Proverbs 21:17 admonishes that the love of wine will result in poverty while Proverbs 23:20-31 repeatedly warns against its consumption and any communion with those indulging in it. As can be seen from the many references found in the book, Proverbs' perspective concerning wine and strong drink is entirely negative—the only exception being the statement in Prov. 31:6, 7, which in turn should be understood as an exercise in irony, employed by the wise mother of Lemuel to teach more effectively one of the main points of royal responsibility in ancient Israel: to judge fairly and to give a voice to those who are downtrodden and powerless. Both the immediate, as well as the larger context, suggest this interpretation, which is also in harmony with other scriptural advice concerning the use or abuse of alcohol.

> The text is an ironic statement which means, "If you are going to give alcoholic beverages to anyone, then give strong drink to him who is perishing to relieve him of his misery."

Gerald A. Klingbeil

References

[1]The translation of the term "strong drink" (*shekar*) follows the translation of the NKJV. Another translation of the term is "beer" (NIV). The term denotes an alcoholic beverage that is not based on grapes but most probably involved a fermentation process based upon grains. However, it should not be forgotten that this beverage is no distilled liquor. Distillation is a relatively late development in the history of alcoholic beverages.

[2]Talmud, Sanhedrin 43a.

[3]S. Bacchiocchi, *Wine in the Bible* (Berrien Springs, MI: Biblical Perspectives, 1989), 235.

DOES ISAIAH 7:14 REFER TO A VIRGIN OR A "YOUNG WOMAN"?

Therefore, the Lord Himself will give you a sign: Behold, a virgin will be with child and bear a son and she will call his name Immanuel. Isaiah 7:14.

The meaning of the Hebrew word for "virgin" (*almah*) is problematic. As the various Bible versions illustrate, the issue is whether the word refers to a young woman (RSV, NRSV, NJB, JPS) or to a virgin (KJV, NKJV, NIV, ASV, CEV).

The historical context – This promise of a son is found in the context of the Syro-Ephraimite crisis (734-733 B.C.). A coalition of the kings of Israel and Aram attempted to overthrow Ahaz, king of Judah, and replace him with Tabeel, a puppet ruler, who was amenable to their anti-Assyrian political plans. This overthrow posed a mortal threat to Judah and the Davidic dynasty, arousing great fear in the nation (Isa 7:2). God sent Isaiah and his son Shear-Jashub to allay Ahaz's fears – the threat will vanish. But there was also a challenge to place absolute faith in Yahweh and be entirely dependent on Him (7:4-9). This was really a confrontation between politics and religion. Ahaz could join the futile anti-Assyrian campaign or he could appeal to Assyria for protection. These were the political options. Isaiah held out a third option – rely on God only. This demand for faith is highlighted in verse 9b, "If you do not stand firm in your faith, you will not stand at all" (NIV). Such faith is an attitude of settled trust and confidence in God. Indeed, Shear-Jashub, whose name meant "a remnant shall return," was a visible exhortation for Ahaz to trust in God alone and form no political alliances. Furthermore, in verse 10, Ahaz was invited to ask for a sign of extraordinary magnitude from Yahweh as an authentication of Yahweh's prophecy in verses 4-9. His refusal, pious as it appears, indicates that he did not want to align himself with Yahweh. God refutes this obstinacy with the *almah* prophecy.

The meaning of the Hebrew word *almah* – Singular and plural forms of the Hebrew word *almah* are used nine times in the Old Testament (Gen 24:43; Exod 2:8; 1 Chron 15:20; Ps 68:25; Prov 30:19; Song 1:3; 6:8; Isa

7:14) but never in a context in which its exact meaning may be determined precisely. The Septuagint (LXX) translates ʿalmah with *parthenos*, the Greek word for "virgin," and the Latin Bible (Vulgate) uses *virgo*, which also means "virgin." Later Greek versions, however, use *neanis*, a "young woman, presumably of marriageable maturity. Both translations are possible. Interestingly, while Isaiah uses *bethulah*, the Hebrew word for "virgin," five times in his book (23:4, 12; 37:22; 47:1; 62:5), he does not use it in chapter 7.

The "virgin" identified – A survey of opinions indicates a wide variety of interpretations for ʿalmah: a cultic bride, the young queen or consort of the king, Zion, a symbol of Israel, the Immanuel clan, Isaiah's wife, an unidentified young woman, and the virgin Mary. In the immediate context, ʿalmah may refer to Isaiah's wife or a specific, though unidentified young woman, whose child will not grow up before God dispatches Judah's enemies (Isa 7:16). But as a telescoped prophecy extending beyond Ahaz's time, it may also refer to a virgin for two reasons: (1) The New Testament interpretation (Matt 1:22, 23) certainly takes it this way. Matthew quotes Isaiah 7:14 almost word for word, using the Greek word *parthenos* (virgin) to translate the Hebrew ʿalmah. He interprets Isaiah's prophecy as being fulfilled specifically in Mary – the definite article refers to a particular virgin – certainly a virgin who was "overshadowed" (Luke 1:35) by the Holy Spirit, and whose son was Immanuel "God with us" (Matt 1:18-21). (2) Ahaz was commanded to ask Yahweh for an extraordinary sign, something beyond human expectation, as a confirmation of God's faithfulness (Isa 7:10, 11). His refusal led to the prophecy of the ʿalmah giving birth. A young woman of marriageable age giving birth is not extraordinary, but a virgin doing so is beyond human expectation. This fits the prophetic scenario with Mary quite well.

> While Isaiah uses *bethulah*, the Hebrew word for "virgin," five times in his book, he does not use it in chapter 7.

Conclusion – It is reasonable to conclude, therefore, that the ʿalmah in Isaiah 7:14 refers to Isaiah's wife or a young woman in the immediate context, the time of Ahaz, and to a virgin in the extended context, the time of Jesus.

Kenneth Mulzac

DID THE HEBREWS BELIEVE THE EARTH HAD FOUR "CORNERS?"

And He will lift up a standard for the nations, and will assemble the banished ones of Israel, And will gather the dispersed of Judah from the four corners of the earth. Isaiah 11:12.

And you, son of man, thus says the Lord God to the land of Israel, "An end! The end is coming on the four corners of the land." Ezekiel 7:2.

There are only two texts that can be used in support of the idea that the earth has four corners – Isaiah 11:12 and Ezekiel 7:2. The two key Hebrew phrases in both texts contain the words: *'arba^c kanphot*—literally "four wings." It would be a mistake to assume that four literal 90-degree angled corners are intended. When the ancient Hebrews intended to describe an object with a literal 90-degree angled corner, such as the corner of a house (Job 1:19), the corner of a street (Prov 7:8) or the four corners of an altar (Exod 27:2), the common word that was employed was *pinnah*, "corner."

"The phrase, 'four corners,' as expressive of the whole earth or country, occurs in inscriptions of the Old Akkadian and Old Babylonian period (c. 2300 B.C.). (M. C. Tenney, ed., *The Zondervan Pictorial Encyclopedia of the Bible*, 5 vols. [Grand Rapids, MI: Zondervan, 1975], s. v. "Corners of the Earth").

Ancient Near Eastern idioms – A recent study shows that the idea that the earth had four literal corners did not exist in Mesopotamia either. Rather, they saw the earth as a circle; to indicate the four cardinal directions (north, south, east, and west), they used a symbol of four equal triangles within a circle, the bases of which formed a square within the circle; they sometimes described this as "The Circle of the Four Corners." Parallel expressions with the same meaning include "the Circle of the Four Winds," "The Circle of the Four Regions," or more simply, "The Circle of the

218

Winds."[1] It referred not to four corners of the earth, but to the directions of the four winds. "The four regions of the earth's surface are well known from historical inscriptions and literary texts, where the four regions comprise the entire earth's surface."[2] This latter understanding perfectly fits the context of Isaiah 11:12 and Ezekiel 7:2.

Randall W. Younker

References

[1]Wayne Horowitz, *Mesopotamian Cosmic Geography*, Mesopotamian Civilizations 8 (Winona Lake, IN: Eisenbrauns, 1998), 324, 325.

[2]Ibid., 204, 205.

A page from the Isaiah Scroll (ca. 125 B.C.) found at Qumran.

DOES *FOREVER* MEAN EVERLASTING PUNISHMENT?

It will not be quenched night or day; its smoke shall go up forever; from generation to generation it shall be desolate; none shall pass through it forever and ever. Isaiah 34:10.

This verse and its immediate context, especially "the day of the Lord's vengeance" in verse eight, seem to suggest that there is an ever-burning hell that has been established by God Himself, where He executes permanent judgment on the wicked and the unfaithful.

God's worldwide judgment against the nations – Isaiah 34 uses the destruction of Sennacherib's army in Hezekiah's days (Isaiah 37) as an illustration of God's worldwide judgment against the nations of this world (vv. 1-4). The prophet here vividly portrays the terrible fate of the wicked.

He beholds the great day of slaughter, when the wicked perish and their corpses are scattered about like those of Sennacherib's army after the visit of the destroying angel of the Lord (ch. 37:36). In the destruction of the Assyrian army he sees promise of the fate of all the hosts of evil that fight against God.[1]

From verse five on, Edom stands as a representative of all the nations, the name being almost symbolic for the whole world. The hatred that the world has for the people of God was exemplified by the nation of Edom (the descendents of Esau) in its hatred of Israel (see Num 20:18, 20; 1 Sam 14:47; 1 Kgs 11:14). Verses nine and ten describe what the land of Edom will be like after God's judgment has descended upon it; Edom's streams shall be turned into pitch and its soil into brimstone (v. 9). In other words, an awful judgment awaits those who trouble God's people.

The meaning of "forever" – The key to a correct understanding of the verse under investigation is the Hebrew term *ʿolam*, usually translated as "eternal" or "forever." The basic meaning of this term is "farthest or distant time;" it does not necessarily mean eternal, without end. Like other Hebrew words for time, *ʿolam* is closely linked to the occurrence of events and describes these events in relation to their duration. Most often it refers "to a future of limited duration, i.e. to conditions that will exist continuously throughout a limited period of time, often a single life span."[2] In other words, the meaning of *olam* is dependent on its subject. If the subject is God who is immortal (1 Tim 6:1), or something he has created to last forever (e.g., the earth has been established "forever," Ps 78:69; 104:5), then *olam* refers to a time without end. If, however, the subject is people, who do not have immortality, or things that are not created to last eternally, then *olam* refers to a limited time period. For example, the people were to believe Moses "forever" (Exod 19:9); the slave in Exodus 21:6 was to serve his master "forever;" and Samuel remained in the tabernacle "forever" (1 Sam 1:22). The meaning of "forever" is each time "as long as that person lives." In the case of Jonah, "forever" only lasted three days (Jonah 2:6)

> Just like the "eternal fire" that destroyed Sodom (Jude 7), the everlasting fire that will destroy the wicked and Satan in the final judgment will be of a limited duration, but its effect will be eternal.

According to Scripture, the redeemed will receive immortality (1 Cor 15:50-54) at the Second Advent. In Matthew 25:46, therefore, "eternal life" is life without end, whereas the "everlasting punishment" of the wicked or the "everlasting fire" in verse 41 is of a limited nature since the wicked do not have immortality. Just like the "eternal fire" that destroyed Sodom (Jude 7), the everlasting fire that will destroy the wicked and Satan in the final judgment will be of a limited duration but its effect will be eternal.

An eternally-burning hellfire is not biblical – In Isaiah 34:10, in the context of God's judgment against Edom, the prophet describes the land of Edom after the judgment of God: "From generation to generation it [the land of Edom] shall lie waste." The text does not deal with or provide support for the idea of an eternally-burning hellfire. The history of philosophy tells us that this idea actually originated with the Greeks, who first thought that *Hades* is the dwelling place of the dead and later added the idea that some needed to get their just punishment there in the afterlife, since they had not received it during their lifetime. This philosophy was later adopted by some Church Fathers and by the medieval Church who added further details such as purgatory. As a result many Christians believe in a place in the underworld where the wicked dead are being tortured continually.

221

The notion of an ever burning hell is not biblical. In addition to the linguistic evidence referred to above, a second key to a correct interpretation of Isaiah 34:10 is the character of God. Would a God who says in Ezekiel 18:23 that He has no pleasure in the death of the wicked find satisfaction in the perpetual torment of men, women, and children burning in the fires of hell? Does a God of mercy have a specific location in the universe where the wicked are being punished by dreadful and horrid pains forever and ever? There is no indication in Scripture that such a place exists or is being planned for the future. The biblical terms *sheol* (Heb.) and *Hades* (Gr.) are designations for the realm of the dead but not a place of torment for the wicked dead. When we take the biblical teaching of life after death into account that says that the dead are not in a state of consciousness and that there is no such thing as an immortal soul (Eccl 9:5.6; Ps 146:4), it should be clear that the idea of an ever burning hell contradicts the clear teaching of the Bible.

Winfried Vogel

References

[1]Francis D. Nichol, *The Seventh-day Adventist Bible Commentary*, 7 vols. (Washington, D.C.: Review and Herald, 1978), 4:230.

[2]Anthony Tomasino, "ᶜolam," *New International Dictionary of Old Testament Theology and Exegesis*, ed. Willem A. VanGemeren, 5 vols. (Grand Rapids, MI: Zondervan, 1997), 3:347.

God often comforts us, not by changing the circumstances of our lives, but by changing our attitude towards them.

Anonymous

DOES THE LORD CREATE EVIL?

The One forming light and creating darkness, causing well being and creating calamity; I am the LORD who does all these. Isaiah 45:7.

In the King James Version the text reads, "I form the light, and create darkness: I make peace, and create evil: I the LORD do all these things." The assertion in this text is so bold that the early Christian heretic Marcion used this text to prove that the God of the Old Testament is different from the God of the New. This passage and other texts (cf. Amos 3:6; Jer 18:11; Lam 3:38) seem to describe God as the author of evil. The problem is: how can a perfect and just God, who is upright and without injustice (Deut 32:4), who does not take pleasure in wickedness and in whom is found no evil (Ps 5:4), who has thoughts of peace and not of calamity (Jer 29:11), who is light and in whom is no darkness (1 John 1:5), and who cannot even be tempted by evil (Jas 1:13), be the author of evil?

God's Sovereignty – The context of this statement makes clear that God's ultimate sovereignty over this world and His people is affirmed. In His sovereignty, God used even the Persian king Cyrus as His servant to bring deliverance and judgment (Isa 45:1, 2). Thus, "light" and "darkness" here describe not so much the cycle of day and night but stand for "deliverance" and "judgment" through which salvation comes to the people of God. When God delivers His people, He can at the same time bring judgment and through it calamity on nations, as He did in the case of Babylon through Cyrus.

The meaning of "evil" – The Hebrew word for evil (ra^c) is used in different ways in the Bible. It can mean "evil" as in "the tree of the knowledge of good and evil" (Gen 2:9, 17). In other places it is translated as "disaster" (Jer 26:3, NIV), "ruin" (2 Sam 15:14, NIV), or "wickedness" (Gen 6:5, KJV). The context in Isaiah 45 indicates that the best translation may be "calamity" (NASB and NKJV) or "disaster" (NIV). Contextually, this verse is dealing with God's supreme sovereignty in judgment, deliverance, and His rule over the earth. Furthermore, it should be noted that the evil spoken of in this text (and in similar passages above) can refer to the evil of punishment or natural disaster and not necessarily to moral evil. God does not create the evil of sin. God is love (1 John 4: 8, 16). "Every good gift and every perfect gift is from above, and cometh down from the Father of lights, with whom is no variableness, neither shadow of turning" (Jas 1:17 KVJ).

God is not the author of evil – God is not the author or originator of evil. Such an act would be totally contradictory to His whole nature and character as revealed in Scripture. However, God is able to use things (even bad things) in the natural world for His own purposes, and He can use other people, such as King Cyrus who knew nothing as yet of the only true God, to accomplish His ultimate purpose to save. In biblical thinking any disaster falls

> In Hebrew thought God is commonly credited with doing what He does not prevent from happening.

within the sovereign will of God, even though God is not the author of that evil. In Hebrew thought, God is commonly credited with actively doing that which in Western thought we would say He permits or does not prevent from happening. If God allowed it, He "did" it, the biblical writers would say. God permits evil things, but He never promotes evil. God is responsible for creating moral beings with a free will and the possibility of its misuse, but He is not the author of evil. It is the moral creatures, with their power of free choice, who are responsible for sin and evil.

Frank M. Hasel

I find the doing of the will of God leaves me no time for disputing about His plans.

George MacDonald

WILL THERE BE DEATH IN THE NEW EARTH?

No longer will there be in it an infant *who lives but a few* days, or an old man who does not live out his days; For the youth will die at the age of one hundred and the one who does not reach the age of one hundred shall be *thought* accursed. Isa 65:20.

The problem with this text is our understanding of the context, Isaiah 65:17-25. The whole passage contains one of the most beloved descriptions of what life in the new earth will be like. God will create a new heavens and a new earth (v. 17). There will be no more weeping and crying there (v. 19). God's people will build houses and live in them; they will plant vineyards and eat their fruit (v. 21). Then there is the glorious climax, "'The wolf and the lamb shall graze together, and the lion shall eat straw like the ox; and dust shall be the serpent's food. They shall do no evil or harm in all My holy mountain,' says the LORD" (v. 25).

What troubles people about this text is the presence of death in paradise (v. 20). God's people will live long in this new earth, "as the days of a tree" (v. 22), but they will not live forever. How can this be harmonized with the "forever" of other biblical texts (Dan 7:18; Joel 3:20; Mic 4:5; 1 Thess 4:17; Rev 22:5)? The key to resolving this problem is to explore briefly the historical context in which the prophecy of Isaiah 65 was given.

The Babylonian exile and the return – The central theme of Isaiah through Malachi is the exile of God's people to Babylon, followed by their eventual return to the land promised to Abraham. This "Exile and Return Theme" is dominant in the writing of the prophets, whether they wrote before, during, or after the Exile. They prophesy that the return from Babylon would be accompanied by a threefold transformation of reality. In Ezekiel 36, for example, God planned to transform *human society* by restoring Israel to her land and by her witness to the nations (Ezek 36:24, 28, 33-36, see also Mic 4:1-5, Isa 2:2-5; 11:2-5). He would transform *human nature* with a new heart and a new spirit (Ezek 36:25-27; see also Jer 31:31-34; Joel 2:28, 29; Isa 35:5, 6). And He would eventually transform *the natural world* itself, banishing hunger and violence (Ezek 36:30, 35, see also Isa 11:6-9; 35:1, 2, 7; Ezek 47:1-12).

225

Unlike the Flood story and the Book of Revelation, in which the end of the world means the full, physical destruction of the planet, the end envisaged in the classical prophets would come within history and geography. God would intervene mightily within history to transform society, human nature, and the natural world. This end is usually described in the context of the exile to, and return from, Babylon.

The danger in this, is that later readers would try to universalize these early prophecies and expect *every* detail to be fulfilled at some time in the future. Instead we should allow that in the New Testament the picture in Isaiah 65 is a type of a much larger antitype.

"The failure of Israel made impossible the fulfillment of these prophecies according to the original intent. Nevertheless the purposes of Jehovah will move forward to their complete fulfillment (see PK 705, 706). There will be new heavens and a new earth, but the manner in which they will be ushered in is somewhat different now that the purposes of God, instead of being accomplished through Israel, the chosen nation, will be accomplished through the Christian church (see PK 713, 714)." (F. D. Nichol, ed., Seventh-day *Adventist Bible Commentary*, 4:332).

The meaning of "new heavens and a new earth" – Throughout Isaiah 56-66 the primary concern of these chapters is the restoration of Judah following the Babylonian captivity. Isaiah 65:20, therefore, needs to be understood in light of the triple transformation of reality that was promised to begin at the time when God's people would return from Babylon. This triple transformation would take place within history, within the time, place, and circumstances of the prophetic writers. Though the "new heavens and new earth" of Isaiah 65:17, at first glance, sound very much like Revelation 21:1, in which God destroys the earth before creating it anew, the peaceful conditions outlined in Isaiah 65 are more in harmony with life on this earth than with the eternal state of immortality. Death is still present (v. 20) in this "new" world.

The whole context of Isaiah 65:20 points to the restoration of Judah in Palestine, following the Exile, rather than to a renewal of the whole earth. While Isaiah 65:17 speaks about the creation of "new heavens and a new earth," the next verse confines this creation to "Jerusalem" and "her people." Isaiah 66, which again refers to the new heavens and a new earth (v.

226

22), describes God's servants as proclaiming His glory among the Gentiles and bringing back other Israelite brothers to Jerusalem (vv. 19, 20). This could have taken place only within the context of Old Testament history.

God's power in creating heaven and earth is repeatedly mentioned in Isaiah (37:16; 40:22; 42:5, 44:24; 45:18; etc.), and each time it is in the context of the salvation of His people from captivity. Furthermore, in Isaiah 51:16 the deliverance of the captives from Babylon (v. 11) is expressed metaphorically as planting the heavens and laying the foundations of the earth. Thus in Isaiah 65:17 the creation of "new heavens and a new earth" must in the first instance be understood figuratively and not literally. The book of Revelation, however, uses this language to describe the full renovation of the earth through re-creation as portrayed in Revelation 21 and 22.

Summary – Isaiah 65:20 is a "problem text" when read from a New Testament mind-set, but it makes perfect sense in the setting of what might have been after Judah's return from the Babylonian Exile. Although God would intervene in spectacular fashion, according to the prophets, the fullness of paradise would be restored only a little at a time. In the wake of Christ's first advent, the book of Revelation portrays a much more sudden picture of transformation at the End.

Jon K. Paulien

The Bible is its own expositor. One passage will prove to be a key that will unlock other passages, and in this way light will be shed upon the hidden meaning of the word.

CE 85

IS THE NEW COVENANT IN JEREMIAH REALLY NEW?

"Behold, days are coming," declares the LORD, "when I will make a new covenant with the house of Israel and with the house of Judah, not like the covenant which I made with their fathers in the day I took them by the hand to bring them out of the land of Egypt. . . . But this is the covenant which I will make with the house of Israel after those days," declares the LORD, "I will put My law within them, and on their heart I will write it; and I will be their God, and they shall be My people." Jeremiah 31:31-34.

Many Christians today distinguish between the "covenant of works" of the Old Testament or "old covenant" and the "covenant of grace" of the New Testament or "new covenant."[1] The two words *works* and *grace* indicate for many interpreters the radical distinction between two ways of salvation. But is this distinction warranted? Is there a radical difference between the old and new covenants with separate approaches to salvation?

The prophets and the new covenant – There is really only one covenant between God and man – the everlasting covenant, the covenant of grace. God has always had only one way of saving humanity—by grace. Jeremiah 31:31-34, which is repeated almost word for word in Hebrews 8, holds several key elements that emphasize lines of continuity between the old and new covenants. Before discussing these elements of continuity, it is important to recognize that although the "new covenant" is designated as "new" for the first time in Jeremiah 31:31, other prophets had already spoken before the time of Jeremiah about this new covenant (Hos 2:18-20). Mention of the new covenant also brings to mind the rich statements in the Old Testament about the new heart. For example, the Lord says, "I will give them a heart to know Me" (Jer 24:7) and "one heart and one way" (Jer 32:39). God will "take the heart of stone out of their flesh and give them a heart of flesh" (Ezek 11:19) and will give "a new heart" and "a new spirit" (Ezek 36:26). These statements remind us of the change that will take place when the new covenant comes into effect in the lives of human beings.

Continuity between the old and the new covenants – Comparisons between the "old covenant," which God made with ancient Israel on Mount

Sinai, and the "new covenant" indicate several lines of continuity.

1. *God is the same in both* – "I will make a covenant." It is always the saving God who initiates that which is new and seeks to bring salvation to those who distort His plan or who reject His great gift. It is for this reason that one can speak of the biblical God as the covenant-making God. The biblical God is the initiator of salvation.

2. *The partners are the same in both* – The new covenant is explicitly announced by the prophet as being made with "the house of Israel and the house of Judah," or simply with "the house of Israel" (see Jer 31:31, 33). Although some have taken this to mean that the "new covenant" was only for ancient Israel, in history this has not been the case. The antediluvian covenant was to save not only Noah and his family but all life through the ark. So also God's salvation was offered to Abraham and his seed "to be a blessing to all nations" (Gen 12:3).

> "When discussing old covenant/new covenant concepts, Paul often had in mind not two historical divisions of spiritual history represented by the Old and New Testaments, but rather two vastly different religious experiences" (Skip MacCarty, *In Granite or Ingrained?*, [Berrien Springs, MI: Andrews University Press], 81).

3. *The law in both covenants is the same* – The statement in the new covenant promise about God's law is also of pivotal significance. A common element in the prior covenants made with Adam, Abraham, and particularly in the covenant made with ancient Israel on Mount Sinai is also the law of God. God's law, appropriately called here in Jeremiah "my law" (Jer 31:33, cf. Ps 89:30; Isa 51:7; Jer 6:19; Ezek 22:26; Hos 8:12), was God's law at Sinai, written on tablets of stone (see Exod 24:12; 31:18; 34:1, 28). The tablets of stone were actually sometimes called "the covenant" (see 1 Kgs 8:21). This law of God is not faulty and was not done away with to be replaced by grace. God's law is immutable and eternal (Matt 5:17, 18).

4. *The Law within—written on hearts* – This is not exclusively a New Testament concept. After Moses repeats the law to the second generation of Israelites, he says "You shall love the LORD your God with all your heart and with all your soul and with all your might" (Deut 6:5; see also 30:6, 11-14). Other passages indicate that this is a complete internalization of God's law. Repeatedly we find that this is accomplished "with all your heart and soul"

(Deut 4:29; 6:5; 10:12; 11:13, 18; 13:3; 26:16; 30:2, 6, 10). The people are told to circumcise the foreskin of their hearts and be stiff-necked no longer (Deut 10:16).

This activity of God in writing His law upon the human heart is His marvelous work of grace within us. It is His work to write the law on the heart through His Holy Spirit. Thus the continuity between the members of the "old covenant" and "new covenant" community is not by blood or through physical descent from Abraham but through every person who chooses and allows God to write His law inwardly, making it part of the total will of the believer so that he or she may obey God by faith.

> "Under the new covenant, the conditions by which eternal life may be gained are the same as under the old—perfect obedience. Under the old covenant, there were many offenses of a daring, presumptuous character, for which there was no atonement specified by law. In the new and better covenant, Christ has fulfilled the law for the transgressors of law, if they receive Him by faith as a personal Saviour. 'As many as received *him,* to them gave he power to become the sons of God.' Mercy and forgiveness are the reward of all who come to Christ trusting in His merits to take away their sins. In the better covenant we are cleansed from sin by the blood of Christ (Letter 276, 1904, E. G. White, *Seventh-day Adventist Bible Commentary*, 7:931).

5. *"I will be their God and they will be my people"* – The purpose of covenanting is this: "I will be their God, and they shall be my people" (Jer 31:33; compare 7:23; 32:38). The Sinai covenant was described by the same formula (see Exod 6:7; Lev 26:12; Deut 26:16-19; etc). God's purpose for His people is that this promised relationship, so short-lived for ancient Israel, shall be renewed and restored and made permanent.

The new elements in the new covenant – In view of these points of continuity, what then is the difference between the old and the new covenants?

1. What was completely new in the new covenant was the confirmation and ratification of the covenant by the blood of Christ. The promise of the covenant remained unfulfilled until the coming of Jesus.

2. The Gentiles who formerly did not believe but who now accepted

the gospel were grafted in to the Israel of faith, a community open to all believers irrespective of their ethnic origin (Rom 11:13-24; Eph 2:12-19). Christ is mediating the "new covenant" (Heb 9:15) for all believers irrespective of whether they are Jews or Gentiles, male or female (Gal 3:28). The Old Testament covenant that was made with ethnic Israel is in the New Testament universalized for the whole human race.

The meaning of "old" and "new" covenant – In English the opposite of "new" is "old." The word "old" implies prior existence or continued usage for a long time. It also frequently designates something antiquated in the sense of something that has fallen into disuse or is out-of-date. We should be careful not to superimpose modern-day meanings upon biblical usage when it comes to understanding the intent, purpose, and design of biblical language.

> The "new covenant" is simply a "renewed" or "restored" covenant, now having characteristics not present in the same way or quality as before.

The term new, with regard to the "new covenant" in Jeremiah 31:31, is the Hebrew term *chadash*. This Hebrew term means: (1) "to renew" or "to restore"; and (2) something "new" that was not yet present in the same quality or way before. Reflecting both senses, the "new covenant" is simply a "renewed" or "restored" covenant, now having characteristics not present in the same way or quality as before. The apostle Paul in 2 Corinthians 3:6 suggests that the "new covenant" is a covenant of the Spirit, in contrast to the "old covenant," which was a written code: "We serve in newness of the Spirit and not in oldness of the letter" (Rom 7:6). What Paul seems to be emphasizing here is that the "written code" (2 Cor 3:6, RSV) is the letter of the law in the sense of that which is outside of the person and not yet written within. As long as the "written code" remains external and not written within by the Spirit, it could bring only condemnation. The law written within is the changing of the heart which saves. Here the Spirit sent by Jesus Christ gives life; He writes the law upon the heart and thus internalizes the law within the person. Thus the newness of the covenant is characterized most effectively by the word "better" in Hebrews 8:6.

Only one gospel – It should be emphasized that the New Testament does not preach a new gospel. Galatians 1:6-9 and Hebrews 4:2 make it abundantly clear that there is only one gospel. To make a radical distinction between the "old" and "new" covenants would be to create two separate methods of salvation, one through the law and the other through grace.

> The covenant that God made with His people at Sinai is to be our refuge and defense. . . . This covenant is of just as much force today as it was when the Lord made it with ancient Israel" (AG 142).

Paul forcefully argues in 2 Timothy 3:14, 15, "You, however, continue in the things you have learned and become convinced of, knowing from whom you have learned them, and that from childhood you have known the sacred writings which are able to give you the wisdom that leads to salvation through faith which is in Christ Jesus." The Scriptures to which Paul refers include the Old Testament. Thus the whole Bible is the basis for salvation (2 Tim 3:16).

Conclusion – The covenant that God offered to His people throughout history was the same everlasting covenant. The words "old" and "new," in relation to the covenants, refer to the responses and experiences of the people, not to different ways of God's plan of salvation. Jeremiah emphasizes that when a person lives the new covenant experience he or she has the law of God in his or her heart. The law is no longer just external, written on stone. And just as each person must experience God's covenant individually, internalizing it into one's heart and soul, so does that covenant become new with each new person and each new generation.

Michael G. Hasel

References

[1]This article is based on Gerhard F. Hasel and Michael G. Hasel, *The Promise: God's Everlasting Covenant* (Nampa, ID: Pacific Press, 2002); cf. M. G. Hasel, "Old and New: Continuity and Discontinuity in God's Everlasting Covenant," *Ministry* (March, 2007), 18-21, 23.

WAS THE PROPHECY AGAINST TYRE
ACTUALLY FULFILLED?

Therefore, thus says the Lord God, "Behold, I am against you, O Tyre, and I will bring up many nations against you, as the sea brings up its waves. And they will destroy the walls of Tyre and break down her towers; and I will scrape her debris from her and make her a bare rock. . . . You will be built no more." Ezekiel 26:3, 4, 14.

The basic problem with this text is this: If Ezekiel predicted that Tyre would be destroyed and never rebuilt again, why do we have a thriving modern city in Lebanon by that name? Was this prediction actually fulfilled?

The Literary Structure – The literary structure of Ezekiel 26:3-14, dealing with two different conquerors of Tyre (the "many nations" and "the army of Nebuchadnezzar"), is informative and helpful in understanding this prophecy. [1] Verses 3-6 and 12-14 deal with the many nations; verses 7-11 with Nebuchadnezzar.

Yahweh will bring up many nations like sea waves (v. 3)
> THEY will destroy walls and towers; rubble is scraped; Tyre is made a bare rock (v. 4)
> Tyre will be a place to spread fishnets, it will be plunder for the nations (pl.) (v. 5)
> Her settlements will be slain by the sword. THEY will know that I am Yahweh (v. 6)

>> Yahweh will bring Nebuchadnezzar with many people (v. 7
>> HE will ravage her settlements with the sword and lay siege to the city (v. 8)
>> HE will set up battering rams and will destroy Tyre's defenses (v. 9
>> HE will enter the gates of the city with wagons and chariots (v. 10)
>> HE will kill her people and break down her pillars (v. 11)

> THEY will plunder her wealth and destroy her walls and houses (v. 12)
> THEY will throw stones, timbers and rubble into the sea (v. 12)
I [God] will put an end to songs and music (v. 13)
I [God] will make you into a bare rock, a place to spread fishnets.
Tyre will never be rebuilt. "I the Lord have spoken." (v. 14)

233

The passage begins with Yahweh bringing "many nations" up against Tyre like sea waves. The plural used in verses 3-6 indicates that more than one nation would rise up against Tyre. In the center section Nebuchadnezzar appears. Here only the singular "he" is used. Then in verses 12-14 we come again to a general statement and the use of the plural followed by a reference to God as the ultimate one who causes the nations to bring judgment on Tyre.

Historical Fulfillment – Ancient Tyre consisted of "Old Tyre," which stood on the mainland and the island city about one-third of a mile (600 m) offshore. According to the Jewish historian Josephus, Nebuchadnezzar besieged Tyre for 13 years before the mainland city submitted to Babylonian rule. In 332, Alexander the Great laid siege to the island city for seven months and captured it only because he built a causeway to the island by scraping "Old Tyre" to bedrock and using the rubble to get out to the island, just as Ezekiel 26:4 and 12 describe. But this was not the end of the city according to Ezekiel. Ezekiel 26:3-6 predicts that many nations will come against Tyre

> Alexander the Great built a causeway to the island by scraping "Old Tyre" to bedrock.

like sea waves. Although verse 4 perfectly describes the actions of Alexander, it appears that we are dealing here with a literary structure that could include other conquerors besides Nebuchadnezzar and Alexander, both of whom fulfilled certain other aspects of the prophecy.

Subsequent nations continued to conquer Tyre (the Ptolemies, Seleucids, Romans, Arabs, Crusaders, Mamluk Muslims) like waves against the city harbor just as the Bible describes. In the nineteenth century there was nothing on the island city of Tyre except a place to cast nets. Even in the early 1900s, Hasting's *Dictionary of the Bible* referred to Tyre as "a stagnant village in a stagnant Turkey."[2]

The Modern City of Tyre – To refer to the modern city as a rebuilding of biblical Tyre is not valid for a number of reasons: First, the ancient city of Tyre was not rebuilt after the Mamluk conquest. We must remember that there were several "Tyres" even in ancient times. There was "Old Tyre" on the mainland, which was conquered by Nebuchadnezzar; then there was the island city that survived and continued to flourish until it was defeated by Alexander in the way described in Ezekiel. While a modern city may have been built around the ancient ruins of "Old Tyre," extending even out along the causeway, this was not the prominent ancient city that had national and international prominence and influence. The island city destroyed by Alexander remains uninhabited today except for fishermen who cast their nets there, as Ezekiel 26:14 predicted.

Second, from an archaeological and historical perspective, the ancient island city of Tyre is in ruins. It was destroyed by successive kingdoms just as the Bible describes. The same can be said for the city of Jericho. Four sites were called "Jericho" throughout history: (1) the Old Testament *tell* or mound, (2) the New Testament site of Herod's palace, (3) the Muslim city, and (4) the city today. While all bear the name "Jericho" it is clear from an archaeological standpoint that the ancient Old Testament *tell* or "mound of ruins" is precisely that today – a destroyed city that has not been rebuilt.

Conclusion – A careful analysis of Ezekiel 26:3-14 reveals the following: (1) The text does not say Nebuchadnezzar would conquer all of Tyre, i.e. the island city. It does specifically predict that Nebuchadnezzar would besiege the *mainland* city (v. 8-12). But Nebuchadnezzar was not completely successful in taking off its wealth in the spoils of war. Rather here the text moves back to plural pronouns indicating multiple nations accomplishing the economic devastation of Tyre. This is what Ezekiel 29:17, 18 implies. There is no contradiction.(2) Rubble from mainland Tyre would be put into the sea. This part of the prophecy was fulfilled in 332 BC by Alexander's army. (3) The total physical destruction of Tyre would be accomplished gradually by one nation after another. (4) In the end, Tyre would be destroyed down to bare rock and never rebuilt. The final destruction took place in AD 1291, almost two thousand years after Ezekiel was written by the Mamluks. The prophecy was ultimately fulfilled as indicated by Ezekiel.

Michael G. Hasel

"Modern-day Tyre is a fishing town with a harbor, built down the coast from the ancient site. Ancient Tyre is now a barren rock that the local fishermen use to spread their nets to dry, just as Ezekiel had said (verse 4, 14). Its once-imposing walls and gates are no more (verse 14), although the ancient causeway built by the Greek army still remains, like these other details, as a testimony to the specific fulfillment of Ezekiel's prophecy." (Randall Price, *The Stones Cry Out* [Eugene, OR: Harvest House, 1997], 255).

References

[1]See Paul D. Ferguson, "Tyre – Prophecy Fulfilled," *Bible and Spade* 19/2 (2006): 48-58.

[2]James Hasting's *Dictionary of the Bible* (Edinburgh: Clark, 1911), 825.

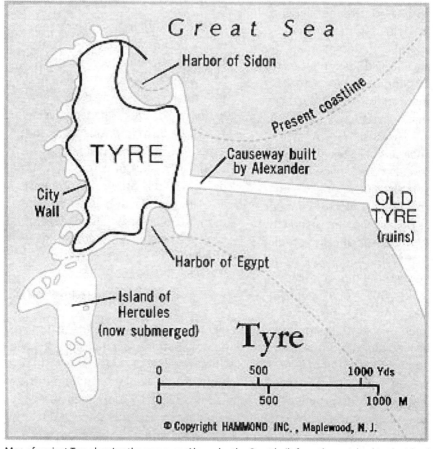

Map of ancient Tyre showing the causeway Alexander the Great built from the mainland to the island city.

WHO ARE GOG AND MAGOG IN PROPHECY?

And you, son of man, prophesy against Gog, and say, Thus says the Lord God, "Behold, I am against you, O Gog, prince of Rosh, Meshech, and Tubal; and I shall turn you around, drive you on, take you up from the remotest parts of the north, and bring you against the mountains of Israel. And I shall strike your bow from your left hand, and dash down your arrows from your right hand. You shall fall on the mountains of Israel, you and all your troops, and the peoples who are with you; I shall give you as food to every kind of predatory bird and beast of the field. You will fall on the open field; for it is I who have spoken," declares the Lord God. "And I shall send fire upon Magog and those who inhabit the coastlands in safety; and they will know that I am the LORD." Ezekiel 39:1-6.

The prophet Ezekiel, after the tragic fall of Jerusalem in 586 B.C., presents a unique prophecy concerning Gog that has stirred a bewildering number of different interpretations, e.g., *The New Scofield Bible* claims that Gog refers to Russia and a literal war in the time of the end.[1]

Summary of Ezekiel's prophecy – Sometime after Israel's return from the Assyrian-Babylonian captivity (Ezek 38:8, 16), from the far north (38:6, 15; 39:2), Gog and his allies will launch an attack against Israel, who is living securely in the Promised Land (38:8, 9, 12, 14). However, divine judgment (38:18-22; 39:2-6, 17, 20) will destroy Gog and his confederacy (38:22; 39:4, 11); thus Israel, (39:7, 22, 28) and all nations will know that Yahweh is God (38:16, 23; 39:6b, 7, 13b, 21, 28), and His holiness will be vindicated (38:16b, 23; 39:7, 27).

This prophecy was never fulfilled literally – On the basis of known historical documents, one can safely conclude that there is no event in the history of Israel that matches Ezekiel's prophecy.[2] If there is no historical fulfillment of an Old Testament prophecy, one must especially carefully study *if* and *how* the New Testament interprets such a prophecy. The principal thoughts of Ezekiel 38 and 39 can be summarized in two points: (1) a confederacy of enemies attacks God's people; and (2) God intervenes on behalf of His people.[3]

The New Testament apocalyptic fulfillment – Apart from the prophecy in Ezekiel, the only other place where reference is made to Gog and Magog together is in the last book of the Bible. Revelation 20:8-10 contains a description of a fulfillment of Ezekiel's prophecy on Gog and his antagonistic forces. The names of Gog and Magog are employed in Revelation to designate all the foes of God before their destruction. The consummation depicts the last judgment of God when Satan, the arch-enemy of God, is destroyed with all his allies, because he stood behind every rebellion in all of its forms from the very beginning. In Revelation 20, Gog and Magog are not a confederacy of one country or a group of several nations, but a universal symbol for all evil powers who oppose God.

> Gog, the prince of Rosh, Meshech and Tubal, has been identified with Gyges of Lydia, a certain Gaga in the Armana letters, Gagi a ruler of the city of Sabi, and with Gagi a Babylonian deity. "The linkage with peoples at the extremities of the known world (Ezek 38:5-6; cf. Rev 20:8) suggests that we are to regard them as eschatological figures rather than as a historically identifiable king, etc. This is the interpretation in Rev. 20:8 and rabbinic literature. The popular identification of Rosh with Russia, Meshech with Moscow and Tubal with Tobolski in Siberia has nothing to commend it from the standpoint of hermeneutics" (J. D. Douglas, et al, eds., *The New Bible Dictionary* [Wheaton, IL: Tyndale House, 1982], s.v. "Gog and Magog").

The definition of Gog and Magog becomes clear: At the end of time, Gog and Magog are not historical names, but a cipher, a code, or a symbol for the antagonistic forces of evil fighting against God, His people, and His law, which will be defeated during the final consummation of time; thus the prophecy about Gog and Magog no longer anticipates a literal war in Palestine against historical Israel as a nation. The main tone of Ezekiel's prophecy is comforting. It not only reveals the final defeat of God's enemies but primarily demonstrates God's wonderful love and care for His people, as well as His sovereignty, victory, greatness, and power.

Jiří Moskala

References

[1]For a detailed discussion of Ezekiel's prophecy on Gog and Magog, see Jiri Moskala, "Toward the Fulfillment of the Gog and Magog Prophecy of Ezekiel 38-39," *Journal of the Adventist Theological Society* 18.2 (2007): 243-273.

[2]It does not mean that this prophecy concerning Gog could not occur exactly as predicted; one can envision the historical, literal fulfillment of Gog's prophecy in the context of Messianic expectations and Israel's faithfulness to God's leadership and His word. Nevertheless, we need to recognize that many Old Testament classical prophecies were conditional, and because "the conditions were never met, the predictions were not fulfilled in literal Israel" (*Seventh-day Adventist Bible Commentary*, 4:709). For the detailed ideal scenario of what would have happened to Israel, Jerusalem, and the temple if they had been faithful to God, see Richard M. Davidson, "Interpreting Old Testament Prophecy," *Understanding Scripture: An Adventist Approach*, Biblical Research Institute Studies, vol. 1, ed. George W. Reid (Silver Spring, MD: Biblical Research Institute, General Conference of Seventh-day Adventists, 2006), 193-200.

[3]On how to interpret classical and apocalyptic prophecies and how to apply typological principles, see Davidson, "Interpreting Old Testament Prophecy," 183-204.

A BIT OF THE BOOK

A bit of the Book in the morning,
To order my onward way,
A bit of the Book in the evening,
To hallow the end of the day.

Margaret E. Sangster

WHY SHOULD THE SEVEN TIMES IN DANIEL 4 NOT BE INTERPRETED WITH THE YEAR-DAY PRINCIPLE?

This is the interpretation, O king, and this is the decree of the Most High, which has come upon my lord the king: that you be driven away from mankind, and your dwelling place be with the beasts of the field, and you be given grass to eat like cattle and be drenched with the dew of heaven; and seven periods of time will pass over you, until you recognize that the Most High is ruler over the realm of mankind, and bestows it on whomever He wishes. Daniel 4: 24, 25.

Daniel chapter 4 contains one of the most remarkable stories in the Bible. It is a public testimony by one of the greatest kings of ancient times, telling of his pride, humiliation, and ultimate conversion to the king of heaven. Nebuchadnezzar's life, prior to this event, was one long success story. By military might he had subdued all the surrounding nations; and at his feet bowed the representatives of all nations. But at the height of his power God brought him low.

"Seven periods of time" refer to seven literal years – "Seven periods of time will pass over you." The Aramaic word ʿiddan "time," which appears thirteen times in Daniel, can refer to "time" in general as in 2:8, "I know for certain that you are bargaining for time," to a specific point of time as in 3:5 "at the moment (ʿiddan) you hear the sound of the horn," or to a certain number of years, as in 7:25, "they will be given into his hand for a time, times, and half a time," i.e., three and a half prophetic years, as a comparison with Revelation 12:6 and 14 indicates. In Daniel 4:16, 23, 25, and 32 the "seven times," however, refers to seven literal years in the life of the king.

Reason why the year-day principle is not used – The reason the year-day principle is not used in this chapter is the fact that Daniel 4 is a historical chapter, not an apocalyptic one as are chapters 7-12. Daniel clearly says that the prophecy was fulfilled upon Nebuchadnezzar, "All *this* happened to Nebuchadnezzar the king" (4:28). Furthermore, twelve months later after Nebuchadnezzar had boasted, "Is this not Babylon the great, which I myself have built" (4:30) we are told in verse 33, "Immediately the word concerning Nebuchadnezzar was fulfilled; and he was driven away from mankind and began eating grass like cattle, and his body was drenched with the dew of heaven, until his hair had grown like eagles' *feathers* and his nails like birds' *claws*." In the fulfillment of the prophecy "when Nebuchadnezzar glorified himself, and did not give praise to God, he was made an example before the world of how God regards this spirit of self exaltation" (RH June 18, 1889). In verse 34 we have the end of the "seven periods

> The reason the year-day principle is not used in this chapter is the fact that Daniel 4 is a historical chapter, not an apocalyptic one.

of times" when Nebuchadnezzar was restored to his kingdom, indicating that the prophecy was fulfilled in his lifetime.

Summary – there is no indication in the text that the seven times of Daniel 4:25 refer to any time period other than the seven years of Nebuchadnezzar's insanity. Daniel 4 is a story of warning to us all: if we make our happiness depend on anything less than heaven, we invite destruction.

Gerhard Pfandl

A portion of the Ishtar Gate from Babylon. The tiles were taken from Babylon and reassembled in the Pergamon Museum in Berlin.

DOES THE LITTLE HORN COME OUT OF ONE OF THE GOAT'S FOUR HORNS OR FROM THE FOUR WINDS?

Then the male goat magnified *himself* exceedingly. But as soon as he was mighty, the large horn was broken; and in its place there came up four conspicuous *horns* toward the four winds of heaven. And out of one of them came forth a rather small horn which grew exceedingly great toward the south, toward the east, and toward the Beautiful *Land*. Daniel 8:8, 9.

In the vision in Daniel 8, the prophet sees a ram with two horns and a male goat with a large horn between his eyes in mortal combat (vv. 3-7). In verse 20 he is told that the ram is a symbol for Medo-Persia and the male goat a symbol for Greece. The large horn, the angel explains, represents the first king, i.e., Alexander the Great. Daniel then sees the large horn being broken and four horns taking its place. From history we know that after the death of Alexander the Great, the Grecian Empire was divided up by Alexander's generals (the four horns) into four parts. Following the appearance of the four horns, a small horn comes on the scene. The question is from where does this little horn come?

Like most commentators on Daniel, Seventh-day Adventist interpreters have traditionally seen the little horn coming out of one of the four horns of the male goat. In recent decades, however, most Adventist interpreters have opted for the four winds as the origin of the little horn. Since the little horn is not attached to an animal, the question is how can a horn by itself represent a political power on the world stage? While a horn by itself is certainly unusual, it is not a singular occurrence. In Zechariah 1:18, the prophet sees in vision four unattached horns that represent the political powers that "scattered Judah, Israel, and Jerusalem" (v. 19). Thus, for the little horn in Daniel 8 to come out of one of the four winds is scripturally possible.

The origin of the little horn from the four winds – The evidence for the little horn's appearance from one of the four winds is as follows:

First, the phrase "the four winds of heaven" in Daniel 8:8 is the nearest possible antecedent to "out of one of them" in verse 9, indicating that the little horn comes from one the four winds of heaven, which is a metaphor for the four cardinal directions of the compass (Jer 49:36; Zech 2:6).

Second, the structural arrangement of the vision report in Daniel 8 places the horn on the same level as the previous two animals. The vision consists of three main parts: the description of the ram (vv. 3-4), the goat (vv. 5-8), and the little horn (vv. 9-11). Each part shows the same pattern of introduction and movement, resulting in absolute power and self-magnification, followed by a downfall. In each of the initial statements, the main actor (ram, goat, or little horn) is introduced in relation to a geographic term or location and its first activity is described as a movement in a geographic direction. Such a pattern requires that "one of them" refers to one of the four winds of heaven.

> "The little horn, we are told, is to come out of one of the four winds of heaven (vs. 8). Which wind it is, is immediately indicated: he will wax great toward the south, east, and toward Palestine. To do this, he will have to start in the north and west." (A. E. Bloomfield, *The End of Days* [Minneapolis, MN: Bethany Fellowship, Inc., 1966], 165).

Third, the parallel order of the protagonists in the visions of Daniel 7 and Daniel 8 does not allow for a sequential connection between the four horns of the male goat in 8:8 and the horn in 8:9. The bear-like beast (two sides, three ribs in its mouth, devours much flesh; 7:5) and the ram (two horns, butting in three directions, no other beast could defy him; 8:3-4) represent the same kingdom – Medo Persia. The leopard-like beast (four wings, four heads; 7:6) and the male goat (flies without touching ground, four horns; 8:5, 8) also represent one and the same kingdom – Greece. An equivalent animal to the fourth beast in Daniel 7 does not appear in Daniel 8. Because the little horn in Daniel 7 originates from the fourth beast (Rome) and the fourth beast does not refer to the same power as the male goat in Daniel 8, the little horn in Daniel 8 cannot come from one of the horns of the male goat (Greece). Rather the starting point of its expansion is one of the four winds of heaven.

Finally, the Hebrew verb *yatza'*, "come forth," in Daniel 8:9 is frequently used to describe the activity of movement in reference to location, often in a military sense, which parallels the verbs used for the activities of the ram and the male goat. *Yatza'* is not used to describe the growing of a horn, an activity usually designated by *'alah*, "come up" (cf. 8:3, 8).

Conclusion – The grammatical construction of verses 8 and 9, the structural arrangement in the vision of Daniel 8, and the parallelism between chapters 7 and 8 in the book of Daniel preclude the interpretation that the little horn in Daniel 8 comes out of one of the four horns of the male goat. Rather, the little horn comes from one of the directions of the compass, i.e., from the west.

Martin Pröbstle

Messianic Prophecies

The Messiah was to:
- Be born in Bethlehem — Micah 5:2, Matthew 2:1; Luke 2:4-7
- Be born of a virgin — Isaiah 7:14; Matthew 1:21-23
- Be a descendant of Abraham — Genesis 12:1-3; 22:18; Matthew 1:1; Galatians 3:16
- Be of the tribe of Judah — Genesis 49:10; Luke 3:23, 33; Hebrews 7:14
- Be of the house of David — 2 Samuel 7:12-16; Matthew 1:1
- Be taken to Egypt — Hosea 11:1; Matthew 2:14, 15
- Be heralded by a messenger of the Lord — Isaiah 40:3-5; Matthew 3:1-3
- Be anointed by the Holy Spirit — Isaiah 11:2; Matthew 3:16, 17
- Enter Jerusalem as a king on a donkey — Zechariah 9:9; Matthew 21:4-9
- Be rejected by the Jews — Psalm 118:22; 1 Peter 2:7
- Die a humiliating death (Psalm 22; Isaiah 53) involving:
  - rejection — Isaiah 53:3; John 1:10, 11; 7:5,48
  - betrayal by a friend — Psalm 41:9; Luke 22:3, 4; John 13:18
  - being sold for 30 pieces of silver — Zechariah 11:12; Matthew 26:14, 15
  - being silent before His accusers — Isaiah 53:7; Matthew 27:12-14
  - being mocked — Psalm 22:7, 8; Matthew 27:31
  - being beaten — Isaiah 52:14; Matthew 27:26
  - being spit upon — Isaiah 50:6; Matthew 27:30
  - having His hands and feet pierced — Psalm 22:16; Matthew 27:31
  - being crucified with thieves — Isaiah 53:12; Matthew 27:38
  - praying for His persecutors — Isaiah 53:12; Luke 23:34
  - being pierced in His side — Zechariah 12:10; John 19:34
  - being given gall and vinegar to drink — Psalm 69:21, Matthew 27:34, Luke 23:36
  - no broken bones — Psalm 34:20; John 19:32-36
  - being buried in a rich man's tomb — Isaiah 53:9; Matthew 27:57-60
  - casting lots for His garments — Psalm 22:18; John 19:23, 24
- Rise from the dead — Psalm 16:10; Mark 16:6; Acts 2:31
- Ascend into Heaven — Psalm 68:18; Acts 1:9
- Sit down at the right hand of God — Psalm 110:1; Hebrews 1:3

WHO IS THE LITTLE HORN IN DANIEL 8?

Then the male goat magnified *himself* exceedingly. But as soon as he was mighty, the large horn was broken; and in its place there came up four conspicuous *horns* toward the four winds of heaven. And out of one of them came forth a rather small horn which grew exceedingly great toward the south, toward the east, and toward the Beautiful *Land*. Daniel 8:8, 9.

The debate about the identity of the little horn power has a long history. Most recent interpreters have settled on the Syrian king Antiochus IV Epiphanes (175-164 B.C.) who persecuted the Jews and desecrated the temple in Jerusalem. Others identify the little horn with the Roman Empire or the papacy. Among Seventh-day Adventists, two views can be found. Some believe that just as the little horn in Daniel 7 represents the papacy, so the little horn in Daniel 8 is also a symbol only of the papacy.[1] Others consider the little horn in Daniel 8 as a symbol of both pagan and papal Rome.[2]

The little horn is a political power – The little horn in Daniel 8, according to most Adventist interpreters, first represents imperial Rome. It "grew exceedingly great toward the south [Egypt], toward the east [the Seleucid Empire], and toward the Glorious *Land* [Palestine]" (8:9). During the first century B.C., imperial Rome succeeded in establishing its supremacy over every kingdom in the eastern half of the Mediterranean world – Syria became a Roman province in 64 B.C., Palestine in 63 B.C., and Egypt in 30 B.C. That it "grew up to the host of heaven" and "cast down some of the host and some of the stars to the ground" (8:10) seems to be a reference to its warring against the Jewish people and the early Christians.[3]

The little horn is a religious power – The little horn in Daniel 8 is not only a political power but also a religious power, for it is not only portrayed with military terminology but also in priestly and religious terms, acting like a priest and a god (8:11, 12). The horn shows an intense interest in worship that none of the previous powers exhibits. It interferes with the worship and priestly function of the divine commander of the host (8:11; cf. Josh 5:13-15) and takes over His rights. It removes "the daily" (Heb. *tamid*), *the* regular sanctuary service, from the divine commander, only to put itself in charge over it. Since the agent of the sanctuary activity (*tamid*) is a priest, often the high priest, the horn acts as a (high) priest and commands its own host which it set up over "the daily" (Dan 8:11, 12).

Daniel 8:23-25 describes the horn as a powerful king in wisdom terminology: it understands riddles, has success, and exhibits insight. While elsewhere in Daniel, wisdom terminology is used exclusively for God and those upon whom He bestows it, the king's wisdom is intentionally contrasted to divine wisdom. The blasphemous king is typified as a pious evil one.

In sum, the little horn acts as another prince of the host that wages a religious war against the divine priest and His host. The little horn appears to be an earthly instrument of Satan; therefore, it is said to be "mighty, but not by his *own* power" (Dan 8:24), and its activity becomes indicative of a cosmic war that is fought on two levels, the earthly and the heavenly.

> **The "Daily"** – The term "daily" (Heb. *tamid*) refers to Christ's continual priestly mediation in the heavenly sanctuary (Heb 7:25; 8:1, 2), inasmuch as the word "daily" appears in connection with the sanctuary. And the "taking away of the daily" by the little horn (papal Rome) "represents the introduction of such papal innovations as the mediating priesthood, the sacrifice of the mass, the confessional, and the worship of Mary, by which it has successfully taken away knowledge of, and reliance upon, the continual ministry of Christ in the heavenly sanctuary, and rendered that ministry inoperative in the lives of millions of professed Christians" (*Questions on Doctrine*, 255-257).

The little horn in history – The little horn does not come from one of the goat's four horns (i.e., from one of the Greek kingdoms that followed the break-up of Alexander's empire)[4] but functions on the same level as the ram (Medo-Persia) and the he-goat (Greece) and, therefore, must historically be identified as Rome, which followed the kingdoms of Medo-Persia (Dan 8:20) and Greece (8:21). Thus, the horn symbol represents either imperial Rome (8:9, 10) as well as papal Rome (8:11, 12), or papal Rome only. The focus of the vision, however, is on papal Rome and its religious war.

Contrary to popular opinion, the little horn cannot refer to Antiochus IV in the second century B.C., for he was part of the Seleucid kingdom represented by one of the four horns in 8:8. There are other reasons as well why the little horn refers to Rome and not to Antiochus IV Epiphanes: (1) The growth and self-magnification of the horn is much greater than that of the previous powers. Antiochus IV was never greater than Greece or Medo-Persia, but Rome was. (2) The temporal sequence of the kingdoms in Daniel 7 and 8 shows that the power symbolized by the little horn should originate from imperial Rome (the fourth animal in Dan 7)[5] and reach the end time. Because the term "vision" in 8:13 refers to the entire vision in 8:3-11 (see 8:1, 2, 13, 15), the 2300 evenings and mornings in 8:14 have to be understood as covering the time span from Medo-Persia to the end time. (3) Striking similarities show that the "horn" in Daniel 8 and the one in Daniel 7 represent the same power (see box). Because in Daniel 7 the horn and its characteristics clearly point to the Roman Church, so the horn symbol in Daniel 8 must also.[6] (4) Jesus suggested, in His time, that the

Parallels between the little horns in Daniel 7 and 8

1. Both receive the same name – 7:8; 8:9
2. Both are little in the beginning – 7:8; 8:9
3. Both become great later on – 7:20; 8:9-11
4. Both are persecuting powers – 7:21, 25; 8:10, 24
5. Both are self-exalting and blasphemous – 7:8, 20, 25; 8:10, 11, 25
6. Both oppose God – 7:8, 11, 20, 25; 8:11, 12, 25
7. Both target God's people – 7:25; 8:10, 24
8. Both have aspects of their activity delineated by prophetic time – 7:25; 8:13, 14
9. Both extend until the time of the end – 7:25-27; 8:17, 19
10. Both are supernaturally destroyed – 7:11, 26; 8:25

abomination of desolation was still future (Matt 24:15; Dan 9:27); He did not consider Antiochus to be the desolator mentioned in Daniel.[7]

Martin Pröbstle

References

[1] For the following reasons some believe that the little horn in Daniel 8 is a symbol only of the papacy. First, using the same symbol of a "small horn" in a vision that is structurally and thematically closely linked to the vision in Daniel 7 suggests that the horn in Daniel 8 represents the same historic entity as the horn in Daniel 7. This is regarded as a consistent symbolic interpretation. Second, the vision in Daniel 8 shows an increasingly prominent cultic focus so that, when the horn appears, terminology related to the sanctuary is used: "The beauty" against which the little horn grew (8:9) points to such a connotation because the term is closely connected to the sanctuary (see the phrase "the beautiful Holy Mountain" in 11:45; cf. Isa 11:9). In Daniel 7 such a targeting of the sanctuary is described only for the little horn, which represents papal Rome. Third, the vision's interpretation in Daniel 8:23-25 mentions a king, who, like the horn in the vision, attacks both the holy people and God, activities that represent papal Rome. Nothing in 8:23-25 seems to be interpretable as pagan Rome. According to this view, the vision in Daniel 8 seems to emphasize that the little horn is different from the previous two political powers. The absence of the fourth beast of Daniel 7 in this vision is to keep the attention of the readers solely on the ram, the goat, and especially the religious horn power. See Martin Pröbstle, "Truth and Terror: A Text-Oriented Analysis of Daniel 8:9-14" (Ph.D. dissertation, Andrews University, 2006), pp. 623, 624; cf. Jacques B. Doukhan, *Daniel: The Vision of the End* (Berrien Springs, MI: Andrews University Press, 1987), pp. 23-25, 28.

[2] Gerhard F. Hasel, "The 'Little Horn,' the Heavenly Sanctuary, and the Time of the End: A Study of Daniel 8:9-14," *Symposium on Daniel*, Daniel and Revelation Committee Series, ed. Frank B Holbrook (Washington D.C.: Biblical Research Institute, 1986), 378-461; C. Mervyn Maxwell, *God Cares*, 2 vols. (Nampa, ID: Pacific Press, 1981), 155-189.

[3] Maxwell, 160, 161.

[4] See the article "Does the Little Horn Come out of One of the Goat's Four Horns or from the Four Winds"? by M. Pröbstle in this volume.

[5] In Daniel 7 the little horn comes out of the fourth beast, which represents Rome, and continues for 1260 years (Dan 7:8, 25).

[6] For example, the little horn comes forth from the fourth animal, having a Roman nature (7:8); it emerges among ten kingdoms and uproots three of them, symbolizing papal Rome's conflict with the Germanic tribes (7:8); saints are given into the horn's power for a time period that fits only the medieval dominance of papal Rome (7:25); and papal Rome attempted to change times and law (7:25).

[7] See the article "What Did Jesus Mean by 'This Generation'?" by Richard Davidson, in this volume.

WHAT IS THE "CLEANSING OF THE SANCTUARY" IN DANIEL 8:14?

And he said unto me, Unto two thousand and three hundred days; then shall the sanctuary be cleansed. Daniel 8:14, KJV.

Traditionally, Seventh-day Adventists have used this text from the King James Version to support the doctrine of the investigative or pre-advent judgment. A literal translation of the text would be, "He said to me: 'Unto 2,300 evenings-mornings and then the sanctuary will be justified.'"

According to Leviticus 16, the ancient Israelite sanctuary was ritually cleansed each year on the Day of Atonement in the sense that the accumulated sins of God's people were removed from the sanctuary in a final stage of atonement. So, Adventists have interpreted Daniel 8:14 as an end-time fulfillment of that event. However, critics of this view have argued that the Hebrew word *nitsdaq* means legally "justified," not ritually "cleansed," and have pointed out that no form of the word *nitsdaq* appears in Leviticus 16. Therefore, they conclude that the restoration or justification of the sanctuary in Daniel 8:14 is not an end-time equivalent of the Day of Atonement.

The Day of Atonement in Israel – Apart from the question of *nitsdaq*, contextual factors indicate a strong thematic connection between Leviticus 16 and Daniel 7 and 8. The Day of Atonement was Israel's yearly judgment day. At this time, God reaffirmed His relationship with those who showed loyalty to Him in order to receive the benefit of having their sins purged from His sanctuary (Lev 16:29-31). On the other hand, God condemned those who were disloyal (23:29, 30). The loyal would enjoy the Promised Land, which the Lord had given to Israel, but the disloyal would be removed from among His people (compare the blessings and curses in Leviticus 26).

The Day of Atonement in Daniel 7 and 8 – Daniel 7 depicts an end-time, pre-advent judgment that vindicates God's faithful people (7:9-14, 22) and rewards them with the promised dominion of this world (7:27) but condemns those who rebel against Him, especially the oppressive "little horn" power (7:26). At the same time, this judgment vindicates God before the universe in the way He has dealt with sin and sinners.

249

Daniel 8 presents an overlapping parallel to Daniel 7 (see below), predicting a succession of earthly kingdoms culminating in a regime symbolized by a "little horn." It is clear that the two chapters portray the same flow of history from different angles. While God's answer to the problem of the horn power in Daniel 7 is the judgment, in Daniel 8 the solution is to justify God's sanctuary (v. 14). The judgment in Daniel 7 and the cleansing of the sanctuary in Daniel 8, which occupy the same positions in the parallel accounts, are functionally equivalent: they refer to the same event.

> While God's answer to the problem of the horn power in Daniel 7 is the judgment, in Daniel 8 the solution is to justify God's sanctuary.

PARALLELS BETWEEN DANIEL 7 & 8

DEMONSTRATING THE SIGNIFICANT LINK BETWEEN
THE PRE-ADVENT SESSION OF THE JUDGMENT,
AND THE "CLEANSING OF THE SANCTUARY"
OF DANIEL 8:14.

DANIEL 7	DANIEL 8
LION (BABYLON)	(BABYLON OMITTED)
BEAR (MEDO-PERSIA)	**RAM** (MEDO-PERSIA)
LEOPARD (GREECE)	**HE-GOAT** (GREECE)
FOURTH BEAST (PAGAN ROME)	**LITTLE HORN** (ROME, PAGAN & PAPAL)
TEN HORNS (10 KINGDOMS)	WARRED AGAINST CHRIST. CAST DOWN SANCTUARY.
LITTLE HORN (PAPAL ROME)	CONTINUED TO THE "TIME OF THE END."
THE NEXT GREAT EVENT?	THE NEXT GREAT EVENT?
THE JUDGMENT SITS	**THE SANCTUARY IS CLEANSED**
THE LITTLE HORN'S DOMINION TAKEN AWAY.	THE LITTLE HORN "BROKEN WITHOUT HAND."
THE SAINTS OF THE MOST HIGH POSSESS THE KINGDOM.	CHAPTERS 9-12 ARE A CONTINUATION OF GABRIEL'S INTERPRETATION, BEGUN IN CHAPTER 8, AND CLIMAXING IN THE FINAL DELIVERANCE OF GOD'S PEOPLE.

(Frank Breaden, *New Pictorial Aid for Bible Study*, Warburton, Vic., Australia: Signs Publishing Company, 1987)

What kind of event could be described both as a divine judgment between loyal and disloyal followers and as a justifying of God's sanctuary? In the Bible there is only one possibility: the Day of Atonement. But in Daniel, this event occurs long after the earthly temple in Jerusalem is gone (what happens in 8:11-14 occurs after the destruction of the temple in 9:26-27). So the end-time judgment must cleanse or justify God's sanctuary in heaven (compare Heb 8-9; Rev 4-5; 11:19).

Leviticus 16 and Daniel 8:14 – Overlapping terminology links Daniel 8:14 to Leviticus 16. For one thing, both speak of God's sanctuary (Heb. *qodesh*). More significantly, the Hebrew word *nitsdaq*, "justified" (Dan 8:14), has an indirect but illuminating connection to Leviticus 16. *Nitsdaq* comes from the word *tsadaq*, which means to "be (in the) right" or to "be just" (Job 9:15, 20; Ps 19:9; 51:4; 143:2; Isa 43:9, 26, etc.). In Job 4:17, one who is "just" (*tsadaq*) before God is "clean" (*taher*) from blame, that is, "vindicated." Here the two terms for "just" and "clean" function as synonyms in a parallel construction that expresses the same idea in different ways. Compare the fact that "blameless" also may be expressed by *naqiy* (Exod 21:28; 23:7; 2 Sam 14:9), which also can mean "clean" (Ps 24:4).

In the context of Daniel 7 and 8, justifying God's sanctuary headquarters, which

> While the pre-advent judgment has reference to the little horn, this judgment seeks "to vindicate God's people, as is seen in Daniel 7, where the saints are judged and acquitted. God's people remain in an attitude of complete dependence on God under the most distressing circumstances. The records of their lives are examined and their sins are blotted out; at the same time the names of false believers are removed from the books (cf. Exod 4:33; Lev 23:29, 39). Those whose names are preserved in the books, including the dead saints, inherit the kingdom (Dan. 7:22; 12:1, 2). Thus the sanctuary is cleansed." (Ángel M. Rodríguez, "The Sanctuary" in R. Dederen, *Handbook of Seventh-Day Adventist Theology* [Hagerstown, MD: Review and Herald, 2000], 395, 397).

represents His authority and government, means that God is vindicated as just or blameless when He judges between loyal people and the disloyal, who have acted in "rebellion" (Dan 8:12). So it is appropriate to regard this vindication as a kind of (legal) cleansing, which explains why the 1988 Jewish Publication Society version renders the end of Daniel 8:14: "then the sanctuary shall be cleansed," in agreement with the Septuagint and the King James Version.

Leviticus 16 calls for a ritual "cleansing" of the Israelite sanctuary, including "cleansing" (*taher*) its outer altar (v. 19), through applications of sacrificial blood by the high priest. This removal of sins and impurities from God's earthly headquarters represents the restoration or justification of His sanctuary: God's government is vindicated as just when He reaffirms loyal people whom He has already forgiven throughout the year (cf. Lev 4-5) and when He rejects those who have committed "rebellious sins" (Lev 16:16).

We have found that legal cleansing or vindication links Daniel 8:14 specifically to Leviticus 16 and that this concept is expressed by the synonymous terms *tsadaq* (Dan 8:14) and *taher* (Lev 16:19). The word *pesha*, "rebellion/rebellious sin," also specifically connects Daniel 8:12 and Leviticus 16. In all the sanctuary instructions of the Pentateuch, this word occurs only in Leviticus 16:16, 21.

An additional allusion to Leviticus 16 appears in Daniel's vision of a ram and a male goat (Dan 8:3-8). These are the categories of animals sacrificed in the same group of rituals only on the Day of Atonement (Lev 16:5, 15, 24)

Interpretation – The Day of Atonement (Lev 16) background to Daniel 8:14 teaches us the meaning and function of justifying (or legally cleansing/vindicating) God's sanctuary in heaven. After a first stage of atonement in which God forgave repentant Israelites who brought their sacrifices to His sanctuary throughout the year (Lev 4:20, 26, 31, 35, etc.), the Day of Atonement provided a second and final major stage of atonement. This second stage cleanses the sanctuary from the sins of the people, representing the fact that God as Judge was vindicated, cleared of judicial responsibility that He had incurred by forgiving guilty people (cf. 2 Sam 14:9), which a just judge normally should not do (Deut 25:1; 1 Kgs 8:32). The ultimate sacrifice of Christ, to which the animal sacrifices throughout the year and on the Day of Atonement pointed, makes it possible for God to be just when He justifies (through forgiveness) those who believe (Rom 3:26).

The question that remains after forgiveness is: Do those whom God has forgiven really continue to believe (cf. Col 1:21-23) so that He can be just when He saves them? He answers this question through an end-time judgment (Dan 7) that vindicates Him (Dan 8) by demonstrating that He indeed saves only loyal people whose faith endures. The two stages of atonement ensure that God grants only full mercy with full justice. Thus God keeps justice and mercy, the two sides of His character of love (Exod 34:6, 7; 1 John 4:8), in perfect balance (Ps 85:10).

Conclusion – It is true that in Daniel 8:14, *nitsdaq* literally means "justified." It is also true that this term does not appear in Leviticus 16 or in any other Day of Atonement passage (Lev 23:26-32; Num 29:7-11). However, there is decisive evidence that the event predicted in Daniel 8:14 is the end-time judgment (cf. 7:9-14) to which the ancient Day of Atonement pointed forward. This event plays a crucial role in salvation history by cleansing the heavenly sanctuary from the sins of the people, thereby vindicating God's character. In other words, the judgment demonstrates that His judgments are just.[1]

Roy E. Gane

References

[1]For further study, see Roy Gane, *Who's Afraid of the Judgment? The Good News About Christ's Work in the Heavenly Sanctuary* (Nampa, ID: Pacific Press, 2006), and other works cited there.

William Miller proclaiming the Second Advent in 1843/44

ARE THE 2300 EVENINGS AND MORNINGS IN DANIEL 8:14 LITERAL OR SYMBOLIC DAYS?

And he said to me, "For 2,300 evenings *and* mornings; then the holy place will be properly restored." Daniel 8:14.

Most interpreters understand the 2,300 evenings and mornings to be literal days. Why do Seventh-day Adventists believe that they are symbolic and should be interpreted according to the year-day principle, as 2300 years?

The vision is symbolic – The vision in Daniel 8:1-14 is the climactic conclusion of the symbolic presentations in the book. Daniel in vision is transported to Susa, where, at the river Ulai, he watches a ram being defeated by a goat. The symbolism is explained in verse 20 – the ram represents Medo-Persia and the goat the Grecian kingdom of Alexander, who is the notable horn between the eyes of the goat (v. 5). At the height of the goat's strength the notable horn is broken, and four other horns appear in its place. Commentators generally agree that the four horns represent the four divisions of the Grecian kingdom after the death of Alexander the Great (see vv. 21, 22). Next, Daniel sees a little horn that grows very great and becomes very active – it casts some of the host of heaven to the ground; it exalts itself as high as the Prince of the host; it takes away the daily from Him; and casts God's truth to the ground.

The little horn is Rome – Most commentators identify the little horn in Daniel 8 with the Seleucid king Antiochus Epiphanes. However, according to history, the power that followed Medo-Persia and Greece on the world stage was Rome; first imperial and then ecclesiastical Rome. That the little horn must be a symbol for Rome and not for Antiochus Epiphanes is made clear by the text itself. The ram (Medo-Persia) it says "became great" (8:4); the goat (Greece) "grew very great" (8:8); but the little horn "grew exceedingly great" (8:9). The only power that became greater than Greece was Rome. Antiochus Epiphanes was a fairly insignificant king in one of the four divisions of the Grecian kingdom after the death of Alexander.

The activities of papal Rome – The activities of the little horn refer first to the persecution of Christians by the Roman emperors (Dan 8:10) and then to the deeds of apostate Christianity (8:11, 12). By openly assuming the office of Christ as mediator between God and humanity, the papacy exalted itself against the Prince of the host and fulfilled 2 Thessalonians 2:4. And by placing the intercession for human beings into the hands of priests, through the confessional and the mass[1], the papacy usurped Christ's heavenly ministry (the daily). Instead of going directly to Christ, people began to go to the priests, to the saints, or to Mary. Finally, by forbidding the common people to read the Scriptures in their mother-tongue and without the explanatory notes of the church during most of Christian history,[2] and by placing the Scriptures on the same level as church tradition, the papacy has cast God's truth (His Word) to the ground.

The symbolic meaning of the 2300 evenings and mornings – In Daniel 8:13 the question is asked, "Until when will be the vision?" "Until when" focuses on the termination point of the vision. Thus the question concerns the whole vision from the time of the ram (Medo-Persia), through the activities of the little horn, to the time of the end (8:17). Because all of the activities of the ram, the goat, and the little horn have covered more than two millennia, it is highly unlikely that the timespan of 2300 evenings and mornings refers to a short timespan of somewhat more than six literal years. Such an understanding of the 2300 evenings and mornings simply does not fit the context. Because the vision is full of symbols (ram, goat, little horn) a symbolic meaning of the time element seems required.

> The activities of the ram, the goat, and the little horn cover more than two millennia; the timespan of 2300 evenings and mornings, therefore, cannot refer to a short time of just six literal years and a few months.

The prophecies in Daniel 7, 8, and 10-12 all lead up to the "time of the end" (8:17; 11:35, 40; 12:4, 9), which is followed by the resurrection (12:2) and the setting up of God's everlasting kingdom (7:27). Looking at the sweep of history, described in these prophecies that extend from the prophet in the sixth century B.C. to our time and beyond, a literal time period of little more than six years is out of harmony with the rest of the vision. Therefore, the prophetic-time period of the 2300 evenings and mornings should be seen as standing for 2300 years of actual historical time.

Daniel 9 is the key to the interpretation – The prophecies of Daniel 8 and 9 are interconnected. In Daniel 9 we find that (1) the same angel revisits Daniel (v. 21); (2) Daniel recalls the former vision in Daniel 8 (v. 21); (3) Gabriel comes to give Daniel understanding of the previous vision (v. 23); and (4) the time element not explained in Daniel 8 is now the topic in Daniel 9 (v. 24).

The Jewish commentator Rabbi Hersh Goldwurm recognizes this interconnectedness and says in regard to the expression "understand the vision [mar'eh]" in 9:23, "This refers to Daniel's vision in chapter 8 in which the part which disturbed him so (v. 14) is characterized in vv. 16-26 as a mar'eh."[3]

> **The primary meaning of the Hebrew word *chatak*, translated "determined," is "cut off."**

Conservative Christians throughout history have seen Daniel 9 as a Messianic prophecy and have interpreted the 70 weeks as 490 years spanning the time from the Persian Empire to the Messiah. According to Daniel 9:24, "Seventy weeks are determined for your people." Bible scholars acknowledge that the primary meaning of the Hebrew word *chatak*, translated "determined" is "cut " or "cut off."[4] For example, R. Newell says, "The Hebrew word used here . . . has the literal connotation of 'cutting off' in the sense of severing from a larger portion."[5] The seventy weeks are cut off from the only other time element mentioned in the context – the 2300 evenings and mornings in Daniel 8:14.[6] Thus, because the 70 weeks are 490 years, the 2300 evenings and mornings from which the 490 years are cut off must be also 2300 years.[7]

There is good contextual evidence, therefore, for interpreting the 2300 evenings and mornings as symbolic days that need to be interpreted by the year-day principle as 2300 years.

Gerhard Pfandl

References

[1]According to the *Catechism of the Catholic Church* (New York: Doubleday, 1995) "The bread and wine are brought to the altar; they will be offered by the priest in the name of Christ in the Eucharistic sacrifice in which they will become his body and blood" (# 1350). It is claimed that the sacrifice on the cross and the

sacrifice of the Eucharist are one single sacrifice, "'The victim is one and the same: the same now offers through the ministry of the priests, who then offered himself on the cross; only the manner of offering is different.' 'In this divine sacrifice which is celebrated in the Mass, the same Christ who offered himself once in a bloody manner on the altar of the cross is contained and is offered in an unbloody manner" (#1367). Modern Catholic theologians in ecumenical discussions try to explain that this in no way minimizes the sacrifice on the cross, but the language and the perception in the minds of the worshipers is clear – Christ is sacrificed in every mass.

[2]As recently as the pontificate of Pius XI (1922-39), all editions of the Scripture were prohibited to be read, kept, sold, or translated, except those that have passed the censorship of the Bishops and contain explanatory notes by the Fathers of the Church.

[3]Rabbi Hersh Goldwurm, *Daniel*, The ArtScroll Tanach Series (Brooklyn, NY: Masorah Publications, Ltd., 1998), 258.

[4]"This root is common in medieval and modern Heb. With the primary sense 'cut' and the secondary meaning 'decide, pronounce a sentence.'" (Willem A. VanGemeren, ed., *New International Dictionary of the Old Testament Theology and Exegesis*, 5 vols. [Grand Rapids, MI: Zondervan, 1997], 2:323).

[5]R. Newell, *Daniel* (Chicago, IL: Moody Press, 1962), 137.

[6]The fact that both prophecies begin in the time of the Medo-Persians indicates that the 490 years are "cut off" from the beginning and not from the end of the 2300-year period.

[7]Some commentators claim that the 2300 evenings and mornings refer to 2300 evening and morning sacrifices arriving at 1,150 days. However, the biblical term for the daily sacrifices is always "morning and evening" sacrifices (Num 28:4; 1 Chron 16:40; 23:30; 2 Chron 2:4; 13:11) not "evening and morning." Furthermore, the phrase "evening and morning" in the Creation story (Gen 1:5, 8, 13, etc.) clearly indicates one full day. Hence the 2300 evenings and mornings in Daniel 8:14 are 2300 days.

As we near the close of this world's history, the prophecies recorded by Daniel demand our special attention, as they relate to the very time in which we are living.

PK 547

WHAT IS THE RELATIONSHIP BETWEEN THE 2300 EVENING-MORNINGS OF DANIEL 8:14 AND THE 70 WEEKS OF DANIEL 9:24-26?

He said to me, "For 2,300 evenings and mornings; then the holy place will be properly restored." Daniel 8:14.

"Seventy weeks have been decreed for your people and your holy city, to finish the transgression, to make an end of sin, to make atonement for iniquity, to bring in everlasting righteousness, to seal up vision and prophecy and to anoint the most holy *place*. So you are to know and discern that from the issuing of a decree to restore and rebuild Jerusalem until Messiah the Prince *there will be* seven weeks and sixty-two weeks; it will be built again, with plaza and moat, even in times of distress. Then after the sixty-two weeks the Messiah will be cut off and have nothing, and the people of the prince who is to come will destroy the city and the sanctuary." Daniel 9:24-26.

Commentators today generally see no connection between the two prophecies and apply Daniel 8:14 to the time of Antiochus IV Epiphanes (175-164 BC) and Daniel 9:24-27 to the time of the first advent of Christ.

Links between Daniel 8 and 9 – Links between chapters 8 and 9 come in several categories. First, the symbols of Daniel 8 start off with the Persian ram (8:1-5, 20), and the decree to rebuild Jerusalem (Dan 9:25) was given by a Persian king. Thus, the time periods of both of these prophecies start in the Persian period.

Second, the question that precedes the time period in Daniel 8:14 asks, "How long (or until when) is the vision. . . ." The vision is not just about the four things listed in 8:13 that were done by the little horn, it is about everything from the Persian ram onwards. This understanding means that the time period of the vision in 8:13, 14 starts somewhere in the general period of Persia. The 70 weeks of Daniel 9:24-27 begin at a specific point in time in that Persian period, at the time when a Persian king gave a decree for the rebuilding of the city of Jerusalem.

Third, the standard pattern in the book of Daniel is that a symbolic vision is followed by an explanation. There is, however, no symbolic vision in Daniel 9 to precede the explanation given there. This break in the pattern has the effect of placing the explanation in Daniel 9:24-27 up against the vision and explanation of Daniel 8 in terms of the normal format of the prophecies in the book.

As has been pointed out, the explanations of the symbolic visions in Daniel 7 and 8 have distinct literary parallels:[1]

Messenger Interpreter	Daniel 7	Literary Unit	Daniel 8	Messenger Interpreter
	vv. 1-14	Symbolic Vision	vv. 1-14	
Angel in heaven	vv. 15-18	Explanation I	vv. 15-27	Gabriel on earth
Angel in heaven	vv. 19-22	Explanation II	Dan 9:24-27	Gabriel on earth
Angel in heaven	vv. 23-27	Explanation III	Dan 11:1-12:4	Angel on earth (probably Gabriel)

There are three distinct sections in the explanation to the vision in Daniel 7, and there are three distinct sections to the explanation of the symbolic vision in Daniel 8. As the last symbolic vision in the book, Daniel 8 requires a longer and more detailed explanation than Daniel 7. That longer explanation shows up in the last half of Daniel 8 and again in the didactic prophecies of Daniel 9 and 11. This format strengthens the relationship of Daniel 9:24-27 to Daniel 8:1-14 as part of its explanation.

Fourth, there is a relatively standard position for the time elements in the prophecies of Daniel. They usually come at or towards the end of those prophecies. There is a reason for this. Time cannot be symbolized in the same way that a nation or a people can. Thus it must be given in a didactic explanation that, of necessity, follows after the symbolic vision. This format is true of the 3-1/2 times in Daniel 7:25, the 2300 evening-mornings in Daniel 8:14, and the times cited in Daniel 12:7, 11

> The Jewish commentator Rabbi Hersh Goldwurm, after citing the words of Gabriel in Daniel 9:23, "understand the vision," explains, "this [vision] refers to Daniel's vision in chapter 8 in which the part which disturbed him so (v. 14) is characterized in vs. 16-26 as a mar'eh."(Hersh Goldwurm, *Daniel* [Brooklyn, NY: Mesorah Publications, 1979], 258).

259

and 12. But the 70 weeks of Daniel 9 come right at the beginning of that prophecy in verse 24. This placement has the literary structural effect of juxtaposing the 70 weeks directly up against the 2300 days of the preceding symbolic vision in Daniel 8.

Fifth, as has been noted in the outline above, the angel Gabriel is common to both explanations in Daniel 8 and 9. In addition, when he gave the explanation in Daniel 9, he pointed back to Daniel 8, saying that this prophetic word that he brought would explain the preceding vision: "Therefore, consider the message [which I bring you now] and understand the vision [which you have seen previously]" (Dan 9:23 NIV, with the author's parenthetic insertions). Quite clearly then, Gabriel points Daniel back to the vision of chapter 8, with the word or message that he brought at the time of Daniel 9.

Sixth, in the English translations of Daniel 9:23, the Hebrew word translated "vision" is Hebrew *mar'eh*. There is another Hebrew word for vision used in these prophecies, and it is *chazon*, which we have seen previously in Daniel 8:1-2 and 13. That is the word for the vision that contains the animals and other symbols between those two references. Hebrew *mar'eh* has another shade of meaning; it refers to a vision in which there is the appearance of one or more personal beings. This meaning is evident in Daniel 10:5-6 in which Daniel saw a theophany, a personal appearance of God. This manifestation he refers to as a *mar'eh* or an "appearance" vision in 10:7.

This distinction is utilized at the end of the explanation of Daniel 8, where verse 26 says, "The [*mar'eh*] vision of the *evenings* and the *mornings* which has been *told* is true, but seal up the [*chazon*] vision, for it is for many days" (emphasis author's). A distinction is made here between the symbolic vision, the *chazon* of verses 1-12, and the appearance vision or *mar'eh* in which the two angels talk about the evenings and mornings. So when Gabriel is talking about the *mar'eh* vision in 9:23, he is talking more specifically about the time given in Daniel 8:13, 14. He is not saying that this prophecy in Daniel 9:24 about the Jews will explain what is said about the Persians, Greeks, and Romans in Daniel 8:1-12. In this way the 70 weeks of Dan 9:24 is specifically connected with the 2300 evening-mornings of Daniel 8:14.

Seventh, the first verb in Dan 9:24 says that the 70 weeks are "cut off" or "decreed, determined" upon the Jewish people and the city of Jerusalem. Most English versions of the Bible utilize the latter translation. The question is whether this is the original meaning intended by the author.

The verbal root present here, *chatak*, is used only once in the whole Bible. That means we need to look to post-Old Testament Hebrew to see how it was used there. In eight out of nine times in Mishnaic Hebrew, [2] the meaning given there is "cut."[3] For example, if a sacrificial animal had an ulcer on its leg, the ulcer was to be "cut out," an expression using this verbal root. Only once does it carry the meaning of "decree," in a commentary on the decree made by Ahasuerus in the book of Esther. The context of Daniel 9 indicates that "cut" is the best meaning to be employed in verse 24. Because the 70 weeks are units of time, they should be cut off from another unit of time, the preceding one to which they are connected through the lines of evidence discussed above, the 2300 evening-mornings. Hence the 70 weeks are cut off from the beginning of the 2300 days. "Since in explaining 'the vision,' Gabriel gave a beginning point only for the 490 years (Daniel 9:23, 25), the 2,300 years must begin at the same point."[4]

"Seventy weeks are determined for your people and for your holy city" (Dan 9:24). "All scholars agree that the primary meaning of the word [are determined] is 'to cut,' or 'to cut off,' and it is so rendered in the early translations of Daniel into Greek and Latin. . . . No Semitic scholar denies that this is its primary meaning. But the English translators, not seeing any connection between this period of seventy weeks and the longer period of 2300 days, and thus seeing nothing from which this period of seventy weeks could literally be cut off, gave the word its secondary meaning of 'decreed,' or 'determined,' or 'assigned.' (George McCready Price, *The Greatest of the Prophets* [Mountain View, CA: Pacific Press, 1955], 230).

Conclusion – Seven points have been noted that show that the visions of Daniel 8 and 9 are closely linked. The same angel, Gabriel, is the interpreter, returning in the vision of chapter 9 to complete his explanation of the vision in chapter 8.

William H. Shea

References

[1]Donn Leatherman, "Structural Considerations Regarding the Relation of Daniel 8 and Daniel 9," *The Cosmic Battle for Planet Earth*, eds. J. Moskala and R. du Preez (Berrien Springs, MI: Andrews University, 2003), 293-306.

[2]Hebrew used by the Rabbis in the time of Jesus. The Mishnah (compiled about A.D. 200), the first written compendium of Judaism's Oral Law, is part of the Talmud, a collection of Jewish law and tradition.

[3]Marcus Jastrow, *Dictionary of the Targumim, the Talmud Babli and Yerushalmi, and the Midrashic Literature* (Reprint, Peabody, MA: Hendrickson Publishers, 2005)

[4]Roy Gane, *Who is Afraid of the Judgment*? (Nampa, ID: Pacific Press, 2006), 66.

Striding lions of glazed brick, decorated the "Processional" way in ancient Babylon.

WHO IS MICHAEL IN DANIEL 12:1?

Now at that time Michael, the great prince who stands *guard* over the sons of your people, will arise. And there will be a time of distress such as never occurred since there was a nation until that time; and at that time your people, everyone who is found written in the book, will be rescued. Daniel 12:1.

Most Christians today believe that Michael is an angelic being. Some, however, throughout church history, have identified Michael as Christ. Reasons for this identification are:

The resurrection at the Second Coming – The first three verses of Daniel 12 describe the end of the conflict that is discussed at length in chapter 11. The resurrection mentioned in 12:2 indicates that when Michael stands up to deliver his people the great controversy between Christ and Satan is coming to an end. From the New Testament we know that the resurrection takes place in connection with the Second Coming when Christ comes to deliver His people (Matt 24:29-31; 1 Thess 4:15-17; 1 Cor 15:50-55). Thus the parallelism between Daniel 12:1-2 and the New Testament passages, describing the resurrection, provides a hint that the figure of Michael may not be just an angel but Christ Himself.

"What seems to emerge from the designations and functions of Michael in Daniel 10 and 12 is that he is more than an angelic figure. He exhibits the functions and prerogatives of divinity. Michael is accorded a degree of distinct personal identity, dignity, rank, and authority not elsewhere accorded to an angelic being. He is filling a role as historical and eschatological warrior and executor of judgment assigned only to God elsewhere in the OT." (Lewis O. Anderson, Jr., "The Michael Figure in the Book of Daniel," unpublished Th.D. dissertation, Andrews University, 1997, 433).

The meaning of the name Michael – The name "Michael," which means "Who is like God," is another indicator. No one is like God except the Son of God (John 10:30), who intercedes for His people (1 John 2:1, 2; Heb 7:25). Jewish literature describes Michael as the highest of the angels and identifies him with the "Angel of Yahweh" frequently mentioned in the Old Testament as a divine being. This "angel" (Exod 23:23) could pardon transgressions, and God's "name was in him" (v. 21). As forgiveness of sin is the prerogative of God (Mark 2:7), the conclusion seems inevitable that "My angel" (Exod 23:23) is a member of the Godhead. In Daniel 10:21, Michael is called "your prince," i.e., the prince of God's people. In Isaiah 9:6, Jesus the Messiah is called the "Prince of Peace;" in Daniel 8:25, He is "the Prince of princes," and in Daniel 9:25, He is identified as "Messiah the Prince." Thus the conclusion seems justified that in the Old Testament there was One with God who was known as "Michael," "the angel of the Lord," or "My angel," who was also called "My Son" (Ps 2:7).

> Jesus and Michael are the only beings in Scripture called "archangel."

Jesus and Michael are called archangel – In the New Testament Jesus is called "archangel" (1 Thess 4:16) meaning "chief of the angels," and in Jude 9 Michael is called archangel. The prefix "arch" goes back to the Greek *word arche,* which can mean "beginning" as in Mark 1:1; "the first cause," as in Revelation 3:14; or "ruler, authority," as in 1 Corinthians 15:24. *Arche* is also used in connection with the Messiah in the Greek translation (Septuagint) of Isaiah 9:6 in which the "government [*arche*] is upon His [the Messiah's] shoulder." Another title given to Jesus in the New Testament is *archegos,* translated as "Prince" (Acts 3:15; 5:31), "author" (Heb 12:2), or "captain" (Heb 2:10, KJV). The basic meaning is "he who is the first, who stands at the head, who leads."

Many Bible commentators throughout history, e.g., Matthew Henry, Adam Clarke, and John P. Lange, have also identified Michael with Christ, as has Ellen G. White: "Michael, or Christ, with the angels that buried Moses, came down from heaven, after he [Moses] had remained in the grave a short time, and resurrected him and took him to heaven" (SR 173).

There is good biblical and historical evidence that Jesus Christ is Michael the archangel. He is also the Angel of the Lord, the Prince or Captain of the Lord's host and deliverer of His people.

Gerhard Pfandl

New Testament Texts

WHAT DOES JESUS MEAN WHEN HE SAYS
WE ARE TO BE "PERFECT"?

Therefore you are to be perfect, as your heavenly Father is perfect. Matthew 5:48.

How can human beings be as perfect as the heavenly Father is perfect? God is a sinless being; since the Fall, human beings are sinful creatures by nature (Eph 2:3). In what way can they ever be perfect as the Father is perfect? What does Jesus mean?

The Sermon on the Mount – The powerful words of Jesus in Matthew 5:48 form the conclusion of the second section of the Sermon on the Mount. The entire Sermon is Matthew 5-7, but this section extends from 5:17 through 5:48. The section divides into a preamble in which Jesus insists that He did not come to abolish the law and the Prophets; rather, He came to fulfill them. This preamble is followed by a series of six contrasting statements, or antitheses, in which Jesus quotes an Old Testament verse or a traditional saying, with the form, "You have heard that it was said . . ." followed by the contrast, "But I say to you . . ." (Matt 5:21, 22).

"He tells us to be perfect as He is, in the same manner. We are to be centers of light and blessing to our little circle, even as He is to the universe. We have nothing of ourselves, but the light of His love shines upon us, and we are to reflect its brightness. 'In His borrowed goodness good,' we may be perfect in our sphere, even as God is perfect in His" (MB 77).

One might suppose that an antithesis would suggest a rejection of the Old Testament idea, replacing it with a new teaching from Jesus. On the contrary, Jesus in each case deepens the application of the teaching of Old Testament Scripture. He thereby illustrates His insistence that His purpose was not to do away with the Old Testament maxims, but rather to demonstrate the depth and far reaching application of God's ancient commands.

Loving one's enemies – The last of the antitheses is in 5:43-48, dealing with the question of loving one's enemies. Jesus quotes a portion of Leviticus 19:18, "You shall love your neighbor," but evidently appends to it a traditional statement, "and hate your enemy." Jesus then counters this statement with His famous maxim that we are to love our enemies and pray for our persecutors. The Master goes on to state that carrying out these actions toward our enemies results in us being or becoming sons of our Father in heaven, "because He makes His sun shine on the evil and the good, and sends rain on the just and the unjust." Loving enemies, then, is to emulate the action of God.

Jesus goes on to express a contrast to God's magnanimous actions by referring to those who love only those who love them, or love only their brothers. This behavior, He says, is no better than what tax collectors and the Gentiles do, people generally thought to be outside the purview of Biblical religion. We are thus given a contrast of behaviors and groups – God with love, care, and concern for both good and bad people, on the one hand, and tax collectors and Gentiles with concern and love only for themselves on the other. All this is followed by our verse above calling disciples to perfection, even as their Father in heaven is perfect.

> The Greek term for perfection means "fully developed, mature, having obtained the end or purpose."

Understanding the context of Matthew 5:48 is essential for comprehending the meaning of the text. Within the last of the antitheses, perfection is defined not as the absence of defects, not as the rooting out of all moral failure, but rather as the extension of love to the group farthest from us – our enemies. Again, within the entire group of antitheses, the call to perfection in 5:48 does contain a sense of the deepest moral purity – for instance redefining murder as hatred and adultery as the lustful look and negating the practice of both.

Faced with these superlatives, we might be tempted to simply give up on discipleship altogether or else to take the approach of the second century A.D. author of the *Didache* who alludes to this verse in chapter 6 verse 2 of his work, "For if you can bear the whole yoke of the Lord, you shall be perfect; but if you cannot, do what you can." Or we may go even as far as some who insist that Jesus did not mean what He said, perfection is impossible and besides that unnecessary, since the Christian is saved by grace.

The meaning of "perfect" – But we lose something deeply important if we take any of these "less than" routes. The Greek term for perfection in Matthew 5:48 is *teleios*, which means "perfect, without defect, complete, fully developed, mature, having obtained the end or purpose."[1] When a thing is full grown and has reached its goal, it is called *teleios*, "perfect." The Christian life has a goal. It is pointed toward heaven. The upward call of the gospel is distinct (Phil 3:12-14). God accepts us wherever He finds us, but He never leaves us there. He takes us on a journey to Christian maturity. The command of Jesus expresses the fruition of that journey. To accept the command is to accept the journey and to walk within His will. The goal of perfection – of Christian maturity, of being like our Father in heaven – is given to us not to discourage but to serve as our guiding star in a world of moral darkness.

Tom Shepherd

References

[1]See William Arndt, and F. Wilbur Gingrich, *A Greek-English Lexicon of the New Testament and Other Early Christian Literature* (Cambridge: University of Chicago Press, 1957), s.v. *teleios*.

Good habits are not made on birthdays, nor Christian character at the new year. The workshop of character is everyday life. The uneventful and commonplace hour is where the battle is lost or won.
Maltbie D. Babcock

WHAT IS THE UNPARDONABLE SIN?

> Therefore I say to you, any sin and blasphemy shall be forgiven peo-
> ple, but blasphemy against the Spirit shall not be forgiven. Who-
> ever speaks a word against the Son of Man, it shall be forgiven him;
> but whoever speaks against the Holy Spirit, it shall not be forgiven
> him, either in this age, or in the *age* to come. Matthew 12:31, 32.

The difficulty of this passage is a matter of understanding the nature of
the sin which is described as being unpardonable. What constitutes blasphemy against the Holy Spirit or speaking against the Holy Spirit, and why
is this sin considered unpardonable? If every other sin and blasphemy is
pardonable, why is this one sin not pardonable? Why is it worse to speak
against the Holy Spirit than to speak against Jesus Christ, the Son of Man?

Conflicts between Jesus and the Pharisees – We need to begin by looking at the context of the passage, to see what Jesus was talking about, to
whom, and under what circumstances. Our text in Matthew 12 and Mark
3:28, 29 (the parallel passage) describes a conflict between Jesus and the
Pharisees. Matthew begins with the Pharisees confronting Jesus about
plucking and eating grain on the Sabbath, which they held to be unlawful
(Matt 12:2). From there, Jesus enters a synagogue and heals a man with a
withered hand. Again, the Pharisees accuse Him of Sabbath breaking, and
at the end of the incident they go out and take counsel against Him how
they might destroy Him (vv. 10, 14). Jesus then withdraws and heals all the
sick among the multitudes that follow Him, warning them against unneces-
sarily invoking the wrath of the Jewish leaders by making His deeds known
(vv. 15-16). Yet when a demon-possessed blind and mute man was brought
to Him for healing and was healed, the people were amazed and could not
restrain themselves from asking, "Could this be the Son of David?" (vv.
22-23). By this rhetorical question, they were implying that Jesus was giving evidence that He was the promised Messiah. When this saying was re-
hearsed in the ears of the Pharisees, they retorted, "It is only by Beelzebub,
the prince of demons, that this fellow drives out demons" (v. 24, NIV). They
could not deny the miracle, so they tried to credit it to demonic powers (cf.
Mark 3:30). Jesus responded that it could not be so, since a house divided

against itself cannot stand (vv. 25, 26). Instead He credited His expelling of the demons to the power of the Holy Spirit, as evidence that the kingdom of God was present in their midst (v. 28), despite their rejection of it. "He who is not with Me is against Me," Jesus declared (v. 30).

The work of the Holy Spirit – The conflict between Jesus and the Pharisees is the context in which Jesus pronounces the words in our text. In Greek, these words begin with the expression *dia touto*, which means "because of this" or "for this reason." It was their defiant and persistent opposition to Christ that was the reason why He felt the need to express Himself so clearly and forcefully to them about the dangers of their active resistance to the work of the Holy Spirit on their hearts. By attributing the power of Jesus to demons instead of to the Holy Spirit, the Pharisees were denying the work of the Holy Spirit in the ministry of Jesus.

> "No one need look upon the sin against the Holy Ghost as something mysterious and indefinable. The sin against the Holy Ghost is the sin of persistent refusal to respond to the invitation to repent" (FLB 58).

It is the work of the Holy Spirit to bring conviction of sin, of righteousness, and of judgment (John 16:8). If the work of the Holy Spirit is persistently resisted, there can be no conviction in regard to these essentials with reference to salvation. The Holy Spirit convicts people of sin when they do not believe in Jesus (John 16:9). In the face of indisputable evidence, the Pharisees chose not to believe in Jesus and sought every opportunity to defeat His influence and even to destroy Him. By so doing, they were rejecting the work of the Holy Spirit in their lives. They were hardening their hearts to His convicting voice, and the result was that they were increasingly insensitive to that voice. One cannot speak against the Holy Spirit while at the same time remaining sensitive to His voice and responsive to the conviction He attempts to instill.

A similar experience may be described in 1 Timothy 4:2 regarding those who have their consciences seared with a hot iron, i.e., rendered insensitive to the promptings of the Holy Spirit. In Hebrews 6:4-6, there is a most serious warning against turning away from the truth after having been enlightened by receiving the gift of the Holy Spirit. We are told that it is impossible to renew such persons again to repentance — although, as Jesus taught in Matthew 19:26, what is impossible with men is still possible with God — because they willfully, with full knowledge, participate as it were in crucifying again the Son of God and putting Him to open shame.[1] This is what is meant by the unpardonable sin.

The nature of the unpardonable sin – The sin referred to in Matthew 12:31, 32 is not an act of carelessness, ignorance, or mere unbelief, but a persistent, defiant refusal to accept the indisputable evidence of the work of God's Spirit as good, speaking of it as if it were evil and resisting the Spirit's work in the heart. Even speaking against Jesus is a forgivable sin (Matt 12:32), but one should beware of speaking persistently against the One whose work it is to bring conviction of sin. The only sin that cannot be forgiven is the one that is not confessed and forsaken and for which forgiveness is not sought. If one is concerned about having committed the unpardonable sin, that concern is in itself patent evidence that the Holy Spirit is bringing conviction to the heart and that the person has not done so, for the one who has already commited the unpardonable sin would never care about it. The appeal found in Hebrews 3:7-9 is pertinent here: "Therefore, as the Holy Spirit says, "Today, when you hear his voice, do not harden your hearts as in the rebellion, on the day of testing in the wilderness, where your fathers put me to the test and saw my works for forty years" (RSV).

Edwin Reynolds

References

[1]See McVay on Hebrews 6:4-6 in this volume.

The mysteries of the Bible, so far from being an argument against it, are among the strongest evidences of its divine inspiration.
Ed 170

IS PETER THE ROCK ON WHICH
JESUS BUILT THE CHURCH?

I also say to you that you are Peter, and upon this rock I will build My church; and the gates of Hades will not overpower it. Matthew 16:18.

Since at least the time of Pope Leo I (fifth century) this text has been used by Roman Catholics to support the claim that Christ made Peter the head of the church, that Peter was the first bishop of Rome, and that the pope as his successor is the divinely appointed leader of the Christian church. If Jesus is not telling Peter that the Christian church will be built on him, what is He saying?

The historical context – Jesus made this statement to Peter when He and His disciples were in the region of Caesarea Philippi. The Lord asked His disciples who people were saying He was. They responded with names like John the Baptist, Elijah, Jeremiah, or one of the other prophets. Then Jesus asked them the pointed question, "'But who do you say that I am?'" (16:15) Peter responded with the clear answer, "'You are the Christ, the Son of the Living God.'" Jesus blessed Peter for the answer, noting that it was a revelation from His Father in heaven, and then made the statement in the text above.

A play on words – In order to understand this text it is important to recognize that it contains a play on words – a pun – and that it alludes to words previously spoken. First, let us consider the pun. The name "Peter" in Greek is *petros*. We get the English name "Peter" from an almost direct transliteration of the Greek. But there is another Greek word in this verse – *petra,* which means "rock."[1] The play on words, then, goes like this – "You are Peter (*petros*) and on this rock (*petra)* I will build my church." But what is the *petra* on which Jesus built the church?

The meaning of *petra* – *Petra* is used 15 times in the New Testament, and it is instructive to understand the way Jesus and the New Testament authors use the term. *Petra* is used to refer to a rock serving as a sufficiently strong foundation to protect a house built on it from storms (Matt 7:24, 25; Luke 6:48). It is the term used of the splitting of rocks during the earthquake at the time of Jesus' death (Matt 27:51), and of the stony tomb where the Lord lay for 3 days (Matt 27:60, Mark 15:46). It refers to the stony ground where there was not enough soil for the seeds to grow (Luke 8:6, 13), and it is the term for the Stone of Stumbling over which Israel stumbled in not accepting Jesus as the Messiah (Rom 9:33, 1 Pet 2:8). It is used of the stone from which Israel drank in the desert (1 Cor 10:4), and of the cornerstone of the church (1 Peter 2:7). It is the term used in parallel with "mountains," referring to the place in which the wicked hide at the time of Christ's second coming and to what they ask to fall on them in order to hide them from the wrath of the Lamb (Rev 6:15, 16).

Several characteristics of *petra* become apparent from this overview of New Testament usage. As a literal term, *petra* generally refers to rather massive or stable stones that either bear a great deal of weight or are part of a mountain (as in the Lord's tomb, the rocks splitting, or the mountains and rocks in Revelation).

> "The word Peter signifies a stone,—a rolling stone. Peter was not the rock upon which the church was founded. The gates of hell did prevail against him when he denied his Lord with cursing and swearing. The church was built upon One against whom the gates of hell could not prevail" (DA 412).

However, quite a few of the usages of the word *petra* are clearly symbolic, meaning that the term stands for something else. In the parable of the soil, Jesus uses different types of ground to symbolize different types of people and their response to the gospel (Luke 8:4-8). Further symbolic usage of the term includes the reference to the house built on the rock (Matt 7:24-27; Luke 6:47-49), the Stone of Stumbling, the Cornerstone (Rom 9:33, 1 Peter 2:7, 8), and the spiritual rock from which Israel drank in the desert (1 Cor 10:4) – all of which are referred to Christ by the New Testament authors.

The symbolic use of *petra* – Matthew 16:18 is a case in which Jesus uses *petra* symbolically, because it is quite clear that He is not referring to some large stone foundation upon which He intended to build a literal church structure. The question is, to what does the symbol refer? Here the play on words and the allusion to previous words help interpret the term. *Petros* and *petra* are masculine and feminine forms of the same term respectively. Although Jesus probably spoke these words in Aramaic and the word in both cases would then be the same (*kepha*), Matthew utilizes the distinction in Greek to explain unambiguously what Jesus meant. In response to Peter,

Jesus says, "You are Peter (*petros*) and on this Rock (*petra*) I will build my church." Does He mean that Peter is the rock on which the church would be founded? This meaning is unlikely for two reasons. First, Peter was overcome by Satan soon after his confession, in verse 16 (see Matt 16:23), and later when he denied Jesus three times at His trial (see Matt 27:69-75). If Peter were the *petra* then Jesus' words were not fulfilled. It took the reinstatement by Jesus for Peter to reenter the ministry (see John 21). Second, that Peter is not the rock is confirmed by three other symbolic uses of the term *petra* in the New Testament, all referring to Christ as we noticed above. It is instructive that Peter himself, in making use of the symbol of a rock (*petra*), links this symbol to Jesus, not to himself (see 1 Peter 2:7, 8). It is also helpful to note that in the Old Testament the word "rock" is often used as a metaphor for God (see box).

> Some of the Old Testament texts that use the word "rock" for God:
> Deuteronomy 32:15 "Then he [Israel] forsook God who made him, and scorned the Rock of his salvation."
> Deuteronomy 32:18 "You neglected the Rock who begot you, and forgot the God who gave you birth."
> 2 Samuel 22:2 "The LORD is my rock and my fortress and my deliverer."
> 2 Samuel 22:47 "The LORD lives, and blessed be my rock; and exalted be God, the rock of my salvation,"
> Psalm 18:2 "The LORD is my rock and my fortress and my deliverer, My God, my rock, in whom I take refuge."
> Psalm 31:3 "For Thou art my rock and my fortress."
> Psalm 42:9 "I will say to God my rock, "Why hast Thou forgotten me?""

Conclusion – If the Christian Church were founded on one of the disciples or on a mere human confession, we would have all the difficulties and inconsistencies of human failure, sin, and weakness in the foundation. The Church's vision of its destiny would reach only as high as human insight could imagine. However, this is not the case. The Church is founded on Jesus Christ. His grace and forgiveness expressed at the cross are the source of its existence. His High Priesthood is the assurance of its standing with God, and His promise to return is the vision of its destiny.

Tom Shepherd

References

[1]See F. W. Danker, *A Greek-English Lexicon of the New Testament and Other Early Christian Literature,* third ed. (Chicago, IL: University of Chicago Press, 2000), s.v. *petra*.

Ancient synagogue in Capernaum

DID JESUS GIVE THE CHURCH THE AUTHORITY TO FORGIVE SINS?

And I will give you the keys of the kingdom of heaven; and whatever you bind on earth will be bound in heaven, and whatever you loose on earth will be loosed in heaven. Matthew 16:19, NKJV.

Matthew 16:19 is a part of Jesus' words to Peter in connection with the confession he made in the vicinity of Caesarea Philippi. In responding to Jesus' question, "Who do you say that I am?" Peter made this statement on behalf of all the disciples, "You are the Christ [Messiah]" (Matt 16:15, 16). This confession was met by Jesus with the following address to Peter: "Blessed are you, Simon Barjona, because flesh and blood did not reveal *this* to you, but My Father who is in heaven. I also say to you that you are Peter, and upon this rock I will build My church; and the gates of Hades will not overpower it" (16:17, 18). Then follows the text under investigation.

The rock on which the church is built is Christ – This passage has been a subject of debate among Christians particularly since the Protestant Reformation. Jesus' saying to Peter has been used by the Roman Catholic Church to support the claims of the popes that they are the successors of Peter who was appointed by Jesus as the leader of the Christian church. However, there is nothing in this text, nor in the rest of the New Testament, to suggest that Peter is the rock on which the church is built. In order to withstand the gates of hell, the church obviously had to be built on a firmer foundation than a human being, including Peter (cf. Matt 16:21-23). The foundation of the church is Christ Himself (1 Cor 3:11; Eph 2:20; 1 Pet 2:4).

The authority of "binding" and "loosing" belongs to the church – In Matthew 16:19, Jesus was addressing Peter, but what was said to Peter in chapter 16 was also said in 18:18 to the church. The authority of "binding" and "loosing" has thus been given to the whole body of Christ and not to a particular individual within the church.

The context of Matthew 18 suggests that the authority of "binding" and "loosing" refers to the church's responsibility of disciplining the members. However, Matthew 16:19 and 18:18 do not provide the church with unlimited power with regard to disciplining and forgiving. The correct translation of Matthew 16:19 reads: "Whatever you bind on earth *shall have been bound* in heaven, and whatever you loose on earth *shall have been loosed* in heaven" (NASB). The text does not suggest that the church has been granted absolute authority to forgive or to refuse to forgive the offenses of its members. Rather, what Jesus emphasized in the text is that the church's decisions must reflect the decisions already made in heaven (not vice versa). To forgive somebody's sins is the sole prerogative of God made possible through Jesus' death on the cross. God's disposition to forgive should set the standard for those who are appointed to exercise the authority to discipline church members.

The text places upon the church a great responsibility. In disciplining members, church officers must not be governed by personal preferences or prejudices. If the sinning member repents, the church must readily forgive by following the example of the Father in heaven. However, if the sinning brother or sister stubbornly refuses to repent, the church must implement church discipline as a last redemptive attempt to bring about repentance. It is interesting that the word "to disfellowship" or "to cast out" (Gr. *ekballo*; cf. John 9:34, 35; 3 John 10) is not used here. Rather, Jesus said, the church has to relate to the unrepentant member as to "a Gentile and a tax collector." What Jesus meant was that the church should treat him or her as it does a sinner in the world, making every effort to bring him or her back into the fellowship of believers. Recall that in the Gospels, the Gentiles and tax collectors were the subjects of Je-

> "The real difficulty Protestants have with the Roman Catholic teaching concerning Peter is the notion of sole apostolic succession emanating from Peter as the first bishop of Rome. This dogma is anachronistic for Matthew, who knows nothing about Peter being the first pope or of the primacy of Rome over other Christian churches. Matthew would not have endorsed the idea of Peter's infallibility or sole authority in the church, since Peter speaks as a representative of the other apostles and often makes mistakes (15:15; 16:16; 17:4,25; 18:21; 19:27; 26:33-35; cf. Acts 11:1-18; Gal. 2:11-14). In 18:18, binding and loosing is a function of the church, not Peter" (David L. Turner, *Matthew*, Baker Exegetical Commentary on the New Testament [Grand Rapids, MI: Baker Academic, 2008], 407).

sus' earnest love, and He made great efforts to save them (Luke 15:1, 2).

Forgiveness of sins by a priest is not biblical – Some comments are necessary with regard to Jesus' statement in John 20:23: "If you forgive the sins of any, *their sins* have been forgiven them; if you retain the sins of any, they have been retained" (NKJV). Once again Jesus indicates that the church's actions must reflect the actions already made in heaven. This text has been taken by some Christians to support the practice of auricular confession or the remission of sins by a priest, but there is nothing in the text that would suggest such a practice.

The forgiveness Jesus refers to in this text must be defined by its context. After His resurrection, Jesus appears to the disciples and says to them: "As the Father has sent me, I also send you" (John 20:21). Then He empowers them with the Holy Spirit, commissioning them to go out to the world and to forgive, or not to forgive, sins: "If you forgive the sins of any, their sins have been forgiven them; if you retain the sins of any, they have been retained" (20:23). Luke reports a similar statement of Jesus in the same context: "That repentance for forgiveness of sins would be proclaimed in His name to all the nations, beginning from Jerusalem" (24:47). This statement adds further insight into the meaning of John 20:21-23. It suggests that Jesus did not authorize the church to forgive sins as such but to proclaim the message of *God's* forgiveness to the world, e. g., at Pentecost the gospel of forgiveness was proclaimed by Peter (Acts 2:38). The church has a responsibility to proclaim forgiveness to those who respond to the gospel by accepting them into the fellowship of believers. On the other hand, the church is commissioned to convey the message of judgment to those who reject the call to repentance, because they have chosen to remain in their sinful condition.

> Jesus did not authorize the church to forgive sins as such but to proclaim the message of God's forgiveness to the world.

Ranko Stefanovic

DID JESUS PERMIT DIVORCE AND REMARRIAGE?

And I say to you, "whoever divorces his wife, except for immorality, and marries another woman, commits adultery." Matthew 19:9.

According to this text, Jesus seems to reject remarriage in any form after a divorce. When dealing with texts in the Synoptic Gospels (Matthew, Mark, and Luke), one must read a text in its immediate context as well as in comparison with parallel texts in the other two.

The hardness of heart – The context of Matthew 19:1-10 is very rich. One aspect that stands out specifically is the issue of hardness of hearts, introduced by Jesus Himself in verse 8. The Pharisees show clear evidence of hard hearts, because they look for reasons that would allow them to get out of marriage. But even Jesus' disciples have a hard time accepting Jesus' teaching on marriage. They suggest to stay single and not to marry if marriage is indissoluble (v. 10). They too cannot think of marriage in terms other than divorce. This hardness of hearts is manifested a little later when they encounter the children brought to Jesus in order to be blessed, and they scold them (v. 13).

For the rich, such as the rich young ruler, it is difficult to enter the kingdom of God because of their hardness of hearts (Matt 19: 21-23). Peter's question about the reward of following Jesus may point to hardness of heart (v. 27). In the parable of the laborers in the vineyard (20:1-16), those who have worked all day long are not content with the generosity of the landowner. They have an evil eye and a hard heart.

Already in Matthew 18 hardness of hearts occurs. The disciples have been warned not to despise the little ones (vv. 6, 10), which may include the vulnerable ones in society, especially women. Chapter 18 ends with the warning that the Heavenly Father will hand over to torture those who do not forgive their neighbors from their heart (vv. 34, 35). The unforgiving servant is an example of a hardhearted person par excellence, and it is interesting that this motif is developed in the following passage dealing with divorce and remarriage. Instead of forgiving their spouses, there are people, such as the Pharisees, who look only for loopholes and possibilities to get out of their marriages and leave their partners.

Jesus and the Pharisees – The conversation between Jesus and the Pharisees started with the Pharisees asking Jesus about reasons for divorce. Probably, they wanted to draw Jesus into the controversy between the more liberal rabbinical school of Hillel, according to whom a man could divorce his wife for any reason, and the more conservative school of Shammai, who taught that divorce was only allowed on grounds of adultery. Maybe they even hoped Jesus would touch on the case of Herod's being married to Herodias and make Herod His enemy (Matt 14:3, 4). This was a highly political issue and had cost John the Baptist his life.

An important word in Matthew 19:3 is *apoluo*, which in this context means "to send away" or "to divorce." It is used twice by the Pharisees (vv. 3, 7), and twice by Jesus (vv. 8, 9). Jesus, however, uses it only in His second answer. In His first answer He uses the term *chorizo* (v. 6) to express the concept of divorce. Jesus clearly says "No" to divorce. In verse 6 no exception is listed, in verse 9 a single possible exception is mentioned.

Jesus' view of marriage – Starting with verse 4 of Matthew 19, Jesus answers the question of the Pharisees. He develops God's perspective on marriage, an institution that together with the rest of creation was very good. Jesus' first answer to the Pharisees (vv. 4-6) begins with a question, "Have you not read that He who created *them* from the beginning made them male and female?" This question refers to two Old Testament texts (Gen 1:27; 5:2). Then follows the statement that "a man shall leave his father and mother, and shall cleave to his wife; and the two shall become one flesh" (Matt 19:5). At the beginning of verse 6, the previous thought is repeated, "Consequently they are no longer two, but one flesh." And the text concludes with an imperative, "What therefore God has joined together, let no man separate." Thus, twice we hear about "two" humans who have "become one" (Matt 19:5b and 6a). Does Jesus

> He who gave Eve to Adam as a help-meet performed His first miracle at a marriage festival. In the festal hall where friends and kindred rejoiced together, Christ began His public ministry. Thus He sanctioned marriage, recognizing it as an institution that He Himself had established. He ordained that men and women should be united in holy wedlock, to rear families whose members, crowned with honor, should be recognized as members of the family above (AH 99).

give any reasons for divorce? No, the Creation order does not allow divorce for any reason.

Mattew 19:5 begins with the phrase "and [He] said" referring to God. God Himself, the highest possible authority, has ordained that a man leave his parents and, together with his wife, form a new union. The phrase "one flesh" points in a special way to the physical union of the spouses. However, the term "flesh" stands for the entire personality and cannot be limited to the physical sphere only. Therefore, adultery is so dramatic. It fractures the wonderful union between husband and wife.

The term "one" stresses union and unity. Two beings, a man and a woman, become one. By making this statement Jesus rejects homosexuality as well as polygamy. To leave one's parents, to live together, and to become one flesh are human actions that, in a hidden way, express the joining of the man and woman together by God. Every legitimate marriage is a joining together by God. Therefore, we are not allowed to divorce our spouse. Jesus clearly takes position against divorce.

The issue of divorce – The Pharisees respond to Jesus by asking why Moses gave a certificate of divorce, if divorce is not permitted. By referring to Deuteronomy 24:1, they may have wished to undo Genesis 1 and 2 in support of a lax practice of divorce. But Jesus explains how the biblical passages relate to each other. In Matthew 19:9 we hear his final conclusion: With divorce, humans destroy God's work.

The Pharisees claim that Moses has commanded (*eneteilato*) to give one's wife a bill of divorce if she has committed some indecency. Jesus is much more precise: Moses has permitted (*epetrepsen*) divorce but he has not commanded it. ". . . but from the beginning it has not been this way." Divorce is not part of God's original plan.

In verse 6, Jesus categorically denies divorce. In verse 9, He adds that even if someone gets a divorce against the clear testimony of Scripture, he or she is not free. In Matthew 5:32, a divorced woman marrying again, except for adultery of her husband, commits adultery—obviously she is still considered to be married. In Matthew 19:9, a husband marrying another woman commits adultery—he is still married, if the exception clause does not apply. According to Mark 10:12, divorce was initiated not only by men but also by women.

Matthew 19:9 allows for only one reason of divorce. This is *porneia* – sexual immorality. But even in such a case the context urges us to forgive our partner and let go of our hard-heartedness. The different aspects of *porneia* include prostitution, premarital sexual relations, adultery, incest, and homosexuality; in short, all sexual relations outside of marriage.

The question that remains is whether or not the exception clause refers to divorce only or also to remarriage.

(1) "Whoever divorces his wife,

except for porneia, commits adultery" (Matt 19:9).

(2) and marries another,

(1) Divorcing one's spouse and remarrying is adultery. Therefore, it can be assumed that the exception clause found right between (1) and (2) refers to remarriage after divorce. The exception clause makes little sense if the spouse not having been involved in *porneia* would not have the right to remarry. A legitimate divorce allows for a legitimate remarriage. Because in the time of Jesus, as well as during Old Testament times, remarriage after a divorce was permitted, one would expect a similar situation for the New Testament. Otherwise, the New Testament would need to state clearly that a new order had been established.

Although with His exception clause Jesus allows for divorce and remarriage in one specific case, the point of His message is the permanence of marriage.

Implications for today – When God constituted marriage it was understood to be a lifelong union between one man and one woman in which the two would complement each other and would contribute to each other's well being.

Jesus has reinforced the permanence of marriage. Divorce destroys what God has joined together and is against God's will. In the case that a divorce takes place anyway—except for *porneia*– biblically there is only the possibility of remaining single or of being reconciled to the spouse. A person who gets a divorce for any reason other than fornication and remarries commits adultery and violates God's laws. This is also true for someone who marries a divorced person, if this person has not been divorced on grounds of *porneia* committed by the spouse.

The only reason for which a church member can divorce his or her spouse is fornication. If a spouse commits fornication, the other spouse who was not involved in such an act may get a divorce. However, even in this case the ideal is reconciliation. If reconciliation is not possible, the spouse not involved in actual fornication may remarry.

When a marriage falls apart, the church is also always affected. Therefore, the church must apply preventive care and must react in a balanced and biblical way. Not to react at all may be irresponsible. The goal of the church's involvement must be to help, to bring about healing, and to assist those who otherwise may get lost. In some cases, this may include church discipline and removing a person from church membership. On the other hand, the church cannot forever stigmatize those who have committed a sexual sin. Following God, the church neither takes sin lightly nor does she refuse to forgive and grant another chance to those who have missed the mark.

"A woman may be legally divorced from her husband by the laws of the land and yet not divorced in the sight of God and according to the higher law. There is only one sin, which is adultery, which can place the husband or wife in a position where they can be free from the marriage vow in the sight of God. Although the laws of the land may grant a divorce, yet they are husband and wife still in the Bible light, according to the laws of God" (AH 344).

All believers are called to turn away from hard-heartedness, to work on their marriages, to grant forgiveness and new beginnings, and to set an example of what a Christian marriage is all about. Where conditions are unhealthy, the Christian solution is to change the conditions, not the partner. Even in cases that seem to be hopeless, we remember that the Lord who has risen from the dead can also resurrect our marriages to new life.

Ekkehardt Mueller

The Bible is worth all other books which have ever been printed
Patrick Henry

HAVE THE SIGNS IN THE SUN, MOON, AND STARS
ALREADY HAPPENED?

But immediately after the tribulation of those days the sun will be darkened, and the moon will not give its light, and the stars will fall from the sky, and the powers of the heavens will be shaken. Matthew 24:29.

To understand this verse, it will be helpful to look at the larger structure of the chapter in some detail in order to identify the tribulation period after which these signs appear. Jesus' discourse begins with His prediction of the temple's destruction (vv. 1, 2), which prompted the disciples to ask when this would all happen. To the disciples, who were soon to be surprised by Christ's death, the lengthy reply Jesus gave must have seemed rather mysterious. In fact, after the resurrection, they asked Him "Lord, is it at this time You are restoring the kingdom to Israel?" (Acts 1:6). In answer, Jesus made clear that we should not expect God to provide us a *timeline* of future events (Acts 1:7). Attempts to find such a prophetic timetable in Matthew 24 have complicated the interpretation of this chapter. Actually, Jesus' discourse has just two main focal points: the destruction of Jerusalem and the end of the world.

The structure of Matthew 24 – The prediction of the destruction of Jerusalem with its temple was made centuries before by Daniel, whose prophecy Jesus urges us to read and understand (Matt 24:15; cf. Dan 9:26). It appears that the disciples, upon hearing Jesus say that the temple would be destroyed, thought that this event would signal the end-time. But because the final days of earth's history were far in the future, the disciples were unknowingly asking two separate questions: (1) "When will these things be?" (i.e., the destruction of the temple) and (2) "What will be the sign of your coming and of the end of the world?" (v. 3).

Careful study of Jesus' reply shows that it has two main parts, corresponding to these two questions.[1] This structure is evident from the repetition of events at two different junctures of His discourse, including the appearance of false Christs (vv. 5, 23, 24) and false prophets (vv. 11, 24), tribulation (vv. 9, 21), and various upheavals of nature (vv. 7, 29). Also, in the first part of His discourse, Jesus warns us that the "end" is not yet (v. 6), that it is only the "beginning of birth pangs" (v. 8). The analogy with childbirth in itself may suggest two different time periods. Just as false labor contractions appear less significant compared to the final ones preceding the actual birth, so the events connected with the destruction of Jerusalem only faintly foreshadowed the end-time events.

> The New Testament almost always uses the term "tribulation" to refer to the persecution of God's people by human authorities and powers.

Each of the two parts of the discourse culminate with a judgment period of highly significant events. The first part culminates with the "abomination of desolation" that believers will recognize as the signal to flee Jerusalem in order to escape the city's impending destruction (vv. 15-20; cf. Luke 21:20). The second part, marked by the end of the "great tribulation," culminates with omens in the sun, moon, and stars, that believers will recognize as the signal "that the final judgment has already begun" and to watch and prepare for the coming of the Son of Man (vv. 29-31).[2]

The great tribulation – The nature of the great tribulation and the cosmic phenomena that follow it contrast sharply with the more generalized descriptions earlier in the discourse. There Jesus warns His followers that they will suffer tribulation and persecution and that, as a result, many will fall away (vv. 9, 10). Later, however, Jesus refers to a "great tribulation" like no period before it. In fact, those days are so severe that they will be cut short for the sake of the elect (vv. 21, 22).[3] Both of these references to tribulation involve the persecution of those who remain faithful to Jesus. The second reference to tribulation, which comes in the second part of the discourse, should not be confused with the time of God's wrath when the seven last plagues are poured out, identified in the book of Revelation as God's judgment on the wicked.[4] The New Testament almost always uses the term "tribulation" to refer to the persecution of God's people by human authorities and powers, and this is clearly its meaning in Matthew 24.

The first mention of tribulation seems to refer to the severe persecution of faithful Christians by pagan Roman emperors from the first to the fourth century (cf. Rev 1:9; 2:9, 10). But this tribulation was sporadic and more limited in place and time compared to the protracted and systematic persecution of faithful believers during the 1260-year period from A.D. 538 to 1798 (Dan 7:25; Rev 12:6, 14), made possible by the church's acquisition of imperial power. This second period of persecution, here called the "great tribulation," was cut short by the neutralization of the persecuting power of the papacy during the French Revolution and the establishment of church-state separation by the United States in the eighteenth century (Rev 13:3, 11). Because this "great tribulation" is cut short by God's providential intervention (cf. Mark 13:20), it cannot refer to the plague-judgments on wickedness during the time of trouble but must instead refer to the tribulation and persecution by earthly powers of God's faithful people.

Omens in the sun, moon, and stars – It is after the great tribulation (Matt 24:29/Mark 13:24) that the cosmic phenomena appear and the time of watching for the coming of the Son of Man begins (Matt 24:42-44). In view of the connection of these omens in the sun, moon, and stars with the end of the great tribulation, we should look for them toward the end of the eighteenth century. It is also important to notice that

> "At the close of the great papal persecution, Christ declared, the sun should be darkened, and the moon should not give her light. Next, the stars should fall from heaven" (DA 632).

the *sequence* sun-moon-stars is the same everywhere these phenomena are mentioned in the New Testament (Matt 24:29; Mark 13:24; Luke 21:25; Rev 6:12, 13). This fixed sequence suggests that a specific rather than a more general fulfillment is expected.

In view of the expected timing and sequence of these phenomena, the so-called "Dark Day" of May 19, 1780, when candles were needed at noon and a smoky haze obscured the moon, fits well with the description of Jesus that the sun and moon would be darkened. This event was followed some decades later by the great Leonid meteor shower of November 13, 1833, in which an estimated sixty thousand meteors an hour were observed, giving birth to the new science of meteor astronomy.[5] These natural phenomena, spanning a brief period from the late eighteenth, to early nineteenth, centuries remain unequaled in North America in terms of religious impact, intensity, and visibility.[6] In view of their significance, sequence, and timing, they constitute the most likely fulfillment of the prophecy of Jesus in Matthew 24. While there is some indication that similar signs may immediately precede the Second Advent,[7] the passing years since the fulfillment of the prophecy about the sun, moon, and stars make the warning with which Jesus concludes this part of the discourse that much more relevant: "For this reason you also must be ready; for the Son of Man is coming at an hour when you do not think He will" (24:44).

Clinton Wahlen

References

[1] See also the chapter by Richard Davidson on Matthew 24:34 in this volume.

[2] Richard M. Davidson, "The Second Advent and the Fullness of Time," *Ministry* 73 (June-July 2000): 45.

[3] Cf. Ibid., 47 n. 25 which suggests in line with Matthew 24:29/Mark 13:24 that these signs appear *after* the tribulation, which ceased "about 1750" (cf. Mark 13:19-20).

[4] The great tribulation and cosmic phenomena described by Jesus and similar descriptions by John (Rev 6:12-14; 7:14) are quite different from references in Revelation to the seven last plagues or "time of trouble" immediately preceding the Second Advent. The period of the plagues is called the time of "God's wrath" (15:1, 7; 16:1, etc.) and should not be confused with the satanic-inspired fury or tribulation which is directed not at the wicked but against God's people (12:12-16).

[5] Regarding the Dark Day, see Joseph Dow, *History of Hampton*, online: http://www.hampton.lib.nh.us/HAMPTON/history/dow/chap12/dow12_14.htm, while the information about meteors and meteor showers is given by *Astronomy* magazine, online: http://www.astronomy.com/asy/default.aspx?c=a&id=2109, both accessed February 2, 2009.

[6] C. Mervyn Maxwell says, "They [the signs of Matt 24:29] occurred where people lived who could take appropriate notice of them. They stimulated wide reflection. They played a distinct part in alerting those who had 'ears to hear' to the commencement of the final judgment and the arrival of the end time" (*God Cares*, 2 vols. [Nampa, ID: Pacific Press, 1985], 2:214).

[7] See Joel 3:15, 16 (cf. 2:10); Tim Poirier, "The End of a Sign, or a Sign of the End?" *Adventist Review*, November 13, 2008, 21.

WHAT DID JESUS MEAN BY "THIS GENERATION"?

"Truly I say to you, this generation will not pass away until all these things take place." Matthew 24:34.

Matthew 24:34 has been regarded as one of the most difficult passages in the New Testament. C. S. Lewis called this passage "the most embarrassing verse in the Bible."[1] This verse has been frequently cited by Jews, Muslims, and agnostics as one of the main arguments against Christ, Christianity, and the New Testament. If Jesus predicted that He would come again in His generation, as many have interpreted Matthew 24:34 to teach, then His prediction clearly failed, and the veracity of His Messianic claims, of Christianity in general, and of the New Testament Scriptures, is called into question. Did Jesus mistakenly predict that His second advent would come in the first century?

Many nineteenth-century Adventists saw this passage as appearing in the context of the signs of Christ's second coming, in verses 27–51, and interpreted it as a promise that Christ would surely come within the lifetime of those who witnessed the cosmic signs connected with the Great Second Advent Awakening of the late eighteenth and early nineteenth centuries. The passing of time, and the death of the eyewitnesses of these signs brought disillusionment to many in the early Seventh-day Adventist movement. The question remains: has the prophecy of Matthew 24:34 failed?

The meaning of "these things" – The key to unlocking the meaning of Matthew 24:34, and of the whole chapter, is found in the pattern of words used in the historical context of verses 1-3. In verse 1 the disciples pointed out to Jesus the magnificent buildings of the Jerusalem temple, and in verse 2, Jesus responds, "Do you not see all these things [*tauta*]? Assuredly I say to you, not one stone shall be left here upon another, that shall not be thrown down." In this verse the Greek word *tauta*, translated as "these things," clearly refers to the Jerusalem temple in the context of its imminent destruction. Then in verse 3, as Jesus sat on the Mount of Olives overlooking the temple, the disciples came to Him privately, and asked, "Tell us, when will these things [*tauta*] be? And what will be the sign of your coming [*parousia*] and of the end [*synteleia*] of the age?"

289

Note that the disciples ask two basic questions: (1) regarding the *tauta* ("these things"), which from the context of the previous verse refers clearly to the destruction of the Jerusalem temple; and (2) regarding the sign of the *parousia* ("coming") and of the *synteleia* ("end") of the age. These terms elsewhere in Matthew always refer to Christ's second coming.[2] The disciples, with their dimmed understanding of Jesus' Messianic mission, probably did not distinguish between these two events in their minds, but it is evident that Jesus draws a careful distinction in His Olivet discourse, based upon the very terminology that He and the disciples had used. Throughout Matthew 24 the term *tauta* "these things" consistently refers to events connected with the destruction of Jerusalem, and the terms *parousia* "coming" and *synteleia* "end" refer to events connected with the second advent of Christ.[3]

"These things" as a reference to Christ's generation – In light of this pattern that is followed throughout the chapter, we are ready to look more closely at verse 34: "Assuredly, I say to you, this generation will by no means pass away till all these things [*tauta*] are fulfilled." To what do "these things" refer? Consistent with usage elsewhere in the chapter, it refers to the events leading up to and including the destruction of Jerusalem and not to Christ's second coming.

> In Matthew 24 "these things" consistently refers to events connected with the destruction of Jerusalem.

Further confirmation that verse 34 is referring to the generation of the first century A.D., and not to the generation at the end of the world, comes from an analysis of the whole phrase "this generation" (*he genea haute*). A look at the usage of this phrase elsewhere in Matthew's Gospel reveals that invariably the phrase denotes Jesus' contemporary generation (see Matthew 11:16; 12:41, 42, 45; 23:36).

Finally, if one views Matthew 24:34 in the larger context of Jesus' woes upon the scribes and Pharisees, in the previous chapter, there is a close parallel to the very wording of Jesus' prediction. In Matthew 23, the context is clearly the condemnation of the Jewish leaders for rejecting Jesus, with the pronouncement of doom upon national Israel as a socio-political entity: "See, your house is left to you desolate" (v. 38). In the previous verse comes the parallel with our passage: "Truly, I say to you, all these things [*tauta*] will come upon this generation [*epi ten genean tauten*]" (v. 36).

"This generation" and the destruction of Jerusalem – If one takes the phrase "this generation" to refer to Jesus' contemporary generation, those to whom He was speaking in A.D. 31, and if one assumes the length of a

---

Signs fulfilled prior to the destruction of Jerusalem in A.D. 70:

a) False Messiahs: Menahem, Theudas, and others convinced thousands of followers of their Messianic claims (Josephus, *Wars,* 2.17.8, 9; *Antiquities* 20.5.1 17.10.6, 7).

b) Wars— In those days Israel was filled with wars and rumours of wars, due in part to the fanatic actions of the Zealots (Josephus, *Wars,* 2:17).

c) Natural catastrophes—A famine under Claudius (A.D. 49) mentioned in Acts 11:28; a pestilence in Rome, in A.D. 65 (Tacitus, *Annals,* 16:13); earthquakes (Acts 16:26; Josephus, *Wars,* 4:286, 287).

d) Persecutions—At that time the Christians suffered repeated persecutions, from the stoning of Stephen to the terrible persecution under Nero. (cf. Acts 12, 14, etc.).

---

generation in biblical thought to be about forty years,[4] then the destruction of Jerusalem (A.D. 70) takes place exactly on time just before Jesus' generation passes away (A.D. 31 + 40 years ≈ A.D. 70).

In summary, then, Matthew 24:34 states that "this generation," i.e., the generation contemporary with Jesus, would not pass away until all "these things," i.e., events leading up to, and including, the destruction of Jerusalem in A.D. 70, would be fulfilled. And since verse 34 does not refer to the Second Advent, the prophecy has not *failed,* but was *fulfilled,* in the first century A.D., right on time!

Richard M. Davidson

References

[1]C. S. Lewis, "The World's Last Night," in *The Essential C. S. Lewis,* ed. Lyle W. Dorsett (New York, NY: Touchstone, Simon and Schuster, 1996), 385.

[2]The Greek word *parousia* ("coming") occurs in Matthew only in chap. 24 (vv. 3, 27, 37, 39), all clearly referring to Christ's second coming in glory. For the consistent use of the term *synteleia* ("end") in Matthew with reference to the "end of the age" (second advent of Christ), see Matthew 13:39, 40, 49; 28:20.

[3]For detailed analysis of this consistent usage of terminology in Matthew 24, see Richard Davidson, "'This Generation Shall Not Pass' (Matt 24:34): Failed Or Fulfilled Prophecy?" in *The Cosmic Battle for Planet Earth: Essays in Honor of Norman R. Gulley,* eds. Ronald A. G. Du Preez and Jiří Moskala (Berrien Springs, MI: Old Testament Department, Seventh-day Adventist Theological Seminary, Andrews University, 2003), 307–319.

[4]Note especially the wilderness generation at the time of the Exodus that passed off the scene in forty years (Num 14:29-34; 32:11, 12; Deut 1:34, 35). It seems likely that Jesus borrowed the phrase "this evil generation" (Matthew 12:45) from its usage in Deuteronomy 1:35, in which it refers to the generation that passed away in forty years, and the shortened version "this generation" probably also harks back to this Old Testament usage.

Jerusalem

DO THE WICKED BURN FOREVER IN HELL?

These will go away into eternal punishment, but the righteous into eternal life. Matthew 25:46.

This text uses the word "eternal" twice, the first time it is applied to the punishment of the wicked, the second time it refers to the eternal life of the righteous. If "eternal life" means a life without end, should not the "eternal punishment" also be without end?

The Sheep and the Goats – Matthew 25:46 is the conclusion of Jesus' parable or story of the Sheep and the Goats (Matt 25:31-46). The story depicts the Lord's second coming wherein He divides "the nations"[1] into two clear groups – the Sheep and the Goats. The Sheep are placed on the Master's right and the Goats on the left. Twice in the story the Sheep are identified as the righteous (vv. 37 and 46). The Goats are never specifically identified, though they are obviously a group opposite to the Sheep. Both the Sheep and the Goats address Jesus as Lord and actually give fairly similar responses to His words to them.

Jesus addresses the Sheep first, calling them blessed and inviting them to enter the Kingdom prepared for them from the foundation of the world. The reason they are invited to enter is that they have cared for Him in the person of the poor and needy. The Goats, on the other hand, are called accursed[2] and are condemned to "the eternal fire that has been prepared for the devil and his angels" (v. 41). The reason for the harsh judgment on the Goats is their lack of concern for the poor and needy – which Jesus indicates is the same as not serving or helping Him.

Two approaches to life – We can see that Jesus presents two very contrary destinies, based on two very different approaches to life in the present world. Those who bless and help others with their time and resources are headed toward an eternal kingdom of joy and blessedness. Those who neglect to help others around them are unaware not only of the needs of these "least" individuals but also of the fact that in so doing they are neglecting Jesus Himself.[3] Jesus said they are headed toward something God never intended for people – eternal punishment.

Eternal punishment – But just what is this "eternal punishment" to which the Goats are consigned? The term "punishment" used here is *kolasis*, a fairly rare word in the New Testament, used only here in Matthew 25:46 and in 1 John 4:18. It comes from a root that means "to trim," "lop," "mutilate," "punish," "chastise." It has the idea of cutting off what is unnecessary. To be punished by God is to be cut off. It is a consistent teaching of Scripture that the wicked will be punished by the Almighty (Gen 6-9; Ezek 18; Rom 1; Heb 10:29; 2 Pet 2:9; Rev 20). It may not be this which troubles as much as the idea of a punishment that continues throughout eternity. Thus the word "eternal" is the more crucial one in the phrase "eternal punishment."

> The sinners of Sodom are "set forth for an example, suffering the vengeance of eternal fire" [Jude 7]. The passage *defines* "eternal fire." It is a fire from God which destroys sinners totally and forever. (Edward W. Fudge, *The Fire That Consumes* [Houston, TX: Providential Press, 1982], 287).

The term "eternal" used here is *aionios*. Its Old Testament counterpart is the Hebrew term *ᶜolam*. Both terms can mean "eternal, everlasting" or "for a lifetime, as long as life lasts" depending on what they modify. In Exodus 21:6, a servant who loves his master will serve him *ᶜolam* (forever = all his life). In Jude 7, Sodom and Gomorrah undergo the punishment of *aionios* fire (eternal fire). Obviously, Sodom and Gomorrah are no longer burning; thus the fire was eternal only in the sense of a final or on-going result, not in the sense of a fire that is still burning or will burn into eternity.

This leads to the question of how the term *aionios* is used in Matthew. He uses the term "eternal" six times (18:8, 19:16, 29, 25:41, 46 [twice]). Three times the term is linked to "life" (thus "eternal life"), and three times it is linked to "fire" or "punishment." Eternal life is the reward of the righteous and clearly indicates unending existence. The punishment of the wicked being "eternal fire" many assume to be unending existence in an ever-burning hell.

Eternal fire – However, a closer examination of Matthew's use of the term "fire" suggests another perspective. Matthew uses the word "fire" (Gr. *pyr*) a total of twelve times.[4] Almost all of these occurrences are linked with the idea of judgment. Especially instructive are the agricultural metaphors used by John the Baptist in Matthew 3:10-12 and by Jesus in the parable of the wheat and the tares in 13:24-30, 36-43. In both cases there is a division made between the good and the bad. The good items are pre-served, while the bad items are burned up with fire. The term "burned up" in Greek is *katakaio* which means "to consume," "burn up." The chaff (3:10-12) or the tares (13:36-43) are consumed by a fire that is unquench-able (3:12). It is not the chaff or tares that endures forever. Since they are combustible they are consumed. But the fire is eternal in its effects. (cf. Mark 9:42-50 with the reference to the worm that does not die and the fire that is not quenched).[5] It is instructive to note in this regard that Jesus does not call the wicked eternal, but rather the fire. The wicked are consumed by the eternal fire (just like the chaff or the tares), and the effect is eternal punishment, not *eternal punishing*.

The issue of immortality – The above conclusion is sup-ported by the fact that the righteous will receive immor-tality only at the first resurrec-tion (1 Cor 15:50-54). Therefore, "eternal life" will be a life without end (Rev 21:4), whereas the unrighteous, who do not have, or receive, immortality (Eccl 9:5, 6; 2 Thess 2:9, 10), cannot suffer eternally because they are mor-tal. Their punishment is the second death (Rev 2:11; 20:6, 14; 21:8). While the righteous can look forward to a life of eternal bliss, the expectation of the wicked is the fire of judgment that will consume them (Heb 10:27).

> The wicked are consumed by the eternal fire and the effect is eternal punishment, not *eternal punishing*.

Summary – Putting this all together we see that the punishment the wicked receive is something they bring on themselves by neglecting the needy around them. This links them to the devil and his angels in heading toward just punishment from God. The punishment will involve destruc-tion by fire, but the fire itself, while eternal in effect, will not burn on for-ever because the wicked are not immortal (cf. Mal 4:1-3).

Tom Shepherd

References

[1]This term in the New Testament often refers to Gentiles. However, at this point in Matthew it seems to include all of mankind, including Israel and the Church. Cf. Donald Hagner, *Matthew 14-28,* Word Biblical Commentary, vol. 33b (Dallas, TX: Word Books, 1995), 742.

[2]The Greek term is a form of the verb *kataraomai,* which means "to curse." It is used only here in Matthew but also appears in Mark 11:21, Luke 6:28, Romans 12:14, and James 3:9. Compare the concept of being accursed by God in Deuteronomy 21:23.

[3]We might object that the story says nothing of salvation by grace through faith apart from works (Eph 2:8, 9), and indeed, it seems to suggest salvation by good deeds to the needy. But such would be a misunderstanding of both Jesus and Paul. The biblical perspective on human nature is that we act out in our life what we are inside (cf. Matt 7:15-20 "by their fruits you will know them"). Paul suggests the same in Eph 2:8-10 where faith is followed by good deeds which God prepared beforehand for us to walk in (cf. also James 2:14-26). It is a consistent teaching of Scripture that we are judged by our deeds (2 Cor 5:10, Matt 16:27, Prov 24:12).

[4]Matthew 3:10, 11, 12; 5:22; 7:19; 13:40, 42, 50; 17:15; 18:8, 9; 25:41.

[5]Jesus' mention of the undying worm and unquenchable fire in connection with the punishment of the wicked quotes Isaiah 66:24. The two images convey the same message: the worm will not die and the fire will not be quenched until the corpse is fully consumed, that is, the destruction of the wicked will be total.

St Catherine's monastery at the foot of Mount Sinai where Constantine von Tischendorf in 1844 found the Codex Sinaiticus (ca. A.D. 350) containing parts of the Old Testament in Greek (LXX) and the complete New Testament.

ARE THE JEWS TODAY RESPONSIBLE FOR
THE DEATH OF CHRIST?

And all the people answered and said, "His blood *be* on us and on our children!" Matthew 27:25.

Despite the Jewish flavor of Matthew's Gospel, this declaration has been used to justify vicious anti-Jewish sentiments and behavior throughout Christian history. Taken at face value, however, it indicates only that those directly involved in the crucifixion of Christ accept responsibility for His death. The oath itself is unremarkable. Many similar declarations are found in both the Old and New Testaments.[1]

The status of Israel – But the question also involves the status of Israel as a nation. The ominous utterance of Jesus that the kingdom (represented by the vineyard in the parable) would be "taken away" from some and given to others (Matt. 21:43) and the blood-curdling prediction that the scribes and Pharisees would "fill up" the measure of their fathers' guilt by killing those Jesus would send to them (23:29-36) both seem to suggest that blame for the crucifixion rests with the whole nation. Furthermore, the immediate context of 27:25 juxtaposes the confession of Judas that he has betrayed innocent blood (27:4) with Pilate's washing his hands of the matter. This is followed immediately by "all the people" readily accepting responsibility for Jesus' death.

On the other hand, it is the religious leaders of Israel, not the whole nation, who are singled out in Jesus' pronouncements of doom in chapter 23. Furthermore, the verse immediately after the so-called "self-cursing" of 27:25 underscores clearly Pilate's own responsibility. The Roman governor has already had Jesus whipped and scourged. Now he hands Him over to be crucified, something only Pilate has the power to do (27:26). Further on, we see the Pharisees, chief priests, and elders, more than the crowd, to be the real culprits (v. 41). In fact, it is these who are said to have brought Jesus to Pilate in the first place (vv. 1, 3, 6, 12) and who incite the crowds to have Jesus crucified (v. 20; cf. 16:21).

The salvation of individual Jews – While with the rejection of the Messiah Israel as a nation lost its privilege of being God's representatives here on earth, individual Jews were attracted to Jesus and followed Him. According to Matthew, crowds flocked to Jesus and followed Him in His travels throughout Israel (4:25; 8:1; 14:13; 19:2; 20:29). They were amazed at His teaching (7:28) and marveled at His power to heal (9:8, 33, 34; 15:31). When Jesus entered Jerusalem, they were shouting His praises (21:8, 9, 11), even causing the leaders to be afraid to arrest Him openly (21:46; 26:5). Only as a result of the Jewish leaders' influence did their attitude change (27:20).

Even Matthew's reference to "all the people" (27:25) does not refer to the whole nation.[2] Israel is divided as a result of the ministry of Jesus. We find this division pictured clearly by Matthew in three ways. First, the synagogues in Israel alternate between those receptive to Jesus (4:23; 9:35; 13:54) and those that oppose Him (12:9-14; 13:54-57; cf. 23:34).

> "There will be many converted from among the Jews, and these converts will aid in preparing the way of the Lord, and making straight in the desert a highway for our God. Converted Jews are to have an important part to act in the great preparations to be made in the future to receive Christ, our Prince" (Ev 579).

Second, the other parable about a vineyard in Matthew 21 describes the people of Israel in terms of two very different "sons" representing two conflicting attitudes toward Jesus (21:28-32). Third, Jerusalem itself is divided (e.g., 20:18; 21:9-11). The implication is that, as a result, the city would not remain standing (12:25). The reference to burning up the city of those who refuse to attend the wedding of the king's son makes the implication even stronger (22:7). Finally, Jesus weeps over Jerusalem because its people were unwilling to be drawn to Jesus and accept Him as the Messiah (23:37). Jesus pronounces doom upon the city and the temple ("your house") as a result of His awareness that it is here that He will be condemned, scourged, and led away to be crucified. Just as the shedding of innocent blood contributed to the city's destruction by Babylon, so now it will eventuate in its destruction by Rome.

"All the people" – In harmony with the immediate context of the chapter and the larger context of the book, the most natural way to understand "all the people" in Matthew 27:25 is as a reference to those present at the time who were calling for Jesus' crucifixion. Obviously the whole nation was not packed into the city square that day. At most, "all the people" refers to those who lived in Jerusalem, together with those who came for the Passover that year and their immediate children. In fact, it is primarily these who would suffer the calamities mentioned in 24:15-19 when Roman armies would lay siege to Jerusalem and ultimately destroy it. Jesus' prediction of this tragic event in Matthew 23:38, 39 alludes to Psalm 118:26. The exclamation, "Blessed is the one who comes in the name of the Lord," seems to have been understood at the time as a reference to the coming Messianic kingdom. By quoting Scripture, Jesus points forward to His second advent when the roles will be reversed and the religious leaders will acquiesce and admit His Messiahship (cf. Matt 26:64). Then Jesus will execute judgment upon those who now judge Him. As in Matthew 24 which follows these verses, the judgment on Jerusalem and the judgment

> "Those who live in this day are not accountable for the deeds of those who crucified the Son of God" (RH April 11, 1893).

at the end of the world are blended. Echoing these words of Jesus, John views "those who pierced him" as being among the ones present when Jesus returns in the clouds (Rev. 1:7). Judgment, then, falls on those Jews who rejected Jesus. Their condemnation is announced already by Jesus but its realization will not come until He returns in glory. "Then those who prayed 'His blood be on us, and on our children,' will receive the answer to their prayer" (DA 739).

Salvation is open to all – Matthew makes clear that, after the resurrection, salvation must be proclaimed not only to the Jews but also now to all nations (Matt 28:19). According to the Book of Acts thousands of Jews repented of their role in the crucifixion, turned to Jesus, and received forgiveness (Acts 2:36-41; 4:4), including many priests (6:7). God is no respecter of persons or nations. Salvation is open to everyone (Acts 10:34, 35; Rom 2:11; 10:12, 13; Gal 3:28, 29). While Jews throughout history are not held responsible for putting Christ to death, they, like any other human being, will be held accountable for rejecting Him as Savior (Matt10:32-34). On the other hand, Jews who now accept Jesus as Messiah can be reincorporated into the true Israel of God (Rom 11:23-26; Gal 6:15, 16).

Clinton Wahlen

References

[1] Josh 2:19, 20; 2 Sam. 1:16; 1 Kgs 2:31-33; Jer. 26:8, 9 (also spoken by "all the people"), 12, 15; Ezek 18:13; 33:4-6; Acts 18:6.

[2] The word for "people" (*laos*) in Matthew is used in various ways and never clearly means the Jews as a whole.

The Miracles of Jesus

Healing physical ailments	Matthew	Mark	Luke	John
A leper	8:2, 3	1:40-42	5:12, 13	
The centurion's servant	8:5-13		7:1-10	
Peter's mother-in-law	8:14, 15	1:30, 31	4:38, 39	
Two possessed Gardarenes	8:28-34	5:1-15	8:28-35	
A paralyzed man	9:2-7	2:3-12	5:18-25	
The woman with a blood loss	9:20-22	5:25-29	8:43-48	
Two blind men	9:27-31			
A man dumb and possessed	9:32, 33		11:14	
The man with a withered hand	12:10-13	3:1-5	6:6-10	
A man blind, dumb, and possessed	12:22			
A Canaanite woman's daughter	15:21-28	7:24-30		
The boy with epilepsy	17:14-18	9:17-29	9:38-43	
Bartimaeus and another blind man	20:29-34	10:46-52	18:35-43	
A possessed man in the synagogue		1:23-26	4:33-35	
A deaf and dumb man		7:31-37		
The blind man at Bethsaida		8:22-26		
A bent-over woman			13:11-13	
A man with dropsy			14:1-4	
Ten lepers			17:11-19	
Malchus' ear			22:50, 51	
The official's son atCapernaum				4:46-54
The sick man at the pool of Bethesda				5:1-9
The man born blind				9:1-41
Command over the forces of nature				
Calming the storm	8:23-27	4:37-41	8:22-25	
Walking on water	14:25	6:48-51		6:19-21
5,000 people fed	14:15-21	6:35-44	9:12-17	6:5-13
4,000 people fed	15:32-38	8:1-9		
Coin in the fish's mouth	17:24-27			
The withered fig tree	21:18-22	11:12-26		
A catch of fish			5:1-11	
Water turned into wine				2:1-11
Another catch of fish				21:1-11
Raising the dead				
Jairus' daughter	9:18-25	5:22-42	8:41-56	
Widow's son at Nain			7:11-15	
Lazarus				11:1-44

DID JESUS MAKE ALL FOODS CLEAN?

Do you not understand that whatever goes into the man from outside cannot defile him; because it does not go into his heart, but into his stomach, and is eliminated? (*Thus He* declared all foods clean). Mark 7:18, 19.

This passage is frequently quoted to prove that Christ in the New Testament abolished the distinction between clean and unclean meat used as food. It is argued that the laws concerning clean and unclean meat in Leviticus 11 are part of the Old Testament ceremonial system and, therefore, no longer binding on Christians.

A problem of translation – Mark 7:1-23 is all about the issue of purity. It begins with the Pharisees and some scribes accusing the disciples of disregarding "the tradition of the elders" and eating with defiled hands (vv. 1-5). Jesus answers these two charges in order (vv. 6-13 and vv. 14-23, respectively), addressing first the Pharisees, then the crowd, and, finally, the disciples.

The problem with verse 19 boils down to a problem of translation. Even so-called "literal" or "word-for-word" translations offer essentially a paraphrase of the last part of the verse. The Greek text says nothing about "declaring" foods clean. Nor is there any indication that Mark has inserted a comment about what Jesus meant.[1] More faithful to the underlying Greek text is the NKJV, which translates the last part of the verse as follows: "thus purifying all foods." However, even if we accept the above translation, the meaning of the passage ultimately hinges on the answer to two questions: (1) What is meant by "purifying" (or "declaring foods 'clean'")? and (2) What is meant by "foods"?

The meaning of "purifying" – The only other place where Mark mentions purifying is in connection with the ritual purification of the leper (1:40-42). Earlier controversies over food in Mark's Gospel concern not the *biblical* prohibition against eating unclean meat but whether or not the *Pharisaic traditions* related to food are obligatory (2:13-28). So also here, the issue concerns not the biblical laws themselves but their correct interpretation.[2] As we have seen, the controversy with which the chapter begins is *not* about unclean food but ritually defiled hands. Jesus responds by insisting that God's Word must take precedence over human tradition. This point is repeatedly stressed in verses 3-13. Jesus further emphasizes it by quoting Isaiah 29:13 in verses 6-7. This prepares the way for His pronouncement on purity in v. 15.

In Acts 10–11, the same basic concern with ritual defilement causes Peter to hesitate in visiting Cornelius, a Gentile. Only through further divine revelation did it become clear to the early Christians that Gentiles also could be fully cleansed through faith alone and receive the Holy Spirit. Circumcision and traditional Jewish ritual requirements were no longer necessary.

Mark's version of the story (which is also found in Matt 15) contrasts what is on the *outside,* which cannot defile a person (Mark 7:15) with what is on the *inside,* which can defile (vv. 21, 23). Thus it is made especially clear that external washings only cleanse the surface and that the kind of defilement these washings treat is only skin deep. That is why verse 2 describes defiled hands as "unwashed," meaning not that they were physically dirty but that they were ritually impure—which is why verses 3 and 4 class this washing of hands with other Jewish rituals. By contrast, verses 20-23 emphasize what is inside a person, the thoughts and intents of one's heart (cf. Matt. 23:25, 26; Heb. 4:12).

The scope of the defilement – In addition to the *source* (inner versus outer defilement), the *scope* of the defilement is also vital. The ritual washings only pertain to "defiled hands" (Mark 7:2, 5) while a more serious kind of defilement affects the whole person (vv. 15, 18, 20, 23). The words used for defilement, *koinos* and the related verb *koinoo,* are unusual.[3] Neither is used in the Greek Septuagint translation of the Old Testament for the unclean animals of Leviticus 11 and Deuteronomy 14. The word *koinos* normally refers to what is "public" or "common."[4] The Pharisees, however, used it in a pejorative sense to mean a state of defilement caused by contact with the common people, whom they considered less careful than themselves in taking appropriate safeguards against ritual defilement. That is why verse 4 tells us that some Jews, when returning from the marketplace, would not eat unless they first immersed themselves (the word is *baptizein,* from which the English word "baptize" is derived). Jesus rejects this Pharisaic distinction by pronouncing all foods *ritually* pure.[5]

The meaning of 'foods' — We should not automatically assume that, by calling "all foods" pure, blanket permission is being given to eat anything that anyone might consider to be food. It certainly does not condone cannibalism. Neither does it condone eating the unclean meats forbidden by the Old Testament. After all, why would verses 6-13 of Mark 7 so emphasize obeying God's commandments if verses 14-19 announced the abolition of God's laws regarding clean and unclean meats? In fact, a study of ancient literature suggests that Jews did not describe as "food" things they considered inappropriate to eat.[6] Therefore, it is unlikely that the reference to "foods" in verse 19 would include unclean sources. It seems more reasonable to understand it as rejecting the idea that food should be considered impure simply because it comes from untrustworthy (mainly Gentile) sources.[7] Such an interpretation also makes good sense of the larger context since this passage then neatly prepares the way for the description of Jesus' work among Gentiles that immediately follows it (7:24–8:10). It also helps explain why the disciples seem unable to anticipate another feeding miracle, which would primarily benefit Gentiles (8:4) and why Jesus reprimands the disciples for failing to understand (8:17-21), warning them specifically about the "leaven of the Pharisees."

> Jesus rejects the idea that, under certain circumstances, even "clean" food can be ritually defiled and unfit to eat.

Summary — Jesus rejects the idea that, under certain circumstances, even "clean" food can be ritually defiled and unfit to eat. He does not abolish the biblical distinction between clean and unclean meat. Had Jesus meant this, it is truly remarkable that His words failed to impact Christian faith and practice for some two hundred years.[8]

Jesus' warning is applicable also today. Whenever an outward conformity to religious forms begins to eclipse the importance of inward consecration and the obedience to God's Word that springs from it, the leavening influence of Pharisaism is at work and a genuine Christian experience is at risk.

Clinton Wahlen

References

[1]When Mark *does* introduce his own comments, he generally makes this quite clear with some sort of signaling phrase (as he does, for example, in verses 2, 3, 11, and 34 of this same chapter). Taking the last phrase of verse 19 as a comment by Mark was first suggested by Origen (*Comm. Matt* 11.12.36-39). The idea has been followed by many modern versions, which place the supposed comment in parentheses or simply outside of quotation marks to distinguish it from the preceding saying of Jesus (a notable exception to this practice is the ASV).

[2]The antithesis between the divine and human is frequently found in Mark (e.g., 8:33; 10:9; 11:27, 30, 32; 12:14).

[3]In the Gospels, the adjective and verb forms appear together only in Mark 7. The terminology is occasionally in the Maccabaean literature, e.g., 1 Macc. 1:47, 62; 4 Macc. 7:6. Especially significant is the first reference which, by its separate mention of swine, appears to distinguish unclean animals from clean animals that have been ritually defiled.

[4]E.g., LXX Prov. 1:14; 2 Macc. 4:5; 9:21; Acts 2:44; Jude 3.

[5]The assertion that purity concerns, in connection with ordinary food, were a later innovation ignores important evidence, not only from the Rabbinic sources but also from the New Testament itself (e.g., Luke 11:38). The Pentateuch stipulates that clean meat, derived from improperly slaughtered animals, is impure (Lev. 11:40; 17:15) and that it defiles anyone who eats it. Even more stringent practices were followed by the Jews who lived at Qumran (see 1QS V.13-14; VIII.16-18). So, it is not hard to imagine a somewhat more lenient practice prevailing among the Pharisees.

[6]When unclean meats are intended, qualifications are normally included (e.g., Josephus, *Antiquities of the Jews* 4.139, 'strange food'; 4 Macc. 1:34, 'any sort of food at all that is forbidden to us under the Law').

[7]Exceptions to this rule are spelled out in Acts 15:20; 1 Cor. 10:28 (implicit already in Dan. 1:8-16).

[8]A brief examination of Christian thought on the subject of unclean foods shows that the issue does not appear to be settled before the middle of the third century. See the helpful survey of Jiří Moskala, *The Laws of Clean and Unclean Animals of Leviticus 11: Their Nature, Theology, and Rationale*, Adventist Theological Society Dissertation Series, vol. 4 (Berrien Springs, MI: Adventist Theological Society Publications, 2000), 31-52.

DID JESUS CALL A WOMAN A "DOG"?

And He was saying to her, "Let the children be satisfied first, for it is not good to take the children's bread and throw it to the dogs." Mark 7:27

The difficulties readers have with this text concerns the apparently harsh and insensitive language employed by Jesus in His description of Gentiles, His seeming reluctance to help a Gentile woman in need, and the irregular manner in which He changed His mind.

Jesus and the Jewish attitude toward Gentiles – The story of the Syrophoenician woman (Mark 7:24-30) is part of a narrative in which Jesus extends His mission to those living in Tyre, Sidon, and the Decapolis (Mark 7:24 – 8:10). It is part of a larger section that highlights the twin themes of Jesus' capacity to offer "bread" and of the disciples' hardheartedness and lack of understanding as to the meaning of this "bread-supplying" ability of Jesus (Mark 6:30 – 8:21).

"This was the only miracle that Jesus wrought while on this journey. It was for the performance of this act that He went to the borders of Tyre and Sidon. He wished to relieve the afflicted woman, and at the same time to leave an example in His work of mercy toward one of a despised people for the benefit of His disciples when He should no longer be with them. He wished to lead them from their Jewish exclusiveness to be interested in working for others besides their own people" (DA 402).

This miracle story has several links with the rest of the chapter and the next: (1) In the controversy with the Pharisees and scribes (Mark 7:1-23), Jesus challenges their traditional beliefs of defiled *objects* (i.e., the disciples hands; Mark 7:1-5), teaching that true defilement comes from within the human heart, not without (Mark 7:20-23); in the Syrophoenician woman's story, Jesus challenges Jewish notions of defiled *persons* (i.e., the Gentiles), demonstrating, through the healing of the woman's daughter, God's love and impartiality to all persons (cf. Acts 10:34-35); (2) The history of salvation perspective, which denotes Israel's priority with respect to the Gentiles (Mark 7:27a; cf. Matt 10:5, 6; 15:24; Rom 1:16) is illustrated in the two feeding stories: In the first, five thousand Jews are fed (Mark 6:30-44); in the second, four thousand Gentiles (Mark 8:1-10); (3) The resolute faith of the Syrophoenician woman contrasts strikingly with the Jewish religious leaders' resistance and unbelief (Mark 7:1-23; 8:11-13) as well as with the disciples' unbending attitude and incomprehension (Mark 6:52; 7:17-18; 8:16-21). The paradoxical results of the proclamation of the kingdom, encapsulated by this story and its narrative context, prefigures the typical responses of the Jews and Gentiles to the proclamation of the gospel found in the book of Acts.

The fundamental purpose of the election of Israel – It is important to interpret this story of the Gentile woman within the framework of the history of salvation. The sovereign election of Israel had one fundamental purpose: God established a covenant with Abraham and his descendants in order to bring a blessing to "all the families of the earth" (Gen 12:1-3). The Old Testament repeatedly alludes to this essential mission of Israel (Isa 19:19-25; 42:1, 6; 49:5, 6; 60:1-22; 61:1-11; Mic 4:1 – 5:15; Zech 8:20-23). As Israel's Messiah, Jesus came to renew and reconstitute the people of God so that they might at last fulfill their divinely intended mission to bless Gentiles (Luke 2:30-32; John 12:20-26).

Jesus teaches His disciples a lesson – Given Jesus' mission to gather to Himself the restored people of God in order to bring to fulfillment the Abrahamic covenant, His decision to enter into the predominantly Gentile territory of Phoenicia (Mark 7:24) was doubtless motivated by a desire to teach His disciples the lesson that He had come to save both Jews and Gentiles. The nation of Israel, in her pride and exclusivism, had demonstrably neglected to carry out this divine task. The initial silence of Jesus toward the Gentile woman, "he answered her not a word" (Matt 15:23) and His statement concerning the priority of Israel, "Let the children be satisfied first" (Mark 7:27), bring this issue to the forefront.

Jesus' words, "it is not good to take the children's bread and throw it to the dogs" should not be interpreted as responses of a churlish Jesus unwilling to help a forlorn Gentile woman; on the contrary, Jesus displays for the benefit of the disciples the typical Jewish animosity toward the pagan world in front of His disciples so that they might have a graphic depiction of how *not* to relate to heathens. In Jewish tradition the term "dogs" was typically employed by Jews to speak pejoratively of Gentiles; the biblical references to dogs (2 Sam 16:9; Ps 22:16; Matt 7:6; Phil 3:2; 2 Pet 2:22; Rev 22:15) are uniformly negative.[1] However, it is possible that Jesus' use of the diminutive form of the word "dogs" (*kynariois*) might refer to household pets and not to the wandering scavenging mongrels.[2] The use of *kynariois* would thus substantially mitigate the harshness of His saying.

Jewish prejudice had erected barriers that precluded social interaction between Jews and Gentiles; Jesus wanted these barriers broken down, for God's love is not limited to any nation or race.

The Gentile woman's response to Jesus, "Lord, even the dogs under the table eat

> Jesus symbolically represents the typical Jewish animosity toward the pagan world in front of His disciples so that they might have a graphic depiction of how *not* to relate to heathens.

from the crumbs of the children" (Mark 7:28), suggests an awareness of salvation history. Addressing Jesus with the theologically rich title of "Lord," the woman employs His brief parable to her advantage, preserving His characterization of Jews as the "children" of God (Exod 4:22; Deut 14:1; Isa 1:2) and Gentiles as "dogs." While she acknowledges the children's privilege to be fed first, at the same time, she insists that the dogs are able to obtain bread from the crumbs that fall from the table. Stated theologically, as Israel's Messiah strives to restore the people of God, the blessings that initially are given to Israel will also overflow to the Gentiles. Displaying a remarkable humility and understanding of the economy of salvation, the woman relentlessly pursues her request to have her "grievously demon possessed" daughter healed. On account of her steadfast faith, Jesus casts out the demon, healing her daughter from a distance (7:29-30).

Conclusion – The story of the Syrophoenician woman reveals the overarching biblical portrait of a gracious and loving God seeking to reconcile estranged Jews *and Gentiles* through the redemptive work of His Son, Jesus Christ. A true outsider – a woman, an "unclean" Gentile from the notorious pagans of Syrian Phoenicia – not only perceives Jesus' worldwide mission to all persons but also receives, through her indefatigable faith, a remarkable experience of God's mercy.

Leo Ranzolin, Jr.

References

[1]Joel Marcus, *Mark 1 – 8*, Anchor Bible 27A (New York, NY: Doubleday, 2000), 463-464.

[2]See James R. Edwards, *The Gospel According to Mark*, The Pillar New Testament Commentary (Grand Rapids, MI: Eerdmans, 2002), 219-21.

The Parables of Jesus

	Matthew	Mark	Luke
Lamp under a bushel	5:14, 15	4:21, 22	8:16; 11:33
Houses on rock and on sand	7:24-27		6:47-49
New cloth on old garment	9:16	2:21	5:36
New wine in old wineskins	9:17	2:22	5:37, 38
Sower and different soils	13:3-8	4:3-8	8:5-8
Wheat and tares	13:24-30		
Mustard seed	13: 31, 32	4:30-32	13:18, 19
Leaven	13:33		
Hidden treasure	13:44		
Pearl of great price	13:45, 46		
Fishing net	13:47, 48		
Lost sheep	18:12, 13		15:4-6
Unmerciful servant	18:23-34		
Workers in the vineyard	20:1-16		
Two sons	21:28-31		
Wicked tenants	21:33-41	12:1-9	20:9-16
Man without wedding garment	22:2-14		
Fig-tree as sign of summer	24:32, 33	13:28, 29	21:29-32
Ten virgins	25:1-13		
Different talents	25:14-30		19:12-27
Sheep and goats	25:31-36		
Growing seed		4:26-29	
Moneylender and debtors			7:41-43
Good Samaritan			10:30-37
Friend in need			11:5-8
Rich fool			12:16-21
Watchful servants			12:35-40
Faithful steward			12:42-48
Fig-tree without figs			13:6-9
Places of honor at the wedding feast			14:7-14
Great banquet and reluctant guests			14:16-24
Counting the cost			14:28-33
Lost coin			15:8-10
Lost son			15:11-32
Dishonest steward			16:1-8
Rich man and Lazarus			16:19-31
The master and his servant			17:7-10
The persistent widow and the unrighteous judge			18:2-5
The Pharisee and the tax collector			18:10-14

DOES THE PARABLE OF THE RICH MAN AND LAZARUS TEACH THE IMMORTALITY OF THE SOUL?

Now the poor man died and was carried away by the angels to Abraham's bosom; and the rich man also died and was buried. In Hades he lifted up his eyes, being in torment, and saw Abraham far away and Lazarus in his bosom. Luke 16:22, 23.

This parable is frequently referred to as one of the biblical proof texts for the immortality of the soul. The poor man is in Abraham's bosom, i.e., in paradise and the rich man is suffering in hell while his brothers are still alive here on earth. This interpretation seems to be contrary to the general teaching of Scripture that the dead do not know anything (Eccl 9:5).

The parable of the Rich Man and Lazarus appears only in Luke 16. It is unique in that it is the only parable of Jesus that tells of events in the afterlife, and it is the only parable that includes a personal name (Lazarus). The majority of Luke 16 deals with the subject of wealth, and this parable has much to say on the topic.

The setting of the parable – The first scene of the parable tells of the vastly different positions in life of two men – a rich man and a poor man named Lazarus.[1] The rich man lives sumptuously while Lazarus is covered with sores and longs to be satisfied from the things falling from the rich man's table. Instead, his sores are licked by dogs.

Upon death, the poor man is carried to the bosom of Abraham where he finds repose, while the rich man is simply buried. However, the scene quickly develops into the rich man in the torments of hellfire calling on "Father Abraham" to send Lazarus with at least a drop of water to cool his burning tongue. It is the smallest of requests for mercy – just the tip of the finger dipped in water to cool the rich man's tongue, not the entire body.

But Abraham refuses the request on two grounds – the rich man had good things in his earthly life while Lazarus had a bad life, and now the roles are reversed with Lazarus comforted and the rich man tormented. Secondly, Abraham notes that a great gulf has been fixed between them so that no one can pass from one side to the other.

The rich man then pleads that Lazarus be sent back to warn his brothers. Again Abraham refuses, making reference to the testimony of Moses and the Prophets. But the rich man refuses to be put off and states that if someone were to rise from the dead with the message, then surely his brothers would change and avoid the torments of hell. Abraham responds that if they did not listen to Moses and the Prophets, neither would they listen if someone were to rise from the dead. With these words the parable comes to a close. But what does it all mean?

The parable teaches the use of resources – Because this parable is linked in Luke 16 with other teachings on the use of financial resources, it makes a great deal of sense to see it as dealing with the same issue. When we use this assumption to look at the teaching of the story, many points in the parable become clear. First, the rich man and Lazarus are at opposite poles in regards to financial resources. The first part of the story illustrates this graphically. Second, in the parable their roles are reversed in the hereafter, again with opposite poles invoked – heaven versus hell. The rich man illustrates the teaching of Luke 16:9-13 – if you do not use your resources to bless others, you cannot expect to receive the true riches and a home in the eternal dwellings. Many in Jesus' day thought that riches were a sign of God's favor, and poverty of His displeasure. Jesus addressed this false theology through this parable showing that the "reward" for the rich was opposite of what they expected. If you do not use your resources to bless others, you cannot expect to receive the true riches and eternal dwellings.

> Details in parables must be interpreted carefully. The parable of the rich man and Lazarus has three clear points: (1) the rich have a responsibility to help the poor in this life; (2) the Scriptures are a sufficient witness to lead us to repent and to follow the Bible's ethic; and (3) there is no chance for change after death; you will receive the reward you deserve.

Death and the Question of the Soul – Does the parable go further and teach that the dead are conscious and receive their eternal reward upon death? Several lines of evidence point away from such a conclusion:

1. Elsewhere in the Gospels Jesus refers to death as a sleep from which He awakens people (Matt 9:24; Mark 5:39; John 11:11, 12, see also Acts

7:60; 13:36; 1 Cor 11:30; 15:6, 18, 20, 51; 1 Thess 4:13-15 and 2 Pet 3:4). This teaching of death as a sleep appears not only in the other Gospels and the writings of Peter and Paul but also in Luke 8:52.

2. According to the parable the rich man after he died had "eyes" and a "tongue," that is, very real bodily parts. He asked that Lazarus "dip the tip of his finger in water." This corporeal state is contrary to the concept of immortal souls leaving the body at death.

3. If this is a literal account of the afterlife, then heaven and hell are near enough for a conversation to be held between the inhabitants of heaven and hell. Not a very desirable situation for either party.

4. To use this parable to prove that men receive their rewards at death would mean that Christ contradicted Himself when He said in another place that the righteous and the wicked receive their reward at the Second Coming (Matt 16:27; 25:31-46; Luke 11:31,32).

5. The Old Testament writers are very emphatic in stating that the dead, righteous and wicked alike, lie silent and unconscious in the grave until the resurrection day. See Job 14:12; Psalm 115:17; Eccl 9:5, 6, 10.

These lines of evidence point toward the idea that, in the parable of the rich man and Lazarus, Jesus simply uses a popular story about life after death, as a graphic way of illustrating the truth that the gospel makes a claim upon our lives and even our resources. The Jewish historian Josephus (1 century A.D.) in his "Discourse to the Greeks Concerning Hades" describes heaven and hell in very similar terms to the parable in Luke 16. [2]

> Jesus uses a popular story about life after death as a graphic way of illustrating the truth that the gospel makes a claim upon our lives and even our resources.

We disregard the needs of others around us at the peril of our eternal salvation. It is not that helping them saves us, but rather that the change of heart the gospel works in us will of necessity show itself in outward deeds of grace and kindness.

Tom Shepherd

References

[1]Because names provide specificity and imply importance, it is instructive that the rich man is never named in the story. Normally we would expect the rich man to be named and the beggar to be nameless. The reversal of expectation will become a major theme in the story.

[2]See William Whiston, translator, *The Works of Josephus* (Peabody, MA: Hendrickson, 1987), 813, 814.

Josephus's Discourse to the Greeks Concerning Hades

For there is one descent into this region [Hades], at whose *gate* we believe there stands an archangel with an host; which *gate* when those pass through that are conducted down by the angels appointed over souls, they do not go the same way; but the just are guided to the *right hand,* and are led with hymns, sung by the *angels* appointed over that place, unto a region of *light,* in which the just have dwelt from the beginning of the world; . . . while they wait for that rest and *eternal new life in heaven,* which is to succeed this region. This place we call *The Bosom of Abraham.*

But as to the unjust, they are dragged by force to the *left hand* . . . into the neighborhood of hell itself; who, when they are hard by it, continually hear the noise of it, and do not stand clear of the hot vapor itself; but when they have a near view of this spectacle, as of a terrible and exceeding great prospect of fire, they are struck with a fearful expectation of a future judgment, and in effect punished thereby: and not only so, but where they see the place of *the fathers* and of the just, even hereby are they punished; for a *chaos* deep and large is fixed between them; insomuch that a just man that hath compassion upon them cannot be admitted, nor can one that is unjust, if he were bold enough to attempt it, pass over it. (William Whiston, translator, *The Works of Josephus* [Peabody, MA: Hendrickson, 1987], p. 813, 814).

DID THE THIEF ON THE CROSS GO TO PARADISE
THE DAY HE DIED?

And He [Jesus] said to him, "Truly I say to you, today you shall be with Me in Paradise." Luke 23:43.

Jesus' promise to the thief on the cross in Luke 23:43 has traditionally been used as a major proof for the immortality of the soul; that is, the belief that the spirit or soul of the faithful dead has conscious existence in heaven before the resurrection. According to this view, which is shared by the vast majority of Christians, when the penitent criminal asked Jesus to be remembered in His kingdom, he was assured that he would be in paradise that very day.

The punctuation of the text – The problem depends on how Jesus' statement is punctuated. If the comma is placed before "today," as most translations do, then the passage reads: "Truly I tell you, *today* you *will be* with me in paradise." But if the comma is placed after "today," then Jesus would simply have said: "Truly I *tell* you *today*, you will be with me in paradise." What did Jesus actually mean?

In the early Christian centuries, New Testament manuscripts were written without separation between words and sentences, and little or no punctuation at all was used to indicate how the text should be read. The comma, for example, was introduced as late as the ninth century. In any case, the presence of a comma, or any other punctuation mark, in Greek manuscripts reveals only the current understanding of a passage's meaning. Thus, when Luke 23:43 was punctuated, the comma was placed before "today" not for grammatical reasons, but for the theological conviction, prevailing at the time, that the final reward of the faithful who die comes at death.

The alternative translation – There is unequivocal evidence that this interpretation was not the only way this passage was understood in the early centuries of the church. Ancient translations, citations by church writers, and even specific signs in Greek manuscripts bear witness to the fact that the alternative reading had in fact several supporters in early Christianity (see box, p. 314). And contrary to what is often claimed, placing the comma after "today" does not make the word "today" superfluous. It has correctly been argued that the use of "today" to introduce or to close a statement is only a Semitic idiom intended to intensify the significance and solemnity of the statement that either will follow or has just been made. In fact, this idiom is rather common in Scripture; in Deuteronomy alone there are over forty examples of expressions such as, "I teach you *today*," "I set before you *today*," "I give you *today*," "I command you *today*," "I testify against you *today*," and "I declare to you *today*" (e.g., 4:26; 6:6; 7:11; 8:19; 11:26, 32; 30:18, 19; 32:46; cf.; Acts 20:26; 26:2). This expression and other biblical Semitisms were familiar to Luke through the Septuagint, the Greek translation of the Old Testament used by the early Christians.

> The reading "Truly I tell you *today*, you will be with me in paradise" is found in the Curetonian Syriac, one of the earliest translations of the New Testament whose text goes back to the second century. It is also found in church writers, such as Ephraem of the fourth century, and Cassian and Hesychius of the fifth century. This reading is also found in two independent apocryphal works probably of the fourth century, the *Acts of Pilate* and *Christ's Descent into Hell*.

Scriptural evidence – To establish the meaning of Jesus' statement on the cross, it is important to look at the overall biblical teaching regarding the time when the saved will enter upon their reward in paradise. By "paradise," there should be no question that Jesus meant heaven (2 Cor 12:2-4) or the eternal habitation of the redeemed in the New Jerusalem in which the tree of life and the throne of God will be found (Rev 2:7; 22:1-5). In another passage, Jesus refers to the many dwelling places in God's house and to the time when He would come again to take His own to Himself (John 14:1-3). At that time, He would invite His followers to inherit the kingdom prepared for them from the beginning of the world (Matt 25:31-34). This event will be a glorious moment of reunion in which the final and complete celebration of deliverance from sin will take place (Luke 22:14-18).

The bestowal of immortality – Paul teaches that believers who die will come forth from their graves at Jesus' second coming (1 Cor 15:20-23) when the gift of immortality will be bestowed on them (vv. 51-55). The resurrected righteous and the righteous living will then be caught up together to meet Jesus in the air, and so they will be with Him forever (1 Thess 4:17). It is important to notice that, according to Paul, it is Jesus' resurrection, not

His death, that gives the righteous hope for life after death (1 Cor 15:16-19; Rom 10:9). It would have been strange, therefore, if Jesus had promised the thief that they would be together in paradise that very day. Moreover, the Bible also clearly teaches that on the day He died, Christ went into the grave (Luke 23:50-54; Acts 2:31, 32; 13:29-31). To argue that only Christ's body went into the grave while His Spirit ascended to heaven is to ignore that early in the resurrection morning Jesus told Mary not to hold on to Him because He had not yet gone to the Father (John 20:17).

> Placing the comma after "today" is a Semitic idiom emphasizing the significance of the announcement.

The meaning of the Passage – It does not seem appropriate, therefore, to conclude that Jesus promised that both He and the penitent thief would be together in paradise the day they died. If the comma is placed before "today," it becomes virtually impossible to reconcile this passage with what the Bible teaches elsewhere, including what Jesus Himself taught, concerning the time when the faithful dead receive their final reward. Placing the comma after "today" is a Semitic idiom emphasizing the significance of the announcement.

Finally, there is also ample historical evidence to demonstrate that this way of understanding the passage is neither new nor illegitimate. Important segments of the early church accepted the reading, "Truly I tell you *today*, you will be with me in paradise," even after belief in the immortality of the soul had become predominant in Christianity.

The thief asked Jesus to be remembered in His kingdom. Apart from his surrender to Jesus in the final moment of his life, there is nothing special in his request about Jesus' kingdom. One should not make the mistake of thinking that he fully understood the teachings of Jesus on the subject. But, however basic his Messianic ideas may have been, Jesus did not promise him immediate and conscious fellowship in heaven after death. By using "today" after "I tell you," the Savior made a solemn promise and so brought comfort and hope to that dying man's heart but without specifying when that promise would be fulfilled.

Wilson Paroschi

315

HAS THE LAW OF MOSES BEEN REPLACED
BY THE GRACE OF JESUS?

For the Law was given through Moses; grace and truth were realized through Jesus Christ. John 1:17.

This is no small question. The answer to it serves as a key for the interpretation of the Gospel of John. It also determines, to a large degree,
how we understand the relationship between the Old and the New Testaments. And it has a fundamental and formative effect on our personal
Christian walk, answering the significant question – Must I obey the commands found in the law? But in order to speak to all these important issues, we begin with the original context of the question in the Gospel of
John, chapter 1.

A hymn about Jesus Christ – The Gospel of John opens with a beautiful
hymn about who Jesus Christ is. It is written in four stanzas. The first stanza
(1:1-5) tells of His eternal existence, creative power, and light-filled life. The
second stanza (1:6-8) compares and contrasts Him with John the Baptist,
giving interesting parallels to the first stanza (i. e. whereas the Word [Jesus
Christ] *was with God*, John was *sent by God*). Jesus is always presented as
superior to John.

The third stanza (John 1:9-13) describes the way people respond to
Jesus–either in rejection or acceptance, with God's power giving new birth
to believers. The fourth and final stanza (1:14-18) describes the incarnation
of Jesus–"the Word became flesh and tented among us"[1] –and the believers' response to this revelation. John testifies that Jesus has priority above
him, "the one who comes after me was before me" (1:15). Believers testify
that they all have received from His fullness and grace upon grace (1:16).
This brings us to our text in question, verse 17, in which Moses is reported
as the agent through whom the law came and Jesus Christ is described
as the one through whom grace and truth came. The hymn concludes in
verse 18 with a reaffirmation of the intimate connection between God the
Father and Jesus Christ the Son–"No one has seen God at any time. The
only begotten God who is in the bosom of the Father is the one who has
explained Him."

Christ the agent of grace and truth – Verse 17 of John 1 focuses attention on Jesus Christ. He is the agent through whom the blessings of grace and of truth have come to us. Whatever else we may say of the passage, this truth is a clear and wonderful blessing in our life. But what is the relationship of the first part of the verse dealing with Moses to the last part of the verse dealing with Jesus? Do the two parts complement each other or do they stand in contrast to each other? In other words, as stated in the question above–has the law of Moses been replaced by the grace of Jesus?

The best way to answer this question is to place John 1:17 within its setting in the fourth stanza of the hymn (1:14-18). The stanza begins with the rather unique statement of verse 14 – "The Word became flesh." What is distinctive here is the shift in the verb used to describe Jesus Christ. In previous verses He is described using a common verb "to be" in Greek–*eimi*. This verb suggests eternal existence in this context, especially in contrast to the verb "come to be –*ginomai*– used to describe John the Baptist in verse 6. Jesus, the Word, *was*, but John the Baptist *came to be*. Jesus is eternal; John had a set time of beginning.

But in verse 14 of John 1 the hymn now says of the Word that He "became flesh." The eternal Word of God stepped into human existence. The Apostle applies that other verb–*ginomai*–to Jesus Christ–He *came to be* flesh. John further stresses

> "For Christians who have been brought up with a negative view of the law of Moses derived from a misreading of Paul and an unnecessary bifurcation of law and grace, the temptation is to read this verse [John 1:17] as a negative slap at the law. But such is hardly the intention of the evangelist. In the Gospel of John, Moses in regarded as a positive servant of God (e.g., 5:45-47; 6:32; 7:19-23). The problem for Jesus in this Gospel was not with Moses and the law; the problem was with disobedient Jews who *misused* Moses and the law (e.g., 6:31-32; 9:28-29)" (Gerald L. Borchert, *John 1-11*, The New American Commentary [Nashville, TN: Broadman & Holman, 2002], 123).

this idea by saying that the Word "pitched his tent" among us, He dwelt among us. It is a clear allusion to Exodus 25:8 in which God tells the Israelites "Let them construct a sanctuary for Me, that I may dwell among them." Seeing the glory of the unique Son of God is like seeing the fiery pillar of cloud over the Old Testament sanctuary. Christ becoming human is God with us, as Matthew tells us, Emmanuel (Matt 1:23).

Grace piling up on grace – The appearance of God's glory in Scripture (the technical term is theophany) calls for human response. This response is exactly what happens in John 1:15, 16 as both John and "we," the church, respond to the glorious light of God's Son in human flesh. The last phrase in verse 16 expresses the abundance–"grace piling up on grace. "[2] But it seems the apostle wanted to express this ever increasing abundance of grace in more detail, and so he wrote verse 17.

John 1:17 begins with the word "because" in Greek–*hoti*. This word indicates the reason for, or explanation of, what has been said before. Verse 16 explains the super abundance of God's grace to us. Verse 17 clarifies it in more detail. A literal translation from Greek would be as follows:

Because the Law was given through Moses,
the grace and the truth came to be through Jesus Christ.

Several important concepts jump out at us. First, we have noted already that the "because" at the beginning of the verse creates a link to verse 16 as an explanation. Whatever "grace piling up on grace" means in verse 16, it must be that verse 17 explains it or "unpacks" it. Second, verse 17 has two parts that stand in parallel to each other. The law is placed in parallel with "the grace and the truth" (both terms have the definite article in Greek, just as law does), and Moses is placed in parallel with Jesus Christ. Third, there is no conjunction between the first and second parts of verse 17–no "and, although, but, either, or. " The technical term for this grammatical construction is asyndeton, which means the omission of a conjunction that would normally join clauses. It is often used for effect to stress the concepts so described–"I came, I saw, I conquered" instead of "I came and I saw and I conquered." It seems the apostle wants to stress the two phrases in a dramatic way.

So what does this suggest? In verse 16 the apostle stresses that we all have received a super abundance of grace from the overflowing fullness of Jesus Christ. In verse 17 we are suddenly told that the law was given through Moses. Why? Was it somehow bad or something that needed to be removed? No, it was part of the revelation of God given in the Old Testament to bless His people. That old revelation was good. But the new revelation in Jesus is even better, more glorious (cf. 2 Cor 3:4-18). Before,

God revealed Himself in a cloudy pillar of fire; now He has come in the flesh. Before, we could not see His face; now we can see Him in His Son. "The theory that vs. 17 contrasts the absence of enduring love in the law with presence of enduring love in Jesus Christ does not seem to do justice to John's honorific reference to Moses (i 45, iii 14, v. 46). Rather v. 17 contrasts the enduring love shown in the law with the supreme example of enduring love shown in Jesus. "[3]

Conclusion – Has the law of Moses been replaced by the grace of Jesus? No; law and grace do not oppose each other; they work hand in hand. law shows us our need; grace supplies it. Grace provides our pardon; law points out our duty. The Old Testament predicts the coming Deliverer; the New Testament fulfills this prediction. The Gospel of John does not pit Jesus against the law of Moses. Instead, the Lord opposes the misinterpretation of the law by the religious leaders of His day. This continues to have relevance today. It is vital that we understand that our personal walk within the grace of the Lord Jesus involves obedience to the law that God gave through Moses. The light was glorious at Sinai; it is even more glorious at the cross. The Master died that we might live for Him in obedience to His commands.

> Law and grace do not oppose each other, they work hand in hand. Law shows us our need, grace supplies it. Grace provides our pardon, Law points out our duty.

Tom Shepherd

References

[1] All translations are my own unless otherwise noted.

[2] This phrase holds a very important place in the interpretation of verse 17. The Greek is *charin anti charitos*. Some interpreters see the use of the Greek word *anti* ("opposite, instead of, in place of, upon") as indicating a contrast– the grace of Jesus *in place of* the law of Moses. The problem with this position is twofold. First, It would be grace in place of grace, not grace in place of law. Second, the Jewish writer Philo from the first century A.D. gives an example of this usage (Philo, *Poster. Cain.* 145), which clearly illustrates understanding the phrase as "grace upon grace." See W. Bauer, W. F. Arndt, F. W. Gingrich, and F. Danker, *A Greek-English*

Lexicon of the New Testament and Other Early Christian Literature, second edition (Chicago, IL: University of Chicago Press, 1979), s.v. *anti*.

[3]Raymond Brown, *John I-XII,* Anchor Bible Commentary vol. 29 (Garden City, NY: Doubleday, 1966), 16.

This papyrus (P52), dated to A.D. 125, and containing portions of John 18, is the oldest extant New Testament manuscript.

WHAT KIND OF WINE DID JESUS MAKE AT CANA?

[The headwaiter said to the bridegroom] "Every man serves the good wine first, and when *men* have drunk freely, *then* that which is poorer; you have kept the good wine until now." John 2:10.

The miracle of turning water into wine, the first recorded miracle of Jesus, is mentioned only in John (2:1-11). The question is, what kind of wine did Jesus make – fermented wine or grape juice? While the miracle is described in the briefest of terms, it is clearly implied that all the water in the jars became wine, totalling well over one hundred gallons (ca. 400 liter).[1] Was the wine fermented? Such a quantity of fine wine would be enough to intoxicate even one hundred guests a day for several days. Did Jesus lay the basis for a drunkfest? It is helpful to recall that, on the cross, Jesus himself refused wine when it was offered (Mark 15:23).[2]

Ancient wine-preservation methods – The Greek word translated "wine" in verses 3, 9, and 10 (*oinos*) can refer to either fermented or unfermented wine.[3] In order, then, to determine what kind of beverage is meant we must consider other important points from the text and from the historical context. Judging from the translation of verse 10, the master of the festivities seems to imply that fermented wine was being served because he refers to the normal practice of serving inferior wine only after everyone is drunk. But if that is the meaning, his speech would fall on deaf (and drunk) ears since no one should care at this point in the celebration anyway! In fact, however, the word "drink" (Gr. *methusko*) need not imply drinking too much or drunkenness as many versions suggest. In this passage it simply means that all the guests have "drunk well."[4] Only when everyone has had plenty of the best quality drink is the inferior kind served. Clearly, the words themselves do not tell us whether the wine is fermented or unfermented. We must look elsewhere for an answer to this question.

Some argue that, in ancient Israel, it was impossible to hermetically seal grape juice before fermentation would set in to some extent. This is a serious question. Did methods exist to preserve grape juice for long periods of time? While information on this point from first-century Jewish sources is limited, we have good evidence from Greek and Roman writers of the time about methods of preservation:

> Grape juice could be boiled down into a jelly. This would be pressed into a clay pot until all the air was removed. Then a thin layer of olive oil across the top would preserve the contents for months or even years. At a later date, the preserves could be mixed with water for use. The end result would be unfermented.[5]

The "wine" Jesus made – However, even if it was possible to keep juice from fermenting for long periods of time, is it really likely that no wine was served at this wedding celebration in Cana? An even more important question is, what drink would be so desirable that the master of the festivities felt compelled to make such a speech? To many people today, it seems preposterous that the guests at such an occasion could be satisfied with grape juice. But the Jewish culture of that time is not ours. For one thing, girls normally got married at the tender age of just twelve or thirteen. The groom may not have been much older. Highly fermented wine could have led rather easily to drunkenness and disorder which pious Jews, concerned with purification as the massive jars indicate that they were (2:6), would have scrupulously sought to avoid on such occasions.[6] There is even evidence from ancient writers of a preference for drinks with little or no alcohol. "Pliny expressly says that a 'good wine' was one that

> "The wine which Christ provided for the feast, and that which He gave to the disciples as a symbol of His own blood, was the pure juice of the grape. To this the prophet Isaiah refers when he speaks of the new wine 'in the cluster,' and says, 'Destroy it not; for a blessing is in it.'" Isaiah 65:8. (DA 149).

was destitute of spirit."[7] The Greeks recommended diluting wine with at least three or four parts water.[8] The "best" wine seems to have been that which was the freshest and touched the least by fermentation, because it could be enjoyed in greater quantities for a longer period of time.[9]

This miracle was also, according to John, the first time Christ manifested His "glory" (v. 11; cf. 1:14). More than simply "icing" on the wedding cake, it shows Jesus' "new wine" ministry outshining and outclassing the traditions of Judaism (cf. Mark 2:22). Imagine the wonder of tasting "wine" fresh from the Creator Himself! Its quality must have surpassed even the juice from grapes of the most select vintage. Through this first miracle, Jesus announces His intention not just to reform but to transform, not merely to make the old better but to make it new.

Clinton Wahlen

References

[1] The capacity of the stone jars is estimated at two or three "measures." A measure equals about nine gallons (ca. 38 liter; 72 sextarii, Josephus, *Ant.* 8.57; 15.314) so that each jar could hold between 18 and 27 gallons (ca. 68 and 102 liters).

[2] While he had already promised not to drink of the "fruit of the vine" until he would drink it with his followers in the kingdom of God (Mark 14:25 parr), it seems that the main reason was not to becloud his mind (DA 746). Significantly, the Babylonian Talmud refers to the practice in Jerusalem of giving drugged wine to those about to be executed in order to dull the pain (*b.Sanh.* 43a).

[3] In Ephesians 5:18; LXX Psalm 74:9 [ET 75:8]; Proverbs 23:31; Isaiah 28:7 *oinos* refers to fermented wine and it refers to unfermented wine in Matthew 9:17; Mark 2:22; LXX Judges. 19:19; Joel 2:24; Isaiah 16:10.

[4] This is how the word is translated by H. Preisker, "*methē, methuō, methusos, methuskomai*," *Theological Dictionary of the New Testament*, 4:547.

[5] Jon Paulien, *John: Jesus Gives Life to a New Generation* (The Abundant Life Bible Amplifier; Boise, ID: Pacific Press, 1995), 70. See also Samuele Bacchiocchi, *Wine in the Bible: A Biblical Study on the Use of Alcoholic Beverages*, 127, 28.

[6] The Hebrew Bible's characterization of wine and "strong drink" as a source of moral confusion and inappropriate behavior (e.g., Gen 9:21; 19:32; Prov 20:1; 21:17; 23:31-35; Isa 5:11, 12; 28:7) was not lost on the Jews of the time or Christians in the first century (Gal 5:21; Eph 5:18; 1 Pet 4:3).

[7] Albert Barnes, *Notes on the New Testament: Explanatory and Practical, Luke-John* (London, 1875; reprint, Grand Rapids, MI: Baker, 1949), 193.

[8] See James Grout, "Wine," *Encyclopaedia Romana*. Online: http://penelope.uchicago.edu/~grout/encyclopaedia_romana/wine/wine.html; accessed 2 Feb 2010.

[9] Bacchiocchi, 123, citing among others Pliny, *Natural History*, 14, 28 and Plutarch, *Symposiacs*, 8, 7.

WHY DID THE JEWS ACCUSE JESUS OF BREAKING THE SABBATH?

For this reason therefore the Jews were seeking all the more to kill Him, because He not only was breaking the Sabbath, but also was calling God His own Father, making Himself equal with God. John 5:18

Christians have at times pointed to this text to claim that Jesus abolished the Sabbath of the fourth commandment by working on the Sabbath. The Jews, therefore, accused Him of Sabbath breaking. Did Jesus in fact break the fourth commandment or did He break only some human-made Jewish laws?

The immediate context of John 5:18 is the healing on the Sabbath at the Pool of Bethesda, of the cripple who had suffered for 38 years. Jesus healed him and told him to get up, take up his bed, and walk (5:8). When the Pharisees met the man they accused him, and by implication also Jesus, of breaking the Sabbath.

Which commandment did Jesus break? – Which commandment did the Jews have in mind when they accused Jesus of breaking the Sabbath? Jeremiah 17:21, 22 states, "Thus says the LORD, 'Take heed for yourselves, and do not carry any load on the Sabbath day or bring anything in through the gates of Jerusalem. You shall not bring a load out of your houses on the Sabbath day nor do any work." Or was the commandment one of the rabbinic traditions added for the purpose of protecting or putting a fence around the Sabbath?

The charge of breaking the Sabbath is a misunderstanding of the very nature of both Jesus' identity and the purpose of the Sabbath. The Jews expressed their concerns to the man who was healed by telling him explicitly, in John 5:10, "It is not permissible for you to carry your pallet." At issue was a specific rabbinic regulation about the Sabbath; Jesus did not disregard, replace, or abolish the Sabbath itself.

One of the thirty-nine rabbinic prohibitions for the Sabbath forbade Jews to transport an object from one place to another.[1] Another regulation specifically prohibited the carrying of an empty bed. This was based on the Mishnaic[2] passage that declared that if a man carries "a living person in a bed, [he] is exempt even on account of [taking out] the bed, for the bed is secondary to him."[3] Jews could carry a man in a bed but not a bed by itself.

Conflict over traditions – It seems that Jesus deliberately challenged the Jewish traditions. He sought to free the Sabbath from burdensome restrictions and make it a day of spiritual freedom and joy. By healing a man on the Sabbath, He provoked a hostile reaction on the part of the Jews. Furthermore, Jesus chose the Sabbath to demonstrate His divine power. The verses following John 5:18, focusing on His divine identity, are in accordance with His mighty acts, in particular that of healing a lame person. The discourse that follows His sign is a revelation of His divine status

> **Jesus deliberately challenged the Jewish traditions.**

and His relationship to the Father. At stake is not only the validity of the Sabbath, per se, but rather the scope of Jesus' authority.

It needs to be remembered that the story is told in the Gospel of John, the Gospel whose overall purpose is to affirm the divine authority of Jesus. And He declared that it is lawful to do good on the Sabbath day. His followers were not to observe the Sabbath according to the rabbinic rules but rather as a day of helpful service after the pattern of Jesus. And the same is true today; whoever observes the Sabbath merely as a legalistic requirement will never receive the blessing God wants to bestow. Thus, neither Jesus nor the church rejected the Sabbath as such, but they did reject the human-made rules for observing it.

Ganoune Diop

References

[1]Jacob Neusner, *The Mishnah – New Translation* (Yale: University Press, 1988), Shabbat 7:2.

[2]The Mishnah is a Jewish law book from the time of Christ.

[3]Neusner, Mishnah. Shabbat 10:5.

WAS THE MEETING IN ACTS 20:7
A SUNDAY WORSHIP SERVICE?

And on the first day of the week, when we were gathered together to break bread, Paul *began* talking to them, intending to leave the next day, and he prolonged his message until midnight. Acts 20:7.

Many commentators over the years have suggested that Acts 20:7 is the earliest solid evidence that the early Christians kept Sunday as a special day of worship. This argument however was not Luke's intention in the passage. As a piece of a much larger story, this descriptive sentence can best be understood by viewing it in the context of Luke's panoramic portrayal of Jesus' work of bringing salvation, first as a Man on earth and later by means of the Holy Spirit through His chosen apostles.

Paul on his way to Jerusalem – In Acts 20 the apostle Paul, who had faithfully followed Jesus' model of teaching and disciple-making, was nearing the end of his work and was beginning his own journey toward Jerusalem where, like Jesus, he would soon face trials and suffering (Acts 20:22, 23; 21:10-14;). As Paul turned his steps toward Jerusalem he went out of his way to bring encouragement to various groups of disciples he had raised up earlier, including the group in Troas as described in Acts 20:6-12.

While Luke makes only brief note of several of the cities Paul visited at this time, he chooses to give a vivid report of one particular event in Troas. By describing the incredible resurrection of Eutychus from the dead after his sleep-induced fall from an upper-story window, Luke demonstrates that Paul was indeed explicitly carrying forward the ministry of Jesus — even to raising the dead. Acts 20:7, the sentence under study, is not placed in the narrative on its own account but to set the scene for this main event. Nevertheless, because of the questions and claims made regarding its interpretation by later Christians, it is worth considering the sentence phrase by phrase in order to learn what it does, and does not, say.

"Paul was talking with them" – This is the central statement of the verse, introducing the ongoing action around which the story of Eutychus takes shape. All the other parts of the sentence function to give more information about this interaction — telling when, why, and how long the dialogue went on. Consulting the meaning of the Greek word for "talk," *dialegomai*, we learn that Paul is not preaching a sermon to those in Troas but "dialoguing" or having a discussion with them.

"On the first day of the week" – The phrase literally reads "the first from the Sabbath." This is an example of the use by Luke and other early Christian literature of the term *sabbaton* in reference to an ordinary seven-day week (cf. Luke 18:12; *Didache*[1] 8:1). As he so often did in his account of Paul's journey to Jerusalem (Acts 20:6, 15; 21:1, 4, 5, 7, 8, 10, 15), Luke chose to note the time in which this important event occurred. The story may have taken place on a "Sunday" as modern Westerners, along with Greco-Romans like Luke's audience, might naturally assume. (John 20:19 clearly refers to a Sunday night in this way, and Luke himself also begins at dawn in reckoning the hours of the day in Acts 2:15 and elsewhere.) On the other hand, it is very possible that Luke was here using the Jewish reckoning in which a day is made up of an evening and then a morning (Gen 1:5; Luke 23:54). From this perspective Paul would have remained in Troas in order to faithfully keep the Sabbath, and then taken the opportunity for a Saturday night farewell meeting[2] with his friends before setting out first thing Sunday morning for his next destination. In either case Luke leaves no doubt that the raising of Eutychus, like the raising of Jesus, happened "on the first day" of the week — another remarkable parallel between the story of Paul and the story of Jesus.

In evaluating this passage as an evidence of early Christian Sundaykeeping, the eminent church historian, Augustus Neander, remarks: "The passage is not entirely convincing, because the impending departure of the apostle may have united the little Church in a brotherly parting-meal, on occasion of which the apostle delivered his last address, although there was no particular celebration of a Sunday in the case" (*The General History of the Christian Religion and Church,* vol. 1 [London: Henry G. Bohn, 1851], 337).

"When we were gathered together to break bread" – People "gathered together" (Gk. *synago*) for all kinds of reasons in Luke and Acts (Luke 22:66; Acts 4:31; 15:6, 30). Gathering to break bread was a common occurrence for Christian believers, not at all limited to a particular day or place. The meals Jesus shared with people in the most diverse of situations were an important theme in the Gospel of Luke. The specific Greek phrase used in Acts 20:7 for "breaking bread" (*klasai arton*) is used repeatedly in Luke's writings, usually in reference to an ordinary meal. On the Thursday night of Passover Jesus "broke bread" with His disciples and instructed them to continue doing so in remembrance of Him (Luke 22:19). The earliest converts in Jerusalem "broke bread" daily from house to house (Acts 2:42, 46) and Paul "broke bread" just before his ship was wrecked (Acts 27:34-36). The apparent reason for the particular gathering and breaking of bread in Troas is suggested in the following phrase.

> Gathering to break bread was a common occurrence for Christian believers, not at all limited to a particular day or place.

"Intending to leave the next day" – Paul was about to continue his trip to Jerusalem, and, because of this, he wished to have one last conversation with those in Troas. As with each group of believers he had visited thus far, Paul had been exhorting and encouraging his friends in Troas and no doubt had much he still wished to say. Therefore since there was no certainty if or when they would see each other again, Luke adds, "he prolonged his message until midnight."

No new day of worship instituted – With this necessary introduction, Luke's readers are now prepared to understand how it happened that Eutychus came to be sitting in an upper-room window in the middle of the night nodding off to sleep and finally plunging to his death in the street below (Acts 20:9). Neither here, nor in any other place does Luke give any indication that believers ought to gather in a regular way on the first day of the week to break bread or to listen to a sermon. Although his declared purpose in writing was to provide for Theophilus and his friends "certainty about what they had been taught" (Luke 1:4), Luke makes no effort to provide certainty of such a momentous change as a shift to a new day of worship. Rather, Luke mentions the believers' dialogue and breaking of bread in passing in order to set the scene for the mighty miracle of the raising of Eutychus through which God demonstrated once again His continued presence in the ministry of Paul and in His growing church.

Teresa Reeve

References

[1]The *Didache* is a Christian document dating from the fourth century.
[2]Cf. Good News Translation.

The Story of the Septuagint (LXX)

Following Alexander the Great's conquest of the countries in the Middle East, the Greek language became the common language in the conquered lands. Many Jews abandoned Aramaic in favor of Greek, particularly in such Hellenistic centers as Alexandria in Egypt.

It was during the reign of Ptolemy Philadelphus (285-246 B.C.) that the Jews in Alexandria were in need of a Greek translation of the Old Testament because they no longer used and understood Hebrew. A standard Greek version was produced, known as the Septuagint (LXX) the Greek word for "seventy." The story is told that the librarian at Alexandria persuaded Ptolemy to translate the Torah into Greek for use by Alexandrian Jews. As a result, six translators were selected from each of the twelve tribes, and the translation was completed in just seventy-two days. The details of this story are undoubtedly fictitious, but the letter does relate the authentic fact that the Septuagint was translated for the use of the Greek-speaking Jews of Alexandria. The early Christians freely used the Septuagint in the propagation and defense of their faith.

The Septuagint differs from the Hebrew canon in the quality of its translation as well as its contents and arrangement. In addition to the twenty-two books of the Hebrew Old Testament, the Septuagint contained a number of books that were circulated in the Greek-speaking world, but they were never part of the Hebrew canon. The Septuagint was generally loyal to the readings of the original Hebrew text and it is important for a number of reasons: (1) It bridged the religious gap between the Hebrew- and Greek-speaking peoples as it met the needs of Alexandrian Jews; (2) it bridged the historical gap between the Hebrew Old Testament of the Jews and the Greek-speaking Christians who used the Septuagint with their New Testament; and (3) it set a precedent for missionaries to make translations of the Scriptures into various languages and dialects. (Adapted from N. L. Geisler and W. E. Nix, *A General Introduction to the Bible* [Chicago, MI: Moody Press, 1986], 530).

WHAT IS THE WRATH OF GOD AND
HOW IS IT MANIFESTED?

For the wrath of God is revealed from heaven against all ungodliness and unrighteousness of men who suppress the truth in unrighteousness. Romans 1:18.

Does God experience emotional and arbitrary outbursts of rage against human beings? Is Paul in this passage associating the God of Jesus Christ with the pagan idea of angry deities who have to be placated? What is the wrath of God mentioned by Paul here?

All humanity is lost – After presenting his greetings and the purpose of the letter (Rom 1:1-17), Paul describes the human condition apart from the influence of the gospel (1:18-3:20). Without the power of God's transforming grace, all humanity remains sinful and lost.

> The sinful human condition provokes God's wrath, but at the same time allows God to offer humanity His grace.

The manifestation of God's wrath (1:18) and the revelation of God's righteousness (1:17) are presented in parallel, as complementary aspects of God's action. The sinful human condition provokes God's wrath, but at the same time it moves God to offer humanity His grace. His diagnosis and His cure go hand in hand.

The argument in Romans 1:18-3:20 is presented in a series of concentric circles, proceeding from the general to the particular. Verse 18 starts with the outermost circle, beginning with a universal indictment: all people stand condemned under the wrath of God. This indictment is the "heading" of the passage.

In the first subsection (Rom 1:18-32), Paul presents the general topic "All human beings are accountable to God for sin." First (vv. 18-20) Paul announces the revelation of God's wrath and justifies it: God cannot but react when people commit ungodly and unjust acts, suppressing the truth and ignoring God. Then (vv. 21-23), the apostle announces the progressive stages in the rejection of God by human beings. And finally (vv. 24-32), he describes in detail the moral consequences of this rejection. In Romans 1:18-32 Paul deals specifically with the moral degradation of the Gentiles. In the next section he focuses explicitly on the Jews (see 2:1-11, 17-29).

The language of Paul – It is interesting to observe that the Greek word used by Paul in Romans 1:18 for "wrath" is *orge*, and not *thymos*. The word *orge* refers mainly to an emotion that may be a positive reaction of anger against a situation of injustice (cf. Mark 3:5; Luke 21:23; Eph 2:3, etc.). The Greek word *thymos*, however, is used more for describing the negative type of anger, the destructive wrath. For example, King Herod was "furious" (*thymoomai*) and gave orders to kill all the little boys in Bethlehem (Matt 2:16; cf. Luke 4:28; Acts 19:28).

In reference to God, *thymos* is used only in Romans 2:8 and several times in the book of Revelation (14:10, 19; 15:1; 16:1, 19; 19:15), but the context is always the time of the final judgment. When God's mercy is withdrawn from the world and probation is closed, then God's wrath (*thymos*), represented by the seven last plagues, is poured out upon the world.

> **Divine wrath describes God's radical rejection of sin.**

The verb "reveal" (Rom 1:18) in the present tense denotes that God is presently revealing something to humanity, besides, or even through, the preaching of the gospel. God's wrath (*orge*) is provoked by constant human transgression. This foolish rejection of grace is repeated in every generation, by every individual. Thus, all human beings are in desperate need of the transforming power of the gospel.

The fact that God's wrath is being revealed "from heaven" implies "the majesty of an angry God and His all-seeing eye and the wide extent of His wrath: whatever is under heaven, and not yet under the Gospel, is under his wrath."[1]

The phrase "all ungodliness and unrighteousness of men" is all-embracing. The term "ungodliness" (*asebeia*) stands for "lack of respect to God" and the word "unrighteousness" (*adikia*) means "wickedness," and "injustice." The pair, "ungodliness and unrighteousness," found already in the LXX[2] (Ps 73:6; Prov 11:5), is governed here by the adjective "all" (*pasan*), summing up the total depravity[3] of humanity. These two terms encompass the violation of the two parts of the Decalogue. The subject is further developed in Romans 1:18-32, following this same sequence: apostasy from

God leads to immorality in life.

"Truth" for Paul is not simply something to which one must give mental assent: truth is something to be done and obeyed (Rom 2:8). To reject God is to "suppress" the truth.

The verb "suppress" (*katecho*) means here "to hold back," "to hold captive," "to hinder," "to withdraw," "to stifle" (cf. Luke 4:42; 2 Thess 2:6, 7). How the truth about God is held captive by human beings, who are imposing on others a false idea of God, is explained in Romans 1:19-32.

The meaning of God's wrath in Romans 1 – The context makes clear that the word "wrath" applied to God in the phrase "the wrath of God" (*orge theou*) must not be compared to any human passion. Paul, with other biblical authors, here applies to God this anthropomorphism because human language does not have a better word. The Biblical authors speak of divine wrath in order to describe God's radical rejection of sin.

In the Bible, wrath is an essential and inalienable aspect of God's character. For God cannot look with indifference on the destruction of His Creation nor on the destroyed lives of His creatures. The notion of divine wrath is rooted in the Old Testament (2 Kgs 22:13; 2 Chron 12:12; Ezra 10:14; Ps 78:31; Isa 13:13; 26:20, etc.). Associated with the final judgment and "the day of the Lord" (Zeph 1:14-18), God's wrath generally expresses God's eschatological retribution for sin. Paul recalls here, however, that God's wrath is also manifested in the course of history. "God's wrath" is the term Paul uses to describe

> "Through a manifestation of His anger God wants men and women to come to their senses and turn from their evil conduct (Jer. 36:7; Isa. 42:25; 12:1). Therefore, it is wrong and irresponsible to take the wrath of God and paint a picture of fear in the minds of people."—F. Hasel, "The Wrath of God" (Biblical Research Institute website).

the process of inevitable retribution that comes into operation when the laws of God are transgressed. Thus, as explained in Romans 1:24, 26, 28, "God reveals His wrath by turning impenitent men over to the inevitable results of their rebellion."[4] In a certain sense, as F. Schiller[5] has famously said, "The history of the world is already the judgment of the world."

God's wrath denotes the expected divine reaction to human sin – The term "wrath" applied here to God denotes the expected divine reaction to human sinful conduct and evil. "The wrath of God against sin, [is] the terrible manifestation of His displeasure because of iniquity . . ." (DA 753).

If one side of the gospel reveals God's will to save sinners, inviting them to accept His plan of salvation through faith in His Messiah (Rom 1:17), the other side reveals God's wrath, that is, His condemnation of sin in the lives of all those who reject His plan. If the status of those who accept the gospel is a status under God's grace (3:21-31), the status of humanity without grace remains a status under God's wrath. We could say that "wrath" expresses what humanity deserves while "grace" expresses what God does instead. The gospel always includes deliverance from wrath.

Roberto Badenas

References

[1]J. A. Bengel, *Gnomon of the New Testament*, 5 vols., 1742, quoted by Douglas J. Moo, *The Epistle to the Romans* (Grand Rapids, MI: Eerdmans, 1996), 102.

[2]The Roman numeral LXX (70) is a symbol for the Septuagint, the second century B.C. Greek translation of the Old Testament (see p. 329).

[3]Total depravity does not mean that human beings are as bad as bad can be but that every faculty of a person, his body as well as his mind, is affected by sin.

[4]F. D. Nichol, ed., Seventh-*day Adventist Bible Commentary,* 7 vols. (Washington D.C.: Review and Herald, 1980), 6:477.

[5]Friedrich Schiller (1759–1805) was a famous German poet and dramatist.

Never should the Bible be studied without prayer. Before opening its pages, we should ask for the enlightenment of the Holy Spirit, and it will be given.

CE 59

DOES PAUL CONDEMN HOMOSEXUALITY AS SIN?

For this reason God gave them over to degrading passions; for their women exchanged the natural function for that which is unnatural, and in the same way also the men abandoned the natural function of the woman and burned in their desire toward one another, men with men committing indecent acts and receiving in their own persons the due penalty of their error. Romans 1:26, 27.

While most Christians hold that these texts describe homosexuality and reject it in all its forms, considering it to be sin, others acknowledge that the passage is dealing with homosexuality but suggest that the issue here is idolatry and pederasty and that Paul could not have taken into account sexual orientation as we know it today. Furthermore, it is argued that the reference to nature should be understood in the following way:

In describing homosexuality as 'against nature' (Rom 1:26 KJV), Paul does not condemn homosexual orientation or any committed mutual relationship. Instead, he condemns the perversion of what comes naturally. It is 'against nature' for homosexuals to practice heterosexuality or for heterosexuals to practice homosexuality. Paul does not condemn people for having been born homosexual, nor does he condemn the homosexual orientation (inversion).[1]

The issue in Roman 1:26, 27 is not whether Paul addresses homosexuality and considers it to be sin. That it is sin can be taken for granted. The issue is whether or not homosexuality in Romans 1 includes all forms of homosexuality and has a universal scope.

Homosexuality in the time of Paul – The ancients not only knew what has been called "contingent homosexuals"(people who are not true homosexuals, such as teenagers and adults who are bored with heterosexuality and get involved with members of the same sex) and most probably "situational homosexuals" (people who for the lack of heterosexual encounters resort to homosexual acts), but they also had some idea or concept of "constitutional homosexuality" (homosexuality that is said to be permanent and may be part of some people's constitution). The notion, at least that a person is attracted to the same sex because of his or her constitution is found in Plato's androgynous myth.

> In this myth Plato explains that primal man was dual. He had four hands, four feet, two faces and two privy parts, that is, like two people back to back–their faces in opposite directions. Some of these dual, primal creatures were male in both parts, others were female in both parts and yet others (a third sex) part male and part female. These primal creatures were so strong that they became insolent, attacking the gods. Because of their continued insolence, Zeus divided these dual four-legged creatures into two-legged creatures. A dual male became two males, a dual female two females and the male-female (androgynous) became a male and a female. On this basis he accounts for the differing sexual desires apparent in society, for each creature searches out its own or opposite kind, according to its original orientation. When dual parts encounter each other they fall in love. By the creation of this myth Plato attempts to explain the attraction some men and women have for persons of the same sex.[2]

It is hardly possible that Paul, who was an educated man and who even quoted Greek authors (e.g., Acts 17:28; Titus 1:12), would not have known Plato's myth and the concept of innate homosexuality. Therefore, there is little justification for the view that Paul was referring to violent or exploitative homosexuality or to pederasty only and not to permanent, caring, one-partner, same-gender relationships supposedly because they were not known in his time.

> **Since Paul does not distinguish different forms of homosexuality, he seems to reject all cases of same-sex intercourse.**

A. C. Thiselton declares: "Paul witnessed around him *both* abusive relationships of power or money *and* examples of 'genuine love' between males. We must not misunderstand Paul's 'worldly' knowledge."[3]

The universal nature of Paul's statement – The context of Romans 1:26, 27 is universal in nature. In Romans 1 Paul shows that all Gentiles are sinners; he presents a catalogue of their vices (Rom 1:21-32). Because his Jewish listeners would have applauded him, Paul in Romans 2 points out that the Jews are also sinners. And in Romans 3 he concludes that all people are sinners and that all are dependent on God's grace as revealed in Christ's sacrifice on our behalf. In Romans 6 Paul elaborates on the fact that all of us have been slaves to sin but that in Jesus we can be set free from sin (6:18). Paul's argument is not limited to humanity in the first century A.D., but encompasses people in all ages. Therefore, the list of vices that includes homosexuality is not limited to a special period of time but is applicable also today. Since Paul does not distinguish different forms of homosexuality, he seems to reject all cases of same-sex intercourse.

Homosexuality and God's creation – The background for the discussion of homosexuality in Romans 1 is Creation. In Romans 1:20 the Creation of the world and God's created works are referred to. Paul's argument is that God can be known through creation but that although the Gentiles "knew God, they did not honor him as God" (Rom 1:21). God was replaced by gods that were nothing more than images of created beings, human beings and animals. The list of creatures and the reference to an image in Romans 1:23 echos Genesis 1:24-26. Romans 1:25 points out that the Gentiles worshiped created things instead of the Creator. Furthermore, Romans 1:26, 27 seems to echo Genesis 1:27 by concentrating on the same terms, namely "male" (*arsen*) and "female" (*thelus*), instead of using the terms "man" and "woman." Since Creation is so clearly referred to in the preceding verses, homosexuality must be understood in the context of Creation. "Idolatry and same-sex intercourse together constitute an assault on the work of the creator in nature"[4] no matter which form of homosexuality it is. The Creation account points out God's intention for man and woman, which is monogamous heterosexual marriage (cf. Mark 10:6-8).

> The Creation account points out God's intention for man and woman, which is monogamous heterosexual marriage.

Paul's choice of words – Romans 1:26, 27 states that God allowed people to exercise their free will even if the result would be shameful and lead to self-destruction. After a description of lesbianism, male homosexuality is addressed. The Greek word *chresis* (use) is found in the New Testament only in Romans 1:26, 27; in the context of Romans 1 *chresis* must be understood as sexual intercourse. The last part of verse 32 mentions the punishment that these sinners receive.

The argument that the phrase "the natural intercourse" and its opposite "against nature" in Romans 1:26, 27 are describing what is natural to an individual is unsubstantiated. Nowhere is the term *physis* (nature, natural) used in such a sense. In the letter to the Romans itself the noun is found seven times.[5] However, the phrase *para physin* (against nature) occurs only twice (Rom 1:26; 11:24). In Romans 11:24 Paul refers to an olive tree that is wild "by nature" (*kata physin*). Branches were cut off from this wild olive tree and grafted into the cultivated olive tree "against nature" (*para physin*). *Kata physin* (by nature) then means being in harmony with the created order. On the other hand, *para physin* (against nature) refers to what is contrary to the order intended by the Creator.[6] This understanding corresponds with Romans 1, in which Creation is the background for the discussion of idolatry, homosexuality, and other vices. Here, activities and behavior described as being "against nature" imply a negative moral judgment. " Homosexual practice is a violation of the natural order (as determined by God)."[7] This includes all forms of homosexuality.

The laws against homosexuality are universal – Although Paul lived fifteen hundred years after the giving of the law through Moses, obviously the moral law is–in his opinion–still applicable to New Testament times. The mention of adult homosexual intercourse in verse 27 is dependent on Leviticus 18 and 20. Paul even goes a step further by including female same-gender activity, which was not mentioned in the Old Testament. Dealing with the objection that Romans 1 "identifies a temporary Jewish purity rule rather than a universal moral principle," J.B. De Young insightfully remarks, "God cannot consign the Gentiles to punishment for breaking a Jewish purity law."[8] And since God does punish the Gentiles (Rom 1:27), the laws of Leviticus 18 and 20 must have a moral quality and be universal in nature.

The fact that Paul adds lesbianism to male homosexuality supports the point that Paul considers all homosexual relationships as sin. "Lesbian intercourse in antiquity normally did not conform to the male pederastic model or entail cultic associations or prostitution."[9] It was not exploitative. Therefore, non-exploitative but caring homosexual partnerships must be included in the sins mentioned in Romans 1.

That Paul was not so much concerned with coercion in a homosexual relationship can be derived from Romans 1:27: "men, leaving the natural use of the woman, burned in their lust for one another, men with men committing what is shameful, and receiving in themselves the penalty of their error." Obviously in such a homoerotic union, both partners lust for each other. Both of them are responsible for their actions, and both of them receive the penalty. God is not so unfair that He would punish a young boy who has been forced to play the female in a homosexual relationship, whether by being raped or by being forced into a pederastic relationship.

Homosexuality in Romans 1 is not limited to a certain time or culture or to certain homosexual forms. The universal context of Romans 1–3 shows that it is sinful behavior in any age and in any culture.

Implications – By pointing out that all forms of homosexuality are sin, our passage warns us not to get involved in such behavior. If we are already so involved, we are called to give it up. In 1 Corinthians 6:9-11, Paul records that some Christians had experienced such a change. However, Romans 1 and its context do not call us to hate, despise, blame, or ridicule sinners. All of us have sinned and need the salvation offered to us by Christ.

> Homosexuality in Romans 1 is not limited to a certain time or culture or to certain homosexual forms.

Therefore, as Christians, we should respect all people whether heterosexuals or homosexuals and acknowledge that all human beings are creatures of the heavenly Father whom He loves and who are valuable in His sight. We are opposed to scorning or abusing homosexuals. We love sinners but separate ourselves from sin. We are called upon to support the prevention of homosexuality and to care for homosexuals in various ways, which in some cases may include following Jesus' advice, outlined in Matthew 18:15-20, in order to save them for the kingdom of God (1 Cor 5:1-5). We support transformation and growth into God's ideal; and we also support those who are struggling with sin but reach out toward God.[10]

Ekkehardt Mueller

References

[1]James B. De Young, *Homosexuality: Contemporary Claims Examined in the Light of the Bible and Other Ancient Literature and Law* (Grand Rapids, MI: Kregel Publications, 2000), 10.

[2]Ronald M. Springett, *Homosexuality in History and the Scriptures* (Silver Spring, MD: Biblical Research Institute of the General Conference, 1988), 97, 98.

[3]Anthony C. Thiselton, *The First Epistle to the Corinthians*, The New International Greek Testament Commentary (Grand Rapids, MI: Wm B. Eerdmans Publishing Company, 2000), 452.

[4]Dan O. Via and Robert A. J. Gagnon, *Homosexuality and the Bible: Two Views* (Minneapolis, MN: Fortress Press, 2003), 78.

[5]Rom 1:26; 2:14, 27; 11:21, 24, 24, 24.

[6]Joseph A. Fitzmyer, suggests: ". . . in the context of vv. 19-23, 'nature' also expresses for him [Paul] the order intended by the Creator, the order that is manifest in God's creation or, specifically in this case, the order seen in the function of the sexual organs themselves, which were ordained for an expression of love between man and woman and for the procreation of children. Paul now speaks of the deviant exchange of those organs as a use *para physin*" (*Romans*, The Anchor Bible, vol. 33 [New York, NY: Doubleday, 1992], 286).

[7]James D. G. Dunn, *Romans 1-8*, Word Biblical Commentary 38A (Dallas, TX: Word Books, Publisher, 1988), 74.

[8]De Young, 159.

[9]Via and Gagnon, 80.

[10]Cf. "Seventh-day Adventist Position Statement on Homosexuality," *Statements, Guidelines and other documents* (Silver Spring, MD: General Conference, 2005), 58. This statement was voted by the General Conference Executive Committee on October 3, 1999, in Silver Spring, Maryland.

The Colosseum in Rome where many Christians lost their lives.

DOES ROMANS 5:12 TEACH ORIGINAL SIN?

Therefore, just as through one man sin entered into the world, and death through sin, and so death spread to all men, because all sinned. Romans 5:12.

"What is original sin?" Is it inherited guilt from Adam, or is it our sinful nature, our tendencies or propensities to sin that also have their origin in Adam—or both? What is the teaching of Romans 5:12?

The sin of Adam – Romans 5:12 is the first half of a comparison (the second half is usually seen in v. 18). This verse, as well as 5:13-19, has been an anchor point for the doctrine of original sin. There have been diverse interpretations of the precise nature of this sin, but all views have one thing in common: Original sin refers not to personal sins but to what lies behind them, namely the sin of Adam. According to some, the term "sin" in Romans 5:12 denotes the inherited sin of Adam: "In Adam's fall, we sinned all. " It could be argued that this view helps to explain why every person without exception has sinned and comes short of God's glory (3:23). It could also be argued that by showing the utter lostness of all human beings, it exalts the grace of God as the only way to salvation. However, there are important negatives as well that make such a position untenable. In this case the immediate and larger contexts of the passage need to be carefully explored, as well as the teaching of Paul on the topic of salvation.

A faulty interpretation – First, the advocates of original sin, in the sense of inherited guilt, have often supported a faulty interpretation of Romans 5:12. Some, like Augustine, have argued that what is ordinarily translated "because," before "all have sinned," should be translated "in whom" and referred to Adam. But in the sentence the pronoun "whom" is too far from the phrase "one man" (Adam). What sense does it make to read, "Just as sin came into the world through one man, and death came through sin, and so death spread to all *in whom* all sinned"? Furthermore, the Greek expression used in the text (*eph ho*, a shortened form of *epi touto hoti* which means "for the reason that") simply means "because. "

Second, the phrase "in Adam" is not found in Romans 5:12-19. It is often argued that the phrase is implicit in the statement "all have sinned

340

[in Adam]," in analogy with 1 Corinthians 15:22 ("For as all die in Adam . . . "). But "implicit" is not good enough. The phrase "all have sinned" was employed by Paul in Romans 3:23 to summarize not what we did "in Adam" but the history of the actual sins of all humanity from Adam on. The fact that Romans 5:12-21 is about Adam and Christ and the effects of their deeds alone does not deny the reality that the actions of other human beings are addressed in the text. Paul uses the singular phrase "one trespass" to refer to the one sin of Adam (5:15, 17), but he also uses the plural form "many trespasses," to refer to the personal sins of the race (5:16). In the same passages Paul also refers to the law at Sinai (5:13, 20) and indicates that the effect of the coming of God's good law among sinful, rebellious people was the multiplication of transgressions (5:20; note 7:8, 11).

Third, the text also requires personal involvement in the salvation that Christ obtained for us. Paul speaks about the many "who *receive* the abundance of grace and the free gift of righteousness" (5:17). This is a pointer to the personal faith of these people and fits well with Paul's teaching in Romans on righteousness (justification) by faith and our personal union with Christ in His death and resurrection through baptism.

Fourth, in terms of sin we have a two-sided emphasis in Romans 5:12: Adam's sin and our sins. Paul says that death entered the world through the sin of one, and it spread to all because of *the sins of all*. The text does emphasize the inseparability of everyone's sin from the sin of Adam. In other words, what Adam did is the fountainhead for what everyone does and the results that follow. Adam's fall unleashed the reality of sin into the world, and we all have personally submitted to it. In other words, Adam influenced the course that all of us have taken. This is what

> "Adventists do not stress the idea of original sin in the sense that personal, individual moral guilt adheres to Adam's descendants because of his sin" (John Fowler, "Sin" in *Handbook of Seventh-Day Adventist Theology*, ed. R. Dederen [Hagerstown, MD: Review and Herald, 2000], 265).

Paul means in Romans 5:19 when he declares that through the disobedience of Adam many (all) became sinners. This statement refers not to the imputation of Adam's sin to us, as some contend, but to the fact that, because we are born with a sinful nature, we become persons who actively participate in sin. We ratify our connection with Adam's sin by our sins.

This is confirmed by the immediately following verse that emphasizes the abounding of sin as "transgression," a term that refers to a deliberate violation of God's revealed will.

Finally, textually and theologically speaking, it is death that comes to all of us as a result of the sin of Adam, not his own personal sin. This is physical and spiritual death—a state of separation from God that makes sin inevitable for the descendents of Adam and Eve. Sin reigns through death in that fallen humanity cannot resist the power of sin. Consequently, we also are subject to condemnation (Rom 5:16, 18) and eternal death (5:15, 17). Perhaps we could say that inasmuch as Adam's sin, through our fallen nature and death, works itself out in our personal lives, the concept of original sin, as inherited tendencies to sin, is true.

> "The result of the eating of the tree of knowledge of good and evil is manifest in every man's experience. There is in his nature a bent to evil, a force which, unaided, he cannot resist" (Ed 29).

God's grace, the antidote to "original sin" – However, that "original sin" cannot block the possibility of obedience to God through the power of Christ's sacrifice. The antidote to both the power and guilt of sin is the justifying, sanctifying grace of God that makes us new. As Romans 6:1–7:6 argues, God's grace disallows continuance in sin as the lord of our life (6:2). Rather, through our baptismal union with Christ in His death and resurrection, we walk in newness of life (6:3-4), and slavery to sin as our lord is over (6:6, 16-18). Christ becomes our Lord (7:4) and we bear fruit for God (7:6). When we cry out to Christ for redemption from this sin-prone body of death (7:24), we can say "Thanks be to God" (7:25), who ends our slavery to sin (6:17). Furthermore, by being incorporated into Christ the Spirit of God comes into our lives, setting us free from the law of sin and death (8:2) and making possible the fulfillment of the righteous requirement of the law by the power of the Spirit (8:3-4).

Ivan T. Blazen

WHAT DOES PAUL MEAN WHEN HE SAYS THAT WE ARE "NOT UNDER LAW BUT UNDER GRACE"?

For sin shall not be master over you, for you are not under law, but under grace. Romans 6:14.

The problem with this passage is that, taken in isolation, it could be misinterpreted as saying that one can overcome sin only if one gets rid of the law and accepts grace in its place. Indeed, the passage has been read to mean that law and grace are contrary to each other. According to John Stott, "Law and grace are the opposing principles of the old and the new orders."[1] Others have gone so far as to portray the law as the cause of sin, if not sin itself. Interpretations like these are unacceptable. They not only go against the overall teaching of the Bible, but they are also contrary to Paul's own statements elsewhere in the letter that speak positively of the law (e.g., Rom 7:12, 16; 1 Tim 1:8). For Paul, law and grace—as the death and resurrection of Christ—are complementary, not opposing institutions.

The Christian and sin – To arrive at the proper understanding of the passage, we must first consider the context. The immediate context, Romans 6:12-14, is a transitional passage linking the larger discussion blocks of verses 1-11 and 15-23, both of which are marked with opening questions. Verses 1-11 open with a question prompted by the preceding discussion in 5:12-21: "Are we to continue in sin that grace might increase?" Paul vigorously denies this possibility. Whatever else Paul wishes us to understand by the statement "for you are not under law, but under grace," he does not want us to think that the reign of grace frees us from obedience to the law. Christians should not remain in sin, because baptism has united them with Christ's death and resurrection. Similarly, verses 15-23 open with a second question that, as the one in 6:1, relates back to the discussion at the end of chapter 5, "Shall we sin because we are not under law but under grace?" Paul again denies this possibility. Christians must remain free of sin by becoming sanctified in Christ.

The age of Adam and the age of Christ – Romans 1-5 make clear that Paul thinks of history in terms of two ages or epochs: the age of Adam and the age of Christ. Unlike the age of Christ, the age of Adam is character-

343

ized by sin. So when, in 3:9, Paul declares that all humans—both Jew and Greek—are *under sin*, he is saying that every human being outside of Christ belongs to the age of Adam. Obviously, the age of Adam continues in history as a parallel reality even after the coming of Christ. What is important for our purpose, however, is that the sharp contrasts drawn between law and faith (3:21-4:21), trespass and grace (5:1-21), and sin and holiness (6:1-23) all express this two-age scheme.

The problem is that under this worldview, the law seems to belong to the age of Adam. Indeed, Paul states clearly that the law no longer performs its condemnatory function (Rom 8:1) in the age of Christ. To prevent the reader from drawing any false inferences about the law, Paul offers two arguments in chapters 6-8. First, Paul argues that the law is not evil. So, after a lengthy argument, Paul affirms the goodness of the law in 7:12, "The law is holy, just, and good." Then, Paul reinforces this affirmation in 8:4 with the statement that the requirements of the law need to be fulfilled. Second, Paul shifts the orientation of his argument from history to human experience. In 5:12-21, Paul focuses on what Christ's death means for history. In chapter 6 he turns his attention to what Christ's death means for our experience. The purpose of 6:12-14 is to mark this shift of focus from history to the human experience in the context of the law.

> Christians must remain free of sin by becoming sanctified in Christ.

The meaning of "under law" and "under grace" – Romans 6:14 begins with the words "for sin shall not be master over you." The future tense of the statement "shall not be master" has given rise to several different interpretations. Some see it not as a command but as a promise, others as an encouragement and assurance. These are good suggestions. What it cannot mean, however, is that we will be presently and instantaneously sinless. The tense of this verse needs to be understood in the light of the admonitions in verses 12, 13, and 19 and the present tense statements in 7:14-25.

The second half of Romans 6:14 states, "for you are not under law, but under grace." The very next verse makes clear that Paul here uses the phrase "under the law" to mean life in the old age of sin and death lived under the condemnation of the law. By contrast, the phrase "under grace" describes life in the new age of righteousness and vitality lived by the renewing power of grace. For Paul follows right on to say: "Do you not know that when you present yourselves to someone *as* slaves for obedience, you are slaves of the one whom you obey, either of sin resulting in death, or of obedience resulting in righteousness? . . . having been freed from sin, you became slaves of righteousness" (vv. 16, 18). So, the statement "for you are not under law" (v. 14) tells the reader that a successful transfer has taken place between the ages.

The two expressions—"under the law" and "under grace"—are best taken as Paul's attempt to elucidate the meaning of baptism in terms of law and grace. The life under the condemnation of the law corresponds to dying, and the life under grace corresponds to the resurrection and the Spirit-filled life in which we receive power to break free from the grip of sin. The immediate purpose of the verse is to define baptism as the means of appropriating the powers of the new age that has dawned in Christ.

The role of baptism – But just how does baptism enable the human being to undergo such a radical change? For Paul, the body is a neutral entity that must be under the control of some sort of spiritual power. This view is what Paul has in mind when he speaks in

> In Romans 6:14 Paul is not referring "to any law in particular but to law as a principle. His point is that Christians are not under law as a way of salvation, but under grace. Law cannot save a sinner, nor can law put an end to sin or its dominion. Law reveals sin (ch. 3:20), and because of the sinfulness of man, law, as it were, causes transgression to increase (ch. 5:20). Law cannot forgive sin, nor can law provide any power to overcome it. The sinner who seeks to be saved under law will find only condemnation and deeper enslavement to sin" (F. D. Nichol, ed., *Seventh-day Adventist Bible Commentary*, 6:541).

the figurative language of "reign" and "slavery." Unlike "the flesh," which in Paul's language refers to our sinful nature, the body can be either good or evil depending on the power it contains. The expression *under law* describes the body under the power of sin. In other words, as long as the power of sin reigns in my life, I am under the condemnation of the law. Similarly, *under grace* means the body has become the dwelling place of the Spirit of the risen Lord. And only in such a state can the law be fulfilled in the life of the believer.

For baptism to transfer the body from the power of sin to the power of

Christ, three conditions must be met. First, we must be baptized in water in a manner that reenacts the death, burial, and resurrection of Christ. Yet, going through the baptismal rite is not enough, because its duration is too brief and, often, our understanding of baptism at the time is incomplete. Second, the initial experience of baptism must be repeatedly remembered in our minds as an experience of dying with Christ to the Old and rising with Him to the New. And finally, our affections and will must become daily identified in sympathy with the affections and will of Christ through a growing faith and love (Gal 2:20).

> Paul uses the phrase *under the law* to mean to live under the condemnation of the law, and by the expression *under grace* he means to live "under the plan that God has offered of salvation from the bondage of sin" (F. D. Nichol, *Answers to Objections*, 82).

P. Richard Choi

References

[1]John R. W. Stott, *Romans: God's Good News for the World* (Downers Grove, IL: InterVarsity Press, 1994), 181.

HOW TO USE THE BIBLE
Read it through,
Pray it in,
Work it out,
Note it down,
Pass it on.
Anonymous

IN WHAT WAY IS CHRIST THE END OF THE LAW?

For Christ is the end of the law for righteousness to everyone who believes. Romans 10:4.

Romans 10:4 has in modern times become one of the most controversial statements in the Pauline Epistles. It is frequently quoted to prove that Christ has put an end to the Old Testament law, including the Decalogue. Dispensationalist writers, who emphasize the difference between "law" and "gospel" and the superiority of the New Testament over the Old, especially make use of Romans 10:4 as the classic proof-text for defending the discontinuity between the Old and New Testaments.

The ambiguity of the terms used by Paul – The uncertainty of the meaning of Romans 10:4 is due, partly, to the ambiguity that surrounds Paul's use of the term "law" (*nomos*) in his writings but, principally, to the complexity of the word *telos,* translated in most of our Bibles as "end," which in Greek has a large range of meanings, from "climax" and "goal" to "fulfillment" and "termination."

Assuming, therefore, that the word *nomos* ("law") always described for Paul a negative reality and giving to *telos* the absolute meaning of "termination," the statement "Christ is the end of the law" in Romans 10:4 has often been interpreted to mean that "Christ has put an end to the law" either because "He has abrogated the Old Testament laws" or because "He has set aside the law as a way of justification."

The context of Romans 10:4 – Romans 10:4 belongs to 9:30-10:21, the central part of the literary unit formed by chapters 9-11. The background of this section is the theological problem of the self-exclusion of most Israelites from the remnant, through their rejection of the Messiah. Basing his arguments on the consistency of God's Word and action, Paul shows that righteousness in the Messianic era –as election in the patriarchal era— does not depend on merits or works, but only on God's grace, manifested through faith in His Messiah. Paul shows, by means of many references to Scripture, that the new situation in Israel was foretold both in the Law and in the Prophets. Therefore, the gospel is not contrary to God's promises but rather the fulfillment of the Hebrew Scriptures.

Christ became for some Israelites the stumbling stone announced by the prophets (Rom 9:33), because they did not follow the law from the perspective of faith but from a perspective of works (9:31, 32) and did not submit to God's righteousness (by acceptance of Christ, 10:2-4). Gentiles, however, believed in Christ and received righteousness (9:30) and status within the new people of God.

The use of the term "law" (*nomos*), in this context (9:31; 10:4, 5), suggests that it refers to the Torah (the Law), as it was generally understood by Paul's Jewish contemporaries, and designates the whole Old Testament, including its revelatory aspects.

The meaning of *telos* "end" – A study of ancient Greek literature shows that *telos* is a dynamic term, with several meanings, but its basic connotations are primarily "teleological" (i. e. indicating direction, purpose, and completion), not temporal. In the time of Paul, *telos* was mainly used for designating the goal, the purpose or the climax of something.

The term *telos*, followed by a word in the genitive form (e.g. "*of* love"), is a phrase specifically used to indicate aim, objective, outcome or result, but not termination. Thus, in 1 Timothy 1:5 it is used in the phrase "the goal of this command is love" (NIV), and in 1 Peter 1:9, it is translated "the goal of your faith, the salvation of your souls."

> In the ancient Greek literature the phrase "end of the law" always denotes the object and purpose of the law, never its abrogation.

In the ancient Greek literature the phrase *telos nomou*, "end of the law," and related expressions always denote the object and purpose of the law, never its abrogation. Therefore, the current translation of Rom 10:4 as "end of the law," in the sense of termination/cessation/abrogation, would be, linguistically speaking, exceptional and hardly – if at all—correct.

Christ as the fulfillment and climax of the law – The first problem with the widespread interpretation "Christ is the end to the law," in the sense that Christ has abolished it, is that the Bible itself contradicts it: Christ clearly stated "Do not think that I have come to abolish the Law or the Prophets; I have not come to abolish them but to fulfill them" (Matt 5:17); and Paul strongly argues in the beginning of his epistle to the Romans, that faith does not nullify the law but rather upholds the law (Rom 3:31).

Second, those who translate the text as "Christ is the end of the law" need to interpret the word *nomos* as though it stood for something more than "law," which must consequently be supplied: "the *validity of the observance of* the law," "the law *understood as legalism*," "the law *in its ritual aspects*," etc. Thus, many scholars interpret Romans 10:4 as "Christ is the end of the law *as a way of salvation*" or something similar. However, this interpretation contradicts a main theme in Romans, namely, that salvation has always been by grace

> # Christ is the climax of the law to bring righteousness to all those who believe, both Jews and Gentiles.

through faith (see especially Rom 3:21-4:13). Therefore Christ could hardly put an end to what never existed.

In fact, the thrust of the passage in its context (Rom 9:30-10:21) does not present Christ in contrast to the law. Thus to translate the phrase as "Christ abrogates the law" (in whatever sense it may be understood) is inconsistent. Christ is, on the contrary, presented as the fulfillment of God's design, in the sense that He is the climax of the law to bring righteousness to all those who believe, both Jews and Gentiles.[1]

This interpretation of Romans 10:4 goes better with the theological argument developed in Romans 9-11, for several reasons: (1) it confirms that "the word of God has not failed," since the Old Testament already pointed to the Messiah for righteousness; (2) it implies that no Israelite has been rejected by God, since in Christ righteousness is available to anyone who ever believes; and (3) it appeals to the unity among Gentiles and Jews, within the new people of God, since in Christ all the believers are united as the eschatological people of God.

> "This verse [Rom 10:4] becomes the key statement and the logical conclusion of the whole passage [10:1-5]. It means that this righteousness that Christ has brought for all is the object and goal to which all along the law has been directed, its true intention and meaning" (R. Badenas, *Christ the End of the Law: Romans 10:4 in Pauline Perspective* [Sheffield: JSOT Press, 1985], 117).

It is therefore biblically and linguistically preferable to take *telos* in its normal meaning of "purpose," "aim" or "object," and to read Romans 10:4

in the sense that the law points to Christ as the climax of the whole Old Testament revelation, both in its ritual and moral ordinances. Christ was the fulfillment of the Old Testament figures and symbols, the culmination of the Torah, the One who was established to bring righteousness to all those who believe.

Roberto Badenas

References

[1]See R. Badenas, *Christ the End of the Law: Romans 10:4 in Pauline Perspective* JSNT Supplement Series 10 (Sheffield: JSOT Press, 1985).

I ONLY KNOW HE DID

I stood beneath a mighty oak
And wondered at its size
How from an acorn it could grow
I never could surmise–
I only know it did.

How God could make the heavens,
The water and the land,
The animals and vegetables,
I cannot understand–
I only know He did.

I do not know how God could come
And cleanse my heart from sin
Through Jesus Christ, His blessed Son,
I only know He did.

Author unknown

Will all Jews be saved?

And so all Israel will be saved; just as it is written, "The Deliverer will come from Zion, He will remove ungodliness from Jacob." Romans 11:26.

In Romans 9–11, Paul deals with the issue of Jews and Gentiles and their respective roles in God's plan of salvation. In contrasting Israel's rejection of Jesus as the Messiah with His acceptance by the Gentiles, the apostle makes the striking statement, "And so all Israel will be saved" (11:26). Taken at face value, these words seem to say that at some time in the future the entire Jewish nation will be saved, and in fact there are quite a number of interpreters who believe just that. They foresee a kind of apocalyptic conversion of the literal nation of Israel and the restoration of the Davidic kingdom right before the second coming of Jesus. Others have argued that "Israel" in this passage stands for the full number of believing Jews through the ages, or the Jewish-Christian remnant. Another interpretation, which goes back to the early Christian centuries, is that "Israel" represents spiritual Israel, that is, the church, which is comprised of Jews and Gentiles. What is Paul trying to say here?

Paul's definition of "Israel" – This affirmation by Paul comes toward the end of a lengthy discussion of the place of ethnic Israel begun in Romans 9, in which Paul acknowledges his lineage, calling his fellow Jews "my kinsmen according to the flesh" (v. 3). At the same time, he modifies the normal definition of Israel away from an exclusively ethnic-based notion by saying "they are not all Israel who are *descended* from Israel; nor are they all children because they are Abraham's descendants, but: 'Through Isaac your descendents will be named.'" (9:6, 7). In other words, God had already made clear to Abraham that a basis other than physical descent defined who would share in the inheritance promised to him, because Ishmael, Abraham's first son, was excluded from the inheritance and sent away together with his mother, Hagar (cf. Gal 4:21-31). Jacob being preferred above Esau, the firstborn, is given as another example to establish the principle that salvation rests on God's gracious election and mercy rather than on works (Rom 9:11). Therefore the way is open not only for Jews but also for Gentiles to be saved (9:24-26).

Ethnic Israel's problem – As Israel's history demonstrates, God repeatedly executed judgment on the nation because of the widespread rejection of God's merciful pleadings through the prophets. As Romans 9 points out, Isaiah refers to only a "remnant" of Israel being saved (vv. 9:27-29).[1] Paul clearly identifies ethnic Israel's problem: they were trusting in their election as God's children and their knowledge and scrupulous performance of the law, which they used to distinguish themselves above the Gentiles as the only ones destined for salvation (Rom 2:17-20; 9:4; Gal 2:11-16; cf. Acts 15:10, 11). The Gentiles, on the other hand, grasped God's promised salvation because they received it as a gift through faith just as Abraham did (Rom 9:30-33; 4:16).

> God made clear to Abraham that a basis other than physical descent defined who would share in the inheritance promised.

This tragic stumbling by Israel obviously pained Paul, because he had already made clear that no one could be justified (and thus saved) based on law (see Rom 3:20): "Brethren, my heart's desire and my prayer to God for them is for their salvation" (10:1). He proceeds to contrast further these two approaches to salvation, one based on law and the other (and only truly effectual approach) based on faith (10:2-17). Paul also addresses the possibility that Israel could be excused through ignorance but dismisses it based on Scriptural proof from David, Moses, and Isaiah (10:18-21)—ethnic Israel is completely without excuse.

Has God rejected Israel? – The next logical question, then, is: Will Israel be lost? Has God rejected His people? (Rom 11:1). Paul answers unequivocally: "God has not rejected His people whom He foreknew" (11:2). It is important to notice that the reason Paul gives for this assurance is *not* that all of ethnic Israel will be saved. As in chapter 9, Paul bases this confident assertion here in chapter 11 on the concept of a remnant (vv. 2-5). If only a remnant will be saved it should be patently obvious that not all Israel will be saved.

How, then, can Paul nevertheless affirm that "all Israel" (Gr. *pas Israel*) will be saved (Rom 11:26)? The key to this dilemma is to recognize that in Romans 9:6 Paul uses the term "Israel" in two different ways: (1) ethnic Israel (i.e., physical descendents of Abraham through Jacob/Israel); and (2)

"Israel" as the totality of God's people (including *some* physical descendents of Abraham but also believing Gentiles). A very common alternative interpretation is that rather than a *broadening* of the definition of Israel in 9:6 there is a *narrowing*, referring to the *elect* among Israel. But was not Israel by definition already elect as God's special people (e.g. Exod 19:5, 6)? Furthermore, we cannot interpret Romans as though Galatians had not yet been written.[2] There Paul clearly refers to "the Israel of God" as broader than ethnic Israel (Gal 6:16), to Isaac as representing also the Gentiles of Galatia (4:28), and to all who "belong to Christ" as "Abraham's descendents, heirs according to promise" (3:29).

Ethnic Israel and salvation – Paul nowhere suggests that all of *ethnic* Israel will be saved. Were he to do so it would be flatly contradicting what he has spent the entire epistle up to this point trying to explain: that salvation has never been based on physical descent from Abraham, Isaac, and Jacob or on the works of the Mosaic law that were expected of all who claimed to be part of the nation of Israel.

At the same time, there is no indication in Romans 9-11 that ethnic Israel *as a whole* will be lost; to the contrary, *some* will certainly be saved. Paul emphasizes this point in two ways: first, by explaining that "not all" (*ou pantes*) of those who are physically descended from Abraham belong to Israel (Rom 9:6-7), which implies that some do;

> **Paul nowhere suggests that all of *ethnic* Israel will be saved.**

and, secondly, by indicating that "not all" (*ou pantes*) of Israel hearkened to the gospel proclaimed by the apostles (10:16), which implies that some did (Paul himself being an example of the latter). Paul makes this point explicit in expressing his hope to save "some" of his fellow Jews (11:14).[3] If he hopes to save *some* he does not expect *all* to be saved. Some "natural branches" (= Jews, 11:21) were broken off of the olive tree (= the believing remnant of Jews, 11:17; cf. v. 5)[4] so that branches from a "wild olive tree" (= Gentiles, 11:17) might be grafted in (11:19). Paul quickly adds that unbelieving Jews are not "once lost, always lost": "they also, if they do not continue in their unbelief, will be grafted in, for God is able to graft them in again" (11:23). In fact, Paul hopes that many will be grafted in again, speaking optimistically of their "acceptance," likening it to resurrection from the dead (11:15; cf. Ezek 37:1-14).

Hardening has happened to *a part* of Israel (i.e. the natural branches that were broken off) in order that "the full number of Gentiles might come in" (Rom 11:25).[5] Come in *to where?* To Israel. Paul makes this explicit in the very next sentence, "And in this way all Israel will be saved" (11:26, ESV). That is, "all Israel" includes both Jews and Gentiles because it is only after the Gentiles enter that Paul can affirm "all Israel" will be saved. In order to establish this point, Paul, in Romans 11:26, 27, quotes two scriptural passages. The first one, Isaiah 59:20, 21, is the climax of the chapter that deals with Israel's disobedience and how *some* of them will be saved through the removal of unbelievers (to use Paul's earlier metaphor, the breaking off of some of the natural branches).[6] The second passage, Isaiah 27:9, underscores that post-exilic salvation will come through God's forgiveness of sin, which, through Jeremiah, God calls a "new covenant" (31:31-34; cf. 59:21). Through Jewish disobedience and rejection of the Messiah, it has been revealed that ethnic Israel is in need of the same mercy as the Gentiles, "For God has shut up all in disobedience so that He may show mercy to all" (Rom 11:32), reiterating the same point made toward the end of his earlier discussion of both Jews and Gentiles as being "under sin" and in need of salvation (3:9; cf. Gal 3:22). Paul wants to make sure the Gentiles in Rome understand that God's mysterious purpose in Israel's hardening was so that salvation might come to them also, lest they think themselves to be wiser than the Jews (Rom 11:25).

> In the closing proclamation of the gospel, when special work is to be done for classes of people hitherto neglected, God expects His messengers to take particular interest in the Jewish people whom they find in all parts of the earth. (AA 381).

Summary – Paul never envisions the salvation of all Jews. Throughout Romans 9-11, he affirms that "some" will be saved. But he also indicates that "part" of ethnic Israel has been hardened and will be saved only "if they do not continue in their unbelief" (11:23). The salvation of "all Israel" refers to both Jews and Gentiles, which was already a part of prophetic expectations. The reincorporation or "grafting in" of Jews who believe back into "Israel" serves to demonstrate God's mercy. An important part of our task today includes reaching out to our Jewish friends with this good news.

Clinton Wahlen

References

[1] On this concept in Scripture, see *Toward A Theology of the Remnant: An Adventist Ecclesiological Perspective* (Silver Spring, MD: Biblical Research Institute, 2009), 23-42, 61-84.

[2] In instructing the Corinthians regarding his collection for the poor in Jerusalem, Paul indicates that he had already given this instruction to the churches in Galatia (1 Cor 16:1). But from Gal 2:10 it seems that the plan for this collection had not yet been conceived and so Galatians must have been written earlier than 1 Corinthians. Romans was written still later, because Paul is already on his way to Jerusalem with the money collected for the poor (Rom 15:25-27).

[3] Paul employs an unusual expression, literally "my flesh" (*mou ten sarka*, translated by the NASB95 "my fellow countrymen"), to stress, on the one hand, solidarity with his fellow Jews and, on the other, that he refers to *ethnic* Israel rather than to a broader notion of "Israel" that includes both Jews and Gentiles.

[4] Compare this image with the image of the remnant, called "the holy seed" (*zera^c qodesh*), as the surviving stump of a tree that has been cut down in Isaiah 6:13.

[5] Author's literal translation.

[6] The Hebrew Bible in Isaiah 59:20 refers to "those who turn from transgression in Jacob" (a positive statement that some in Israel will be saved, cf. Rom 11:23). The Septuagint translation of the same verse (which is here quoted by Paul) describes God removing "ungodliness from Jacob" (a negative statement that some will be removed from Israel). The mention in the previous verse of those who "fear the name of the Lord from the west and His glory from the rising of the sun" (Isa 59:19) may also be in Paul's mind as ultimately referring to the inclusion of Gentiles, but this idea is not explicit.

Converted Jews are to have an important part to act in the great preparations to be made in the future to receive Christ, our Prince.

EV 579

DOES IT MATTER ON WHICH DAY WE WORSHIP?

One man regards one day above another, another regards every day alike. Let each man be fully convinced in his own mind. Romans 14:5.

Many Christians understand this text to mean that it does not matter on which day we worship, Saturday or Sunday, as long as we worship God. Because Jesus rose from the dead on Sunday, most Christians feel justified in worshiping Him on Sunday.

The church in Rome – Unlike Paul's other letters, his letter to the Romans was sent to a church that he had not founded. He had not yet even visited it, though because of the Christian "movement" he knew many people there, as we can see from the greetings in chapter 16. He intended to go to Rome and have fellowship with the church there (Romans 1:9-15). This letter was designed to prepare the way for his visit, because he knew of some troubles the church was having.

We do not know how the church in Rome got started. Some people from Rome were present at Pentecost (Acts 2:10), and they may have carried the gospel message back with them. Some of the people Paul names in chapter 16 may have been the founders. But what is important for understanding our problem verse is to know that the Roman congregation was mixed, consisting of both Jews and Gentiles, and they were not getting along very well. The main theme of the letter to the Romans is how Jews and Gentiles should relate to one another in the Kingdom of Grace; everything else is only supporting arguments. All need salvation, and all are saved the same way.

The background of the problem in Rome – We can reconstruct the background of the problem. In A.D. 49 the emperor Claudius expelled all the Jews from Rome. Aquila and Priscilla came to Corinth and met Paul at this time (Acts 18:1, 2). The Roman historian Suetonius,[1] in a somewhat garbled way, tells us why this happened. The Jewish community was in an uproar because some accepted Christ and others did not. Claudius made no distinction between Christian Jews and non-Christian Jews. His decision was, "Out with all Jews!" But by the time that Paul sent his letter to

Rome, about six or seven years later, the Jews had returned. We know this, because Priscilla (diminutive form of Prisca) and Aquila were back in Rome (Rom 16:3).

Having this information, it is possible to fill in the blanks. The charter members of the church were clearly Jewish. They naturally would have been the church leaders, holding the church offices. But there were also Gentile believers. When the Jews had to leave, the Gentiles stepped in and filled the vacancies. So far, so good; but then the Jews returned, and they most likely expected to pick up where they had left off, continuing their roles as if nothing had happened. One big problem: somebody else was now sitting in that chair! Now you have the ingredients for a classic church fight, and that is just what seems to have happened. But in Christian circles you don't say you are fighting because you want someone's job. No, you say that the other party is guilty of heresy or laxity or some kind of misbehavior. Reading through Romans with this in mind, one can see how Paul leads up to the passage under consideration.

Divisive issues – Basically, the issue in chapter 14 is this: Some believers said that Christians should do all the Jewish things and that the Gentiles were lowering the standards by not doing them. The latter argued that Christians don't need to be bothered with all that. What were the Jewish things in question? One was food (Rom 14:1-4), probably the same issue that Paul deals with in 1 Corinthians 8, in which he also talks about the strong and the weak and about not putting a stumbling block in the way of your brother.

The other thing was special days (Rom 14:5, 6). To what days is Paul referring? Commentators offer differing answers. Some have thought that this issue is about distinguishing between lucky and unlucky days, which was a common superstition in ancient times. But it is hard to believe that Paul would have dealt so gently with such superstitions. Many ancient and modern interpreters have thought that Paul was talking about observing certain days as days of fasting. Pharisees fasted on Mondays and Thursdays, as well as on the Day of Atonement and on other occasions.

> Some believers said that Christians should do all the Jewish things and that the Gentiles were lowering the standards by not doing them.

This interpretation is marginally possible, but in that case we would expect Paul to refer directly to fasting. Still another common interpretation is that Paul is referring to the Sabbath, which along with dietary rules was an important boundary marker of Judaism at that time. But keeping the Sabbath was one of the requirements of the Ten Commandments, which all early Christians upheld. Indeed, the New Testament makes more reference to the Decalogue than the Old Testament does! That includes Paul, who quotes it in Romans 13:9 and provides us with a paraphrase of the Ten Commandments in 1 Timothy 1:8-10.

Special Jewish days – The best interpretation seems to be that Paul was referring to the many special days of the Jewish calendar apart from the weekly Sabbath. They included not only the festivals of the law of Moses, listed in Leviticus 23—Passover, Unleavened Bread, Pentecost, Trumpets, Day of Atonement, and Tabernacles—but also post-Mosaic festivals, such as Purim, and even post-biblical festivals, like the Feast of Dedication (Hanukkah). There was also the observance of the New Moon, the first day of each lunar month. Some of these days were observed as sabbaths, days upon which they rested from work, but distinct from the weekly Sabbath in several ways. They were not commanded in the Decalogue. They were not weekly, but rather annual, events (or in the case of the New Moon, they were monthly), and as such their timing was to some extent dependent upon human judgment, because human authorities determined when each lunar month began, based on testimony that the new moon had been seen.

> "In accord with the analogy of Scripture and particularly the teaching of Paul, Romans 14:5 can properly be regarded as referring to the ceremonial holy days of the Levitical institution. The obligation to observer these is clearly abrogated in the New Testament. . . . To place the Lord's day and the weekly Sabbath in the same category is not only beyond the warrant of exegetical requirements but brings us into conflict with principles that are embedded in the total witness of Scripture" (John Murray, *Romans*, New International Commentary of the Old Testament [Grand Rapids, MI: Eerdmans, 1965], 259).

Making all men one in Christ – It seems best to conclude that while Paul upheld biblical morality for Jews and Gentiles that was based on the Ten Commandments, he intended to diminish the separation between

Jews and Gentiles, making them all one in Christ. That meant regarding as no longer obligatory those Jewish customs that served as boundary markers but which had no moral significance. These included certain dietary scruples and the numerous festivals that were tied to Jewish history and reinforced Jewish identity.

At the same time it is important not to miss Paul's main point. Though the Gentiles who regarded these customs as optional may have been more enlightened than their "weaker" Jewish brethren, it was necessary for them to be sensitive to the religious feelings of those who did not see things their way. In this chapter Paul makes a beautiful appeal for Christian tolerance, one that is still needed today. Christians can disagree and yet sometimes *both* sides may be right! The thing that is wrong is to take the place of God in judging your brother who conscientiously holds to an opinion that is different from yours.

Robert Johnston

References

[1]Suetonius, *Life of Claudius,* Loeb Classical Library (Cambridge, MA: Harvard University Press, 1979), 25.4.

Handwritten Greek manuscript of the New Testament (ca. A.D. 950)

DOES PAUL TEACH THAT ALL THINGS ARE
LAWFUL FOR THE CHRISTIAN?

All things are lawful for me, but not all things are profitable. All things are lawful for me, but I will not be mastered by anything. 1 Corinthians 6:12.

How can everything be lawful for Paul when the law that he upholds (Rom 7:12) clearly forbids many things. Obviously "all things are lawful for me" cannot be taken in an absolute sense. So what is Paul telling us here? What are the limits of a Christian's liberty?

The Christian freedom is limited – The verse under investigation is part of the apostle Paul's detailed argument against sexual immorality found in 1 Corinthians 6:12-20. Whatever else we may think that Paul is saying in this passage, it is crystal clear that he teaches that the Christian cannot be involved in illicit sexual behavior—Christians are not to go to prostitutes! Paul brings many great theological truths to bear on this vital topic—freedom versus slavery, the doctrine of the resurrection, the unity created by sexual intercourse, the way sin infects the body, the doctrine of redemption, and the doctrine of the body temple. He even makes reference to the Godhead in this fight against evil. The problem must have been very significant for Paul to have brought so many great theological truths to bear upon it.

Part of our difficulty with 1 Corinthians 6:12 is determining exactly how Paul makes his argument. We can be clear from the passage in at least general terms that the Corinthian church had some type of problem with sexual immorality. However, commentators differ over just how Paul goes about arguing his point. One of the major battles is whether in 1 Corinthians 6:12 the apostle is simply stating his own concept, "All things are lawful for me," or whether he is quoting a slogan of people in the Corinthian church.

Paul is quoting a slogan in the Corinthian church – If he is quoting his own principle, then the answer to the question above would be, "Yes, all things are lawful for the Christian," though such an answer could easily miss the teaching of this passage. Paul immediately qualifies the statement by stating that not all is beneficial and some things can even overcome or master a person. That is to say, if Paul is stating a principle of his own that all things are lawful for the Christian, he does not mean that the Christian can do whatever he pleases, for that would be harmful and lead to slavery. This position would seem almost to make the statement that "all is lawful" meaningless, for it is immediately modified and qualified with restrictions.

Instead, it seems to make more sense that the first statement of 1 Corinthians 6:12 is a slogan that some people in the Corinthian church were using to excuse their immoral behavior. "All things are lawful for me" was what *they* were saying, *not* the apostle Paul. This slogan represented a libertine perspective that seems to have led to terrible sexual immorality—Christians going to brothels or temple prostitutes. In fact, there are probably three slogans of the Corinthians in this passage.[1] Besides the "All things are lawful for me" slogan in 6:12, there is also "Foods for the stomach and the stomach for foods, and God will destroy both of them," in 6:13, and "Every sin which a person may do is outside the body," in 6:18. In each case Paul counters the implied theology of the slogan, bringing some of his most impressive theology to bear in countering an insidious error that still infects the church today.

Paul's counter arguments – To counter the slogan about all things being lawful, Paul introduces two very gentle sounding propositions. The first is that not everything is beneficial. It would be hard to argue against such an idea. All of us know that some practices cause us trouble—staying up too late at night, eating the wrong kinds of foods, getting into arguments with others; so far, so good. Then Paul quotes the slogan again, "All things are lawful to me," this time presenting a more pointed concept—"but I will not be mastered by anything." Even if one believes in total "freedom," it is clear that some practices just cause trouble. And not only that, one can become enslaved to practices he or she may feel "free" to do. Thus such "freedom" leads to slavery—and Paul illustrates that such "freedom" is no freedom at all, and so must be wrong.

> In response to the Corinthians' sinful laxity, Paul "quotes the slogans they used to justify visiting prostitutes, and adds some correctives. He also tries to instill a proper respect for the body as belonging to the Lord" (Gregory J. Lockwood, *1 Corinthians*, Concordia Commentary [Saint Louis, MO: Concordia Publishing House, 2000], 214).

The apostle similarly dismantles the other slogans. He shows that the

Corinthian argument from design ("Foods for the stomach and the stomach for foods" 6:13–a euphemism for sexual freedom is misapplied because the body is made for the Lord, not for sexual immorality (6:13). And the view that it does not matter what you do with your material body because it is just going to be destroyed anyway ("God will destroy them both" Rom 6:13) is countered with the doctrine of resurrection in Romans 6:14. God will raise our bodies; so it *does* matter what we do with them.

> Even if one believes in total "freedom," it is clear that some practices just cause trouble.

The teaching that every sin is outside the body (a dualistic[2] concept in which the spirit is what matters; the body is nothing), is countered with the idea that sexual sin is against the body (Rom 6:18). Dualism is wrong, as illustrated by (1) the resurrection of Jesus (6:14); (2) the concept that our body is for the Lord (6:13); (3) the union between bodies that occurs in sexual intercourse (6:16); and (4) the concept of the body as a temple (6:19, 20).

Conclusion – Understood in this light, 1 Corinthians 6:12 teaches just the opposite of what many have thought it suggests. Rather than libertinism, Paul teaches Christian responsibility and wisdom. Rather than making allowance for immorality, he teaches dedication to the Lord. Rather than an eschatology of destruction, he teaches an eschatology of resurrection. Rather than dualism, he teaches wholism.[3] This passage contains deeply powerful and numerous theological concepts to counter one problem–immorality. We, the church today, neglect the apostle's teaching on this topic at our own peril.

Tom Shepherd

References

[1]See the discussion about the slogans in Gordon Fee, *The First Epistle to the Corinthians* (Grand Rapids, MI: Eerdmans, 1987), 249-266. The majority of commentators today agree that there are slogans in the passage.

[2]Dualism in this context is the view that the mind and body function separately, without interchange.

[3]Wholism is the teaching that a person is a unity, a whole, not divisible into various parts.

IS IT BETTER TO STAY SINGLE THAN TO GET MARRIED?

But I say to the unmarried and to widows that it is good for them if they remain even as I. But if they do not have self-control, let them marry; for it is better to marry than to burn *with passion*. 1 Corinthians 7:8, 9.

Should Christians, who expect the soon coming of Jesus, stay single so they can devote more time to the work of God? Why did Paul counsel the single people in Corinth to remain single?

It is not a sin to marry – 1 Corinthians 7:8, 9 is one of several places in his writings in which Paul is revealed to be both a man of strong ideals and a pragmatist. Apparently, and for reasons that he spells out, Paul's ideal is that young unmarried Christians should stay that way. But he is also very realistic about human sexuality. Already in this chapter he has pointed out that because married couples who decide to refrain from sex, even for strong religious reasons, are only opening themselves up to the temptations of Satan, they should only make such a decision for a short time (1 Cor 7:5). He is also quite aware that humans are sexual beings, and that for many people a single-lifestyle is not something that they can maintain without being "aflame with passion" (v. 9). Furthermore, he explicitly says, that "it is no sin" to marry (v. 36), and urges those who are already married to remain married (vv. 10, 11), even if their partner is an unbeliever (vv. 12-16).

If, as he says, there is no sin in marriage, and if Paul urges already married people to remain married, why does he suggest that the unmarried remain single? Again for very practical reasons. As he says in verse 26, 27: "I think then that this is good in view of the present distress, that it is good for a man to remain as he is. Are you bound to a wife? Do not seek to be released. Are you released from a wife? Do not seek a wife." Paul even says that he wants single people to be "free from anxieties" (v. 32). The reference to "present distress" implies that his counsel is not for all time.

Persecution of Christians – It is true that many of the things that cause married couples anxiety today were also present at the time that Paul was writing. Just as modern newly-weds, they had to discover a suitable place to live and how to find the money to pay for all the necessities of life. Yet there are also big differences between today and the time of Paul. For example, young parents today have the choice of when to have children. This was not so in the ancient world. The first child was often born within the first year of marriage, at some risk, let it be said, to the health of the mother. But the biggest difference between then and now is that in most parts of the world today it is not particularly dangerous to be a Christian. That was not necessarily true in Paul's day.

Christians were not persecuted in all places at all times. But many examples demonstrate that dangerous persecution could break out at any time. Before he was a Christian, Paul himself had been present when Stephen was martyred (Acts 7:58, 59). After he became a Christian, he had been seriously beaten three times and stoned once because of his faith (2 Cor 11:25). As a Christian missionary he had been continuously in danger of his life (2 Cor 11:26, 27).

> The biggest difference between then and now is that just being a Christian then was sufficient to warrant death.

Others in the early Christian group had met their death because of their faith (e.g. James in Acts 12:1, 2), and many had spent time in prison (e.g. Peter in Acts 12:3-11). At some later time periods, just being a Christian was sufficient to warrant death. For example, on one famous occasion after a big fire had destroyed much of Rome, Nero blamed the fire on the Christians who were living at Rome, and as a result, many who did not escape died rather horrible deaths. Still later widespread persecution broke out right across the Roman Empire, and many Christians who refused to give up their faith died.

Paul the idealist and pragmatist – It was a serious thing to become a Christian, and Paul's advice in 1 Corinthians 7 was given to those living in serious times. Deciding to stand firm and remain a Christian, even if this would result in one's death, was a difficult decision. How much more difficult would that decision be for somebody who was married and if killed would leave young children without support? Paul was right. Considering the times in which they lived, first-century Christians who were single should indeed give serious thought as to whether or not they should marry. Who would want to take on the responsibility of children at such times? Yet, even so, Paul was at heart both a pragmatist and an idealist. He was pragmatic enough to realize that some would prefer to marry even under such conditions, and he was willing to allow that to happen. He was an idealist in that he considered marriage something sacred that should be preserved under the most difficult of circumstances.

What would Paul the pragmatist and idealist say to young unmarried Christians today? He would most likely ask them to consider their circumstances and to act sensibly. Given favorable enough conditions, he would have no problem encouraging them to marry, but he would insist that they should take their marriage vows very seriously. For Paul marriage is "for better or for worse." Vows should be observed in good times and in bad, in sickness and in health. And finally, I have no doubt that Paul would also say that marriage was one of the many important blessings given by God.

Robert K. McIver

Remains of the judgment seat in Corinth where Paul appeared before Gallio (Acts 18:12)

WHY SHOULD WOMEN COVER THEIR HEADS IN CHURCH?

But every woman who has her head uncovered while praying or prophesying disgraces her head, for she is one and the same as the woman whose head is shaved. 1 Corinthians 11:5.

For many years, most Seventh-day Adventists interpreted this verse to mean that women must wear a hat while attending church. Considerable discussion arose when a large number of women – mainly younger women – started to turn up to church without a hat. Today most of the women who attend a Seventh-day Adventist worship service do not wear a hat. Why not?

The meaning of a head-covering in first-century Greece – Why did Paul advise that women should cover their heads at church gatherings? The answer to this question lies in the society of first-century Greece. The role of a respectable married woman in Greece was very circumscribed. She, like her respectable married contemporaries in Palestine, and even in Rome, would not appear in public without wearing a head-covering. A number of Roman female statues from the first century have been found. Generally, a married woman "was portrayed in a long dress with a large mantle drawn around her which she used to cover the back of her head to form the marriage veil."[1] Others had the large mantle drawn over the head epitomizing modesty.[2] It was, obviously, important to have the hair covered. Whether or not a head-covering was worn was considered to be a question of modesty.

The reason for a head-covering in church – Given that background, why would any woman not cover her head in a church gathering? The most likely explanation was that she considered the church members to be part of her extended family. Yet Paul advises that this behavior could easily be misunderstood. He insists that while at church, women should act with the greatest decorum. The issue of decorum crops up several times throughout Paul's letters. In 1 Corinthians 14:26-33, Paul complains that when the church at Corinth gathers together, each has a Psalm, a teaching, a revelation, a tongue. He insists that only one or, at most, three speak in a tongue, and that they do it one after another, not at the same time (vv. 27,

28). Likewise, only one or at most three prophets should speak, and they too should take turns (vv. 29-31). Paul would not have to state these rules unless everybody was presenting their tongue or a teaching or Psalm or prophecy all at the same time! It is little wonder that Paul says that everything must be done decently and in order (1 Cor 14:40). This sense of order clearly was not happening at Corinth. It is reasonable to suspect that Paul considered the lack of a head-covering on women as part of this wider problem. Christians at Corinth were not acting with decorum. Because God is a God of peace not tumult (1 Cor 14:33), Christians should worship in a way suited to His nature – with decorum.

The lesson for today – 1 Corinthians 11:5 is an excellent example of the fact that good biblical interpretation uses the historical context to understand the text. Clearly, Paul's advice was right on target for Christians living in first-century Greece. Modesty required that respectable women should wear a head-covering on public occasions, such as worship. But is wearing a head-covering still necessary today?

"It was customary for women to cover their heads with a veil, as an evidence that they were married, and also as a matter of modesty. . . . For a woman at Corinth to take public part in the services of the church with her head uncovered would give the impression that she acted shamelessly and immodestly, without the adorning of shamefacedness and sobriety (see 1 Tim. 2:9)." (F. D. Nichol, ed., *Seventh-day Adventist Bible Commentary*, 6:756).

Biblical texts have to be taken seriously, even if cultures and customs change. The Ten Commandments, as well as other commands, are still as valid today as they ever were. However, sometimes a directive may be aimed at a specific situation only. How do we know? By whether or not the text or context provide a clue or whether a change can be seen by tracing the topic throughout Scripture. In our case Paul's mention of a custom (v. 16) indicates that he is addressing a specific situation only. However, the underlying principle would still be applicable, even if the details are not.

So what would Paul's advice be to us today? The same principle is clearly applicable. All of us, both women and men, should dress modestly, especially when attending worship. What exactly that means may vary from country to country, and even from culture to culture within that country.

367

But God is still the God of peace, not tumult. When it comes to worship, all things should still be done decently and in order.

Robert K. McIver

References

[1]Bruce W. Winter, *Roman Wives, Roman Widows* (Grand Rapids, MI: W. B. Eerdmans, 2003), 78, 79.
[2]Ibid., 79.

The Apollo temple in Corinth where Paul established a church and labored for 18 months (Acts 18:11).

WHAT ARE THE TONGUES IN 1 CORINTHIANS?

For one who speaks in a tongue speaks not to men but to God; for no one understands him, but he utters mysteries in the Spirit. 1 Corinthians 14:2; RSV.

What was the nature of the tongues Paul mentions in his letter to the Corinthians? Was he referring to an ecstatic or angelic unintelligible speech, comparable to what we encounter in Pentecostal and charismatic circles, or were the tongues in Corinth foreign languages?

The church in Corinth – The Corinthian church, founded by Paul some three years prior to the letter, faced many problems: rivalries among various factions (1 Cor 3:3), gross immorality (1 Cor 5:1), court cases among believers (1 Cor 6:1), marriage problems (1 Cor 7:1), the eating of foods sacrificed to idols (1 Cor 8:1), the improper conduct of women in public worship (1 Cor 11:2-16), abuse of the Lord's supper (1 Cor 11:21), and also misunderstanding regarding the proper function of spiritual gifts, particularly the use of the gift of tongues (1 Cor 14:1-5).

The proper use of spiritual gifts – Tongues are mentioned only in chapters 12-14. These chapters deal with spiritual gifts, one of which is called "[various] kinds of tongues" (1 Cor 12:10, 28) or just "tongues" (1 Cor 12:30). In addition there is the gift of translating tongues (1 Cor 12:10, 30). Paul ends chapter 12 by pointing to something even better than spiritual gifts, namely love. In this connection he states that speaking with human tongues or even angelic tongues is worthless without love (1 Cor 13:1).

In 1 Corinthians 14 Paul continues the discussion of spiritual gifts by focusing on speaking in tongues versus prophecy. However, the real issues are: (1) who is to benefit in a worship context; and (2) the problem of disorder in the worship service. The discussion of tongues must be understood against this background. Who is going to benefit from the exercise of this spiritual gift—the gifted person only or others also (1 Cor 14:2-6, 9)? Paul is clear: The goal must be to edify the church (1 Cor 14:4, 5, 12, 17, 26). Furthermore, for outsiders the impression must be avoided that church members are out of their mind (1 Cor 14:23). Verses 27-40 discuss the problem of disorder in the worship service in Corinth. Paul points out

369

that since spiritual gifts can be controlled by the recipients, only two or three persons should speak in turn and that an interpretation should be provided. If these rules are not maintained, speaking in tongues has no place in the worship service of the Corinthian church. The same is also true for prophecy (1 Cor 14:29-32). Thus, the context makes it clear that the issue is the abuse of spiritual gifts.

Important words – In order to appreciate what 1 Corinthians 14 teaches we need to understand the meaning of some of the key terms. We will briefly study the use of the important Greek words in the Greek translation of the Old Testament (the Septuagint) and in the and New Testament:

"Tongue" (*glossa*) – The Greek term *glossa* stands predominantly for (1) the human organ of the mouth called the tongue (e.g., Ps 22:15, Jas 3:5); (2) languages (Gen 10:5; Acts 2:4), including nations that speak other languages (Zech 8:23; Rev 5:9; and (3) the tongues of fire at Pentecost (Acts 2:3).

> The context in 1 Corinthians makes it clear that the issue is the abuse of spiritual gifts.

"Speak" – The Greek term "to speak" (*laleo*) occurs 34 times in 1 Corinthians. In chapter 14 it is used 10 times with "tongues" and 14 times without it. Each time it is used without "tongues" the act of speaking involves a real language that contains content that can be communicated. Because the very same verb "to speak" is used in the phrase "speak in a tongue" (1 Cor 14:2, 4-6, etc.), it is expected to have the same meaning in every text; otherwise language loses its meaning. In the same context, a word should have the same meaning unless it is clearly redefined. In chapter 14, in which the author goes back and forth between prophecy and speaking in tongues, the word *laleo* should always have the same meaning.[1]

"*Speaking in Tongues*" – How are the words "speaking" and "tongue" in the same context and the phrase "speaking in tongues" used in Scripture? (1) In Wisdom Literature: My tongue speaks (Job 33:2). The tongue of the righteous speaks justice (Ps 37:30; LXX Ps 36:30). "They have spoken against me with a lying tongue" (Ps 109:2; LXX Ps 108:2). (2) In the Prophets: "Indeed, He will speak to this people through stammering lips and a foreign tongue" (Isa 28:11).[2] "They have taught their tongue to speak lies . . ." (Jer 9:5). (3) In the Gospels: "they will speak with new tongues" (Mark 16:17). (4) In Acts: The early Christians "began to speak with other tongues, as the Spirit was giving them utterance" (Acts 2:4). What they spoke were foreign languages: People from different countries said, "we hear them in our own tongues speaking of the mighty deeds of God" (Acts 2:11). Foreign languages are also meant in Acts 10:46 in which Peter, refering to Cornelius and his household says, "They have received the Holy Spirit just as we have." The same applies to Acts 19:6 in which speaking in tongues and prophesying are attributed to those who received the Holy Spirit. (5) In 1 Corinthians: The phrase "speak with tongues" occurs in 1 Corinthians 12:30 as a description of the spiritual gift. In 1 Corinthians 13:1 it is used to describe human language. The disputed texts are primarily found in 1 Corinthians 14. There the phrase is used with "tongue" in the singular ("speaking in a tongue") in 1 Corinthians 14:2, 4, 13, 27 and with "tongue" in the plural ("speaking in tongues") in 1 Corinthians 14:5 (twice), 6, 18, 23, 39. Because "speaking in tongues" refers to foreign languages throughout Scripture, it is hardly conceivable that the phrase in 1 Corinthians 14 should be understood differently from the rest of Scripture, unless there were clear indicators in the text.

"*Mysteries*" – The term "mystery" occurs 28 times in the New Testament, and 21 times it refers to the mystery of the kingdom of heaven and related concepts. Other mysteries are the "the mystery of iniquity" (2 Thess 2:7), "the mystery of the seven stars" (Rev 1:20), or "the mystery of the "harlot" in Revelation 17.

Paul uses the Greek word *mysterion* (mystery) in the singular in 1 Corinthians 2:1 (translated as "testimony"), 2:7 and 15:51. In chapter 2 the mystery is "Jesus Christ crucified" (1 Cor 2:2), i.e., God's saving activity in and through Christ. In chapter 15 the mystery is that not all will die and sleep but that they will be transformed at the Second Coming. The plural "mysteries" is used in 4:1; 13:2; 14:2. In Paul's writings mysteries are truths revealed by God that are related to Christ and the plan of salvation.

"*Spirit*" – In 1 Corinthians *pneuma* (spirit) usually refers to the Holy Spirit, but the word can also describe the human spirit or person (e.g., 1 Cor 2:11; 5:5; 16:18), the spirit of the world (1 Cor 2:12), or various spirits (1 Cor 12:10), probably true and false prophets or teachers, etc. The highest concentration of "spirit" is found in chapter 12. In this chapter, spirit is used once in the plural and eleven times in the singular. Always "spirit" in the singular refers to the Holy Spirit. He is the author of the spiritual gifts. Therefore, it is very natural that 1 Corinthians 14:2, which continues the discussion of spiritual gifts, would refer to the Holy Spirit. Furthermore, when Paul talks about the human spirit, he makes it quite clear. Either he uses qualifiers, such as personal pronouns or appositions, e.g., "of the man" (1 Cor 2:11), or the context of his letter points clearly to the nature of the spirit. Because there is no qualifier in 1 Corinthians 14:2, we assume that Paul refers to the Holy Spirit. This also makes sense with "mystery" being revealed truth.

> "The New Testament use does not support the idea that *glossa* ever refers to ecstatic speech. The only specific example or description of tongues in the entire Bible is Acts 2:4-11 where they are definitely described as normal human languages. . . . Abundant evidence demonstrates that the gift of tongues is the miraculous ability to speak languages previously unknown to the speaker" (Thomas R. Edgar, *Satisfied by the Promise of the Spirit* [Grand Rapids, MI: Kregel, 1996], 153).

Paul and the misuse of the gift in Corinth – On the one hand, Paul wants to encourage the church to use their spiritual gifts; on the other hand, he tries to correct the abuse of the gift of tongues. Instead of using this gift for what it was intended – to evangelize people who speak foreign languages – the Corinthians were using it in church to edify themselves or to gain status. Therefore, Paul says, "For one who speaks in a tongue does not speak to men, but to God; for no one understands." God, of course, understands all languages but the other church members do not.

Arguments in favor of foreign languages – While many sincere Christians believe that Paul in 1 Corinthians is speaking about ecstatic speech, the weight of scriptural evidence favors the view that tongues in 1 Corinthians refers to real languages:

1. The context refers to languages. 1 Corinthians 13:1 uses the unique phrase "tongues of men." This phrase clearly refers to human languages. Paul states a hypothetical case. Even if I spoke foreign languages and were able to communicate the way angels do, without love it would be worthless.

2. Throughout the New Testament the same word *glossa* is used for the gift of tongues. Because in Acts tongues are foreign languages, the tongues in 1 Corinthians should also be understood as foreign languages. Difficult texts should be explained by clear texts, i.e., 1 Corinthians 14 should be interpreted by Acts 2 in which "tongues" clearly mean foreign languages.

3. God works through man's intelligence. The Lord, who warned against babbling on like the heathen (Matt 6:7), would hardly inspire ecstatic

speech that no one could understand.

4. 1 Corinthians 14:21 provides something like a definition of the gift of tongues. In this verse Paul quotes Isaiah 28:11, when it says that God will speak to His people in a foreign, literally "another tongue." The context of Isaiah 28 reveals that the persons speaking the foreign language are the Assyrians. The Septuagint renders the term "foreign tongue" *glossa hetera*. Paul contracts the two words and speaks about *heteroglossoi*. "This comparison is revealing, because it seems to imply that what is happening in Corinth is the same. 'Foreign languages' are brought in by means of the tongues-speakers, but they do not bring about the desired results since they cannot be understood by the hearers."[3] Because foreign languages clearly are in view in 1 Corinthians 14:21, verse 2 must also refer to a real human language. Furthermore, in verse 22, tongues are for a sign to unbelievers as at Pentecost in which real languages were a positive sign for unbelievers, calling them to repentance (Acts 2:38).

> **Because foreign languages clearly are in view in 1 Corinthians 14:21, verse 2 must also refer to a real human language.**

5. The gifts were given for the common good (1 Cor 12:7), which rules out using a gift purely for personal gratification.

6. The divine gift of tongues appeared for the first time at Pentecost as described in Acts 2 where it is clearly presented as foreign languages and was a fulfillment of the prediction made in Mark 16:17. Although the events depicted in Acts 2 happened earlier than the events presented in 1 Corinthians, the letter to the Corinthians was written earlier than Acts. There are a number of connections between 1 Corinthians 14 and Acts 2, as well as other texts in Acts, dealing with the gift of tongues:

(a) There is a similar reaction to the gift of tongues in 1 Corinthians 14:22, 23 and Acts 2:13. People think Christians are mad or drunk.

(b) Speaking in tongues is to serve the mission of the church (1 Cor 14:22; Acts 2:14-41). Tongues are a sign to unbelievers, calling them to repentance. Many are saved; others refuse to follow Jesus. Ecstatic speech would hardly be a sign and could hardly achieve the reported results.

(c) The phrase *lalein heterais glossais* (speak in other tongues) in Acts 2:4 reminds us of the language used to describe those with a foreign language (*en heteroglossois . . . laleso*) in 1 Corinthians 14:21.

(d) In Acts 2, Luke uses the same terminology employed by Paul in 1 Corinthians 12-14 to describe the spiritual gift of speaking in tongues, referring to foreign languages. In Acts 19:6, Luke associates Paul with a situation in which some disciples received this gift. When Paul laid hands on these believers, they received the Holy Spirit and began to speak in tongues and to prophesy. It is hardly conceivable that Luke would understand or use the same phrase differently than Paul did and vice versa.

Summary

Our study indicates that the gift of tongues may best be understood as the gift of speaking foreign languages without having studied them. First Corinthians 14:2 refers to a situation in which someone who speaks a foreign language in a context in which the language is not understood speaks to God only, because God can understand all languages. The gift of tongues in Corinth was a genuine gift of the Holy Spirit, but it was misused. Consequently, the church was instructed by Paul to return to the right use of spiritual gifts so that they could become a blessing and not a hindrance for believers and unbelievers.

Ekkehardt Mueller

References

[1]Raymond F. Collins, (*First Corinthians*, Sacra Pagina Series, Volume 7 [Collegeville, MN: The Liturgical Press, 1999], 492), seems to distinguish between *laleo* (to speak) and *lego* (to say), suggesting that the latter refers to intelligible conversation. However, the terms occur next to each other and, to some degree, interchangeably in 1 Corinthians 9:8; 12:3; 14:21. While Paul and others "speak (*laloumen*) God's wisdom in a mystery" (1Cor 2:7), Paul tells (*lego*) the believers a mystery (1 Cor 15:51).

[2]The Septuagint of Isaiah 29:24; 32:4 also talks about stammering tongues that will learn to speak clearly.

[3]Gerhard F. Hasel, *Speaking in Tongues: Biblical Speaking in Tongues and Contemporary Glossolalia* (Berrien Springs, MI: Adventist Theological Society Publications, 1991), 140.

WHAT DOES PAUL MEAN BY BEING "ABSENT FROM THE BODY AND AT HOME WITH THE LORD"?

We are of good courage, I say, and prefer rather to be absent from the body and to be at home with the Lord. 2 Corinthians 5:8.

This text has been interpreted in different ways but the most common one is along the lines of a conscious intermediate state after death. We will examine the text from the perspective of that particular reading of it. In the context of this passage, Paul is discussing the glorious future of God's people (2 Cor 4:7-18). He acknowledges that, although in this world we suffer and are afflicted, the power of life is already present in Christ's resurrection. For him, what matters is the future glory that will be ours. In 2 Corinthians 1-11, Paul uses several images to discuss our present condition and our future hope.

A tent – The Christian hope is introduced by a description of our present condition. The image of an earthly tent (2 Cor 5:1, 4) designates the mode of our earthly transitory human existence that could come to an end any moment. But the believer is assured that God has for us a "house" not built by human hands. This "house" from God will be our future, permanent, and eternal mode of human existence (2 Cor 5:1). The certainty of this hope is so powerful that Paul uses the present tense ("we have") when referring to it. In our present mode of existence–the tent–we groan and look forward to being clothed with the heavenly dwelling. Then the image changes from that of a dwelling to clothing.

Clothed or naked – Paul proceeds to describe the earthly existence as a garment (5:4). He mentions two possibilities. The first one he dislikes. He does not want to be unclothed; that is to say, he does not want to go through the experience of nakedness before being clothed again. The other possibility is "to be clothed with our dwelling from heaven" (v. 2). By that he means that our present existence will be "swallowed up by life" without experiencing nakedness (5:4c). This is a reference to the transformation Christians will experience at the return of Jesus, not when they die (1 Cor 15:52). Paul does not wish to experience the *state of nakedness* (5:4b).

375

Nakedness as a figure of speech refers to death. Those who die are *naked*, not in the sense that their soul continues to exist in a bodiless state but in the biblical sense of being dispossessed of everything. This sense of dispossession was affirmed by Job when he declared: "Naked I came from my mother's womb, and naked I shall return there" (Job 1:21). Paul uses the term "naked" in 1 Corinthians 15 in the context of a discussion about the resurrection: "What you sow does not come to life unless it dies. And as for what you sow, you do not sow the body that is to be, but a bare [naked] seed, perhaps of wheat or of some other grain. But God gives it a body as he has chosen, and to each kind of seed its own body" (15:36-38, NRSV). The naked grain is the one that, like the tent, will dissolve and die. We can, then, conclude that to be naked is to be dead. Believers could be unclothed (experience nakedness/death) before the return of the Lord, or they could remain clothed (would not experience nakedness/death) and experience the change when "this mortal must put on immortality" (1 Cor 15:53).

> To be at home in the body designates our present existence in this world, our natural condition.

At home in the body – In 2 Corinthians 5:6 Paul uses the image of a home. In that context, to be at home in the body designates our present existence in this world, our natural condition. But according to Paul, being in that natural condition means that we are "away from the Lord." There is a separation between the ascended Lord and the believer in the sense that they exist in different spheres of being—the earthly versus the heavenly. But the distance is not absolute. While we exist in our earthly mode of existence, we can *by faith*, not by sight, walk with the Lord (5:7; cf. 4:18). The implication is that "to be at home with the Lord" means to enjoy full personal fellowship with Him in His immediate presence, in His heavenly sphere. This will take place at the resurrection from the dead (cf. 1 Thess 4:16, 17).

Absent from the body – Paul in our text expresses his deepest desire: He would like to be absent from the body (his natural, earthly human existence) in order "to be at home with the Lord." He is not wishing to die in order to be with the Lord. He already rejected the idea of dying (5:4). He is repeating what he said in 2 Corinthians 5:2. He would like to move from one mode of existence to the other without experiencing death. He even clarifies that we will be judged on the basis of our earthly existence ("for the things done while in the body," [5:10, NIV]). Paul offers a conclusion: "Whether we are at home or away, we make it our aim to please him [the Lord]" (5:9, NRSV). The joy of the Christian in this earthly existence and in the coming world—in this life and in the future life—should always be to please the Lord.

> "To be at home with the Lord" means to enjoy full personal fellowship with Him. This will take place at the resurrection from the dead.

The idea of a bodiless soul or spirit is not found in this passage but is read into it by those who believe in the immortality of the soul. As we have seen, Paul discusses three possibilities (present earthly life, death, future eternal life) and rejects the second one as less desirable. The following chart summarizes his argument:

Present Earthly Life	Death	Future Eternal Life
1. A tent-house	1. Tent-house dissolved	1. Eternal house
2. Clothed with mortality	2. Naked	2. Clothed with life
3. Walking by faith		3. Living by sight
4. At Home in the body		4. At home with the Lord
5. Away from the Lord		5. Away from the body (our earthly mode of existence)
6. Pleasing God		6. Pleasing God

Ángel Manuel Rodríguez

Prayer should be the key of the day and the lock of the night.

George Herbert

WHICH LAW IS THE TUTOR THAT LEADS US TO CHRIST?

Therefore the Law has become our tutor *to lead us* to Christ, so that we may be justified by faith. But now that faith has come, we are no longer under a tutor. Galatians 3:24, 25.

What does Paul mean in Galatians 3:24 that the law was our tutor? What does it tell us about the status of the law? Is the law done away with for the Christian now that faith in Christ has brought maturity?

The meaning of the word "law" – The word "law" legitimately can be said to designate a particular body of commandments, such as the Ten Commandments, but it goes far beyond that. The Greek word "nomos" (law) or its Hebrew antecedent is not confined to a judicial or a purely legal setting. Law, translated from the Hebrew word "Torah," in its most general sense, means "instruction." Unless the context makes reference to explicit commandments, this general meaning of law is to be preferred.

"'The law was our schoolmaster to bring us unto Christ, that we might be justified by faith' (Galatians 3:24). In this scripture, the Holy Spirit through the apostle is speaking especially of the moral law. The law reveals sin to us, and causes us to feel our need of Christ and to flee unto Him for pardon and peace by exercising repentance toward God and faith toward our Lord Jesus Christ" (1SM 234).

The purpose of the law – In Galatians 3:19-29, Paul addresses the purpose of the law and compares it to a tutor. In 3:22, he states that all are confined under sin, hemmed in on all sides, in need of deliverance. This is the circumstance under which the law comes into the picture. The law does not accomplish the actual deliverance. Instead, the law (1) highlights the condition of the sinner; and (2) it points to the One who can make the deliverance a reality. Faith in this Person is mandatory for the deliverance to take place.

The law functions as a tutor – The understanding of the word tutor is often seen as negative. "Tutors were often strict disciplinarians, causing those under their care to yearn for the day when they would be free from their tutor's custody. The law was our tutor which, by showing us our sins, was escorting us to Christ."[1] The Greek word *paidagogos* for "tutor," in verse 24, was used in Greek literature as a referent for one who teaches a child to behave, a private tutor, or a teacher. Etymologically, the word *paidagogos* contains the idea of leading a child. In some settings the tutors were slaves to whom were entrusted the care of children. "In the Hellenistic period, the accompanying role of the *paidagogos* expanded and became nobler; his protection was not exclusively negative. He formed the child's character and morality and even became its private tutor, if not its teacher."[2]

The issue in Galatians is how righteousness is obtained – At issue in the Epistle to the Galatians is the overarching motif of "righteousness by faith." The question is, How is "righteousness" obtained? Is it through the law (any law: ceremonial, moral, etc.) or through faith in Jesus Christ, understood as dependence on His righteousness? In Romans 4:3, Paul unequivocally states that Abraham believed in God, and it was accounted to him for righteousness; faith is the key to righteousness. But righteousness is an attribute of God that He grants to those who believe in Christ Jesus.

> When we receive Christ we are no longer under the condemnation of the law, but we are not free to disregard the law either or else we would come back under its condemnation.

To clarify the source and nature of righteousness, Paul had to address the function of the law. In Galatians 3:21, Paul focuses on the real issue. He specifies that the law is not against the promises of God. He takes this position in order to avoid the charge of being against the law. To the question of verse 19, "what purpose then does the Law serve?" Paul states insightfully that it cannot give life. He emphatically declares "If a law had been given which was able to impart life, then righteousness would indeed have been based on law. But the Scripture has shut up everyone under sin, so that the promise by faith in Jesus Christ might be given to those who believe" (vv. 21, 22). What the law does can, therefore, be compared to that of a tutor who leads to faith in Christ Jesus. When we receive Christ we are no longer under the condemnation of the law, but we are not free to disregard the law either or else we would come back under its condemnation. By accepting Christ we receive power to be obedient to the law (Rom 3:31). Thus Galatians 3:24, 25 give no support to the claim that the law is abolished.

This understanding of the law as leading to Christ is in harmony with Jesus' own teaching in Matthew 5:17 in which the status of the law is at issue. Jesus has not come to abolish the law but to fulfill it, that is, to bring it to its intended goal, to indicate the righteousness of God personified in Jesus (1 Corinthians 1:30).

Ganoune Diop

References

[1]John MacArthur, *The MacArthur Bible Commentary* (Nashville, TN: Thomas Nelson, 2007), 1667.

[2]Ceslas Spicq, *Theological Lexicon of the New Testament*, translated and edited by James D. Ernest, 3 vols. (Peabody, MA: Hendrickson, 1996), 3:2.

We should carefully study the Bible, asking God for the aid of the Holy Spirit, that we may understand His word. We should take one verse, and concentrate the mind on the task of ascertaining the thought which God has put in that verse for us. We should dwell upon the thought until it becomes our own, and we know "what saith the Lord."

DA 390

DID CHRIST ABOLISH THE LAW AT THE CROSS?

[Christ] by abolishing in His flesh the enmity, *which is* the Law of commandments *contained* in ordinances, so that in Himself He might make the two into one new man, *thus* establishing peace. Ephesians 2:15.

To answer the question, Did Christ abolish the law at the cross?, we need to grasp the theme of Ephesians as a whole and then move to the flow of thought in the text's immediate context.

The theme is well summarized in Ephesians 1:9, 10, which declares that God has revealed the mystery of His will in the life and death of Jesus Christ. It is God's desire that all things in heaven and on earth are to be brought into unity in Christ. In spelling out the components of this unity the Epistle teaches that the disunity between God and humankind is to be resolved, the evil powers are to be overcome, and the separation and hostility between human beings is to be ended. The mystery now revealed in the gospel is that Gentiles are to be heirs together with Israel (3:6), the two are to constitute one body, and both are to share together in the promise found in Jesus Christ.

Gentiles become citizens – In Ephesians 2, which supplies the immediate context for 2:15, God's grace is extolled (2:1-10) as the basis for the unity of Jews and Gentiles pictured in 2:11-22. This passage begins with a graphic description of the separated and hopeless state of the Gentiles. On the one hand they are contemptuously called "the uncircumcision" by circumcised Jews (2:11). On the other hand, the Gentiles were "without Christ, aliens from the commonwealth of Israel, strangers to the covenants of promise, having no hope, and without God in the world" (2:12, NRSV).

What a picture of lostness! However, a great reversal is on the way, for verse 13 begins with the word "but" that alters everything preceding. The results of the revolution that the "but" signals are found in Ephesians 2:19-22: the Gentiles are no longer strangers and aliens but citizens with the saints and members of God's household. The house of which they are now a part is built on the foundation of the apostles and prophets with Jesus Christ as the cornerstone. Incredibly, in this new spiritual house or temple they who once were without God will become a dwelling place for God!

Christ united Jews and Gentiles – How is all this to be achieved? Ephesians 2:13-18 shows the way. As in ancient times sacrificial blood was brought to the altar, the place of God's presence, so, by virtue of the blood of Christ, Gentiles have been brought near to the people of God and, together with the Jews, to God himself. The headline of verse 14 is, "Christ is our peace." It is no longer "us and them" but "our." The peace of Christ is the possession of Gentiles as well as Jews. Peace is embodied in Christ, and to be united with Him is to find peace on earth and peace with heaven.

The way to peace is explained in Ephesians 2:14-16. Christ takes decisive action so "that he might create in himself one new humanity in place of the two, thus making peace" (2:15). Jews and Gentiles are made one by three events that take place simultaneously in the Cross. Christ (1) breaks down the wall of partition; (2) puts an end to the hostility; and (3) abolishes "the Law of commandments *contained* in ordinances." The centerpiece is the ending of the hostility that is mentioned not only in verse 14 but also in verse 16 in which, through the death of Christ, the hostility is put

> " 'He has abolished the law of commandments contained in ordinances.' Which means that the way to God now is no longer the way of burnt offerings and the sacrifices and the things that were peculiar and special only to the Jew. It is through Christ and through Him alone." (D. Martyn Lloyd-Jones, *God's Way of Reconciliation*, [Grand Rapids, MI: Baker Book House, 1972], 209).

to death. This is made possible by Christ breaking down the dividing wall that stood between Jews and Gentiles. This wall is defined as the "Law of commandments *contained* in ordinances [or regulations]." These regulations are what gave rise to the separation and hostility between Jews and Gentiles.

The barrier broken down is not the moral law of God – How do we identify the law of commandments *contained* in ordinances that formed a barrier needing to be broken down? It can be confidently asserted that they are not the moral principles found in the law of God. Ephesians 2:15 does not take an antinomian (against the law) position, contemplating the abrogation of God's command to love Him and one's neighbor (Deut 6:4, 5 and Lev 19:18), which is amplified in the Ten Commandments (Exod 20:2-

17) and deepened by Jesus in Matthew 5:17-48, which begins, "I have not come to abolish the law." Did the moral dimension of the law provoke the enmity between Jews and Gentiles so that if the principles of morality were abolished peace would result? What kind of peace would it be if basic standards of love and justice were gone? War instead of peace would be the result!

These are general considerations, but there are also a number of specifics from Ephesians that can be cited to support our conclusion. First, in contrast to the past when we were children of disobedience acting in accord with the prince of the power of the air (2:1-2), we were "created in Christ Jesus for good works which God prepared beforehand to be our way of life" (2:10). Second, these good works not only include the general command to love (4:15; 5:2, 25) but also moral practices that should be followed and immoral practices that should be avoided (4:17–5:20). If moral instruction creates enmity, then Ephesians has rebuilt the wall of partition! Third, and very significantly, the Fifth Commandment concerning honor to parents is spoken of as a principle of continuing validity with a promise of inheriting life attached (6:2, 3). It should be remembered too that there were Gentiles who were attracted to Judaism precisely because of its lofty moral standards.

The "commandments *contained* in ordinances" – If the moral dimension of the law is not intended in Ephesians 2:15, then what is? The "commandments *contained* in ordinances" referred to by Paul have to do with the separation between Israel and the other nations. What was it that the Jews had that visibly separated them from the Gentiles? For one, they had the temple service with the daily sacrifices, regulated by the ceremonial laws and the Jewish regulations later added to it, which very clearly distinguished between Jews and Gentiles.

This can be illustrated by the tumult that arose for Paul in Jerusalem when a group of Jews supposed that he had brought the Gentile Trophimus into the temple. This act was thought to have defiled the temple (Acts 21:28, 29), for the Gentiles were deemed unclean (Acts 10:28). Paul's experience with Trophimus is further clarified by an inscription unearthed in 1871. The inscription marked the separating wall between the court of the Gentiles and the Jewish courts within and threatened death to any Gentile going beyond it. A source of hostility indeed!

It is true that in Old Testament times God called Israel out from the nations to be His special people (Exod 19:5, 6; 1 Kgs 8:53). Various regulations maintained this separation, one of which was the law of circumcision.

383

Paul in Ephesians 2:11 mentions how circumcision functioned divisively because of the way circumcised Jews used the word "uncircumcision" derisively to describe Gentiles. But in Christ circumcision is no longer necessary, for Gentiles as well as Jews can be God's people, and together they constitute one new humanity (2:15), which is neither Jew nor Gentile. Paul in 1 Corinthians 7:19 says that circumcision and uncircumcision are nothing (cf. Gal 6:15); that which counts is the keeping of the commandments of God.

> What is abolished in Ephesians as "the Law of commandments *contained* in ordinances" are the ceremonial laws and legal regulations that made it difficult for Gentiles to become part of God's people.

Not only did the very specific ceremonial laws in the Old Testament separate the Israelites from the other nations but in the Jewish writings of the intertestamental period, in which Jewish laws multiplied, the idea of separation was strongly emphasized (cf. Mark 7:2-5). Those who returned from exile and their descendants were determined never to go into exile again and sought to protect Israel from the influence of the idolatrous pagan cultures surrounding it, thereby strengthening the wall of separation between Jews and Gentiles.

Thus what is abolished in Ephesians as "the Law of commandments *contained* in ordinances" are the ceremonial laws and legal regulations that made it difficult for Gentiles to become part of God's people. When this barrier of separation was overcome by the Cross, which was the fulfillment of the Old Testament ceremonial system and which put to death the hostility (2:16), what emerged was "one new humanity in place of the two, thus making peace" (2:15).

Ivan T. Blazen

ARE WIVES TO SUBMIT TO THEIR HUSBANDS?

Wives, *be subject* to your own husbands, as to the Lord. Ephesians 5:22.

The abuse of women has a long history and many faces. Some statistics indicate that one in four women experience physical, sexual, emotional or psychological abuse in their relationships. Abuse can come in very subtle ways, for example, in the idea that women need to follow blindly their husbands. "My husband said it very eloquently one day," one woman stated. "He said 'I am the master and you are the servant. And when you understand that, we will get along fine.'"[1] And some men feel that Ephesians 5:22 provides the biblical sanction for such an attitude.

The problems with Ephesians 5:22 are the nature of the wife's "submission" to her husband and that of the husband's "headship" of his wife. What did Paul mean when he counseled wives to be subject to their husbands?

The overall theme of Ephesians – Ephesians 5:22 is part of a set of rules for Christian households (5:21 – 6:9) that is concerned with three sets of relationships: wives and husbands, children and parents, and slaves and masters. This set of household duties is itself part of a larger section (chapters 4-6) that consists of Paul's pastoral exhortations to the Ephesians, which are themselves closely tied to the theological explanations of the first half of the epistle (chapters 1-3).

In the early parts of the letter, Paul asserts that humanity is captive to "the ruler of the authority of the air" (YLT) and so is alienated from God (2:1-3; cf. 6:10-20), as well as from one another (2:11-12). Christ's triumph over the cosmic forces of darkness upon the cross (1:7; 2:13, 15-16) has brought this estrangement to an end, bringing about a harmony between God and human beings and establishing unity among believers (2:13-18).

As a result of Christ's victory, Paul in Ephesians 4-6 entreats the community of believers to realize fully the "reconciled life." Members of the "body of Christ" (1:22, 23; 2:16; 4:4, 12, 16; 5:23, 30) ought to yield completely to the mighty transforming work of the Spirit (2:22; 3:16; 4:23, 24,

30; 5:18) so that they might be a community "growing up in every way into him who is the head, Christ . . . in love" (4:15, 16). The Spirit works to effect what Christ's reconciling work provided for – the creation of "a new humanity" comprised of both Jews and Gentiles (2:13-18); this is the body of Christ, the household of God (2:19), and a holy temple (2:21). This universal church is the chief focus of Ephesians, specifically because it reveals to humanity and to "the principalities and powers in the heavenly realms" (3:10) the fullness of God's purposes in history to "re-unify" all of reality in Christ (1:10). The letter is thus characterized by the theme of *unity*, wherein members of the church are continually called upon "to make every effort to keep the unity of the Spirit in the bond of peace" (4:3) so that the church might make manifest, in part, the cosmic unity existing in Christ (1:10).

> "Marriage, a union for life, is a symbol of the union between Christ and His church. The spirit that Christ manifests toward the church is the spirit that husband and wife are to manifest toward each other. Neither husband nor wife is to make a plea for rulership. The Lord has laid down the principle that is to guide in this matter. The husband is to cherish his wife as Christ cherishes the church. And the wife is to respect and love her husband. Both are to cultivate the spirit of kindness, being determined never to grieve or injure the other" (7T 46, 47).

The husband and wife relationship – The instructions to husbands and wives (5:21-33) begin with a call for all believers to "submit to one another in the fear of Christ" (v. 21). Paul introduces the rules for Christian households with this principle of *mutual* submission, which he proceeds to explain. The mutual submission of believers is to be motivated by the "fear of Christ"; this phrase denotes a sense of reverential awe for one who is both Lord and Judge.

The husband and wife relationship is characterized by a distinct and important feature: Christ's relationship to the church functions as the pattern for Paul's treatment of the husband and wife relationship; the apostle repeatedly shifts between these two relationships before bringing them together in verses 31 and 32.

Wives are first addressed with two exhortations to submit themselves to their husbands in everything (vv. 22-24). The rationale for the first exhortation is set forth: "the husband is the head of the wife as also Christ is the head of the church"[2] (v. 23); the second, that "the church is subject to Christ" (v. 24). Applying the Christ-and-Church relationship to the husband-and-wife relationship suggests that the husband takes the role of Christ and the wife the role of the church. As Christ is the head of the church, so the husband is to be the head of the wife; and as the church submits to Christ, so the wife should submit to her husband.

The issue of submission – In the context of Paul's message for husbands and wives, what does submission mean? The word *hypotassein* has the connotation of a subordinate, submissive role. It is used in Titus 2:9 and 1 Peter 2:18 for the submission of slaves to their masters. But in contrast to the slaves who are to be submissive to their masters whether their masters are good or bad (1 Pet 2:18), the wives are to submit "as to the Lord," i.e., "as is fitting in the Lord" (Col 3:18). This submission excludes any servile obedience to the husband if his demands are not in harmony with the Lord's will for the marriage.

> God requires that the wife shall keep the fear and glory of God ever before her. Entire submission is to be made only to the Lord Jesus Christ, who has purchased her as His own child by the infinite price of His life. God has given her a conscience, which she cannot violate with impunity. Her individuality cannot be merged into that of her husband, for she is the purchase of Christ. It is a mistake to imagine that with blind devotion she is to do exactly as her husband says in all things, when she knows that in so doing, injury would be worked for her body and her spirit, which have been ransomed from the slavery of Satan (AH 116).

Husbands love your wives – In Ephesians 5:25-32, Paul proceeds to explicate more fully the true nature of the husband's headship. In two sections – verses 25-27 and verses 28-32 — the apostle exhorts husbands to love their wives. It is noteworthy that the major portion of the marriage code is concerned with the duties of the husband and that they are admonished not to *rule*, but to *love,* their wives.

In the first section (vv. 25-27), Christ's self-giving love for the church functions as the basis for the appeal to husbands to love their wives; earlier in the chapter, Christ's sacrificial love, preeminently demonstrated on the cross, provided the example for all believers to emulate (5:2). Christ's love for the church is made manifest in His sanctifying work on her behalf; He desires to sanctify and cleanse the church of sin (v. 26) so that "he might present her to himself as a radiant church, without blemish or wrinkle or any such thing, but rather that she might be holy and unblemished" (v. 27). The far-reaching extent of Christ's love for the church profoundly impacts the nature of the husband's "headship" of his wife. While the husband is certainly not the agent of his wife's holiness, he ought to walk in the very footsteps of Christ, nurturing and cherishing her, even willing to lay down his own life for her.

In the second section (vv. 28-32), Paul further elaborates on the husbands' duty to love their wives. In light of Christ's love for the church, the apostle entreats the husbands "to love their wives as their own bodies" (v. 28a). Just as husbands are naturally inclined to care for the needs of their own bodies, for "no one ever hated his own flesh, but nourishes it and cherishes it" (v. 29), so husbands ought naturally to demonstrate the love they have for their wives by caring for their needs. Such a course of action ought to be followed because "he who loves his own wife, loves himself" (v. 28b). Paul moves from this discussion of human relationships to a consideration of Christ's intimate union with His "body," the church (vv. 29c-32). Christ also nourishes and cherishes His body, of which all believers are members (vv. 29c, 30). Furthermore, He has a deep-seated union with His body, which is analogous to the "one flesh" union between husband and wife; this spiritual union of Christ and the church is nothing short of a "profound mystery" (vv. 31, 32).

> "Paul ascribes to women a position of subordination in relation to their husbands (cf. 1 Peter 3:1–6). The ethics of Christian relationships within the family are clear when once it is seen that difference and subordination do not in any sense imply inferiority. The submission enjoined upon the wife is of the kind that can be given only between equals, not a servile obedience, but a voluntary submission in the respects in which the man was qualified by his Maker to be head (cf. Gen. 3:16)." (F. D. Nichol, ed., *The Seventh-day Adventist Bible Commentary*, 6:1036).

Paul concludes the marriage code by once again addressing husbands and wives (v. 33). The concluding focus upon the marriage relationship makes clear that the code's fundamental purpose has been to outline the responsibilities involved in the husband/wife relationship through the analogous relationship of Christ with the church. In an exhortation that incorporates previous references concerning the obligations of the husband and wife, Paul declares, "Let each one of you so love his own wife as himself and let the wife fear the husband" (v. 33).

Conclusion – Andrew Lincoln aptly captures the essential meaning of this marriage code:

> "Although all is under the banner of mutual submission, the specific conduct required can be summed up for the wife as submitting to and fearing her husband's loving headship and for the husband as treating his wife with the same care that he expends on himself and, even more, with the quality of love that would enable him to sacrifice his life for her. For both partners there is a Christological motivation which comes mainly through the analogy with Christ and the Church."[3]

For husbands and wives, it is the example of Christ's sacrificial love that functions as the model for believers to emulate. Such a Christological motivation transforms the norms for Christian marriage and discloses a deep, well-considered theology of marriage. If a husband selflessly loves his wife and willingly sacrifices himself and places her needs ahead of his own as Christ did for the church, questions of submission and headship will not be

"The wife is to respect and reverence her husband, and the husband is to love and cherish his wife" (AH 103).

an issue as the husband actualizes Christ's sacrificial love in his relationship with his wife. Interpreted in this light, marriage can be seen as an institution wherein the husband and wife, striving to follow Christ's model of sacrificial love, mutually and lovingly submit to one another (Eph 5:21). Such a marriage displays a "one flesh" unity, demonstrating the kind of unity that is at the heart of God's purposes to re-unify all of humankind and the cosmos (1:10).

Leo Ranzolin, Jr.

References

[1]Taryn Fitsik, "1 in 4 women experience abuse in relationships." http://www.wten.com/Global/story. asp?S=11233097; accessed October 1, 2009.

[2]The word *kephale* (head) does not signify source, prominence, or preeminence, but authority and leadership (Walter Bauer, *A Greek-English Lexicon of the New Testament and other Early Christian Literature*, third edition [Chicago, IL: University of Chicago, 2000], 542).

[3]Andrew T. Lincoln, *Ephesians*, Word Biblical Commentary 42 (Dallas, TX: Word Books, 1990), 389.

The library of Celsus in ancient Ephesus. Paul spent three years in Ephesus working for the Lord (Acts 20:31).

IS THE SEVENTH-DAY SABBATH A "SHADOW OF THINGS TO COME"?

So let no one judge you in food or in drink, or regarding a festival or a new moon or sabbaths, which are a shadow of things to come, but the substance is of Christ. Colossians 2:16, 17, NKJV.

For centuries the clause, "sabbaths, which are a shadow of things to come," has been interpreted by most writers to mean that the seventh-day Sabbath has been abolished and is no longer binding upon Christians.[1] However, those who observe the weekly Sabbath of the Decalogue have generally maintained that the "sabbaths" mentioned here are the ceremonial sabbaths of the ancient Hebrew religion.

Colossians 2:16 begins with the word "so," or "therefore" (KJV), indicating that the caution being sounded arises from what Paul has said in the previous verses. Verses 12 and 13 emphasize the sufficiency of salvation in Jesus Christ. To further emphasize the certainty and fullness of divine forgiveness mentioned in verses 12 and 13, Paul utilizes a legal metaphor in verse 14, namely that God has "wiped out the handwriting (*cheirographon*) of requirements that was against us . . . having nailed it to the cross."

The meaning of the "handwriting" – Suggested identifications of the handwriting are numerous, the most probable being the Mosaic law itself (cf. Eph 2:15). The connected Greek word *dogmasin*, variously translated as "ordinances" (KJV), "requirements"(NKJV), "decrees" (NASB), or "legal demands" (RSV), probably refers to the demands of the Mosaic law. A number of interpreters have concluded that Ephesians 2:15 throws light on Colossians 2:14. In Ephesians we have "the expression 'the Law of the commandments *with its decrees* (*en dogmasin*)', which is clearly a reference to the Mosaic Law."[2]

Nevertheless, because Paul refers to the Old Testament law as *nomos* (Gr. for "law") more than a hundred times in his writings, some have wondered why *nomos* never appears in Colossians, especially if Paul was dealing with the "Mosaic law," as suggested above. The answer to this quandary seems to reside in the following factors: (1) Paul apparently intentionally refrained from using *nomos* so as to avoid the impression that the entire Mosaic law had been abrogated. (2) Since the Decalogue, and the health laws, as well as the universal principles enumerated in the Torah were to continue, Paul utilized the unique phrase "the handwriting of requirements" (*cheirographon tois dogmasin*) to draw attention specifically to the ceremonial law of the Jewish nation. (3) The listing in verse 16 of various elements of this ritual law of Israel serves to corroborate this more carefully nuanced understanding of the "Mosaic law."

> Paul utilized the unique phrase "the handwriting of requirements" to draw attention specifically to the ceremonial law of the Jewish nation.

But, how can the ceremonial laws as given by God through Moses, be classified as really "against us," and "contrary to us," as the text indicates? This concept actually echoes the Hebrew phrase utilized at the time of the proclamation of the Mosaic law, "'Take this Book of the Law . . . that it may be there for a witness against you'" (Deut 31:26). In other words, should Israel depart from the requirements of the Mosaic Law then that law would become a witness, a silent testimony, against their apostasy.

Thus, Colossians 2:14 is a divine declaration that the ritual requirements have come to an end, because Jesus the Messiah has died on the cross as the antitypical fulfillment of the sacrificial system. Verse 15 depicts Christ as a complete conqueror over all His enemies.

Let no one judge you in food or in drink – Texts such as Colossians 1:21, 22, 27, and 2:13 give the distinct impression that the Colossian church was predominantly Gentile, though Jews were certainly present. Based on similarities with the Epistle to the Galatians, it seems that the Colossian "heretics" were Jews or Judaizers, though chapter 2:21 suggests that the restrictions proposed went far beyond the Jewish law. These false teachers were telling the Colossian believers that it was not enough to have accepted Jesus as the Messiah; they needed to keep the Jewish ceremonial law, with its times and seasons, in order to be saved.

Paul's counsel to the Colossians, regarding how to relate to these Judaizing teachers, is strong: "Let no one judge you. . . ." The word "judge" comes from the Greek word *krino,* which means to "pass unfavorable judgment upon."[3] In other words, no one has the right to set himself up as a judge over others because they do not follow certain regulations of the abolished ceremonial law.

Before considering the crucial terms "feast, new moon, sabbath," a brief comment needs to be made regarding the "food and drink" of Colossians 2:16. Since the food and drink come in the context of circumcision and the observance of special days, these words doubtless refer to the meal and drink offerings presented by the Israelites in compliance with the sacrificial system, an example of which can be seen in Leviticus 23:37. Gordon Clark notes, "The context speaks of food and drink, feasts, and new moon, all this is ceremonial."[4]

Meaning of the word "sabbaths" – Careful students of Scripture are aware that in both the Old and the New Testaments the word "sabbath" in the original languages has various meanings. An examination of all 180 occurrences of this "sabbath" terminology in the Bible (i.e., *shabbat* in Hebrew, and either *sabbaton* or *sabbata* in Greek) reveals that the prophets consistently surrounded these terms with definitive linguistic indicators, as well as contextual factors, so as to enable the reader or hearer to quickly recognize what the term "sabbath" refers to in each setting. In both Hebrew and Greek, approximately eighty-five percent of the cases deal with the weekly Sabbath, while the rest refer to something else, such as annual ceremonial sabbaths, or even "weeks." Thus, it is evident that, among other factors, linguistic markers and context would play an important role in rightly identifying the *sabbaths* of Colossians 2:16.

At first glance it may appear as though the "feast, new moon, sabbath" sequence of verse 16 derives from six Old Testament passages (1 Chron 23:29-31; 2 Chron 2:4; 8:12, 13; 31:3; Neh 10:33; and Ezek 45:13-17 in which the Hebrew term *shabbat* does, in fact, refer to the seventh-day Sabbath. However, careful investigation of the original languages clearly militates against the supposition that Paul was quoting from these texts. For example, all six passages actually have at least four parts (not three as seen in Col 2:16); all six specifically indicate that the focus is on sacrifices and not the actual days themselves (which contradicts the emphasis in Col 2:16); and all six include a *daily* offering, a factor not present in Colossians 2:16.

Interestingly, there is one other passage in the Old Testament that may function as an intertextual link–Hosea 2:11. A literal translation of the text is, "Her festival, her new moon, and her sabbath." Note the following areas of agreement between the tripartite phrase of Colossians 2 and that of Hosea 2: Both consist of a three-part grouping; both have the same sequence (first "feast," then "new moon," finally "sabbath"); both passages deal with the *days* per se, and not sacrifices; and both lack the linguistic links crucial for identifying "sabbath" as the seventh day.

In addition, the term "feast" or "festival" in Hosea 2:11 is actually the rather restricted Hebrew term *chag*. Whenever this word is used in connection with Israel's ceremonial law, it always refers to one or more of the *pilgrim* festivals—Passover (including Unleavened Bread), Pentecost, and/ or Tabernacles. Next comes the new moon (*chodesh*), which played such a vital role in determining dates for the other sacred set times. Finally, the phrase "*her* sabbath" (*shabbattah*) identifies this expression as Israel's ceremonial sabbath(s), rather than the weekly Sabbath, which is never spoken of in this manner.

Likewise, linguistic investigation of the similar three terms of Colossians 2:16 uncovers the fact that the Greek term *heorte* (feast) is limited to the identical three annual pilgrim festivals, in which all males were expected to go to Jerusalem for the celebration. While *neomenia* (new moon) indicates the new moon observances, *sabbata* includes the non-pilgrimage "rest times" of Trumpets, Atonement, and, by extension, Sabbatical Years. Hence, Paul was not repeating himself by listing both *heorte* (pilgrim feasts) and *sabbata* ("rest times").

> The sabbaths of Colossians 2:16 refer to the ceremonial sabbaths of the ancient Israelite religion and not to the seventh-day Sabbath of the Decalogue.

In short, the lexicographical data, the linguistic links, and the context all persuasively indicate the similarity of the *pilgrimage, new moon, sabbath* sequence in both Hosea and Colossians. Moreover, this tripartite phrase seems to show evidence of a characteristic of Semitic communication—an inverted parallelism, in which the writer moves from annual to monthly and then again to annual sacred seasons, as follows:

A	"festivals"	=	3	annual pilgrimage feasts
	B "new moons"	=		monthly celebrations
A'	"sabbaths"	=	2	annual & 1 septennial rest

A study of the manner in which Bible translators of the *New English Bible*, the *New King James Version*, and the *Holman Christian Standard*

Bible have rendered all the Greek words for *sabbath* in the New Testament provides some intriguing results. All three versions correctly and consistently understood *sabbaton* or *sabbata* (in nine passages) as identifying the "week." In accord with the linguistic markers and contextual factors, all three Bibles translated *sabbaton* or *sabbata* as "Sabbath" (with a capital "S"), fifty-nine times, so as to identify the seventh day of the week. Only in Colossians 2:16 did these translators render the Greek into English with a lowercase "s"–the "sabbath." This seems to confirm the conclusions of the above investigation that the sabbaths of Colossians 2:16 refer to the ceremonial sabbaths of the ancient Israelite religion and not to the seventh-day Sabbath of the Decalogue. Recognizing the immediate context of Colossians 2:16, Clark states, "All this is ceremonial. Then are not the Sabbaths, here mentioned, ceremonial Sabbaths, and not the creation ordinance?"[5]

The "sabbaths" a "shadow" – "So let no one judge you . . . regarding . . . sabbaths, which are a shadow [Gr. *skia*] of things to come, but the substance [Gr. *soma*] is of Christ" (Col 2:16, 17). There is a widespread scholarly consensus as to the basic meaning of the Greek words *skia* and *soma*. The *skia* is here understood to mean not a literal "shadow," but a "foreshadowing."[6] This is because *skia* is directly linked with the words "things to come" (*ton mellonton*). Colossians 2:17 is very similar to Hebrews 10:1, which says, "The law is only a shadow [skia] of the good things that are coming [*ten mellonton agathon*]—not the realities themselves" (NIV). Frank Holbrook comments on Colossians 2:17 and says:

> The key to the passage is verse 17, which states that these items are a *'shadow of things to come,'* that is, they are *types* which foreshadowed things to come. The law which sets forth a 'shadow of good things to come' is clearly stated . . . . elsewhere to be the sacrificial, or ritual, law of types and ceremonies (see Hebrews 10:1-4). Therefore, all the items in verse 16 being 'shadows,' or types, are *items found in the ritual law* which typified the coming of Christ, His atoning death, and priestly ministry.[7]

Christ's sacrifice is the reality that was foreshadowed by the Passover feast. This is where the other Greek term, *soma*, comes into play. The lexicon describes *soma* (i.e., literally "body") in this context, as *"the thing itself, the reality."*[8] Christ became the reality that the sacred observances prefigured. Hence, The New English Bible correctly renders verse 17 as, "That are only the shadow of the things to come, but the reality is Christ."

The structure, context, and overall flow of the entire passage, beginning in verse 12, demonstrate that the "shadow" of verse 17 refers to the content of both verses 14 and 16. In other words, "Since the context deals with ritual matters, the sabbaths here referred to are the ceremonial sabbaths of the Jewish annual festivals 'which are a shadow,' or type, of which the fulfillments were to come in Christ."[9] Because most of the items listed in verse 16 were intended to help God's people in the Old Testament to look forward to the Messiah, for the Christian to participate in these Jewish celebrations was tantamount to a denial of Jesus' Messiahship.

Various non-sabbatarian writers through the years have recognized the indispensability of taking the context into account when dealing with the "sabbaths" of Colossions 2:16. For example, William Plumer wrote concerning Colossians 2:16, "The context clearly shows that he [i.e., Paul] speaks not of the weekly Sabbath, nor of any institution of the Decalogue, but of matters beside the moral law."[10]

Conclusion – Thus, in response to the question posed at the beginning, "Is the Seventh-day Sabbath a 'Shadow' of Things to Come?," we can say that the compelling weight of linguistic, intertextual, and contextual evidence demonstrates that the sabbaths of Colossians 2:16, 17 refer to the ceremonial sabbaths of the ancient Israelite religious system. In light of the fact that Christ has triumphed over the forces of evil and that the ceremonial law has accomplished its salvific purpose, these ritual regulations have been abolished through Christ's death on the cross and have no significance at all and, thus, should no longer be observed.

W. E. Read's succinct statement forms a fitting conclusion to this study: "The Sabbath of the Lord, the seventh day of the week, is a *memorial*, not a *type*, the memorial looks back; the type looks forward."[11] Hence, the seventh-day Sabbath of the Decalogue should still be kept holy.

Ron du Preez

References

[1]For a brief overview of this trend among both Roman Catholic and Protestant writers and for further substantiation of other points made in this chapter, see Ron du Preez, *Judging the Sabbath: Discovering What Can't Be Found in Colossians 2:16* (Berrien Springs, MI: Andrews University Press, 2008), 1-16.

[2]Charles R. Hume, *Reading Through Colossians and Ephesians* (London: SCM, 1998), 44.

[3]Walter Bauer, *A Greek-English Lexicon of the New Testament and Other Early Christian Literature*, second ed., Frederick William Danker, ed. (Chicago, IL: University of Chicago Press, 1979), 452.

[4]Gordon H. Clark, *Colossians: Another Commentary on an Inexhaustible Message*, Tyndale New Testament Commentaries (Phillipsburgh, N.J.: Presbyterian and Reformed, 1979), 96.

[5]Ibid., 96.

[6]Bauer, 755.

[7]Frank B. Holbrook, "Frank Answers: Did Christ Abolish the Sabbath?" *These Times*, August 1977, 22.

[8]Bauer, 799.

[9]Don F. Neufeld, ed., *Seventh-day Adventist Encyclopedia: M-Z*, second rev. ed., Bobbie Jane Van Dolson and Leo R. Van Dolson, eds. (Hagerstown, MD: Review and Herald, 1996), s.v. "Sabbath." Kenneth Wood commented: "Thus, 'shadows' describes well the various elements of the ceremonial law, including the annual sabbaths, for they pointed forward to Christ's life, ministry, and kingdom as the reality;" Kenneth H. Wood, "The 'Sabbath Days' of Colossians 2:16, 17," in *The Sabbath in Scripture and History*, Kenneth A. Strand, ed. (Washington, D.C.: Review and Herald, 1982), 339.

[10]William S. Plumer, *The Law of God as Contained in the Ten Commandments, Explained and Enforced* (Philadelphia, PA: Presbyterian Board of Education, 1864), 307.

[11]W. E. Read, "More on Colossians 2:14," *Ministry*, January, 47.

What is a home without a Bible?
'Tis a home where daily bread
For the Body is provided
But the soul is never fed.

C. D. Meigs

WHAT DOES THE APOSTLE MEAN WHEN HE SAYS JESUS HAD TO LEARN OBEDIENCE?

Although He was a Son, He learned obedience from the things which He suffered. Hebrews 5:8.

The key problem with this verse is the word "learned." In what sense did Jesus learn? Did He learn the way we learn? Did His learning involve moral correction and development? Also, did He learn through trial and error as we do? Does "perfected" in 5:9 imply imperfection in Jesus' life? And, is suffering a necessary part of spiritual growth?

Jesus our High Priest – To answer these questions, we need to begin with the immediate context, Hebrews 4:14-5:10, which is a long christological section that discusses why Jesus is fit to be our High Priest. The exhortation in 4:14-16 to approach Christ as our High Priest in time of need serves as the section's introduction. Two crucial points appear in this brief introduction to help us avoid misunderstandings about Jesus. The first is that Jesus became like us "in every respect," (v. 15, NRSV). The second is that Jesus is without sin. Our interpretation of 5:8 needs to stay within this perimeter. This brief introduction is followed in 5:1-4 with the qualifications of the earthly high priest. Then in 5:5, 6, there is an announcement of Jesus as the exalted Son, which is achieved through quotations from Psalm 2:7 and 110:4. This announcement is then followed in Hebrews 5:7-10 with Jesus' qualifications to be our High Priest. Clearly, 5:1-10 forms a chiastic structure[1] with the announcement of Jesus' Sonship in verses 5, 6 as its central thrust. For our purpose, though, it is important to note that 5:8 forms part of the explanation of Jesus' qualifications as our High Priest. In other words, the chief concern of 5:8 is not so much over the nature but the function of Jesus.

We also need to consider the broader context of the letter. The description of Jesus' humanity in Hebrews 2:10-18 bears a striking thematic resemblance to 4:14-5:10. Hebrews 2:10-18 clarifies the purpose of Jesus' incarnation: to be perfected through suffering (2:10), to be united with us (vv. 11-14a), to destroy both death and the devil (14b, 15), and to be made a merciful High Priest through suffering and temptation (16, 17).

The most important human suffering – Another important passage is the admonition section of Hebrews 12:1-11, which reveals to us what suffering entails. By simultaneously addressing our suffering and the suffering of Jesus, this section helps us see that suffering involves more than physical suffering. The Crucifixion (12:2a), shame (12:2b), hostility from others (12:3), and temptations to sin (12:4) focus on physical, social, religious, and psychological suffering. But the section's lengthy discussion about suffering as God's discipline (12:5-11) makes clear that the most important human suffering is spiritual. Indeed, many prayers in the psalms reflect this kind of suffering (10:1, 13; 22:1; 42:9, 11; 43:2, 5; 44:23, 24; 49:5; 74:1, 11; 88:14). Asking God "why" in the context of prayer, as Jesus did on the Cross, is not an act of unbelief or rebellion but a way of overcoming mental suffering. We ask God "why" because we want to *believe* God has the power to save us from our sufferings. Moreover, we learn by asking "why." Intense curiosity is what causes us to learn. As we intensely but patiently look for answers with the *practical* intent of reaching deeper levels of obedience, we grow spiritually. Those who cease from asking "why" also cease from learning.

> **The most important human suffering is spiritual.**

Jesus learned obedience – Now we turn to study Hebrews 5:8 in detail. "Although He was a son." The mention of *son* here recalls the words of Psalm 2:7 in Hebrews 1:1-5 and 5:5, which are announcements of Jesus' exalted Sonship. The Son is the preexistent, creative Agent of God, indeed God's very express image. The reason Psalm 2:7 is reintroduced in Hebrews 5:5 is to remind the reader of this fact. The opening clause of 5:8 is best understood to mean "Son of God though he was."[2] The next statement about Jesus' "learning" needs to be read with the understanding that the earthly Jesus was simultaneously the preexistent, exalted Son of God.

"He learned." There is no reason to deny that the earthly Jesus' spiritual knowledge advanced from one stage to another. Luke clearly tells us not only that Jesus "grew" physically but that He "increased" in wisdom (2:40, 52). Luke did not feel that it took away from the perfection of Jesus in any way to suggest that development occurred in His life. Still, the statement "he learned" needs to be understood within the limits set by the author of Hebrews. On one side is the author's earlier statement that the earthly Jesus was without sin (Heb 4:15), and on the other is the notion that He was perfected at the end of His earthly life (5:9, 2:10). It is unnecessary to ask whether Jesus' perfection took shape gradually during His earthly life or whether it was granted to Him all at once at the time of His resurrection and ascension. Either way, it is clear that perfection lay ahead of Jesus during His earthly life. It is also clear in the present context that needing to grow—if that can be called imperfection—is no sin. Indeed, growth and learning are part and parcel of the joy of being human. It is safe to say that, to the very end of His life, the earthly Jesus would have searched for new and better ways to serve and obey God. Moreover, since most of us learn through trial and error, it is easy to think that Jesus also learned this way. It should be clear that Jesus made no errors in His life—moral or otherwise—as it is clear from Hebrews 4:15. At the same time, it should be equally clear that Jesus was often surprised and pained by the callous attitudes of the people He taught and served. Sometimes He even wept. A truly thoughtful human being, He must have learned something from these experiences.

"It was not only on the cross that Christ gave Himself for humanity, not only in the wilderness of temptation and in Gethsemane that He overcame in our behalf. Every day's experience was an outpouring of His life; every day he learned obedience by the things which He suffered. And because the life of Jesus was a life of perfect trust His service for heaven and earth was without failure or faltering. He met and resisted all the temptations that man must meet because in his humanity he relied upon divine power." (*Visitor*, October 2, 1912).

The meaning of obedience – Hebrews 10:5-7 perhaps explains what Jesus' obedience involved. Jesus' obedience was not so much about literal observance of the Ten Commandments as about doing the will of God, whatever it took. This sacrificial theme of obedience is found in other Scriptural passages as well (Phil 2:6-8; Mark 8:31; 10:38; Luke 12:50; John 10:17) but perhaps most clearly in Romans 5:19. The will of God for Jesus was that He should suffer and die in His human body as the sacrifice for the world. The Cross was Jesus' answer to this call of obedience: "A body hast Thou prepared for Me. . . . Behold, I have come to do Thy will, O God" (Heb 10:5, 7). It is also important to note that many also take obedience in Hebrews 5:8 to refer to the "godly fear" in verse 7 (NKJV). If so, godliness is obedience finding expression in suffering.

"From the things which He suffered" or "through what he suffered"

(RSV). In spite of the familiar wordplay learn-suffer (Gr. *emathen-epathen*), the suffering here means more than simply the customary hardship connected with learning. Rather it covers all aspects of suffering mentioned above—physical, religious, social, psychological, and mental. But, admittedly, the notion that Jesus learned and achieved perfection through suffering is a difficult concept for many modern readers. We need to keep in mind that the purpose of this verse is not to glorify suffering but to argue that suffering characterizes human nature in a world of sin. What made the earthly Jesus truly human was His capacity to suffer. This notion of a suffering Jesus sharply contrasts with the heresy of Docetism.[3] According-ing to Docetism, Jesus only appeared to suffer. Hebrews rejects this kind of superficial understanding of Jesus. Jesus was human primarily because of His undiminished capacity to suffer.

> Jesus learned obedience the human way; and yet what he experienced goes far beyond what any human being has or ever will experience.

A theological interpretation – The central thrust of Hebrews 5:8 is—in the words of F. F. Bruce—Jesus learned "just what obedience involved in practice in the conditions of human life on earth."[4] In other words, Jesus learned obedience the human way; and yet what he experienced goes far beyond what any human being has or ever will experience. Hebrews 5:8 is an invitation to see suffering as an opportunity to grow in the Christian life. Our verse is an invitation to accept suffering as the pathway—a Via Dolorosa—to a perfect and compassionate ministry. This is especially true when such a ministry calls for suffering, as it did in the experience of Jesus. Nothing binds humans like a common lot of suffering—be it a concentration camp or a catastrophic tsunami. Our ministry to others can be perfect and compassionate to the degree we allow ourselves to be touched by their sufferings.

P. Richard Choi

References

[1]A chiastic structure, from the Greek letter X (chi), refers to the inverted sequence or crossover of parallel words or ideas in a sentence, or larger literary

unit, e.g., Mark 2:27.

B man   man B'

A Sabbath   Sabbath A'

[2]F. F. Bruce, *The Epistle to the Hebrews*, rev. ed., New International Commentary on the New Testament (Grand Rapids, MI: Eerdmans, 1990), 130.

[3]Docetism was an early heresy in the Christian church that claimed that Jesus was not really human, but only appeared to be a man.

[4]Bruce, 131.

Important New Testament Manuscripts

Among the more than 5000 Greek manuscripts in existence today, the following are the most important witnesses to the New Testament text:

1. **Codex Vaticanus** – written about the middle of the fourth century, and located in the Vatican library in Rome since the 15th century or longer. It is considered to be the most important extant manuscript of the New Testament. It originally contained both Testaments and part of the Apocrypha; the manuscript now lacks most of Genesis and part of the Psalms in the Old Testament, and part of Hebrews and all of Titus, Timothy, Philemon and Revelation in the New Testament.

2. **Codex Sinaiticus** – from the fourth century. It was discovered in 1844 by Constantin von Tischendorf in the Monastery of St. Catherine at the foot of Mt. Sinai. Brought from Mt. Sinai to Russia in 1859, it was purchased in 1933 by the British government from the Soviet government for 100,000 pounds. Originally, it contained the whole of both Testaments. Approximately half of the Greek Old Testament (or Septuagint) survived, along with the complete New Testament and some apocryphal books.

3. **Codex Alexandrinus** – a fifth century manuscript. It was presented in 1627 to King Charles I of England by the Patriarch of Constantinople, who had obtained it in Alexandria. Originally containing both Testaments, it lacks today parts of the Gospels of Matthew and John and Second Corinthians. It is displayed in the British Museum alongside Codex Sinaiticus.

IS FORGIVENESS STILL AVAILABLE FOR THOSE WHO FALL AWAY?

For in the case of those who have once been enlightened and have tasted of the heavenly gift and have been made partakers of the Holy Spirit, and have tasted the good word of God and the powers of the age to come, and then have fallen away, it is impossible to renew them again to repentance, since they again crucify to themselves the Son of God, and put Him to open shame. Hebrews 6:4-6.

Warning passages are important to the structure and the thought of the Epistle to the Hebrews (2:1-4; 3:7–4:13; 5:11–6:12; 10:19-39; 12:14, 29). The apostle is concerned about the spiritual condition of the addressees and employs these warnings, some of them dire ones, to persuade them to re-engage their Christian faith and live out a more decisive Christian commitment. A section of one of these warning passages, Hebrew 6:4-6, has proved especially challenging. The passage describes a group of individuals who have "fallen away" from the Christian faith, and the resulting judgment upon them, in such a strident way that many interpreters find it difficult to take the passage in a straightforward manner.

As a result, a number of questions swirl around the passage: (1) Were the individuals described here once true believers, or did they only masquerade as such? (2) What is the nature of their "falling away"? That is, is their apostasy total or limited in some way? (3) Can the ones who have fallen away never be restored to repentance in an absolute sense or, assuming they turn from their apostasy, could they once again regain Christian belief? (4) What does the passage suggest about sin in the lives of Christians?

The purpose of the warning – The purpose of these dire words of warning should be carefully noted. In the immediate context, the author expresses concern about the spiritual laxity and lack of maturity of the addressees. They should, by this point in their Christian experience, be teachers. Instead, they need to be taught the basics of Christian teaching that include "repentance from acts that lead to death, and . . . faith in

God" (5:11–6:2). In a bid to revive their slackening faith, the apostle puts forward the dire words of warning contained in Hebrew 6:4-6. Having offered these strong words, the author returns to a message of reassurance, carefully stating that "we are confident of better things in your case—things that accompany salvation" (v. 9, NIV). Again, he exhorts them toward "diligence" and making their "hope sure" and away from being "lazy" (vv. 11, 12). So these ominous words are framed by the desire of the apostle for the spiritual health and well being of the addressees. To use these words, then, to discourage or dishearten would be to violate their original context and intention.

Christians who apostatized – In Hebrews 6:4-6, the author describes a specific group of individuals, offering a negative example of apostasy from the Christian faith. It is as if the apostle says, "Do not let this happen to you!" First, the apostle announces that "it is impossible to restore again to repentance" this group of people (v. 4a, NRSV). Then the author describes their former, Christian experience (vv. 4, 5), followed by a description of their condition in apostasy (v. 6).

These people, now apostatized from the Christian faith, once enjoyed the blessings of Christian commitment. The apostle uses four phrases to describe this stage in their experience. These individuals had once: (1) been enlightened; (2) tasted the heavenly gift; (3) shared in the Holy Spirit; and (4) tasted the goodness of the Word of God and the powers of the age to come. Read straightforwardly these phrases add up to the conclusion that these individuals were once full believers, enjoying the most precious and sacred blessings of Christian faith.

> The people referred to in this passage have so decisively turned from their once Christian faith and now are in such opposition to their former commitments that they are forever lost to Christ and to His church.

The current condition of these people, once believers, is then taken up. They have now "fallen away" from the Christian faith. And, in somewhat cryptic fashion, the author says that "they again crucify to themselves the Son of God, and put Him to open shame" (v. 6). Apparently they have not turned quietly away from the Christian faith to take up their former way of life. They most likely have used their Christian experience and their apostasy from it as a platform to cast contempt upon Christian believers, likely belittling their gullibility and lack of sophistication in following the crucified Messiah. In this description, which may owe something to the tradition of Judas as the betrayer of Jesus, the apostle describes total apostasy on the part of this group. They have so decisively turned from their once Christian faith and now are in such opposition to their former commitments that the apostle acknowledges what seems obviously to be true—these individuals are forever lost to Christ and to His church.

The passage likely reflects the narratives of the wilderness wanderings of the Israelites, especially in the description of the blessings once enjoyed. Just as the Israelites enjoyed the "pillar of fire," these once were "enlightened." As the Israelites enjoyed manna from heaven, so these "tasted the heavenly gift" (Heb 6:4). Just as Holy Spirit inspired the Israelites, so these shared in the Spirit. And the apostle seems to extend that background in the illustration he offers in verses 7, 8, using the blessings and curses of Deuteronomy 11 as the basis for it. The positive future he wishes for the addressees is sketched out in verse 7: "Ground that drinks up the rain falling on it repeatedly, and that produces a crop useful to those for whom it is cultivated, receives a blessing from God" (NRSV). The negative, future judgment on the apostates described earlier in verses 4-6 is, in turn, portrayed in verse 8: "But if it produces thorns and thistles, it is worthless and on the verge of being cursed; its end is to be burned over."

> This "passage should be treated as dealing with the unpardonable sin, for only those guilty of this sin cannot be renewed to repentance. This sin ordinarily manifests itself in continued resistance to the call of God and the wooing of the Spirit. It consists in a hardening of the heart, till there is no longer any response to the voice of God. Hence, a person who has sinned against the Spirit has no remorse, no feeling of sorrow for sin, no desire to turn from it, and no conscience that accuses him. If one has a sincere desire to do right, he may confidently believe that there is still hope for him" (F. D. Nichol, ed., *Seventh-day Adventist Bible Commentary*, 7:435).

The nature of the apostasy – In view of our discussion we return to the questions offered at the beginning: (1) *Were the individuals described here once true believers or did they only masquerade as such?* In view of their participation in the highest blessings of Christian faith, it is clear that these individuals were once true believers. (2) *What is the nature of their "falling away"? That is, is their apostasy total or limited in some way?* Their apostasy is total, so total they are "crucifying the Son of God all over again and subjecting him to public disgrace" (v. 6). (3) *Can those ones who have fallen away never be restored to repentance in an absolute sense or, assuming they turn from their apostasy, could they once again regain their Christian belief?* Given the total apostasy of this group of individuals and their activism against Christian faith, the apostle cannot imagine their restoration to Christian faith and fellowship. He acknowledges what seems obviously to be true—they cannot be restored to repentance.[1]

Sin in the lives of Christians – The final question, posed at the beginning of this discussion deserves special attention: *What does the passage suggest about sin in the lives of Christians?* The passage has often been taken to suggest that any sin, committed by Christians after their baptism, leads to loss of salvation and even eternal damnation. This interpretation simply does not follow from this passage. The apostle is not offering here a comment on post-baptismal sin. To learn about God's gracious approach to Christians who sin we should turn to other passages in which that topic is more clearly treated, e.g., 1 John 1:9. In Hebrews 6 the apostle is commenting on the apostasy of a well-defined group of individuals whose falling away from, and opposition to, the Christian faith has been total and public. He is not discussing the failings of Christians. Christians, struggling in their faith commitment, have a High Priest who sympathizes with their weaknesses, offers mercy and grace, and deals gently with them (Heb 4:15–5:3).

Having said that, we must not mute the strength of the apostle's warning nor fail to take it to heart. We are called to full and vigorous faith in the risen Christ. Tepid commitment risks becoming outright apostasy and foreshadows eternal ruin. In the dire warning of Hebrew 6:4-6 we may hear the appealing voice of God, calling us to firm faith in His Son, offering us afresh the "things that accompany salvation" (Heb 6:9).

John K. McVay

References

[1]Most likely the following passages in Hebrews 10:26-31; 12:15-17, 25-29 can be understood in the same way.

WHAT IS THE COVENANT IN HEBREWS?

When He said, "A new *covenant*," He has made the first obsolete. But whatever is becoming obsolete and growing old is ready to disappear. Hebrews 8:13.

"New Covenant" Christians have begun a systematic attack on the Sabbath. The new-covenant theology teaches that the new covenant has released Christians from the Ten Commandment law and that the demise of the old covenant cancels the obligation to keep the Sabbath because it is considered to be ceremonial.

The covenant in the New Testament – The term "covenant" is found 33 times in the New Testament; half of its occurrences (17) are found in the book of Hebrews. In the Gospels, three out of four times the covenant is connected to the blood of Jesus in the context of the Lord's Supper (Matt 26:28; Mark 14:24; Luke 22:20). A number of times Old Testament covenants are mentioned, sometimes without direct reference to the new covenant (Luke 1:72; Acts 3:25; 7:8; Rom 9:4; Eph 2:12). In 2 Corinthians 3 new and old covenants occur in close proximity (vv. 6 and 14). Galatians mentions a human covenant (Gal 3:15), the covenant with Abraham (Gal 3:17), and two contrasting covenants (Gal 4:24). The issue in Galatians is the role of the law in salvation, and the book discusses covenants from an experiential perspective. The outlook of Hebrews is different, taking a historical perspective and focusing on the covenant in relation to the sanctuary, its services, and the promises connected to those services.

The covenant in Hebrews – In Hebrews the word "covenant" is found most frequently in chapters 8-10, which contain the climax of the Letter to the Hebrews. The book quotes the new covenant promise of Jeremiah 31:31-34, in Hebrews 8:8-12, and in an abbreviated form in 10:16-17.

While Hebrews 8 stresses the importance of the new covenant, which empowers Jesus to be our high priest, Hebrews 9 and 10:1-18 contrast the old tabernacle and its service with the heavenly sanctuary and Jesus' sacrifice (e.g., 9:12-14, 18). The better covenant requires a better sacrifice, a better priesthood, and a better sanctuary. The author claims that the new priesthood has come in the person of Jesus and the better sanctuary is the heavenly sanctuary.

In Hebrews 9:4 we hear about the Ark of the Covenant and the tables of the covenant, namely the Ten Commandments. Jesus is called Mediator of a new or better covenant (8:6; 9:15; 12:24). In Hebrews 9:20 we find a quotation from Exodus 24:8, connecting blood (cf. 13:30)–and thus sacrifice–to the covenant, a connection not found in Jeremiah 31.

The old covenant and the new covenant – In Hebrews, the Mosaic covenant is called the first covenant. Although Hebrews draws a clear contrast between this old covenant and the new, better, and eternal covenant (Heb 8:6, 13; 9:15; 13:20), nowhere does the apostle say that the old covenant was bad or detrimental. It was inadequate and, therefore, it needed replacing. However, there are important similarities between the divine covenants:

> "The same theological DNA identity markers that characterize the new covenant—sanctification, reconciliation, mission, and justification—were divinely imprinted in the old covenant as well. . . . what God intended to be different about the new covenant . . . was the faithfulness of the recipients of the covenant" (S. MacCarty, *In Granite or Ingrained?* (Berrien Spring, MI: Andrews University Press, 2007), 53, 59).

1. The partners in both covenants are the same: God and His respective people (Exod 19:5; Heb 8:8-10).

2. In each case, God takes the initiative by establishing the covenant (Exod 34:27; Heb 8:8).

3. All covenants rest on the saving activity of God (Deut 6:20-23; 29; Heb 10:12-17). He saves His people before He enters into a covenant with them. Therefore, one cannot rightfully claim that the Old Testament covenants are based on justification by works and salvation by means of the law, while the new covenant rests on salvation by grace.

4. Although salvation by means of the law was never an option under any of the covenants, these covenants nevertheless maintain that the saved keep God's law as a response to the gift of salvation (Exod 20:2-17; Heb 10:16).

5. In both covenants the blood of the sacrifice is necessary to bring about forgiveness (Lev 17:11; Heb 9:12, 22).

6. All covenants contain promises of blessings (Deut 8:18; 11:8-25; Heb 8:6, 10-12).

7. The presence of God amidst His people or access to God by His people are the goal of the covenants (Deut 29:10-12; Heb 10:16-22).

The new covenant is different from the old covenant and better than the former, because it has (1) a new priesthood; (2) a better and once-for-all sacrifice; (3) a better sanctuary; and (4) a new corporate approach to God in worship. Furthermore, (1) the new covenant is not established with a nation but is universal; (2) with the new covenant there is total forgiveness and assurance; (3) the law is internalized in the covenant people; (4) the new covenant is permanent; (5) it has been ratified with the blood of Jesus; and (6) the new covenant offers real hope and salvation.

The former covenants (the Abrahamic, Sinaitic, and Davidic covenants) contained major elements of the new covenant and were pointing to this new covenant. From that perspective the new covenant was a logical extension of the earlier ones. What is unique about the new is the coming of Christ, which is the central theme of the book of Hebrews.

> "The great law of love revealed in Eden, proclaimed upon Sinai, and in the new covenant written in the heart, is that which binds the human worker to the will of God. If we were left to follow our own inclinations, to go just where our will would lead us, we should fall into Satan's ranks and become possessors of his attributes. Therefore God confines us to His will, which is high, and noble, and elevating" (DA 330).

The new covenant and related concepts – Several concepts are related to the covenant. For example, covenant, sacrifices, priesthood, and the sanctuary belong together. A new covenant also requires a renewal or replacement of these elements. Hebrews talks not only about a better covenant (Heb 7:22) but also about a better hope (Heb 7:19), better promises (Heb 8:6), a better possession (Heb 10:34), a better homeland (Heb 11:16), a better resurrection (Heb 11:35), and something better (Heb 11:40) in addition to the better sacrifices (Heb 9:23), the superior cleansing (Heb 9:13-14), and the permanent royal high priest, exalted above the heavens (Heb 6:20; 7:24, 26; 8:1).

The new covenant has an eschatological dimension. Believers enjoy its blessings here and now. Full realization of most covenant blessings is still future. Benefits of the new covenant include: (1) access to God and being God's people (Heb 8:10; 10:19); (2) knowledge of God (Heb 8:11); (3) being sanctified (Heb 10:10, 14); (4) eternal salvation especially in the context of Christ's second coming (Heb 9:12, 15, 28); (5) a clear conscience (Heb 9:9, 14; 10:2); (6) the internalizing of the law in our hearts and minds (Heb 8:10; 10:16); and (7) forgiveness of sins (Heb 8:12; 9:26, 28; 10:17, 18).

What about the law in the setting of the new covenant? On the one hand, the apostle stresses the necessity of a change of the law (Heb 7:12, 18), which was only a shadow of the things to come (Heb 10:1). This specific system of law was fulfilled in Jesus and done away with at His death. It included the priestly law and the sacrificial system with ritual ablutions and the shedding of the blood of animals. The many sacrifices offered year after year were not able to save the sinners, pointing forward to the new covenant's once-for-all sacrifice and priest, Jesus Christ. On the other hand, in both the old and the new covenant the moral law is included. Under the new covenant it is now written on the hearts. It is internalized, not abolished (Heb 8:10).

> "The law written upon the mind and heart can be none other than the Decalogue. Many believe that Christ instituted a new law or changed the old one, which they designated as the law of love or the law of the Spirit. But the New Testament nowhere reveals such a law. The law of the Spirit is a new way of life, not a new law from God" (E. Heppenstall, "The Covenants and the Law" in *Our Firm Foundation*, 1:480).

Continued validity of the moral law – In the book of Hebrews we find evidence for continued validity of the moral law. First, the reality of sin requires a law that can determine what sin is (Heb 8:12; 12:1). Second, to have a good conscience is dependent on the existence of some kind of standard. Such a standard is not only an inner feeling but an external law. Individuals have a good conscience when they are obeying an existing law (Heb 9:9, 14; 10:2; 13:18). Third, disobedience (Heb 3:18; 4:6, 11) and obedience (Heb 5:9), as well as doing God's will (Heb 10:7; 13:21), presuppose the existence of a law that should be kept. Fourth, since lawlessness is forgiven (Heb 10:17), God wants us to keep His law. The promise that God will write His law into our hearts reminds us of

God's writing the Ten Commandments with His finger on stone tablets (Exod 34:28; 31:18).

Most of the Ten Commandments, as well as their summary in Matthew 22:37-39, are referred to directly or indirectly in the book of Hebrews:

1. Falling away from God into godlessness (Heb 3:12; 6:6; 12:16) may indirectly point to a violation of the first and second commandments (Exod 20:2-3 and 4-6).

2. Hebrews 4 reminds us of the Sabbath commandment (Exod 20:8-11; Deut 5:12-15).

3. The respect that we give to our fathers may hint at the fifth commandment (Heb 12:9; Exod 20:12).

4. The issue of adultery (Heb 13:4) reminds us of the seventh commandment (Exod 20:14).

5. To be content with what one has and not to covet money (Heb 13:5) may point to the tenth commandment (Exod 20:17).

6. Believers have shown love toward God's name (Heb 6:10), which points to the command to love God (Deut 6:5; Matt 22:37).

7. Believers need also to love the Christian brothers (Heb 13:1), which alludes to the command to love one another (John 13:34-35) and, by extension, one's neighbor (Lev 19:18; Matt 22:39).

Conclusion – The new covenant is a qualitatively better covenant; yet, it is in continuity with the previous covenants. It does not present a new way to salvation, different from the Old Testament approach of salvation by grace, but it highlights the fact that Jesus has accomplished it. Neither does the new covenant destroy or make obsolete the moral law of the Ten Commandments; but it internalizes it in the believers. The most important aspect of the new covenant is the person who has ratified it and who ministers in its context. Jesus is the surety, the guarantee of the new covenant (Heb 7:22).

Ekkehardt Mueller

DOES HEBREW 9:8 REFER TO THE MOST HOLY PLACE IN THE HEAVENLY SANCTUARY?

The Holy Spirit was showing by this that the way into the Most Holy Place had not yet been disclosed as long as the first tabernacle was still standing. Hebrews 9:8 (NIV).

At issue in the NIV translation is the Adventist sanctuary teaching. Did Jesus, after His death and resurrection, ascend to the Most Holy Place of the heavenly sanctuary and begin His Day-of-Atonement ministry in AD 31, as some translations of Hebrew 9:8 seem to suggest, or did He not?

The meaning of the Greek *ta hagia* – The most popular versions of Hebrews 9:8 translate the Greek words *ta hagia* as the "Most Holy Place," supporting the idea that Jesus, after His ascension, went straight into the presence of the Father in the Most Holy Place of the heavenly sanctuary. Connected to this belief is the assumption that all His saving work finished at the Cross. The expression "it is finished" of the Cross marked the completion of the atonement, thereby rendering obsolete any reference to a heavenly high-priestly ministry after the cross. Bible versions differ in their translation of *ta hagia*:

KJV: The Holy Ghost this signifying, that the way into the holiest of all was not yet made manifest, while as the first tabernacle was yet standing:

NLT: By these regulations the Holy Spirit revealed that the entrance to the Most Holy Place was not freely open as long as the Tabernacle and the system it represented were still in use.

HCSB: The Holy Spirit was making it clear that the way into the holy of holies had not yet been disclosed while the first tabernacle was still standing.

Several other translations read quite differently:

NASB: The Holy Spirit *is* signifying this, that the way into the holy place has not yet been disclosed, while the outer tabernacle is still standing.

NET: The Holy Spirit is making clear that the way into the holy place had not yet appeared as long as the old tabernacle was standing.

NJB: By this, the Holy Spirit means us to see that as long as the old tent stands, the way into the holy place is not opened up.

Some translations simply have "sanctuary":

NAB: In this way the holy Spirit shows that the way into the sanctuary had not yet been revealed while the outer tabernacle still had its place.

NRSV: By this the Holy Spirit indicates that the way into the sanctuary has not yet been disclosed as long as the first tent is still standing.

REB: By this the Holy Spirit indicates that as long as the outer tent still stands, the way into the sanctuary has not been opened up.

Few versions attempt to be consistent all the way through in translating *ta hagia*. Exceptions to this are the NIV that translates all occurrences of *ta hagia* as "the Most Holy Place," and the REB that translates "sanctuary" in 9:8, 12, 24, and 25.

It has been clearly established that the expression *ta hagia* refers mainly to the

> # The expression *ta hagia* refers mainly to the sanctuary, in general.

sanctuary in general. The Greek translation of the Old Testament (LXX) uses this expression 170 times of which 142 refer to the sanctuary, in general.[1] In 98 places in which *ta hagia* in the LXX is a translation from the Hebrew, 36 times it is a translation of the Hebrew word *miqdash* (sanctuary), which designates a sanctuary, in general.[2]

The purpose of Hebrew 9 – Beyond the different meanings of *ta hagia*, the reader must bear in mind the purpose of this section of the book of

Hebrews. The purpose of chapter 7 is to establish the superiority of Christ's priestly functions over the Aaronic priesthood. The comparison between Christ and the Aaronic priesthood reaches a climax with the affirmation that Jesus, is the guarantor of a better covenant (7:22) and that He is able to save to the uttermost those who approach God through Him (7:25). In chapter 8, after providing a summary of the main point, the preeminence of Christ the High priest, who is sitting at the right of the throne of the majesty on high, the author goes on to elaborate on the content of the New Covenant. Chapter 9 picks up all these themes and weaves them together to illustrate the reality and superiority of the New Covenant to the Old. The point of Hebrews 9 is not to provide a detailed description of either the earthly sanctuary or the heavenly sanctuary. Even when he mentions the rooms and furnishings of the earthly sanctuary, the author specifies that "these we need not discuss in detail" (9:5), showing that the point he is trying to make is something else.

> "It appears that *ta hagia* here [in v. 8] is the heavenly counterpart to *prote skene* ('first tent') or the earthly sanctuary. In this case the author is saying that access to the heavenly sanctuary was historically not available as long as the earthly sanctuary was still standing. To say it differently, before the atoning death of Christ believers had only limited access to God because of the structure and ceremonial of the earthly sanctuary. At the death of Jesus the earthly sanctuary had fulfilled its purpose. Access was now made possible into the heavenly sanctuary." (H. Kiesler, "An Exegesis of Selected Passages" in F. Holbrook, ed., *Issues in the Book of Hebrews*, Daniel and Revelation Committee Series, ed. F. B. Holbrook [Silver Spring, MD: Biblical Research Institute, 1989], 64).

The inauguration of Christ's ministry – While the New Testament clearly teaches that at His ascension Jesus entered into the presence of God (Acts 7:55; Rom 8:34; Eph 1:20; Heb 9:24), this fact does not mean that He began His Day-of-Atonement ministry at that time. The emphasis in Hebrews 9 is on the inauguration of His ministry in the heavenly sanctuary. The death of Christ on the cross opened the way not only for the true sanctuary to be operational, in reference to the ministry of which the cross is a part, but also to its inauguration with the blood of Jesus (9:18). This idea is repeated in 10:19, 20 as a climax of the development: "Since therefore, brethren, we have confidence to enter the holy place by the blood of Jesus, by a new and living way which He inaugurated for us through the veil, that is, His flesh."

Hebrews 9:8 provides a key to understanding what is meant by the use of *ta hagia*. In this text a comparison is made between the earthly sanctuary called "the first tent" and the heavenly sanctuary, the *ta hagia* or "holy places" (plural, ESV). That this is what the author meant is corroborated by verse 24, where it is stated, "For Christ did not enter a sanctuary [*hagia*] made with hands– the representation of the true sanctuary – but into heaven itself, and he appears now in God's presence for us" (NET Heb 9:24).

This comparison, showing the superiority of the heavenly sanctuary over the earthly, is relevant for the author's larger purpose, showing the superiority of Christ's heavenly high-priestly ministry. The focus is neither on the Most Holy nor on the Day of Atonement. In other words, at issue is not the place or the time but the *person* who ministers in the heavenly sanctuary. The explicit statement about the heavenly sanctuary is not about its subdivisions but rather the fact that it is not made with human hands (v. 24); it is a heavenly reality that also needs cleansing by the blood of a better sacrifice. The *time* of this "cleansing" is not specified except that it is to be completed before the Second Advent. The *agent* of this cleansing will come again no longer to deal with sin or atonement but to bring salvation to those who eagerly wait for him. This much he specifies.

Ganoune Diop

References

[1]A Useful statistical study is provided by Alwyn P. Salom. "Ta Hagia in the Epistle to the Hebrews," in *Issues in the Book of Hebrews*. Ed. Frank B. Holbrook. vol. 4 (Silver Spring, MD: Biblical Research Institute, 1989), 219-227. See also Richard M. Davidson, Christ's Entry 'Within the Veil' in Hebrews 6:19, 20: The Old Testament Background," *Andrews University Seminary Studies* 39 (2001):175-190.

[2]Idem, 221, 222.

DOES JAMES TEACH RIGHTEOUSNESS BY WORKS?

You see that a man is justified by works and not by faith alone. James 2:24.

The difficulty this text poses lies in the fact that it seems to contradict the Pauline assertion in Romans 3:28 that a person is justified by faith *apart from works*. Because James is saying that a person is justified by works and not by faith alone, many Protestants, beginning with Martin Luther, have either relegated James to a lesser place in the canon, while elevating Paul's theology, or have sought to make both inspired men say and mean the same thing.

Paul and James – A careful reading of each text in its context will reveal that they neither are contradicting each other nor are they speaking to the same issue. Let's start with Paul. The context of Paul is similar to that of Jesus' conflict with the legalistic party of the Pharisees. Both these Pharisees and some members of the early Christian Church sought salvation through law keeping. Paul's argument is that one is not justified by *legalistic* works (literally in Greek: "works of law"), but by faith.

James' context is entirely different. He is not involved in a polemic with Judaizers (people who tried to lead Christians back into Judaism) who are attempting to gain salvation by the observance of the law. He is not involved in a theological dispute over Jewish observances. His dispute is ethical. His concern is over deeds and acts of mercy and charity. His "works" have to do with his audience's attitude to the poor and marginal in society.

> "True religion" has a social dimension.

The social dimension of faith – The context of James becomes clear when we realize that James 2:24 comes at the end of an extended argument that began in 1:27. James begins with a statement that "true religion" has a social dimension: It involves caring for the poor and marginalized (i.e. orphans and widows). This "true religion" is the equivalent of "works" in 2:24.

As a matter of fact, all of James 2 is an illustration of "religion at work." In the first half (2:1-13), he illustrates this negatively and condemns those who show partiality to the rich and disdain for the poor. In the second half (2:14-26), James states clearly that "faith" *alone* does not save – that is, faith without a strong practical component. This is precisely why he begins in verse 14 with the illustration regarding the person who lacks clothes and food. He argues that telling such a person to go and keep warm and be fed without any action by the well-off person is not helpful.

Faith and works are complimentary – We must make it clear that James is not teaching justification by works. He is not eliminating the element of faith. His argument is that faith and works (which together form true religion) are complimentary and concurrent in the life of the believer. What James is arguing against is a faith that ignores the component of caring for one in need. Thus, a better translation for the phrase in James 2:14 "can faith save him" is "can *that* faith save him?" "Faith" that is disconnected from ethical works is invalid. In James' theological system "works" is not a substitute for faith; it is simply the other side of the salvific coin. You can't have one without the other. Thus James includes the word *alone* in the sentence in 2:24 – "a person is justified [i.e. in a relationship with God] by works and not by faith *alone*."

> "James does not deny that a man is declared righteous by faith. . . However, he does deny that a mere profession of faith alone can justify a man. Good works accompany faith and prove the validity of the faith by which a man is justified. If there are no 'works,' it is evident that genuine faith does not exist" (F. D. Nichol, ed. *Seventh-day Adventist Bible Commentary*, 7:523.

Pedrito Maynard-Reid

The most valuable rules for social and family [interaction] are to be found in the Bible.

AH 423

WHO ARE THE "SPIRITS IN PRISON"
TO WHOM CHRIST PREACHED?

For Christ also died for sins once for all, *the* just for *the* unjust, in order that He might bring us to God, having been put to death in the flesh, but made alive in the spirit; in which also He went and made proclamation to the spirits now in prison, who once were disobedient, when the patience of God kept waiting in the days of Noah, during the construction of the ark, in which a few, that is, eight persons, were brought safely through the water. 1 Peter 3:18-20.

Many Christians believe that during the time between His crucifixion and His resurrection Christ went and preached to the spirits in prison. This proves, for them, that there is an immaterial spirit, the real person, which departs from the body at death. This belief would also suggest that the ungodly in Noah's day received a second chance whereas the rest of the dead did not, unless Jesus preached to the departed of all ages.[1]

The Christian and suffering – Throughout this letter, there are indications that the faith of Peter's readers was being tested (1:6, 7) and that they were being unfairly maligned, abused, and reviled for what they believed (2:12; 3:9, 16; 4:14). The willingness of Jesus to silently endure suffering for their sakes is presented as the ideal for them to emulate in the face of persecution (2:20-23; 3:17, 18). Christ suffered, Peter tells them, in order to "bring you to God" (3:18). Next follows a reference to the death and resurrection of Christ. He was "put to death in the flesh, but made alive in the spirit," i.e., "by the Holy Spirit" (NKJV).

> "The work of the Spirit in antediluvian times was evidently the same as in the time of Christ – the preaching to those who are prisoners of sin, offering them a way of escape" (F. D. Nichol, *Answers to Objections*, 350).

Genesis 6 and a Jewish myth – Some who take the view that Jesus went to the spirits in prison between His resurrection and ascension believe that Jesus went there to proclaim His victory over the powers of evil. They understand the "spirits in prison" as an allusion to a Jewish myth based on Genesis 6:4. According to a pre-Christian, Jewish apocalypse, angelic beings called "Watchers" were tempted by the beauty of earthly women, had sexual relations with them, and produced giants as offspring. Though the Flood supposedly destroyed the bodies of these giants, their existence continued in the form of evil spirits. The vast majority of these spirits were said to have been imprisoned by God until the judgment day (see *1 Enoch* 6:1-7:1; 9:7, 8).

The dead do not receive a second chance – Supposing that Peter alludes to this myth presents numerous problems that we will consider shortly. First, however, it should be noticed that this passage cannot be used to support the idea that Jesus preached to the souls of *all* dead humans as some modern paraphrases of these verses seem to suggest (e.g., *The Message*). 1 Peter 3 is very specific with respect to time. Each phrase of the relevant portion of verse 19 progressively limits the period to which reference is made. Literally, it reads: "once, when the patience of God waited in the days of Noah, while the ark was being built."

Understanding the verse to mean that Christ preached to a select few among the dead in order to give them a second chance for salvation is likewise mistaken. Apart from the fact that it would be unfair, in his second epistle Peter excludes even the possibility that they could still be saved by assuring us that, like the angels who sinned and the inhabitants of Sodom and Gomorrah, God has consigned the ungodly of Noah's time to be punished on the Judgment Day (2 Pet 2:4-9).

Christ visited by means of His Spirit – It is important to note *how* Jesus visited these spirits. According to the most natural and straightforward understanding of verse 19, Jesus went to them by means of *His* Spirit. That Peter was not thinking of Jesus going in a separate, disembodied spiritual state, as some translations suggest (e.g., TEV, TNIV) is clear from the only other reference in the epistle to His Spirit. 1 Peter 1:11 describes how the Spirit of Christ guided the prophets in their foretelling of the salvation that would come through Jesus. Even Noah proclaimed the

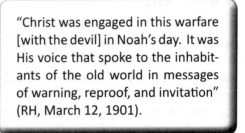

"Christ was engaged in this warfare [with the devil] in Noah's day. It was His voice that spoke to the inhabitants of the old world in messages of warning, reproof, and invitation" (RH, March 12, 1901).

message of salvation. Peter calls him a "herald" or "preacher" (*keryx*) of righteousness (2 Pet 2:5), using a word with the same root as the verb "proclaimed" or "preached" (*kerysso*) in 1 Peter 3:19. In fact, in the New Testament, these words refer almost exclusively to preaching the gospel.[2] Therefore, it seems unlikely that the verse could refer to Jesus' proclamation of His victory over demonic spirits. If these spirits have been defeated and are now imprisoned awaiting Judgment Day, why are there so many references in Acts, the Pauline epistles, and the book of Revelation to an ongoing struggle against evil powers? Surely Peter is not suggesting (as the writer of *1 Enoch* thought) that God imprisoned only some of the evil spirits!

The best understanding of this difficult text is that Jesus *preached* to the spirits in prison by the Holy Spirit who spoke through Noah. Jesus told His disciples that the Spirit would "convict the world of sin" (John 16:8). And just as God's Spirit spoke through the disciples in the first century, so He spoke through Noah in the time of the Flood. Jesus, in the words of Isaiah, said His work included preaching freedom to the prisoners (Luke 4:18; Isa 61:1; cf. Isa 42:7). Calling the people of Noah's day "spirits" sounds strange to modern ears but would not have seemed unusual to the early Christians any more than talking about people as "souls" would be to us today. The word used for spirit (*pneuma*) often has reference to human beings.[3] It is used in 1 Peter 3:19 to underscore the spiritual relation of the people to the message of salvation proclaimed through Noah. The inhabitants of the antediluvian world, though

> "The same Spirit, by which Jesus rose from the dead and spoke through Noah, the prophets, and the apostles, appeals to people today to be saved through the death and resurrection of Christ" (1 Pet 3:22, NIV).

seemingly safe and secure, were actually on "death row" because their world was destined to be destroyed by the flood. Their only hope rested in accepting the warning given through Noah and entering the ark.

Peter's days are compared to Noah's days – Peter wants his readers to recognize the similarity of their time with Noah's day (cf. Matt 24:37-39). He writes to them with an urgency and awareness that it may not be long before Christ returns to judge the world by fire (1 Pet 1:3-7; 4:17; cf. 2 Pet

3:5-7). He seeks to encourage them that, just as Noah and his family stood as a tiny minority against the current of popular opinion, so they, despite being few in number and being unjustly maligned and abused for their faith, have "entered the ark" so to speak through baptism. Peter even calls baptism the *antitypos* or "antitype" of the salvation experienced by those in the ark (1 Pet 3:21).[4] Like Noah and his family, believers can face with confidence the inevitable destruction of this old world, knowing that baptism (being "saved through water") guarantees safe passage to the new world. Peter is quick to add that baptism in itself does not save a person. It is meaningless unless it represents the response of a good conscience toward God. The same Spirit, by which Jesus rose from the dead and spoke through Noah, the prophets, and the apostles, appeals to people today to be saved through the death and resurrection of Christ, since He is now enthroned "at God's right hand with angels, authorities, and [spiritual] powers in submission to Him" (1 Pet 3:22, NIV).

Clinton Wahlen

References

[1]Seventh-day Adventists generally interpret 1 Peter 3:18-20 as outlined in this chapter. In recent years a different interpretation has been put forward that teaches that Jesus at His ascension addressed the fallen angels, the demons, and proclaimed "what is good news for His followers but judgment for the demons 'I, Jesus Christ, am the conqueror. I have gained the victory' (Col 2:15)." Of course, both interpretations deny explicitly the immortality of the soul and are compatible with the Adventist faith, (Ekkehardt Mueller, "1 Peter 3:18-22," *Reflections* 13 [January 2006]: 6).

[2]The exception being Revelation 5:2 and, possibly, Luke1:23. The noun *keryx* elsewhere refers exclusively to Paul as a "herald" of the gospel: 1 Tim 2:7; 2 Tim 1:11; Col 1:23. Another related noun, *kerygma* refers to the gospel procramation itself.

[3]E.g. Num 16:22; 27:16; Ps 76:12 (LXX 75:13); 1 Cor 14:32; Heb 12:23; 1 John 4:1; Rev 22:6.

[4]In a similar way, Paul likens the Israelites' crossing of the Red Sea during their Exodus from Egypt to baptism (1 Cor 10:2).

DOES 1 JOHN 3:9 TEACH THAT CONVERTED CHRISTIANS DO NOT SIN?

No one who is born of God practices sin, because His seed abides in him; and he cannot sin, because he is born of God. 1 John 3:9.

1 John 3:9 sounds pretty frightening to many people because it seems to give the impression that once a person becomes a Christian, he or she will not sin anymore. When they compare this verse to their own experience of making mistakes multiple times and tripping over the same sin again and again, they conclude that either they are not Christians or that John must somehow be wrong in what he says. Either all hope is lost, we just do not understand how to live the Christian life, or the word of God is unreliable, at least in this passage. However, none of these conclusions is necessary.

John's teaching about sin – Two concepts help us to understand 1 John 3:9 better. The first is a broader perspective on the teaching about sin and sinning as presented by the apostle. The most common New Testament words for sin are the Greek noun *hamartia* and the verb *hamartano*. These terms mean failure to achieve a standard, to miss the mark, to err, or to transgress.[1] The verb *hamartano* means "to sin, to do wrong." Nearly twenty-five percent of all its New Testament uses occur in 1 John. Clearly, the subject of sin is very important in this epistle.

What does the apostle teach about sin? According to 1 John 3:4, it is the same as lawlessness ("transgression of the law," KJV). It is expressed as rebellion against God and His commands, to the point that a person who claims that they have not sinned, actually makes God out to be a liar (1:10). Sin is connected with the devil and stands in opposition against God. God and Christ have no connection with sin (3:5, 8, 9), and the same can be said for the Christian in a certain sense. The Christian has experienced sin, but he or she has also experienced the solution to sin. That solution, the apostle states over and over, is the atoning sacrifice of Christ in our place (1:9; 2:1, 2; 3:5; 4:10; 5:16). This sacrifice removes the sinner from the realm of sin and brings him or her into the state of forgiveness and fellowship with God (1:7, 9; 2:2; 4:10). This new state of fellowship with God is separate from the life of the world (another favorite word of the apostle in 1 John; see 2:15-17; 3:1, 13; 4:4-6; 5:4, 5, 19).

The Christian's new relationship toward sin – Twice John tells us that the Christian, the person born of God, does not sin or cannot sin (1 John 3:6, 9). In both cases, he uses the present tense form of the verb *hamartano*. This usage is very significant, because elsewhere in the epistle, when he speaks of the Christian sinning, he uses the aorist[2] tense of the verb (2:1). In Greek, verb tenses do not only contain the idea of the time of an action but also the kind of action. The present tense is often used to express an on-going type of linear action (as a video picture), whereas the aorist or simple past tense often expresses a single event (as a snapshot). The Christian cannot have an ongoing lifestyle of sin, even though he or she may occasionally sin.

"The Lord will recognize every effort you make to reach His ideal for you. When you make a failure, when you are betrayed into sin, do not feel that you cannot pray, that you are not worthy to come before the Lord. 'My little children, these things write I unto you, that ye sin not. And if any man sin, we have an advocate with the Father, Jesus Christ the righteous.' With outstretched arms He waits to welcome the prodigal. Go to Him, and tell Him about your mistakes and failures. Ask Him to strengthen you for fresh endeavor. He will never disappoint you, never abuse your confidence" (MYP 97).

What John tells us through this careful use of Greek tenses and through his extensive theology of sin is that when individuals become Christians they receive a new attitude toward sin. They are forgiven their past when they receive the new birth (1 John 1:7, 9; 2:1, 2; 4:10), and now, born of God, they are to live for Him and, like Him, are to be distant from sin (2:3-6, 15-17, 29; 3:1-3, 7-10, 21, 22; 4:4-14, 17-21; 5:11, 12). That the Christian continues to struggle against sin is plainly taught in such passages as 1:7-10 and 2:1, 2. In fact, those who claim to have no sin remaining in their life are pictured by the apostle as liars and self-deceived (1:6-10). John clearly states that the goal of the Christian must be to overcome sin (2:1, 2). The Christian cannot live a lifestyle of sin (a present tense ongoing experience). That lifestyle is the way of the worldly person. The Christian may still stumble and fall with an individual act of sin (the snapshot experience), but her or she turns to Jesus for forgiveness and cleansing.

The true solution to sin is found in Christ – 1 John teaches us the truth about the problem of sin. The Apostle warns us to beware of the danger of claiming that we no longer have any sin in our life (1:7-10). That claim is self-deception that feels no need, and, where no sense of need exists, the proffered propitiation remains unused (2:2). What a pity to have in hand the inestimable treasure and not recognize or utilize its power!

> The Christian cannot have an ongoing lifestyle of sin, even though he or she may occasionally sin.

The only true solution to sin is found in Christ. We must confess our sins to God who graciously forgives us on the basis of the sacrifice of Christ. This new birth experience sets us on the path that Jesus walked (1 John 2:5, 6) and, though we may stumble, He gets us up again, purifies us, and points us toward the heavenly goal (1:9; 2:2; 3:2, 3). Now we are children of God and, when He appears, we will be like Him, for we will see Him as He is (3:1, 2). What a wonderful assurance of forgiveness and grace!

Tom Shepherd

References

[1] See P. Fiedler, "ἁμαρτία" in *Exegetical Dictionary of the New Testament,* eds., H. Balz and G. Schneider, 3 vols. (Grand Rapids, MI: Eerdmans, 1990), 1:65-69.

[2] The Greek aorist tense is a past tense, but requires the context to determine more precisely the extent of the action. It is usually translated by the English simple past tense.

IS THE TRINITY FOUND IN 1 JOHN 5:7, 8?

For there are three that bear witness, the Spirit and the water and the blood; and the three are in agreement. 1 John 5:8.

In 1 John 5:7, 8 of the King James versions (KJV and NKJV), we find very explicit words supporting the Trinity. In almost all modern English versions, the words supporting the Trinity are missing.

The two readings – In the following KJV reading, the underlined words, called the Johannine comma,[1] are not found in most modern Bible translations:

For there are three that bear record <u>in heaven, the Father, the Word, and the Holy Ghost; and these three are one. And there are three that bear witness in earth</u>, the Spirit, the water, and the blood: and these three agree in one. (1 John 5:7, 8)

Modern translations read, with slight variations, "There are three witnesses, the Spirit, the water, and the blood; and these three agree." (RSV). The words omitted in the modern translations take away a powerful testimony to the doctrine of the Trinity, and it is natural to sense an important loss in regard to a major doctrine of Christianity. Why are these words missing in all modern Bible translations?

The manuscript evidence – Of the more than fifty-six hundred manuscripts containing all or portions of the New Testament, approximately six hundred contain the seven General Epistles,[2] one of which is 1 John. The additional words ("the Johannine Comma") are found in eight of these six hundred manuscripts. The pertinent information about these eight manuscripts is that: (1) None of the manuscripts is among the oldest manuscripts. Four of the eight have the additional words in the margin,[3] and only one of them predates the sixteenth century, coming from the tenth century. Three of the other four are dated in the sixteenth century, and the fourth one is dated in the eighteenth century. (2) None of the Church Fathers ever quoted the Comma, and when we keep in mind the numerous Trinitarian controversies in the third and fourth centuries, it surely would have been used had they known about it. (3) The Comma is not found in any of the ancient versions except in the Latin version. Its earliest appearance in Latin is attributed to a Spaniard in the fourth century. But, of greater significance, the most influential Catholic scholar of the time who translated the Greek text into Latin, Jerome (345-420 A.D.), did not have the Comma in his Latin Vulgate.[4] It showed up in the Latin Vulgate after Jerome's time.

> "It is now believed that the later editions of the Vulgate acquired the passage by the mistake of a scribe who included an exegetical marginal comment in the Bible text that he was copying. The disputed words have been widely used in support of the doctrine of the Trinity, but, in view of such overwhelming evidence against their authenticity, their support is valueless and should not be used" (F. D. Nichol, ed., *The Seventh-day Adventist Bible Commentary*, 7:675).

Furthermore, it would be almost impossible to account for an accidental or deliberate deletion of the Comma in some six hundred manuscripts, given its somber message. Whereas, to find it in a handful of late manuscripts that no doubt followed the later editions of the Latin Vulgate, and therefore added it, is much more likely.

From the Latin Vulgate to the King James Version – The Greek text upon which the KJV is based comes from a revision of the Greek New Testament compiled by the very honest and devout Roman Catholic scholar Erasmus (1466-1536). Erasmus wanted the Scriptures to be sound in all respects, even if it meant going against the Catholic traditions, including the Johannine Comma found in the Latin Bibles.

Erasmus decided to put a New Testament text together that was based on the Greek rather than on the Latin text. Initially, he found four twelfth century Greek manuscripts and later another two. None of the six manuscripts contains the Johannine Comma. Hence, his Greek text was published in 1516, to the chagrin of many, without the Comma.

He was asked repeatedly, "Why have you left out these important statements?" His response was that they were not in the original Greek text. "Show me one Greek manuscript that contains the Comma," he said, "and I will include it in my Greek text." A few years later, a manuscript containing the Comma was produced. "As it now appears, the Greek manuscript had probably been written in Oxford about 1520 by a Franciscan friar named

Froy (or Roy), who took the disputed words from the Latin Vulgate."[5] Erasmus, a man of honor, therefore included the additional words in his 1522 edition of the Greek New Testament. But it was more than this new Greek manuscript that compelled Erasmus to include the Comma in his next edition. Charges were being made against Erasmus that he was an Arian—the denial that Jesus is God—a serious charge. And because Erasmus put the church ahead of himself, he acquiesced by inserting the extra Trinitarian words. He nevertheless continued to hold that the words did not belong in the original.[6]

All subsequent editions of Erasmus' Greek New Testament contained the Johannine Comma. And it was this text, with the addition, that was used by the committee who translated the King James Version in 1611.

Conclusion – The history of the text in the original language shows clearly that the reading in the KJV is inaccurate. Is this a serious charge against the KJV? No! To state that the KJV is inaccurate in this passage is not to state that the KJV as an English Bible should be laid aside. First of all, the differences between the Greek text that the KJV is based upon and the Greek text upon which all modern translations are based come to less than five percent, and *not one major doctrine is affected by this small percentage of disagreement.*

Second, based on years of examining both the ancient Greek manuscripts and the English translations, I conclude unequivocally that both the best and the worst manuscripts

> The best and the worst manuscripts and the best and worst translations still give us an infallible revelation of God's will, and all major doctrines can be supported in all of them.

and the best and worst translations still give us an infallible revelation of God's will, and that all major doctrines can be supported in all of them.

We need to point out too that, apart from this passage, there are other passages, statements based on Greek manuscripts which are not disputed, that support the Trinity. A clear example is Matthew 28:19, ". . . baptizing them in the name of the Father, the Son, and the Holy Spirit." But even this passage from Matthew does not state that they are *One* —this facet was understood only in the fourth century. Thus, we may affirm the doctrine of the Trinity, even if it is a developed understanding based on texts that do not state the doctrine explicitly. We cannot, however, do so based on 1 John 5:7, 8 as it reads in the King James versions.

W. Larry Richards

References

[1]"Comma" is Greek for "short clause."

[2]1, 2, 3 John; 1, 2 Peter; James and Jude.

[3]Marginal notes were generally commentary observations.

[4]In North Africa, Latin Fathers began to use the Comma, and from that time on, its usage continually increased.

[5]Bruce M. Metzger, *The Text of the New Testament* (Oxford: Oxford University Press, 1968), 101.

[6]This sequence of events is recorded in a well-documented article by Joseph M. Levine, "Erasmus and the Problem of the Johannine Comma," *Journal of the History of Thought* 58 (1987); 573-596.

Roman Emperors in New Testament Times

Augustus	31 B.C. to A.D. 14	In his reign Jesus was born
Tiberius	A.D. 14-37	In his reign Jesus was crucified
Caligula	A.D. 37-41	
Claudius	A.D. 41-54	
Nero	A.D. 54-68	In his reign Peter and Paul were executed
Galba	A.D. 68-69	
Vespasian	A.D. 69-79	In his reign Jerusalem was destroyed
Titus	A.D. 79-81	
Domitian	A.D. 81-96	He banished the apostle John to Patmos
Nerva	A.D. 96-98	He freed John who returned to Ephesus

ARE THE EVIL ANGELS KEPT IN A BURNING HELL?

And angels who did not keep their own domain, but abandoned their proper abode, He has kept in eternal bonds under darkness for the judgment of the great day. Jude 6.

The language of Jude 6 has often been understood, or rather misunderstood, to be a reference to hell. "Darkness" is assumed to describe hell's dark and gloomy nature, while "everlasting chains" defines its unending duration. Such an interpretation goes against the biblical teaching of the non-immortality of humans and angels, and the temporary nature of hell.

The Epistle of Jude, written by the brother of Jesus, addresses some of the issues also mentioned in 2 Peter—the threat of heretical teachers in the church and the believer's proper response to that threat. Therefore, reference will be made to 2 Peter, even as we discuss Jude.

Understanding the Language of Jude

To better expound the meaning of Jude 6 we will look at four terms Jude uses: (1) "the judgment of the great day"; (2) "kept" or "reserved"(NKJV); (3) the "eternal bonds" or "chains"; and (4) "darkness."

The judgment of the great day – This is obviously a reference to the final judgment spoken of repeatedly throughout Scripture.[1] In verse 7, Jude compares this judgment to the fire that consumed Sodom and Gomorrah. Furthermore, he uses the verbs "destroyed" (v. 5), and "perished" (v. 11) to describe the fate of the unfaithful of biblical times and of the false teachers he is writing against. He compares them to fruitless trees that are uprooted and are "twice dead" (v. 12). The language reminds us of the words of John the Baptist that fruitless trees will be "cut down and thrown into the fire" (Matt 3:10) and the enacted prophecy of Jesus in which the fruitless fig tree was cursed and withered (Matt 21:19). Nothing in Jude's language and imagery suggests that hell involves prolonged torment. Rather, sin brings death and destruction both in the temporal realm and in the final judgment.

The witness of 2 Peter confirms this picture. In 2 Peter 3:6, the final judgment is compared to the Flood in its encompassing destruction. In

429

verse 7, the final judgment will come with fire that will completely destroy "ungodly men;" and, in verse 10, the picture is even more definitive, "the day of the Lord will come like a thief in the night, in which the heavens will pass away with a roar, and the elements will be destroyed with intense heat, and the earth and its works will be burned up." It is evident, therefore, that both Jude and Peter, just as the rest of the Bible writers, envisaged the final judgment to involve the destruction of the wicked, not their everlasting torment.

Angels are kept for judgment – The angels are "kept or "reserved" for the final judgment. "Kept" translates the Greek verb *"tereo,"* which has no negative connotation, no suggestion of torment or punishment. It simply means that something is being reserved or kept for future reference. In Acts 25:21, Paul asks to be "kept in custody," i.e. not judged, until he appears before Caesar. In Romans 11:4, Paul quotes from the Old Testament in which God "kept"

> Both Jude and Peter, just like the rest of the Bible writers, envisaged the final judgment to involve the destruction of the wicked, not their everlasting torment.

seven thousand people faithful who had not bowed their knee to Baal. In 1 Peter 1:4, God is "reserving" an incorruptible inheritance for all believers. And in 2 Peter 3:7, the earth is being "kept" in its current form until the final judgment.

What this means in the context of Jude 6 is that the fallen angels are being kept in anticipation of the coming judgment. The real punishment is not their current state but the coming judgment. The current binding serves simply as a means to keep the angels in check until the Day of Judgment.

The eternal bonds are symbolic – The eternal bonds or chains with which the fallen angels are bound are obviously symbolic. In Lamentation 3:7, Jeremiah laments the destruction of Jerusalem. He declares that the Lord has made his "chain heavy." In Ezekiel 7:23, God commands that a "chain" be made to bind a land filled with crimes. In 2 Peter 2:4, the "chains" with which the fallen angels are bound are made of darkness. In Revelation 20:1, Satan, the leader of the fallen angels, is bound with a symbolic "chain" and cast to the earth. In Jewish thought, fallen angels were often described as bound with symbolic, not literal, chains. Indeed, throughout the Bible, fallen angels are often active but never are they seen dragging chains behind them. The language of Jude is symbolic. The fallen angels are "chained" in the sense that their freedom of movement and action has been limited by our benevolent God and in this limited state they await the judgment.

Kept under darkness – The fallen angels are kept "under darkness." Contrary to popular assertions, "darkness" is not a description of hell but of the place in which the angels are reserved until the final judgment. According to the unanimous witness of Scripture, fallen angels are now domiciled on this earth. In Matthew 4:8, 9, Satan claims to own all the kingdoms of the earth and offers them to Jesus on condition of worship. In Matthew 12:25, 26, Jesus intimates that Satan has a kingdom located among people; and according

> In Jewish thought, fallen angels were often described as bound with symbolic, not literal, chains.

to Luke 10:18 and Revelation 12:7-10, Satan and his angels were once in heaven but have been cast to earth. In Revelation 2:13, Satan's throne is in Pergamum; and from Revelation 9:1, we know that evil powers seem to dwell in a symbolic bottomless pit or abyss on earth. In Luke 11:24, unclean spirits prefer to dwell among humans but sometimes roam deserted places. Jewish tradition also depicted fallen angels as bound to the earth, in general, or to specific areas on the earth, usually deserted areas.

Places from which the light of God is absent or dimmed are referred to in Scripture as "dark."[2] In fact, the Greek word "*zophos*" (darkness) can refer to "deep gloom," as well as to physical darkness. The fallen angels, without a doubt, lead a deeply gloomy existence. Having rebelled against God (Rev 12:7), they were cast out of their glorious abode in heaven and dwell now on an earth made gloomy through the ravages of sin, anticipating the judgment that they know is coming upon them.

Conclusion – The darkness and everlasting chains of Jude 6 are by no means a description of hell. Rather, we noticed that, for Jude, hell is described in language of destruction, not torment. The "darkness" and "everlasting chains" refer to the current state of the fallen angels in anticipation of the coming judgment. They are currently bound in chains in the sense that God has limited their freedom of movement. They are bound to this earth, away from their original heavenly home. They are in gloomy darkness, because they have been separated from fellowship with God and with unfallen angels and live amongst the ravages of sin they themselves fomented in the first place. Their gloom is the worst kind of gloom they know the judgment that awaits them, their final destruction when God puts an end to sin and sinners.

Kim Papaioannou

References

[1]E.g. Matt 10:15; 11:22; 12:36; Mark 6:11; Luke 11:31; Rom 14:10; 2 Cor 5:10; Heb 10:27; 2 Pet 2:3; 2:9; Rev 20:11-15.
[2]E.g. Num 12:8; Deut 28:29; 1 Sam 2:9; 2 Sam 22:29; Job 3:4-6; 10:22; 12:24-25; 34:22; Pss 18:28; 74:20; Prov 4:19; Eccl 6:4; Isa 5:30; 60:2; Jer 2:31; Lam 3:6; Joel 2:2; Matt 4:16; 6:23; Luke 1:79; 11:34; 12:3; John 1:5; 3:19; 12:46; Acts 26:18; Rom 1:21; 13:12; 2 Cor 6:14; Col 1:13; 1 Pet 2:9; 2 Pet 2:4; Rev 9:2; 16:10.

In the Bible are found the only safe principles of action. It is a transcript of the will of God, an expression of divine wisdom. It opens to man's understanding the great problems of life, and to all who heed its precepts it will prove an unerring guide, keeping them from wasting their lives in misdirected effort.

AA 506

WHO ARE THE 144,000 AND THE GREAT MULTITUDE?

And I heard the number of those who were sealed, one hundred and forty-four thousand sealed from every tribe of the sons of Israel. Revelation 7:4.

After these things I looked, and behold, a great multitude which no one could count from every nation and *all* tribes and peoples and tongues, standing before the throne and before the Lamb, clothed in white robes, and palm branches *were* in their hands. Revelation 7:9.

The number 144,000 is one of the cryptic numbers of Revelation that has caused much speculation. What kind of group are the 144,000? When do they appear? What is their relationship to the great multitude and the remnant? Is 144,000 a literal or figurative number? In Scripture the 144,000 appear under this designation only twice, namely in Revelation 7:1-8 and 14:1-5.

Among Seventh-day Adventists two views prevail concerning the identity of the 144,000. Some believe that the 144,000 and the great multitude are one and the same group. This view is the position outlined in this chapter. Others believe that the great multitude is the redeemed of all ages not just the 144,000.[1] Both views agree, however, that the 144,000 are the saints who will be alive at the Second Coming.

The vision of the seven seals – Revelation 7:1-8 is part of the sixth-seal vision. The sixth seal contains the heavenly signs of Jesus' second coming (6:12-14) and the Day of Lord, which is the Second Advent (6:14-16). The sixth chapter ends with the question: "Who is able to stand?"on the Day of the Lord (6:17). The previous verses (6:15, 16) portray people who are not able to survive that day. On the other hand, Revelation 7 points to people who are able to stand. Thus, Revelation 7 responds to the question of 6:17 telling us that the 144,000 will be able to stand (7:1-8). Following the 144,000, the great multitude (7:9-17) is depicted as serving God in His heavenly sanctuary before His throne (7:15). The 144,000 of Revelation 7 are God's end-time people, apparently those who will be alive when Jesus returns to take His children home.

The great multitude and the 144,000 – What is the relationship between the great multitude and the 144,000? Are they two different groups of people or the same group under different names?[2] The arguments for the latter option seem to be more convincing:

1. In Revelation 5:5 John *hears* about Jesus the Lion but when, in 5:6, he takes a look, he *sees* a lamb. Jesus the Lion is Jesus the Lamb. This phenomenon is repeated in the same vision. In 7:4 John *hears* the number of those being sealed, 144,000, but in 7:9 he actually *sees* that they form a great multitude. The 144,000 and the great multitude are the same group seen from different perspectives.

2. The answer to the question, Who is able to stand? (6:17) is provided by the entire seventh chapter. Both the 144,000 and the great multitude are those who are able to stand. The 144,000 are introduced as an immediate answer to the question of 6:17. They are not further described here and their final destiny is not mentioned. However, the great multitude receives a more detailed description and is depicted as standing before God. The same term "to stand" is used in 6:17 and in 7:9.

> The 144,000 and the great multitude seem to be the same group seen from different perspectives.

3. The 144,000, as well as the great multitude, have to go through difficult times. The 144,000 are sealed before the winds blow and have to endure the succeeding difficulties. The great multitude has come out of the great tribulation.

4. The 144,000 are God's end-time church on earth. The great multitude is the end-time church in heaven. The 144,000 are the fullness of God's militant end-time church, 12x12x1000. This number reminds us of the twelve tribes of Israel and the twelve apostles of the Lamb (Rev 21:12, 14). The number one thousand may point to a military unit in ancient Israel (Num 31:4-6). Thus, the 144,000 represent the church militant of the end-time.[3] The great multitude is the end-time church after the great tribulation. The information on the great multitude complements what was lacking with the 144,000. The sealing of the 144,000 would be incomplete, if it would not lead to the final consummation of the great multitude.

5. The 144,000 are "servants [Gr. *doulos*] of our God" (Rev 7:3). The great multitude "serves" [Gr. *latreuo*] God (7:15). Both Greek words are

used for all the saved in Revelation 22:3 where the redeemed are described as "servants [doulos]" who "shall serve [*latreuo*]" God.

It seems best to understand the 144,000 and the great multitude as the same group. The great multitude does not comprise the redeemed ones of all ages—they are not the focus of Revelation 7—but this does not deny that there will be saved ones from all ages. In fact this is implied in 14:4 by calling the 144,000 first fruits of a larger universal harvest.

The Vision of the Satanic Trinity – Revelation 14:1-5, the second passage in which the 144,000 are found, is part of the central vision of Revelation. It focuses in a special way on the church and her struggles with evil powers. Revelation 12 starts

> The 144,000 are God's end-time church on earth.

with the early church, it describes the persecution of the church during the medieval period, and in verse 17 it introduces the end-time remnant. The following two chapters focus on the end-time people of God and their fate.

Revelation 12:17 describes a remnant; 13:1-10 mentions the saints who will not be involved in the future universal false worship; and in 13:11-18 we meet a group that does not accept the mark of the beast and does not worship the beast or its image. In spite of economic restrictions (they cannot buy or sell) and a death decree aimed at God's faithful remnant, there is a group of survivors – the 144,000 of Revelation 14. Obviously, the remnant, i.e., the saints who do not receive the mark of the beast and do not worship the beast and its image and the 144,000 are the same group. The difference is that the 144,000 are already portrayed as standing with the Lamb on Mt. Zion, whereas the remnant is still found on earth.

The phrase "to make war with" is found in Revelation 12:17 and in 13:7. In 12:17 the war is waged with the remnant. In 13:7 war is waged with the saints. Apparently, the remnant of 12:17 and the saints of 13:7 describe the same group. Revelation 12:17; 13:10; and 14:12 describe the main characteristics of the remnant in different ways.

Rev 12:17	Rev 13:10	Rev 14:12
Keep the commandments		Keep the commandments
Have the testimony of Jesus		
	Patience	Patience
	Faith	Faith of Jesus

According to the context of Revelation 14, the 144,000 have accepted the three angels' messages and have proclaimed them (Rev 14:6-13), a message which will be preached just prior to Jesus' second coming (14:14-20).

Literal or symbolic? – According to Revelation 7 the 144,000 are God's servants who are going to be sealed (7:3). The seal of God on their foreheads points to the fact that they are God's property and that they are protected from apostasy in the final hours of the world's history.[4]

Our study has already indicated that the 144,000 must be understood in a symbolic rather than in a literal way. Here are some additional considerations: The beginning of our passage is clearly symbolic (7:1-3), mentioning the four corners of the world, the four winds of the earth, the sea, the earth, trees, and the seal of God. Also the context (Revelation 6) is largely symbolic. For instance, the apocalyptic riders and the martyrs under the altar are clearly symbolic. The parallel passage in 14:1-5 must also be understood symbolically. It tells us that the 144,000 "have not defiled themselves with women." They are "virgins" and follow the "Lamb." The group does not consist of unmarried men only. The term "woman" is as much a symbol in Revelation as the term "Lamb." Therefore, symbolic language must be expected for 7:4-8.

Thus, the number 144,000 is symbolic and points to the fullness of the people of God. In Old Testament lists we find twelve tribes in addition to the tribe of Levi, which was singled out for service at the sanctuary and was not counted among the twelve. The number twelve was achieved by dividing the tribe of Joseph into Ephraim and Manasseh. However, in Revelation 7 the enumeration of tribes is very unusual. The tribe of Dan is missing. Also whereas Manasseh is mentioned the other son of Joseph, Ephraim, is not mentioned, but Levi is counted. Judah is found in the first place and Benjamin in the last, forming a parenthesis which encompasses the tribes of the former Northern Kingdom. Such a list is not found elsewhere in Scripture and may therefore point to a symbolic number. Moreover, most of the twelve tribes no longer exist today, nor did they exist at the time Revelation was written. Therefore, it would hardly be possible to find 144,000 literal Israelites according to their tribes as listed in Revelation 7 forming God's end-time people. Furthermore, in the New Testament the descendants of Abraham are not restricted to his literal descendants but include all true believers (Rom 4:11-12). Spiritual "Jews" are people whose hearts have been circumcised by the Holy Spirit (Rom 2:28, 29). The 144,000 are such people.

Ekkehardt Mueller

References

[1] F. D. Nichol, ed., *Seventh Day Adventist Bible Commentary,* 7 vols. (Washington, D.C.: Review and Herald Publishing Association, 1978), 7:784.

[2] See, e.g., the great number of names, titles, and symbolic descriptions used for God the Father, Jesus, and the church in Revelation.

[3] Her counterpart is found under the sixth trumpet (9:16), the demonic army of 200 million. The phrase "I heard their number" appears only twice in Revelation (7:4 and 9:16) and contrasts God's army on earth with Satan's army on earth.

[4] See Ezekiel 9:4.

Mosaic above the entrance to the church built on top of the cave where John is supposed to have received the visions recorded in the book of Revelation. John is seen dictating to his pupil Prochoros.

WHO ARE THE TWO WITNESSES IN REVELATION 11?

And I will grant *authority* to my two witnesses, and they will prophesy for twelve hundred and sixty days, clothed in sackcloth. These are the two olive trees and the two lampstands that stand before the Lord of the earth. Revelation 11:3, 4.

As with so many of the apocalyptic images of the book of Revelation, the two witnesses of Revelation 11 cannot be fully understood apart from an awareness of the way in which the author adapts the Old Testament background. The background to this passage is Zechariah 4, in which the Old Testament prophet is shown a solid gold lampstand with a bowl at the top and seven lamps, with seven pipes leading from the bowl to the lamps. Two olive trees stood on the right and the left of the lampstand. These trees supplied oil to the central bowl, which, in turn, supplied the lamps.

The lampstand in Zechariah – The vision of Zechariah has been adapted in Revelation 11 in certain ways. In Revelation 11:4, we have two lampstands instead of the one in Zechariah 4:2, and the two witnesses are both the two lampstands and the two olive trees. In Zechariah 4, the prophet asked the attending angel for an interpretation of the two olive trees, and the angel replied, "These are the two anointed ones, who are standing by the Lord of the whole earth" (v. 14). The expression the "anointed ones" is an interpretation of the Hebrew "sons of oil," meaning those having been anointed with oil, being consecrated for a special function. This special function may be understood in the light of the first answer given by the angel to Zechariah when he inquired as to who the lampstand and the two olive trees represented (v. 4). He was told, "This is the word of the LORD to Zerubbabel saying, 'Not by might nor by power, but by My Spirit,' says the LORD of hosts" (v. 6). In other words, the lampstand whose light is fed by oil from the two olive trees represents the word of the Lord which equips God's servants for their assigned tasks by the power of God's Spirit, as opposed to human might or power. Zerubbabel, the governor of Judea, was not dependent on human power for his task, but was dependent on the power available to him by

God's Spirit as communicated to him through God's Word, or through prophetic revelation.

John's two witnesses: The Old and New Testaments – In Zechariah's vision, there was only one lampstand, the Word of God through the prophets. But by the time of John's vision, two lampstands appear. What could be the significance of having two lampstands instead of one? The two are linked together as one, since both are identified with the two olive trees that feed them with oil. The key to this curious feature has to do, in large part, with the larger context of John's two-witness theology in the book of Revelation. John adheres to the biblical principle expressed in Deuteronomy 19:15: "On the evidence of two or three witnesses a matter shall be confirmed." This principle was reiterated by Jesus (Matt 18:16) as well as by Paul (2 Cor 13:1; 1 Tim 5:19; Heb 10:28). The two witnesses that John cites throughout the book of Revelation are "the word of God and the testimony of Jesus." These two witnesses first appear in Revelation 1:2 as the content of the revelation given to John. In 1:9, John states that it is for these two that he is on Patmos as a "brother and fellow partaker in the tribula-

> "The two witnesses represent the Scriptures of the Old and the New Testament. Both are important testimonies to the origin and perpetuity of the law of God. Both are witnesses also to the plan of salvation. The types, sacrifices, and prophecies of the Old Testament point forward to a Saviour to come. The Gospels and Epistles of the New Testament tell of a Saviour who has come in the exact manner foretold by type and prophecy" (GC 267).

tion and kingdom and perseverance *which are* in Jesus," implying that he has been willing to suffer for the sake of these as they relate to Jesus.

The Word of God signifies the revelation given through the Old Testament prophets, while the testimony of Jesus signifies the revelation given through Jesus and His New Testament apostles and prophets, which supplements and clarifies the Old Testament revelation in the light of the first coming of Jesus Christ. These two witnesses to the truth stand together as a unit in Revelation 11. In fact, they are so conceived as a unit that when they are slain (v. 8), the text Greek twice uses the singular noun "corpse" in verses 8 and 9a to refer to their dead body, before reverting to the plural "corpses" in 9b.

The activities of the two witnesses – Everything that characterizes the one witness characterizes the other, and everything that happens to the one happens to the other. They are prophets (v. 10) who prophesy for 1260 "days" (vv. 3, 6) clothed in sackcloth, signifying darkness or obscurity (6:12; Isa 50:3); mourning and grief (Ezek 27:31; Joel 1:8, 13); distress, rebuke, and disgrace (2 Kgs 19:1, 2); or humility and repentance (1 Chron 21:16, 17; Matt 11:21). The time parallel with the previous verse (Rev 11:2) suggests that there is mourning and grief over the trampling of the holy city during the same period of time. In addition, because these two witnesses are two lampstands, whose function is to give light (cf. Ps 119:130; John 1:9), the sackcloth may signify an obscuring of the light, as though shrouded by sackcloth. In view of the response to their prophesying, in that they were killed and there was great rejoicing over their deaths, the sackcloth could also signify that they were experiencing distress, rebuke, and disgrace in the face of the rejection of their message. Certainly, the picture is of a time when the prophetic word was not going forth with power and efficiency. This was a characteristic of the Dark Ages, a time frequently seen as represented by the prophetic periods of 1260 days or 42 months (Rev 11:2, 3; cf. 12:6,14; 13:5; Dan 7:25; 12:7).[1]

Understanding the two witnesses – We can better understand the two witnesses by reviewing the clues given to us in Revelation 11:5-8. Verse 5 says that if anyone tries to harm the two witnesses, fire comes from their mouths and devours their enemies. Some have seen this as an allusion to the prophet Elijah, but more likely it is an allusion to Jeremiah 5:14: "I will make my words in your mouth a fire, and these people the wood it consumes" (NIV). It is God's word that comes out of their mouths as a devouring fire to consume their enemies. A parallel image is given of Jesus Christ in the Revelation in which He is portrayed with a sharp, double-edged sword coming out of His mouth (Rev 1:16), with which He will strike down the nations (19:15, 21). This sword also represents the Word of God (Heb 4:12), the testimony of Jesus in His mouth (He Himself is called the Word of God in Rev 19:13). This sword, or word, in the mouth of Christ will judge the world.

The authority of the two witnesses – Revelation 11:6 portrays the two witnesses with the authority of the greatest of the Old Testament prophets, Moses and Elijah. Like Elijah, they have authority to shut up the sky so that it will not rain during the time they are prophesying, and like Moses, they have authority to turn the waters into blood and to strike the earth with every kind of plague as often as they want. The use of such figurative language does not mean that the two witnesses *are* Moses and

Elijah but that they have the same authority as the greatest of the ancient prophets. Despite the fact that they prophesy clothed in sackcloth, there is nothing to suggest any weakening of their authority. It is the external circumstances that have changed not the character or authority of the prophetic word.

The death of the two witnesses – Revelation 11:7 states that when the two witnesses have finished their testimony—in other words, when the 1260-day period of their prophesying is drawing to a close—the Beast from the Abyss (cf. 17:8) attacks them and overpowers and kills them. In the light of verse 5, this is an amazing event, for verse 5 declares that anyone who would kill the two witnesses must be killed with fire from their mouths, or judged by the Word of God. This fate is, in fact, what Revelation 20:7-15 goes on to show will happen to those who would harm the two witnesses. Satan and all the wicked will be consumed in the lake of fire after facing the bar of justice before the Great White Throne.

Revelation 11:8 says that the corpse (Gr. singular) of the two witnesses lies in the street of the Great City, which is figuratively called Sodom and Egypt, where their Lord was also crucified. There are two cities in

According to the year-day principle, the "three-and-a-half days" (Rev 11:9), during which the two witnesses are lying dead in the street of the great city, represent three-and-a-half years. "Seventh-day Adventists, who generally understand the beast of v. 7 to represent the First French Republic (1792 to 1804), especially in terms of its antireligious bias, find this prophecy fulfilled during that brief period in French revolutionary history when atheism was at its height. This period may be reckoned from November 10, 1793, when a decree, issued in Paris, abolished religion, to June 17, 1797, when, it is held, the French government removed restrictions against the practice of religion" (F. D. Nichol, *SDA Bible Commentary*, 7:803).

Revelation, the Great City and the Holy City. The former is depicted also as a Great Harlot, while the latter is portrayed as the Bride of the Lamb. The former is usually called Babylon, while the latter is called the New Jerusalem. In this first reference to the Great City in Revelation, it is figuratively called both Sodom and Egypt. Sodom was notorious for its great prosperity, self-indulgence, arrogance, wickedness, immorality, indifference, and inhospitality (Ezek 16:49, 50; 2 Pet 2:6-8; Jude 7). Egypt was notorious for its dominance, arrogance, oppression, denial of the God of heaven, and worship of many created things, including the Pharaoh himself (Exod 5:2; Jer 43:12, 13; 46:8, 25; Ezek 20:7; 23:3, 8, 27; 29:3; 30:13; 32:12; Joel 3:19; Mic 6:4). The Great City is in rebellion against God and oppresses His witnesses. In this context, the two witnesses are killed and scorned.

The resurrection of the two witnesses – In saying that the Great City is "where their Lord was also crucified," the text is saying that the two witnesses are following their Lord in death as they did in life. This is reinforced by the rest of the passage, which points to other ways in which the two witnesses follow in the footsteps of their Lord, the Faithful and True Witness. They are despised by the world in death as well as in life (Rev 11:9, 10). They are resurrected after three-and-a-half days and honored by God, while the amazed world looks on (v. 11). They ascend up to heaven in a cloud and are glorified before their enemies (v. 12). A great earthquake accompanies their resurrection and their enemies are afraid, while God is glorified through these events (v. 13). Historically, the death and resurrection of the two witnesses were fulfilled when, during the French Revolution, atheism reached its height and religion was abolished (November 10, 1793), three and one half years later (June 17, 1797) the French government removed restrictions against the practice of religion, and at the beginning of the nineteenth century various national Bible societies were established.

Conclusion – The two witnesses appear to represent the written word of God, namely the Word of God and the testimony of Jesus, the Old and New Testaments of Scripture. They are the witnesses that Christ left through His Spirit when He ascended to heaven. They are portrayed as prophets who are killed for their straight testimony, just as Jesus was, but who follow in His footsteps in being resurrected, ascending to heaven in a cloud and being glorified before their enemies. The implication seems to be that all those who are witnesses for Christ, like John and his brethren, who have the word of God and the testimony of Jesus, should also expect to share in the experience of Jesus, including martyrdom for their testimony, as well as resurrection, ascension to heaven, and glorification before their enemies (Rev 1:2, 9; 6:9; 12:11, 17; 14:12; 17:6; 19:10; 20:4; 22:8).

Edwin Reynolds

References

[1]In apocalyptic prophecy one day stands for one year. For further explanation of the year-day principle see the chapter "How do Adventists interpret Daniel and Revelation?" in this volume.

Patmos: The island where John wrote the book of Revelation.

WHAT DOES "THE SMOKE OF THEIR TORMENT ASCENDS FOREVER AND EVER" MEAN?

And the smoke of their torment goes up forever and ever; and they have no rest day and night, those who worship the beast and his image, and whoever receives the mark of his name. Revelation 14:11.

Many Bible students interpret this text to mean that the wicked will suffer ongoing, never ending punishment because their souls are immortal. This would mean that a loving God punishes sinners, who have maybe sinned for 70 years or less, throughout eternity. Since this seems not to fit with the concept of a just and righteous God, how should this text be understood?

The expression "forever and ever" in Revelation – The expression "forever and ever" appears thirteen times in the book of Revelation. Nine times it refers to God or the Lamb, ascribing power or glory and dominion to the One who lives forever. The remaining four uses are divided as follows: (a) three times the phrase refers to the final punishment of the wicked (14:11; 19:3; 20:10); and (b) one time it refers to the reward of the redeemed (22:5). Revelation 14:11 best represents the thoughts that describe the punishment meted out to those who are excluded from heaven.

The phrase "and the smoke of their torment rises forever and ever" occurs in the context of God's last warning message to the world. Revelation 14 draws a sharp contrast between those who serve God by keeping His commandments (Rev. 14:12) and those who worship the Beast, God's enemy on earth. It is the nature of the beast worshippers that is under investigation. Is John here speaking of immortal sinners? If so, are the wages of sin not death, but eternal life in hell? According to 2 Timothy 1:10 "Jesus Christ . . . has destroyed death and has brought life and immortality to light through the gospel" (NIV). Since the wicked do not believe the gospel they cannot have immortality. So what does Revelation 14:11 mean?

The meaning of "forever and ever" – What is intended by the words translated "forever and ever"? The Greek word behind both words is *aion* which can be translated as "age" (Matt 12:32; 13:39), "world" (Matt 13:22; 24:3, KJV), "forever" (Luke 1:33, 55; John 6:51), or "never" (John 10:28;

11:26). It is the equivalent of the Hebrew word *'olam* which is generally translated as "forever" (Exod 19:9; 2 Sam 7:29, etc.). However, neither the Hebrew nor the Greek term carry in themselves the sense of endless or everlasting. Their meaning depends on the nature of the subject or entity to which they are applied. If God, who is immortal, or the righteous who receive immortality are the subject, the meaning of *'olam* and *aion* is eternal without end (Gen 21:33; Matt 25:46). If anyone or anything that does not possess immortality is the subject, *'olam* and *aion* refer to a limited time period that can be long or short, i.e., as long as the nature of the subject allows.

Examples of *'olam* and *aion* (*aionios*) – A brief survey of the uses of these words in the Bible will prove helpful:

> **The biblical words for "forever" refer to a limited time period which can be long or short, i.e., as long as the nature of the subject allows.**

1. In Deuteronomy 15:17 a servant who desired to stay with his master was to serve him "forever ['olam]." The NIV translators, aware of the fact that no man can be a slave for eternity, correctly translate the term 'olam with "for life."

2. According to 1 Samuel 1:22, Samuel was to serve in the sanctuary "forever ['olam]." In verse 28 the meaning of 'olam is explained as "for his whole life" (NIV) or "as long as he lives" (RSV).

3. In Jonah 2:6 we are told that Jonah was in the belly of the great fish "forever" ('olam). However, Jonah's "forever" only lasted three days and three nights (1:17).

4. Paul, writing to Philemon regarding the return of his servant Onesimus, said, "Perhaps he was for this reason separated *from you* for a while that you would have him back forever [*aionios*] . . . both in the flesh and in the Lord" (Phlm 15, 16). The NIV says, "that you might have him back for good." This span of time could have been a few years or a few decades until the death of Onesimus.

5. Jude 7 describes the fire that destroyed Sodom and Gomorrah as "eternal [*aionios*] fire." While the effect of that fire was eternal, the actual flames only lasted until everything that could burn was burnt up.

6. Hebrews 5:6 says of Christ, "You are a priest forever [*aion*], according to the order of Melchizedek." Here "forever" clearly means this present age, for most Christian theologians agree that Christ's work as a priest comes to an end when sin has been blotted out, because the work of a

445

priest is to deal with sin (see Heb 2:17 and 5:1).

Thus Revelation 14:11 does not teach that the wicked burn in hell forever. Rather the text declares that the wicked are punished continuously *for as long as they live.* When all wicked beings are finally destroyed the history of sin ends and this *end* lasts forever.

Problems with an eternally burning hell – By teaching that the damned will be tormented continuously for all the ages of eternity, proponents of this view have to deal with certain, perhaps unintended, distortions of the character of God:

"This "eternal destruction" [2 Thess 1:9] will be the extinction of those so sentenced. This retribution will be preceded by penal suffering exactly suited to each degree of guilt by the holy and just God, but that penal suffering within itself is not the ultimate retribution or punishment. There will be an act of destroying, resulting in a destruction that will never end or be reversed. The act of destroying includes penal pains, but they will end. The result of destruction will never be reversed and will never have an end" (E. W. Fudge, *The Fire that Consumes*, Houston, TX: Providental Press, 1982), 47.

1. The Scriptures declare that no man "can keep his own soul alive" (Ps 22:29 KJV). Only God can keep him alive. If God punishes human being eternally, this would mean that God has to give the wicked immortality for the specific purpose of perpetuating their agony. This is a horrific accusation against the God of love portrayed in the Bible.

2. Matthew 10:28 says that God "can destroy both soul and body in hell." Since He can put the wicked out of their misery, why doesn't He do it? Those who believe in the perpetual torturing of sinners portray God as a malevolent being.

3. God created a perfect universe. There was no sin anywhere in His creation. He has promised that the "age to come" will again be free of death; "there shall no longer be *any* mourning, or crying, or pain; the first things have passed away" (Rev 21:4). However, if sinners live forever in pain in some corner of the universe, God does not really accomplish what He set out to do. Sin, pain, and mourning remain, and it would seem that God does not win the Great Controversy. But make no mistake about it: God wins and Satan and his followers lose!

S. Quezada Case

WHAT IS "THE SPIRIT OF PROPHECY"?

And I fell at his feet to worship him. And he said to me, "Do not do that; I am a fellow servant of yours and your brethren who hold the testimony of Jesus; worship God. For the testimony of Jesus is the spirit of prophecy." Revelation 19:10.

What does John the Revelator mean by the term "spirit of prophecy" which appears only once in Scripture? Does the expression "spirit of prophecy" refer to the Holy Spirit with whom all Christians should be filled, or does it refer to a specific gift of the Holy Spirit? Furthermore, why is "the testimony of Jesus" in Revelation 19:10 called "the spirit of prophecy?"

The meaning of "the spirit of prophecy" – The expression "the spirit of prophecy," which occurs only in Revelation 19:10, is nowhere explained in the book. The obvious reason for this lack of explanation is that the first-century Christians to whom Revelation was originally written were very much familiar with the expression. They understood this expression as a reference to the Holy Spirit, who imparts the prophetic gift. Rabbinic Judaism equated the OT expressions "Holy Spirit," "Spirit of God," or "Spirit of Yahweh" with "the Spirit of prophecy." This equation can be seen in the frequent occurrence of this phrase in the Aramaic translation of the Old Testament. For example, Genesis 41:38 in the Aramaic translation says, "Pharaoh said to his servants, 'Can we find a man like this in whom there is *the spirit of prophecy from before the Lord?'"*(Gen 41:38), referring to Joseph. And, in Numbers 27, the Aramaic translation has the Lord saying to Moses, "Take Joshua, son of Nun, a man who has within himself the *spirit of prophecy*, and lay your hand on him" (Num 27:18).

Thus, for first-century readers of Revelation the expression "the spirit of prophecy" meant the Holy Spirit who speaks through specific persons, called prophets, to declare the message revealed and entrusted to them by God. In other words, "the spirit of prophecy" refers to the Holy Spirit who inspires and empowers the prophets to proclaim God's messages to the people (2 Pet 1:21).

The meaning of "the testimony of Jesus" – The text equates "the spirit of prophecy" with "the testimony of Jesus." The expression "the testimony

447

of Jesus" in the original Greek can have the meaning of bearing witness about Jesus, thus the *New American Bible* translates the phrase as "bear witness to Jesus" (Rev 12:17); or it can refer to the testimony that Jesus Himself bore during His life and ministry and after His ascension through His prophets, who had the spirit of prophecy, much as the prophets in ancient times had (cf. 1 Pet 1:11, 12). The context of Revelation suggests the latter. Most translations, therefore, read, "have the testimony of Jesus" (ESV, KJV, NASB, NIV, etc.).

In Revelation 1:2, 9; 12:17 and 20:4 the expression "testimony of Jesus" is each time balanced symmetrically with the expression "the word of God" or the phrase "the commandments of God." "The Word of God" is what God has said; "the commandments of God" are God's commandments and the "testimony of Jesus" is what Jesus said. "The Word of God" in John's time referred to the Old Testament, and the "testimony of Jesus" to what Jesus had taught in the Gospels and through His prophets, such as Peter and Paul. Revelation 19:10, therefore, says, "For the testimony of Jesus is the spirit of prophecy," i.e., the Holy Spirit who bestows the prophetic gift on human beings.

> "'For the testimony or witness of (i.e., borne by) Jesus is (i.e., constitutes) the spirit of prophecy.' This prose marginal comment specifically defines the brethren who hold the testimony of Jesus as possessors of prophetic inspiration. The testimony of Jesus is practically equivalent to Jesus testifying (xxii. 20). It is the self-revelation of Jesus which moves the Christian prophets" (James Moffatt, "The Revelation of St. John the Divine," *The Expositor's Greek Testament,* ed., W. R. Nicoll, 5 vols. (Grand Rapids, MI: Wm. B. Eerdmans, 1980), 5:465.

Thus, the context of the phrase is the key for unlocking the meaning of the statement that "the testimony of Jesus is the spirit of prophecy." The phrase "the testimony of Jesus" indicates that the message the true prophet brings to God's people is not his or her idea. It is rather "the word of God" sent by Christ as His own testimony to the church by means of "the spirit of prophecy." It is referred to as "the spirit of prophecy" because it is the Holy Spirit who inspires and empowers the prophet to speak the words of Christ and to communicate "the testimony of Jesus" to God's people on earth (cf. 2 Pet 1:20, 21).

The prophetic gift in the church – Revelation 19:10 is thus in line with the clear teaching of the rest of the New Testament that the prophets in the church are distinguished as a special group within the church. "The spirit of prophecy" does not refer to all believers in the church but only to those called by God to the prophetic ministry. This fact is especially emphasized in Revelation 22:9: "But he said to me, 'Do not do that. I am a fellow servant of yours and of *your brethren the prophets* and of those who heed the words of this book." In Revelation 19:10, John's "brethren" are those who have the testimony of Jesus through the Spirit of prophecy. This notion

> "The spirit of prophecy" does not refer to all believers in the church but only to those called by God to the prophetic ministry.

is further affirmed in Revelation 22:6: "The Lord God of the spirits of the prophets, sent his angel to show to his servants the things which must soon take place." John the revelator claims in this text to be one of the prophets (as Paul prior to him); he has received a special revelation–"the Word of God"–from God. And he bears witness to "the testimony of Jesus" that was communicated to him through an angel in vision (Rev 1:2).

However, John the revelator obviously does not consider himself to be the last of the prophets; he indicates clearly that the prophetic ministry will continue in the church after the first century. While God may have revealed Himself to individuals throughout the Christian age, Revelation 12:17 makes it clear that God's end-time remnant is characterized by keeping the commandments of God and having "the testimony of Jesus," i.e., the spirit of prophecy or the prophetic gift. In other words, at the time of the end, the remnant church will again have the prophetic gift operating in its midst, as it was in the time of John.

Conclusion – Revelation 19:10 (together with 22:6, 9) provides God's people, living in the closing days of this earth's history, with an assurance of God's special care and guidance through the Holy Spirit working through those called to the prophetic office, just as it was with God's people of old. However, it is not the manifestation of the prophetic gift in their midst only, but also their faithfulness to the prophetic message that separates God's people from the unfaithful at the time of the end.

Ranko Stefanovic

"WASH THEIR ROBES" OR "DO HIS COMMANDMENTS"?

Blessed are those who wash their robes, that they may have the right to the tree of life, and may enter by the gates into the city. Revelation 22:14, NASB.

Blessed *are* they that do His commandments, that they may have the right to the tree of life, and may enter in through the gates into the city. Revelation 22:14, KJV.

For hundreds of years readers of the King James Bible were told that those who do God's commandments have access to the tree of life; most modern versions, however, replace "keeping the commandments" with "those who wash their robes." Which of the two translations is the correct one?

The manuscript evidence – Revelation 22:14 is the seventh and last beatitude of the book (cf. 1:3; 14:13; 16:15; 19:9; 20:6; 22:7, 14). It promises special blessings for the victorious saints in terms of access to the tree of life and entrance into the New Jerusalem. However, Greek manuscripts support two different readings with regard to the characteristics of those referred to in the text as blessed. The earliest known manuscripts that contain this text of Revelation, Codex Sinaiticus and Codex Alexandrinus, dated to the fourth and fifth centuries A.D., refer to the saved saints as the ones who "wash their robes." This reading is adopted by most modern Bible translations. On the other hand, many later manuscripts–the earliest of which are dated to the eighth century A.D.–follow the reading "do his commandments." This reading is preferred by the King James Bible. The ancient versions are divided in their reading of the text. Interestingly, some early Latin patristic authors, such as Tertullian (A.D. 145-220) and Cyprian (A.D. 200-258), used a text that contained "do his commandments."

"Wash their robes" is to be preferred – Thus one might easily observe that the textual evidence is divided. However, although both readings of the text are plausible and might suit the context, the textual evidence obviously favors the reading "wash their robes." Several evidences lead to such a conclusion. First of all, the earliest manuscripts available to us read "wash their robes," while the reading "do his commandments" is attested in very late manuscripts. That Tertullian and Cyprian had access to a text containing the reading "do his commandments" at an early date, although significant, is not necessarily decisive. It suggests only the early date of the circulation of this textual variant in the Latin Church.

Second, the internal evidence supports the reading "wash their robes." Elsewhere in the book of Revelation John refers to the *keeping* (Gr. *tereo*) of the commandments (cf. Rev 12:17; 14:12) or the *keeping* of the words of the book (cf. 1:3; 3:8, 10; 22:7, 9, KJV) rather than the *doing* of the commandments. The reading *"do* [Gr. *poieo*] his commandments" in Revelation 22:14 would thus be very unusual and inconsistent with reference to the keeping of the commandments in the other texts in Revelation.

Finally, the reading "wash their robes" seems to better fit the theology of the book of Revelation. In Revelation 7:14, John describes the victorious

> **Although both readings of the text are plausible and might suit the context, the textual evidence favors the reading "wash their robes."**

saints standing before the throne of God as the ones who have washed their robes and made them white in the blood of the Lamb. However, the concepts of washing the robes and keeping the commandments are closely related in Revelation. Obedience to God by keeping the commandments is the outward characteristic of God's end-time people who have washed their robes (cf. 12:17; 14:12). It is, however, the blood of Christ that provides the grounds for their salvation and their victory over sin (cf. Rev 1:5; 5:9-10; 12:11). Both Revelation 7:14 and 22:14 indicate that only through the washing of their robes in the blood of the Lamb are God's victorious people entitled to the heavenly city and the tree of life.

The reason for the variant reading – The modern Bible versions that follow the reading "wash their robes" are frequently accused of minimizing (or even denying) the importance of keeping God's commandments by those who believe that the King James Version reading "do his commandments" is the correct one. Some sincere Bible readers are thus led to believe that there is a kind of conspiracy among some Bible translators to change the content of the Bible. However, the foregoing discussion indicates that the textual difference in the two readings of Revelation 22:14

is not due to any conspiracy but most likely to a scribal error. In order to explain this clearly, it is necessary to briefly outline the ancient process of copying biblical manuscripts.

No original copy of any book of the Bible (known as "autographs") is known to exist today. The copies of the original biblical books were produced by hand by learned scribes. The copying was very often done under very difficult circumstances. In addition, in the original Greek New Testament manuscripts, there were no chapter and verse divisions. The text was written in capital letters and without spaces between the words. The scribe had to look at a word or phrase on the manuscript he was copying from and then write it down. Or, the scribe would write down what the reader read aloud for him and for other copyists with him. Thus, when copying, the scribe could make mistakes of different kinds. For instance, he would sometimes see or hear a word or phrase and write down another similar to it. This probably explains the variant readings in Revelation 22:14.

> The textual difference in the two readings of Revelation 22:14 is probably due to a scribal error.

A comparison of the two variant texts in Greek shows that the two readings resemble each other; the difference between them is in several letters and they sound similar. "Those who wash their robes" is, in Greek, *hoi plunontes tas stolas*; and "those who do his commandments" is *hoi poiountes tas entolas*. The Greek text (originally written in capital letters and without space between the words), transliterated into English capital letters, shows the close similarity between the two phrases:

HOIPLUNONTESTASSTOLAS

HOIPOIOUNTESTASENTOLAS

One can easily observe that whether a scribe was himself reading the phrase or listening to somebody reading it to him, he could easily substitute "wash their robes" with "do his commandments."

Conclusion – In light of all the facts here presented, we conclude that although both variant texts are possible, the evidence strongly favors the reading "wash their robes" as original. The reading "do his commandments" is probably due to a scribal error. This certainly does not undermine the importance of the keeping of the commandments by God's end-time people, a point that is strongly emphasized elsewhere in Revelation (Rev 22:17; 14:12). John the Revelator himself makes very clear that the breakers of God's law will not have a place in the New Jerusalem (cf. Rev 22:15). No Bible doctrine, including the importance of the commandments, is based on one text; in this case nothing is lost with regard to the importance of keeping the commandments, which God expects from his end-time people.

Ranko Stefanovic

In the Revelation all the books of the Bible meet and end. Here is the complement of the book of Daniel.

AA 585

Bible Statistics (KJV)

Old Testament		New Testament		Bible	
Number of books	39	Number of books	27	Number of books	66
Chapters	929	Chapters	260	Chapters	1,189
Verses	23,145	Verses	7,957	Verses	31,102
Words	609,269	Words	179,011	Words	788,280

(Source: www.thebelieversorganization.org)

Selected Scripture Index

The selected texts are either quoted or they provide additional important information. Page numbers in italics indicate a detailed explanation of the text or passage.

References to Apocrypha and Pseudepigrapha

Subject Index